The South Carolina Roots
of African American Thought

A READER

Edited by

Rhondda Robinson Thomas and Susanna Ashton

THE UNIVERSITY OF SOUTH CAROLINA PRESS

© 2014 University of South Carolina

Published by the University of South Carolina Press
Columbia, South Carolina 29208

www.sc.edu/uscpress

Manufactured in the United States of America

23 22 21 20 19 18 17 16 15 14
10 9 8 7 6 5 4 3 2 1

Library of Congress Cataloging-in-Publication Data
The South Carolina roots of African American thought : a reader /
edited by Susanna Ashton and Rhondda Robinson Thomas.
    pages cm
  Includes bibliographical references and index.
  ISBN 978-1-61117-314-7 (hardbound : alk. paper) 1. American literature—
South Carolina. 2. American literature—African American authors. 3.
South Carolina—Literary collections. I. Ashton, Susanna, 1967– editor
of compilation. II. Thomas, Rhondda Robinson editor of compilation.
  PS558.S6S68 2013
  810.8'09757—dc23

                              2013018490

Contents

PART II   THE TALENTED TENTH

PART III   THE CIVIL RIGHTS LEGACY

Acknowledgments

Susanna Ashton especially offers thanks to her children, South Carolinians all.

Rhondda Robinson Thomas wishes to thank her parents, grandparents, and great-grandparents, who were born in South Carolina.

Many individuals assisted with the mechanics and assembly of this volume. Many more helped sustain our work with their scholarly and emotional support. We would like to thank our families, colleagues, and friends for their encouragement. We are grateful for funding from Clemson University's Department of English, Pearce Center for Professional Communication, and College of Architecture, Arts, and Humanities. We would also like to thank Alex Moore at USC Press; our graduate research assistants, Jake Greene and George Dubose; Georgette Mayo of the Avery Research Center for African American History and Culture for research assistance; Camille Nelson for superb editorial services; and Beverly Pressley for assistance with processing invoices.

The title and concept for this book were initially inspired by William L. Andrews's edited anthology *The North Carolina Roots of African American Literature.* While this volume directs itself toward the evolution of national social, political, and cultural work from its local origins in South Carolina and leaves the project of exploring the particular South Carolina African American literary and artistic influence on national consciousness for another endeavor, the notion of locating the local roots of a national African American cultural form owes much to and honors the conceptual example set by Andrews. We are grateful to follow in his wake.

Permission for the use of the following figures, or access to them, is gratefully acknowledged:

J. Max Barber image, courtesy of the Department of Special Collections and University Archives, W. E. B. Du Bois Library, University of Massachusetts Amherst.

Ty'Sheoma Bethea image, courtesy of Melvin Breeden, LLC.

Septima Poinsette Clark image, courtesy of the Highlander Research and Education Center.

Martin Robison Delany image, courtesy of the William Gladstone Collection at the U.S. Army Military History Institute.

Archibald Grimké image, courtesy of the Moorland-Spingarn Research Center, Howard University.

Francis Grimké image, courtesy of Scurlock Studio Records, Archives Center, National Museum of American History, Behring Center, Smithsonian Institution.

Jesse Jackson image, courtesy of the American Antiquarian Society.

Benjamin Elijah Mays image, courtesy of the Benjamin E. Mays Historic Site and Museum.

Kelly Miller image, courtesy of the Moorland-Spingarn Research Center, Howard University.

Armstrong Williams image, courtesy of Chis Angermann.

Permission for the use of the following texts, or access to them, is gratefully acknowledged:

Ty'Sheoma Bethea, letter, courtesy of Melvin Breeden, LLC.

Mary Jane McLeod Bethune, "Certain Unalienable Rights," from *What the Negro Wants,* edited by Rayford W. Logan. © 1944 by the University of North Carolina Press, renewed 1972 by Rayford W. Logan. Used by permission of the publisher.

Septima Poinsette Clark, "The Role of Women," courtesy of the Copyright Clearance Center, reprinted from *Ready from Within: Septima Clark and the Civil Rights Movement,* published by Africa World Press.

Jim Clyburn, "To Whom Much" and "A Proper Response," courtesy of the Office of Congressman James E. Clyburn.

Marian Wright Edelman, "If the Child is Safe," from *The Measure of Our Success* by Marian Wright Edelman. © 1992 by Marian Wright Edelman. Reprinted by permission of Beacon Press, Boston.

Jane Edna Harris Hunter, "An Opportunity" "My Experience," and "Democracy," courtesy of the Western Reserve Historical Society.

Jesse Jackson, "What Does the Government Owe the Poor?," © 1986 by *Harper's Magazine.* All rights reserved. Reproduced from the April issue by special permission. "Keep Hope Alive," courtesy of the Copyright Clearance Center. Reprinted from *Keep Hope Alive: Jesse Jackson's 1988 Presidential Campaign.*

Randall L. Kennedy, "Nigger: The Strange Career of a Troublesome Word," reprinted from *Nigger: The Strange Career of a Troublesome Word,* by Randall Kennedy.

Benjamin Elijah Mays, "Born to Rebel," reprinted from *Born to Rebel: An Autobiography*, by Benjamin E. Mays, published by the University of Georgia Press.

Eugene Robinson, "This Consequential Presidency," from the *Washington Post*, © January 20, 2009, the *Washington Post*. All rights reserved. Used by permission and protected by the Copyright Laws of the United States. The printing, copying, redistribution, or retrainsmission of the material without express written permission is prohibited. "The Mainstream," from *Disintegration: The Splintering of Black America*, by Eugene Robinson, © 2010 by Eugene Robinson. Used by permission of Doubleday, a division of Random House, Inc.

Armstrong Williams. "The Morality of Race" and "The Virtue of the Sabbath." Courtesy of the Copyright Clearance Center. Reprinted from *Reawakening Virtues*, by Armstrong Williams.

Editorial Note

The reading selections for the various authors represented in this volume have been kept intact as originally published with a few small exceptions in several of the nineteenth- and early twentieth-century documents. In the cases where we found obvious printing or typographical errors in the original publication, we made silent and very minor alterations.

Colloquial terms were retained as originally published. The word "Nigger" was retained as capitalized or not as represented in the original text. Similarly, we retained the original capitalization of "white" and "negro" as was found in the primary documents. Uncommon or inconsistent spellings were generally retained with only a few exceptions when they significantly hindered comprehension.

Scholarly or discursive endnotes have been added to our introductory essays, but endnotes on the reading selections have been kept largely within the limits of definitional glosses. The endnotes for each author/subject will be found at the end of that author's section.

Introduction

ʒ❧

Kelly Miller was not born in the United States. He was, as he put it in
1925, "born in South Carolina when that state was out of the Union."
Miller's bald statement underscores questions of inheritance and
identity shared by all of the writers in this collection. What did it mean
to be an American when one was black and from South Carolina? As this
collection demonstrates, there is no easy answer. And yet the mere act of
questioning such an identity has led to some of the most influential writing
on public policy and personal identity in our nation by black or white writers. South Carolinians have launched questions that have altered America
for the better.

South Carolina has always loomed large in the national imagination,
particularly in terms of political and social policy. Some might even argue
disproportionately large, considering how small the state is in comparison
to others. And yet the fearlessness, the audacity, and the often-astonishing
character of the thinkers and political figures who have hailed from this
region belie its modest size. One might think of Edward Rutledge challenging the condemnation of the slave trade in the initial draft of the Declaration of Independence, John C. Calhoun penning the audacious philosophy
of state nullification, Congressman Preston Brooks caning Senator Charles
Sumner on the floor of the Senate, the Citadel cadets firing shots at Fort

Sumter, Benjamin Tillman using his paramilitary group to terrorize African American citizens, or Senator Strom Thurmond defending segregation. One might even look to the more recent prominence of South Carolina politics in the national eye as evidenced by the attention accorded twenty-first-century figures such as Governor Nikki Haley, former senator Jim DeMint, Senator Lindsey Graham, and Congressman Joe Wilson. Even South Carolina's 2012 Republican presidential primary election, in which voters overwhelmingly bucked the Republican establishment by supporting the renegade candidate Newt Gingrich, demonstrates the contrarian nature that runs through the state's population. South Carolina has always used its passion to influence national debate.

What this collection seeks to address is the singularly narrow way in which that South Carolina character has been defined in the popular imagination, for an equally important tradition parallels the one just mentioned—that of the national prominence and influence of black thinkers, educators, journalists, and policy analysts from South Carolina who have used their experiences in the state to shape their own thinking about the state of the nation. Individuals such as Francis Grimké, Daniel Payne, Mary McLeod Bethune, Benjamin Mays, Kelly Miller, Septima Clark, Eugene Robinson, Marian Wright Edelman, and Jesse Jackson have changed this nation for the better with their questions, challenges, and persistence—all in the proudest South Carolinian tradition.

We introduce each of the nineteen authors in this collection with a supplementary scholarly essay to sketch out the cultural and historical import of their works and to demonstrate how they draw upon and distinguish themselves from one another. These connections exhibit a coherent legacy of engagement, brought on and nurtured by South Carolina traditions. Whether competing or collaborating with one another, these individuals knew they could change their world for the better by recognizing all who had come before and all who would come after them. It is no coincidence that so many of them wrote social histories as well as personal memoirs and narratives. Their witnessing honored their extraordinary experiences in South Carolina.

The excerpts featured in this volume were specifically chosen for their accessibility and for the ways in which the writers' compelling personal life stories might "speak" at many different levels. Indeed, most of these authors were selected precisely because of their ability to translate local concerns or experiences into writings that reached the broadest possible national audience. From Jesse Jackson's speech at the Democratic Convention in 1988 and the Pulitzer Prize–winning newspaper columns of Eugene Robinson to the excerpts from autobiographies by Children's Defense Fund founder Marian Wright Edelman and Morehouse College president Benjamin Mays, these works share a compelling interest in speaking to the general public as well as to the nation's policymakers. Indeed, many of these authors seek to convince lay people that they have the potential to be policymakers themselves.

It should come as no surprise that many of these writers became nationally renowned activists and intellectuals because South Carolina's dominant culture of intense conservatism demanded a response. Social change and political activism on local and national scales is explored with both fury and hope by well-known figures such as Edelman and Jackson and also by lesser-known figures such as Daniel Payne, Jane Edna Hunter, and J. Max Barber. Whether advocating for the abolition of slavery, the need for integration and fundamental civil rights, or the value of education, black South Carolinians have steadily gone out into the world ready to crusade for the causes of the poor and neglected and to live the hopes and dreams of their communities. While some of the featured writers might be placed on the more conservative spectrum of black thought (such as the commentator Armstrong Williams or the social activist Jane Edna Hunter) and others are characterized more easily as radicals (such as the journalist J. Max Barber or the abolitionist John Andrew Jackson), they all share a nuanced complexity that resists easy categorization. Indeed, in several texts selected for this book, authors such as Payne, Kennedy, Robinson, and Mays reflect upon their own development as thinkers and examine different poses, ideologies, and dreams.

These writers hail from across the state, from communities both large and small, and while certain specific regions within South Carolina have been a nexus for African American cultural engagement, most of them nevertheless identify themselves as South Carolinians in the broadest sense rather than seeing themselves solely as Charlestonians or as hailing from Orangeburg. One of the most significant patterns that emerges from this collection, however, is the diasporic nature of these thinkers. With a few notable exceptions, the remarkable public figures we profile were people who either by choice or by circumstance left the state to build their lives and careers. This was, of course, not coincidental. As many of these writers point out, their professional and personal opportunities often were limited in South Carolina. Indeed, in many cases it wasn't until they left the state that their voices could be heard. For men like Daniel Payne and John Andrew Jackson, slavery and political oppression were sufficient catalysts for flight. For the generation of black intellectuals that emerged during Reconstruction and those who emerged during the Progressive Era, opportunities for political influence were initially found in the post–Civil War statehouse, but political reversals soon pushed most of them, with the exception of U.S. Representative Robert Smalls, outside the confines of the Jim Crow South. The activists of the civil rights era are harder to characterize. Congressman James E. Clyburn, for example, has represented South Carolina's Sixth District since 1993 and remains deeply invested, by definition, in his local identity. Yet the necessity of his living in Washington, D.C., is not insignificant to his ability to weave national and local concerns together. Jesse Jackson, who was born and raised in the upstate of South Carolina, represents a more extreme case of the diasporic influence, however. Rarely does he return to or even refer to South Carolina, with very notable exceptions such as in the excerpt from his 1988 Democratic Convention speech.

The texts presented in *The South Carolina Roots of African American Thought* span a spectrum of genres, ideologies, and issues, reflecting South Carolinians' experiences as well as examining the challenges of American life from the South Carolinian's perspective. Some of the selections are acutely autobiographical (such as excerpts from the memoirs of Daniel Payne and Benjamin Mays) and depict early South Carolinian influences upon these individuals' lives. Other selections (such as Kelly Miller's protest pamphlet "The Disgrace of Democracy") do not mention South Carolina at all. In several instances, we have chosen two or more works by a writer in order to demonstrate how the personal translated into the political and how contrast and continuity might be found in such juxtaposition. For example, in his 1988 speech to the Democratic National Convention Jesse Jackson draws an analogy between the quilt his grandmother pieced together to keep his family warm and the coalition that Democrats must stitch together to focus disparate groups on common ground. In *Nigger: The Strange Career of a Troublesome Word* Randall Kennedy recalls how his early encounters with the word "nigger" in South Carolina irrevocably shape his examination of the cultural currency of the controversial term. Both writers exemplify the dual vision that black South Carolinians often bring to critical issues. Indeed, as both insiders and outsiders, all of these commentators share a commitment to speaking truth to power, relentlessly challenging our citizenry and shaping the ways in which African American thought might function and mold a stronger United States.

As a "reader," this volume is shaped with an eye toward conversation and provocative juxtaposition. While the book's contents in no way pose as comprehensive, the authors featured here each exemplify traits that made them stand out as having entirely new stories to tell. Writers primarily known for their literary or artistic craft were not included here, nor were several African American politicians and scholars who, influential though they were and although they continue to be important influences in the state, did not or do not necessarily have a national impact to the degree that most of those represented here had. Noted activists such as Charlotte Forten Grimké and scholars such as William Sinclair and Benjamin Brawley were influential thinkers of their respective generations, to be sure, but space constraints limit our ability to feature all of the writers whose works could have been included in this reader. This volume launches what we hope will be a longer and more extensive consideration in the future of how one of the nation's smallest states has such a disproportionate influence on American thought. Moreover, we hope this reader might even point the way for scholars to further extend and apply our analysis to the many other African Americans from South Carolina whose work has shaped American thought.

While influence and context are never neatly generational, we have nonetheless divided the readings into four chronological parts: "Slavery and Freedom," "The Talented Tenth," "The Civil Rights Legacy," and "The Media Generation." These parts represent a rough logic of generational organization, and one can see most acutely within these parts how public conversation about the role of African Americans by African Americans has been shaped by the black South Carolinians who keep appearing, again and again, in newspaper headlines and national policy discussions, as well as in local community organizations and advocacy groups.

1. Slavery and Abolition

Our "Slavery and Abolition" section focuses on black intellectuals born prior to the Civil War who were embroiled in the ideological debates that foreground the modern civil rights movement. The writers were both freeborn and enslaved, and all took the national stage with a confidence that contradicted their humble beginnings. Daniel Payne overcame challenges arising from the death of his parents and his expulsion from South Carolina after the state outlawed the education of African Americans to become an African Methodist Episcopal (AME) bishop who facilitated enormous institutional growth and weighed in frequently on national deliberations regarding race relations. Archibald and Francis Grimké faced even greater impediments after the death of their father, an indulgent planter who had taken up with their enslaved mother on an isolated lowcountry plantation. After being enslaved by their own relatives, they managed to leave the South after the Civil War and, with the assistance of other, much more sympathetic relatives, attended college and graduate school. They became prominent national activists, Archibald as a politician and civil rights leader and Francis as a Presbyterian minister.[1] Unlike the Grimké brothers, Robert Smalls experienced favor as a slave in the lowcountry before devising a daring escape on a Confederate munitions ship, a feat that catapulted him to national fame and helped launch his long and illustrious political career. John Andrew Jackson's experience in slavery was more brutal than that of Smalls or the Grimké brothers, for he witnessed and experienced horrific acts of violence that eventually impelled him to escape and informed his work as an abolitionist in England and as a social reformer in South Carolina. Unlike the other writers featured in this unit, the black nationalist Martin Delany was freeborn in Virginia but spent considerable time in South Carolina after the Civil War implementing Reconstruction initiatives, opining about the local political landscape in the press, and operating a medical practice.

The South Carolina lowcountry provides a complex sociopolitical nexus for these writers, simultaneously offering a haven for self-improvement and political engagement and a portal of escape from slavery or threats arising from incendiary activism. As a port city, Charleston functioned as an irresistible gateway to freedom for many enslaved African Americans. John Andrew Jackson exploited Charleston's stratified labor force of slaves, free blacks, and whites to find work on the wharf and to escape as a stowaway. He entered the public sphere at an international level in England, where he published his 1862 narrative that detailed the dehumanizing effects of slavery. Robert Smalls, who had also taken advantage of the unstable social environment to escape the lowcountry, nonetheless returned to South Carolina after the Civil War and reconnected with Charleston's merchant network, which provided critical support for his business and political ventures. As a state senator and U.S. representative, Smalls shaped public policy through impassioned, humor-laced, audacious speeches that supported education, decried disenfranchisement, and critiqued antimiscegenation laws and practices. The Grimké brothers were enslaved in the Charleston household of their older half brother (Francis was also hired out for extended periods to a Confederate officer), and after the Civil War one of the many sponsors who took it upon themselves to help these talented young men get out of the state for an education was Martin Delany. Delany, who was already a well-established national figure in the abolitionist movement, was just at that point starting the next phase of his career in Charleston as an officer with the Freedmen's Bureau; he thereafter served as a mercurial political figure in the tumultuous scene of the South Carolina government.

The writings that appear in "Slavery and Abolition," which span a range of genres including personal narrative, letter, essay, and sermon, are representative of the varied rhetorical strategies black South Carolinian thinkers and intellectuals adapted in response to the dramatic advances and setbacks African Americans experienced during and after the Civil War. John Andrew Jackson's *The Experience of a Slave in South Carolina* (1862), an influential slave narrative of the nineteenth century, recounts his daring escape from a slave system in Sumter County that was distinguished by insidious acts of violence. Although Archibald Grimké never published his own slave narrative, he recounted Denmark Vesey's remarkable transformation from slave to insurrectionist in "Right on the Scaffold; or The Martyrs of 1822" (1901), valorizing Vesey as a savvy dissembler at the very moment African American activists were embroiled in a fractious debate regarding the most effective means of launching a national racial uplift strategy. Francis Grimké lent his voice to the debate, outlining a radical, biblically grounded blueprint for African American activism in "The Negro and His Citizenship" (1905). Francis Grimké directed African Americans to adopt the Apostle Paul's strategy of demanding the rights accorded to him as a persecuted Roman citizen as a model for their own response to America's increasingly violent denial of their civil rights. While Delany's "Letter to Frederick Douglass" (1871) illuminates the history of the destructive forces that were unleashed against African Americans during Reconstruction, the excerpt from Payne's *Recollections of Seventy Years* (1888), which details the founding, opening, and forced closing of his antebellum school for African American children in Charleston, serves as a sobering reminder that the roots of Reconstruction's failure in South Carolina stretched deep into its history of contentious race relations.

2. The Talented Tenth

The authors featured in the "Talented Tenth" section came of age in South Carolina during a period that spanned from the height of the Civil War to the dawn of the modern civil rights era, pivotal historical moments that shaped their views and informed their activism. Members of this first free-born generation heeded W. E. B. Du Bois's call to pursue liberal arts education in preparation for uplifting their brethren and changing their nation. Kelly Miller, born in 1863, after South Carolina had seceded from the union, began life in a rebel state that forced conscription into the Confederate Army on his free black father and inadvertently provided freedom through Lincoln's Emancipation Proclamation to his enslaved mother. Miller completed his early education in South Carolina, then finished the college preparatory program at Hampton Institute and earned a bachelor's degree at Howard University before embarking on a remarkable career as a mathematician and reformer. After acquiring his education in South Carolina and Virginia, J. Max Barber, the son of former slaves, headed north in search of opportunities to hone his journalistic skills at black newspapers. Jane Edna Hunter, whose parents were former slaves, overcame an impoverished childhood by taking advantage of educational opportunities in South Carolina's segregated school system before seeking more lucrative employment opportunities in Cleveland.[2] There she persisted doggedly through unanticipated challenges to found the Phillis Wheatley Association (PWA), which addressed the needs of black female migrants and served as a cultural center for black Clevelanders. Benjamin Mays, born of former slaves who established a family farm, pursued an education in South Carolina's segregated public school system despite his father's objections. He went on to study with white students and teachers for the first time at Bates College in Maine, and he earned master's and doctoral degrees from the University of Chicago while beginning his long and remarkable career as an influential educator and administrator. Septima Clark, who was born in 1898, the daughter of a former South Carolina slave and a free black woman, was, of course, significantly younger than the other activists profiled in this section, and her life encompassed challenges and achievements long before the late 1950s. She came to prominence as an educator and advocate for black teachers in the 1920s. By the time the 1950s arrived she was an elder of the civil rights movement and had tirelessly laid the groundwork for the explosive social changes that were to come.

Education not only equipped this generation to become effective advocates of radical social change but also often placed them in a position to improve America's education system by shaping public policy, establishing their own schools, or becoming educators themselves. Barber wielded the *Voice of the Negro,* which was briefly one of the largest and most influential black newspapers in America, as a double-edged sword against injustices perpetrated by the nation against African Americans as well as those perpetrated by enemies from within, particularly the accommodationist views of Booker T. Washington. Hunter took a different path, establishing herself as an influential social activist after relocating to Cleveland during the Great Migration. She connected the service mission of the PWA to the social gospel of the settlement movement, the empowerment objectives of the Young Women's Christian Association, and the home, moral, and civic vision of the National Association of Colored Women's Clubs.

Still other writers devoted their lives to creating educational opportunities for African Americans while simultaneously advancing aggressive civil rights agendas. Kelly Miller, a gifted mathematician, introduced sociology to the curriculum at Howard University and rose through the ranks to become the dean of the College of Liberal Arts. Mary McLeod Bethune redirected her talents as a teacher to the southern mission field after her application for foreign mission service was rejected because of her race. She worked for educational institutions for African American youth in Georgia and South Carolina before founding her own school in Daytona, Florida, which eventually became the co-educational Bethune-Cookman College. As dean of the School of Religion at Howard University, Benjamin Mays substantially improved the program before becoming president of Morehouse College. There, he served as mentor to thousands of African American men, including Martin Luther King Jr., who were transformed into foot soldiers and leaders of the civil rights movement while listening to Mays's weekly chapel homilies. Initially a public school teacher working on Johns Island with impoverished black children, Septima Clark became active in the movement to create equal pay scales for teachers of all races. Starting in 1919, that work led her to increasing involvement in the NAACP and a lifetime of running

Citizenship Schools, leading literacy programs, and mentoring young activists like Rosa Parks (one of her most notable activist protégés), emphasizing the indivisible link between literacy and liberation, which she championed throughout her lifetime. The debt that so many of the young activists owed Clark was paid not by their awards, tributes, and honors but by their own work in continuing the fights she championed. All members of the Talented Tenth generation represented in this collection exploited their connections with prominent white Republicans, civil rights organizations, and renowned activists and reformers to develop institutions that aggressively addressed the needs of the African American community.

Dramatic technological innovations and sociological shifts in the twentieth century enabled the thinkers and intellectuals profiled in "The Talented Tenth" to become media-savvy activists who were increasingly adept at shaping public debate and fashioning distinctive messages, images, and legacies. Jane Edna Hunter self-published her autobiography, *A Nickel and a Prayer;* boosted sales by convincing John Bennett, an influential white patron of the arts, to write a favorable review for the Charleston *News and Courier;* and aggressively marketed the book. In widening the scope of her influence through orations infused with demographic statistics, biblical allusions, and classical literature, she addressed many different groups, including black club women, white college students, and interracial organizations. Kelly Miller, J. Max Barber, and Mary McLeod Bethune, all nationally renowned writers, also harnessed the power of the press in crafting searing editorials and commentary that addressed the ills afflicting African Americans. Miller wrestled with the complexities of regional identity for African Americans in his essay "South Carolina," published in the *Messenger,* and decried the plague of lynching across the nation in "The Disgrace of Democracy," an open letter to President Woodrow Wilson. Both Barber and Bethune lambasted the scourge of race riots that were erupting in northern and southern urban centers. While Barber decried the unmitigated use of violence against African Americans in "The Atlanta Tragedy," an editorial he published in the *Voice of the Negro* about the Atlanta race riots of 1906, Bethune deftly transformed the 1943 race riot in New York into a rallying cry for African Americans in "Certain Unalienable Rights," which was featured in Rayford Logan's seminal anthology *What the Negro Wants.* Other black thinkers embraced life-writing to shape public perceptions of themselves and their communities. Near the end of his illustrious career as an educator, Mays, a prolific writer, wrote a best-selling autobiography that secured his legacy as an activist who was *Born to Rebel.* Clark's award-winning autobiography, *Ready from Within,* performed similar work, solidifying her place in history as the "queen mother of the Civil Rights Movement."[3]

3. The Civil Rights Legacy

In our third section, "The Civil Rights Legacy," we consider the contributions of Jesse Jackson, Marian Wright Edelman, and James Clyburn. Jesse Jackson achieved his greatest fame when he ran for president in 1988 and gave a stirring speech at the Democratic National Convention that brought him international recognition for his oratorical powers and his impassioned ideals. His political career was honed, however, in the civil rights era. Thus we have clustered Jackson, Edelman, and Clyburn in this section because, notwithstanding lifetimes of service that continue up to this day, their experiences in the civil rights movement defined and propelled their ongoing life missions.

That individuals from South Carolina were at the forefront of the civil rights movement should come as no surprise. The intense conservatism of South Carolina from the early to the mid-twentieth century created a cultural atmosphere of segregation and repression that demanded response. Septima Clark and other African American activists daringly forged alliances with white civic leaders to dismantle one such stronghold of prejudice, South Carolina's segregated public education system, thereby subjecting themselves to extreme personal and professional peril. When Clark refused to relinquish her affiliation with the NAACP while fighting to improve working conditions for African American teachers, the Charleston school board fired her. Both black and white activists involved in the South Carolina court case *Briggs v. Elliott,* one of five critical lawsuits that were combined and brought before the Supreme Court in *Brown v. Board of Education,* faced greater tragedy.[4] As petitioners for equal school funding in South Carolina (particularly for buses and buildings for African American schoolchildren), they not only saw their case, represented by NAACP attorney Thurgood Marshall, denied by the lower courts but also suffered from reprisals both financial and violent. The Reverend J. A. Delaine, for example, one of the primary African American instigators of *Briggs v. Elliott,* saw his home burned to the ground. Even the aristocratic white U.S. district judge Julius Waties Waring from Charleston, who had sided with the petitioners, was harassed with cross burnings. South Carolina took the lead in some of the most egregious state-supported Jim Crow practices of the mid-twentieth century, but the courageous partnership of black and white activists of this period to fight such repression nonetheless brought about some of the most explosive social changes the nation was soon to face. For it was Waring's dissenting opinion in *Briggs v. Elliott* that formed the legal foundation of the 1954 decision in *Brown v. Board of Education,* which even uses many of his terms and some of the wording from the South Carolina case.

Seeing the immediate and real effects of courageous legal lobbying and advocacy enabled this civil rights generation to translate its South Carolina experiences into fuel for national and international policy. Careful attention to functional details and structural organization, as opposed to simple uplift and vague speeches, characterizes the practices of all the individuals featured in this part. For while Jesse Jackson might certainly be considered one of the greatest American orators of the twentieth century, his career has also been marked by focused policy analysis. As his 1986 interview in *Harper's* magazine illustrates, his ability to connect moral understanding to specific policy decisions on welfare distribution, for instance, are part of a canny realism that infuses his more lofty rhetoric. While his work encompasses international issues (such as campaigning against South African apartheid and arguing the case for Palestinian statehood), his expertise in combining local with international, moral outrage with pragmatism, and a sense of a shared world with a pride in American exceptionalism has fueled some of his great successes in helping negotiate freedom for hostages in Syria, liberation for Cuban and Cuban American prisoners in Cuba, freedom for hostages held in Kuwait and Iraq, and the release of American servicemen held in Yugoslavia.

Marian Wright Edelman, whose experiences in Mississippi and Washington, D.C., during the 1960s shaped her work with the Children's Defense Fund for the past forty years, similarly created a career that managed to bridge invocations of sentiment with concrete action and output. As our excerpt from her best-selling book *The Measure of Our Success* demonstrates, Edelman's condemnation of and mourning for the unnecessary death of young children due to lack of adult care are never allowed to linger in bathos. She immediately points to lack of engaged government and lack of an engaged community that could have passed a specific law, say, or provided concrete amounts of funding for institutions or programs that could have prevented such suffering. She never ends with simple prayers for action. As a true product of the civil rights generation, she knows that engagement takes practical guidance and that action needs to be challenged wisely in order to be sustained.

The civil rights generation from South Carolina came to embody the heady combination of savvy activism and the gravitas of righteousness. As we can see with the career of Congressman James Clyburn, translating both anger and love into action is a strategic and defining characteristic. He first honed his skills as a member of the NAACP youth movement of the 1950s and melded idealism with a readiness for action in his increasing involvement with social justice throughout the 1960s and 1970s, all the while climbing a professional ladder of government positions. He became the first post-Reconstruction black adviser to a South Carolina governor and the state's human affairs commissioner before finally, in 1992, being elected to Congress, where he still serves. His statements on the challenges faced by the state during the national fiscal crisis of 2010 that we share here are, significantly, framed within a statement he released in response to a young African American girl's letter to Congress about the desperate state of her impoverished middle school in South Carolina (an issue we explore at greater length in our Afterword). That he felt a need to sketch out for us just how sympathy or even vague anger is meaningless without, in this case, an understanding of the specific systemic obstacles that prevent school districts from receiving loans demonstrates the kind of grounded battles he was trained to fight with both ferocity and pragmatic determination.

4. The Media Generation

The starkest ideological differences featured in our collection probably separate the people profiled in our fourth unit, "The Media Generation." Randall Kennedy, a former Rhodes Scholar and currently an endowed professor at Harvard Law School, is one of the preeminent public intellectuals of our time. Eugene Robinson is perhaps the most visible black newspaper journalist in the United States; he uses his media presence, his status as a Pulitzer Prize–winning columnist for the *Washington Post,* and his frequent television appearances to critique politics and culture from a distinctly liberal and yet often idiosyncratic position. And Armstrong Williams's rise, fall, and rebirth in the conservative movement and in the public eye surely demonstrate the determination and astounding confidence we have seen characterize South Carolinians who went before him. The circumstances and visions of these four people are starkly different. And yet they all share the hallmark South Carolinian self-assurance, whether foolhardy or magnificent, that fuels their conviction that words—their words—can make a difference. In each case, such conviction has proved true.

Williams, who discusses his own fall from grace when his career as a political commentator and media figure collapsed under revelations that he had not publicly acknowledged taking large sums of money from the Department of Education to promote President Bush's "No Child Left Behind" policies, himself acknowledges that "it matters how [his] actions as a public figure are perceived." He concedes that, as a journalist, he held a particular position of public trust and violated it by accepting government money. And while he doesn't view the incident as starkly egregious, as many of his critics might, he nonetheless shapes his account of the experience as one in which he became newly aware of what public perception means and how it can and cannot be controlled. As a South Carolinian he writes of trying to find a balance between the private family values he was raised with and the notions of community, identity, and public accountability more broadly.

Both Kennedy and Robinson have chronicled how their identities don't fall into easy public categories of left and right, much less black and white.

Indeed, Kennedy's book *Nigger: The Strange History of a Troublesome Word* in some ways asks what being a freethinking person of color in the United States might truly signify. Similarly, Robinson's writings confront how the static American categories of race and class, which have shaped his own perceptions of self, are absurdly binary in the face of the fluid and real lives of people who regularly identify across seemingly untraversable class and racial boundaries.

The writings we feature in this section showcase individual experiences and concerns, of course. But we also selected these pieces to demonstrate the broader interpretative possibilities that the spectrum of their differences allows. What current connects the brilliant mix of personal and scholarly legal reflections woven so tautly together in Kennedy's brief study of the cultural "career" of a word to Williams's portrait of Sabbath values in his book *Reawakening Virtues. Restoring What Makes America Great* (2011) or to Robinson's project to reinsert the "invisible" black middle class into public discourse in *Disintegration: The Splintering of Black America*? In each case the writer's passion for engaging the personal as a legitimate investment in the political is perhaps one of the clearest markers of what is a vision for a new century.

The Afterword

One telling marker of how these thinkers and intellectuals on the pulse of current events emerges when they discover their own legacies and significance is their discovery of what their public visibility could mean. Young Ty'Sheoma Bethea exemplifies the new generation of African American South Carolinians who enact bold initiatives by linking local issues to national public policy debates. She follows in the footsteps of black South Carolinian activists and thinkers such as Jesse Jackson and James Clyburn, whose experiences in the state's underfunded school system compelled them to develop a public voice. Ty'Sheoma, who was only fourteen years old when she wrote her letter petitioning Congress to allow stimulus money to be directed to her decrepit middle school, could not possibly have anticipated the media attention that was to follow. Yet she exhibited a surprising poise in directing her letter not just to Congress but to a broader public audience that needed to become invested in change.[5] As she wrote to Congress, she also, perhaps, gestured to the world: "If you approve this bill it would not only be our school but also *yours* too" [emphasis added]. Her endearing and honest rhetoric expressed faith in the notion of a national collective interest that she could, even as a young girl, represent.

As South Carolina's conservatism continues to capture national headlines and influence public policy, the voices of African American intellectuals and thinkers remain essential to our understanding of the history and politics of the state and their effect on American life. The writers featured in *The South Carolina Roots of African American Thought* offer a critical counternarrative stretching back into the antebellum period that challenges and reshapes the dominant discourse that characterizes perceptions of South Carolina as a white conservative Republican stronghold. African American thinkers and intellectuals have positioned themselves as both Republicans and Democrats, and they have also aligned themselves with independents, when necessary, to best address injustices locally, nationally, and internationally. The legacy of slavery and oppression in the state has heightened their sensitivities to the plight of marginalized peoples on a global scale. *The South Carolina Roots of African American Thought* showcases the passions emanating from eighteen black thinkers for South Carolina, as well as for the state of the nation and the world. They are representative of African American South Carolinians, whose ideologies and activism enrich the deeply rooted tradition of fervid engagement in public debate to effect change.

NOTES

1. Angelina and Sarah Grimké were sisters of the boys' father and had established prominent careers in the North as abolitionists and advocates for women's rights. When they found out about their young mixed-race nephews, they welcomed Francis and Archibald into the family and assisted them with their education and their careers. The complex family history of these brothers is sketched out in more detail in the essays that are included in their respective chapter units in this volume.

2. Hunter's mother, Harriet Milliner Harris, was born on January 1, 1863, the date that President Abraham Lincoln signed the Emancipation Proclamation. Lincoln had issued a preliminary proclamation four months earlier, on September 22, 1862. In her autobiography, *A Nickel and a Prayer,* Hunter states that her mother escaped "slavery by the narrowest of margins." Hunter, *A Nickel and a Prayer,* 32.

3. Jessie Smith Carney, "Septima Clark," *Notable Black Women,* 189.

4. *Briggs v. Elliott,* 98 F. Supp. 529 (S.C. 1951); *Brown v. Board of Education,* 347 U.S. 483 (1954).

5. Although Bethea addressed her letter to Congress, her principal also forwarded it to President Barack Obama.

Slavery and Abolition

PART I

Daniel Payne
(1811–1893)

ᘒ❦ EDUCATOR, ACTIVIST, CLERGYMAN

"Payne is playing Hell in Charleston."

I n 1865, while the ruins of the South still smoldered, Daniel Payne returned to the state he had been run out of three decades before. Payne,
who had left Charleston in 1835 after his school for black children was
shut down, fearlessly returned to Charleston with nine other missionaries
to establish congregations of the African Methodist Episcopal (AME) Church
in order to provide spiritual, educational, and logistical support to those recovering from lives in bondage.

This bold return would not have surprised anyone who had worked
with or known Payne. His courage, resilience, resourcefulness, and—most of
all—profound dedication to service shaped his entire life; as can be see from
the excerpts here, taken from his thoughtful autobiography, *Recollections of
Seventy Years* (1888), it was his experiences seeing the deprivation and suffering in South Carolina during the early decades of the nineteenth century
that impelled him to a life of religious and educational activism.

Payne was born in 1811 a free black child in Charleston, a status that
had terrible constraints upon it because of the stringent cultural and legal
practices of the period. Orphaned early on, he was nonetheless fortunate
enough to be sponsored by a freeman's benevolent organization, the Minor's

Moralist Society,[1] which paid for a few years of his education at a school for free black children. With enormous dedication and by squeezing in hours to study before and after his labor as a carpenter, he managed to educate himself enough to open his own school at the age of nineteen. Beginning with three free children by day and three adult slaves by night, Payne's school grew to more than sixty students by 1834 and included classes in mathematics, geography, history, grammar, drawing, and even physical education.

In 1834 the state authorities passed legislation forbidding anyone to teach blacks, whether slave or free, and Payne was forced to shut down his school by May 1, 1835. Knowing the legislation was at least partly directed at him, personally (as is discussed later), Payne promptly left Charleston and made his way north with letters of introduction to ministers from a variety of denominations, all attesting to his character and his need for suitable occupation. Once settled in Pennsylvania, he worked with the Philadelphia Vigilance Committee to aid fugitive slaves and during these years began to grapple with shifting personal, political, and spiritual identities as he transitioned through a number of organizations.

Although it was Episcopalians who initially helped him the most as he settled in the north, their focus upon Liberia alienated Payne, who did not wish to go overseas on an African field mission or what he later termed "Ecclesiastical Imperialism."[2] He joined the Lutheran Seminary in Pennsylvania, but his poor eyesight, supposedly the result of having observed an eclipse in earlier years, forced him to drop out. By 1842 he switched allegiances to the African Methodist Episcopal (AME) Church because he thought an independent and successful black church could, by example, counter arguments about racial inferiority. The AME Church became his institutional home for the rest of his life. He quickly rose in its ranks to become its official historiographer in 1848 and a bishop by 1852.

His first wife, Julia A. Farris, died shortly after they were married in 1847. He was married again in 1854 to Eliza Clark of Cincinnati. They had no children; instead of childrearing, Payne threw his considerable energies entirely into service of his nation, his race, and the AME Church.

Payne was instrumental in the founding of Wilberforce University, a Methodist school, in 1856, and in 1863 he helped arrange for the AME Church to take over the university after it had been bankrupted by financial troubles brought on by the Civil War. When much of the campus was burned by Southern sympathizers in 1865, Payne helped raise funds to rebuild and was soon appointed Wilberforce University's president, the first African American university president in the nation.

During Reconstruction he returned to Charleston to help the AME Church expand in the South, and he oversaw its explosive growth to more than fifty thousand new members only a year after he arrived.[3] In his long career thereafter he served as one of the nineteenth century's most influential black spiritual leaders. The motto he established for the AME Church, "God our Father, Christ Our Redeemer, Man Our Brother," served as the AME motto until 2008.[4]

After Payne's death, in 1893, his legacy of mentorship was revered by later generations of black intellectuals. He was eulogized and anthologized in the works of several other writers in this collection, who recognized him as a figure who had changed the possibilities of America for everyone. As Francis Grimké wrote in his introduction to Payne's memoir, "No man of our race has had a wider influence, or has contributed more toward the intellectual, moral, and spiritual elevation of our people than the author of these memoirs."[5]

Payne's narrative shares many characteristics of the nineteenth-century slave narrative: it features an inspirational personal journey from ignorance into knowledge; it chronicles a growing social and political awakening to the idea that injustice and slavery were national issues and not merely personal ones; and it follows the northbound journey of a young man of color from the Deep South. Nonetheless, because Payne was born as a free child of color in Charleston, his narrative differs in other ways quite markedly from the slave narrative tradition. Among other differences, while African American slave narratives of this period commonly feature stock, albeit sincere, references to the links between literacy and spiritual awakening, Payne's narrative addresses both education and religion in a manner that would have been unfamiliar to most enslaved African Americans of his era. He chronicles his own efforts at getting an education so as to then chronicle how his efforts were later directed toward the education of others.

In the chapters from his autobiography, *Recollections of Seventy Years,* represented here, Payne describes how he chose the subjects he taught and, most significant, how he attained the expertise to teach those specialized areas of study. As he powerfully illustrates, this was a formidable task for a young black schoolteacher at the time.

Indeed, one of the reasons to include this discussion of his school curriculum here is to reinsert interest in the natural sciences into the history of African American thought. For while Payne is known today as an educator and as an AME bishop, his broad-ranging interests in all areas of education flesh out a dimension of education's possibilities far beyond the powerful but nonetheless more common discussions of literacy as it is depicted in slave narratives of the mid-nineteenth century. In one of the chapters presented here, Payne even describes sending out students to collect rare caterpillars and, eventually, poisonous snakes—the latter an assignment he soon regrets as it brings him to the attention of white authorities in Charleston just at a historical moment in which black education was itself a new target for suspicion and fear. The son of the wealthy lawyer Lionel Kennedy caught Payne's students collecting snakes and commented, "Payne is playing hell in Charleston."

It should not, perhaps, have surprised Payne to hear a few months later that Lionel Kennedy, the owner of the snake-infested plantation, had helped draft a bill in the General Assembly forbidding anyone to teach black people, whether slave or free, to read or write.[6] While seemingly general, this was nonetheless legislation clearly inspired by, if not directed at, Payne. He was given no choice but to disband his school. As his remarkable account makes clear, this pivotal experience of seeing his work so crushed drove the dedication to overcoming ignorance and oppression that characterized the rest of his life.

The second selection featured here marks a critical speech in the rise of the abolitionist movement and demonstrates the intellectual growth and power Payne had achieved since retreating from Charleston as a mild-mannered, albeit renegade, schoolmaster just a few years earlier. His speech about the danger slavery posed to the entire country is directed nationally but draws its references and force from his South Carolina experiences.

In 1839 Payne, on the occasion of his ordination, spoke to the Franckean Synod of the Lutheran Church in Fordsboro, New York. His stirring speech, which is one of the great texts of the abolitionist movement, effectively persuaded the Synod's leadership to officially support the antislavery position. In his speech he draws upon his personal experience in South Carolina to make his case. As he saw it, slavery was an offense "not because it enslaves the black man, but because it enslaves man." Payne argues that slavery destroys "moral agency"—that is, it destroys one's will or agency to be the moral actor God had intended him to be. For his audience Payne could calculate no more compelling argument.

A sophisticated rhetorician, Payne also raises notions of how power operates in the very real world of civic law by building his case on the obscenity of how slavery could "nullify" God's laws. Such terminology was, of course, calculated to invoke the very recent prominence of South Carolina in the national debates. The 1832 nullification crisis was brought on by South Carolina's resistance to federal tariffs set up after the war of 1812. By July 1832, John C. Calhoun had resigned the vice presidency of the United States to run for the Senate, where he could more effectively promote the notion of the tariff issue's unconstitutionality. A compromise tariff was eventually accepted but not before South Carolina had made military preparations to resist anticipated federal enforcement and had set the stage and the tone for what many increasingly came to see as the inevitable conflict of the Civil

War. Thus when Payne invoked nullification, as he does repeatedly in the this speech, it was both an ironic and a heartfelt move designed to remind his listeners not merely of the offense to God that slavery represented but also of how the particular history of South Carolina's political posing over states' rights had belied the true evil of slavery behind the state's power.

❧ Excerpts from *Recollections of Seventy Years*

Chapter 1: *"Parentage and Ancestry"*

I was born of free parents in the city of Charleston, S.C., on the 24th of February, 1811, in what was then known as Swinton Lane, now called Princess Street. My parents were London and Martha Payne. I remember that my father was a man of brown complexion, of slender frame, and about five feet eight inches high. He was an earnest Christian and a class-leader, having two classes under him—what used to be called the Seekers' Class and the Members' Class.[7] He was a faithful observer of family worship; and often his morning prayers and hymns aroused me, breaking my infant sleep and slumbers. He taught me the alphabet and my monosyllables, and I remember that once he whipped me for neglecting my lessons. After the war of 1812 the city of Charleston was illuminated,[8] and, in order that I might have a clear view of every object, he carried me through the streets with my feet straddling over his shoulders.

It is said that he was born of free parents in the State of Virginia, but, when a mere lad, was decoyed on board a ship with cakes and amused in the cabin until the vessel was out at sea. He was taken into the port of Charleston, and sold as a slave to a house and sign painter. In this condition he lived until he reached manhood, when he purchased his freedom for one thousand dollars.

His father, I am informed, was one of six brothers who served in the Revolution. Their father was an Englishman by the name of Paine. In the early immigration from England to Massachusetts two of the brothers arrived on the shores of New England. One remained in Massachusetts; the other concluded to go and join the colonists at Jamestown, Va. But before parting they agreed to change the letter "i" to "y" in the name of the one who had resolved to identify his fate with that of the Virginia colonists, in order that his descendants might be identified. Thus our family name became Payne.

As far as memory serves me my mother was of light-brown complexion, of middle stature and delicate frame. She told me that her grandmother was of the tribe of Indians known in the early history of the Carolinas as the Catawba Indians.[9] The husband of her grandmother was a black man named Alexander Goings, who was remarkable for great bodily strength and activity. My mother was a woman of amiable disposition, gentle manners, and fervent piety. Her death, which was triumphant, even glorious, was occasioned by consumption. Both parents were members of the Methodist Episcopal Church, and worshiped in Cumberland Street Church.[10]

I was about four and a half years old at the time of my father's death, and about nine and a half when my mother died. After the death of my father it was my mother's invariable custom to take her "little Daniel" by the hand and lead him to the class-meeting, seating him by her side. In this way I became early impressed with strong religious feelings. After her death my grandaunt, Mrs. Sarah Bordeaux, took charge of me. She did much toward stimulating me to attain unto a noble character, and to this day I feel the influence of her godly lessons and holy examples.

Chapter 2: "Childhood and Youth"

As early as 1803 the Minor's Moralist Society was established in the city of Charleston by James Mitchell, Joseph Humphries, William Cooper, Carlos Huger, Thomas S. Bonneau, William Clark, and Richard Holloway—all free colored men. Its object was to educate orphan or indigent colored children, and also to provide for their necessary wants. It consisted of fifty members, who contributed five dollars each at first, and paid thereafter the monthly sum of twenty-five cents each. As many as six children were at one time receiving its care and attention. It continued in existence until 1847, when, from the decease of many useful members and other local causes, it ceased to exist; not, however, without having done much good which continues to manifest itself both in Church and State.

The Hugers (pronounced Hugee) were descendants of the Huguenots. One of the Hugers was Minister to the court of Belgium. During his ministry he heard one of the French missionaries give his experiences in heathen lands. He translated the story and sent it to the Charleston papers. The reading of this aroused in me a great desire to learn the French language—my first ambition to know a foreign tongue.

I was put into this Society's school for two years, when I was about eight years old; after which I was instructed by Mr. Thomas S. Bonneau, the most popular school-master in the city, for about three years. There I learned to spell, read, and write, and "cipher" as far as the "Rule of Three."[11] The chief books used for reading were monographs of the histories of Greece, Rome, and England; while the "Columbian Orator"[12] was the book used for training in the art of speaking. When about twelve years of age I was hired out to a shoe-merchant, with whom I did not stay long. When nearly thirteen years old I was put to the carpenter's trade with my brother-in-law, James Holloway, the eldest son of Mr. Richard Holloway. I spent four and a half years with him. I then spent nine months at the tailor's trade.

It was during the time that I was in the carpenter's shop that I came into possession of the first number of what was then known as the "Self-interpreting Bible,"[13] by Rev. John Brown, of Haddington, Scotland. It was prefaced with a biographical sketch of the great man. The reading of this became the turning-point of my life; for, after reading it, I came to the conclusion to try and be what he was. I said to myself: "If Brown learned Latin, Greek, and Hebrew without a living teacher, why can't I?" This question was answered by: "I'll try." Up to that hour I had never seen a book in Latin, Greek, or Hebrew; but I resolved as soon as I could get them to study them. Meanwhile, I read every book within my reach—among which was the "Scottish Chiefs."[14] Wallace and Bruce became my ideal great men. Having heard of Hayti and the Haytiens, I desired to become a soldier and go to Hayti, which resolution was fixed until changed by a dream in which I was a soldier on the battle-field encountering a tremendous foe. The slaughter was great; the cries of the wounded and dying; the mangled corpses, their hideous looks; the prancing, leaping, and neighing of wounded horses—all conspired to make such a terrible impression upon me of the horrors of war that I foreswore the soldier's life; and again Rev. John Brown,[15] of Haddington, became my ideal man.

I was the child of many prayers. My father dedicated me to the service of God before I was born, declaring that if the Lord would give him a son that son should be consecrated to him, and named after the Prophet Daniel. After my birth I was taken to the house of God, and there again consecrated to his service in the holy ordinance of baptism. From the sanctuary my parents returned home with me, and on bended knees, my pious father holding me in his arms, again dedicated me to the service of the Lord.

Many a time, when the people of God were telling their experience in the divine life, in the class-meeting, I have felt the Spirit of God moving my childish heart. When I was only eight years old such was the effect of a sermon upon my young heart that I went home crying through the streets, and sought the garden and prayed. After my mother's death I was often led by the Spirit to go to the garret to bend the knee and look up into heaven, beseeching the Lord to make me a good boy. Such devotional feelings were always deepened by the contemplation of a moon-lit sky.

In my fifteenth year these impressions were so great that I could no longer cast them off amid my youthful sports, as in former times. I therefore went to the authorities of the Methodist Episcopal Church, and was examined. I was taken into the Society on probation, and assigned to the class of Mr. Samuel Weston,[16] who from that time became the chief religious guide of my youth.

My conversion took place in my eighteenth year. Religion among the members of the Cumberland Street Church had waxed very cold, and Brother

Holloway called a special meeting of all the classes, and inquired what might be done for the revival of God's work. It was decided to meet every Sunday between the morning and evening service in Mr. Bonneau's school-room to pray for a revival. In this place we met Sunday after Sunday. God heard our songs of praise, our prayers of faith, poured out his awakening and converting power upon his waiting children, and many souls were converted and sanctified by it. Of this number I was one. Here I too gave him my *whole heart,* and instantly felt that peace which passeth all understanding and that joy which is unspeakable and full of glory. Several weeks after this event, between twelve and one o'clock one day, I was in my humble chamber, pouring out my prayers into the listening ears of the Saviour, when I felt as if the hands of a man were pressing my two shoulders and a voice speaking within my soul saying: *"I have set thee apart to educate thyself in order that thou mayest be an educator to thy people."* The impression was *irresistible* and *divine;* it gave a new direction to my thoughts and efforts. Then again did the example of the illustrious John Brown, of Haddington, set itself before me.

After this circumstances I resolved to devote every moment of leisure to the study of books, and every cent to the purchase of them. I raised money by making tables, benches, clothes-horses, and "corset-bones,"[17] which I sold on Saturday night in the public market. During my apprenticeship I would eat my meals in a few minutes and spend the remainder of the hour allowed me at breakfast and dinner in reading. After the day's work was done I perused my books till nearly twelve o'clock; and then, keeping a tinder-box, flint, steel, and candle at my bedside, I would awake at four, strike a light, and study till six, when my daily labors began. Thus I went on reading book after book, drawing pictures with crayon, and now and then composing verses. In my nineteenth year I forsook the carpenter's trade for the life of an educator.

Chapter 3: *"The School-Master in the Dark South"*

My first school was opened in 1829 in a house on Tradd Street occupied by one Cæsar Wright. It consisted of his three children, for each of whom he paid me fifty cents a month. I also taught three adult slaves at night, at the same price, thus making my monthly income from teaching only three dollars. This was not sufficient to feed me, but a slave-woman, Mrs. Eleanor Parker, supplied many of my wants. I was happy in my humble employment, but at the end of the year I was so discouraged at the financial result, and by the remarks expressed by envious persons, that I decided to seek some other employment which would yield better pay.

At this juncture a wealthy slave-holder arrived in Charleston, *en route* to the West Indies for his health. Knowing that British law emancipated every slave that put his foot on British soil, he desired to obtain the services of a free young man of color sufficiently intelligent to do his out-of-door business. I was commended to him, and called upon him at the Planters' Hotel.[18] Among the inducements he offered he said: "If you will go with me, the knowledge that you will acquire of men and things will be of far more value to you than the wages I will pay you. Do you know what makes the difference between the master and the slave? *Nothing but superior knowledge.*"

This statement was fatal to his desire to obtain my services, for I instantly said to myself: "If it is true that there is nothing but superior knowledge between the master and the slave, I will not go with you, but will rather go and obtain that knowledge which constitutes the master." As I politely took my leave these words passed through my mind:

> He that flies his Saviour's cross
> Shall meet his Maker's frown.

Then these reflections followed. "In abandoning the school-room am I not fleeing from the cross which the Saviour has imposed upon me? Is not the abandonment of the teacher's work in my case a sin?" The answer was easily found, and I resolved to reopen my school and to inform my patrons to that effect.

On the first of the year 1830 I re-opened my school, which continued to increase in numbers until the room became too small, and I was constrained to procure a more commodious place. This in turn became too small, and one was built for me on Anson Street, by Mr. Robert Howard, in the rear of his yard. This house is still standing (1886). Here I continued to teach until April, 1835.

During the three years of my attendance at the school of Mr. Thomas S. Bonneau I learned how to read, write, and spell; also arithmetic as far as the "Rule of Three." Spelling was a delightful exercise of my boyhood. In this I excelled. Seldom did I lose my place at the head of my class, and he who won it did not occupy it long. History was my great delight. Of geography and map-drawing, English grammar and composition I knew nothing, because they were not taught in any of the schools for colored children. I therefore felt the need of knowledge in these directions; but how was I to obtain it?

I had a geography, but had never seen an atlas, and, what was more, I knew not how or where to get one. Fortunately for me, one day as I was sitting on the piazza endeavoring to learn some lesson, a woman entered the gate and approached me with a book in her hand. Said she: "Don't you want to buy this book?" Taking it, I opened it, and to my great joy I beheld the colored maps of an atlas—the very thing I needed. Said I: "What will you take for it?" The woman had found it on the street, and replied: "Whatever you choose to give." All that I could command at the time was a York shilling (twelve and one-half cents in silver coin), so I gave it to her, and rejoiced over my prize. Immediately I went to work with my geography and atlas, and in about six months was able to construct maps on the Mercator's and globular projection.[19] After I had acquired this ability I introduced geography and map-drawing into my school. At the same time with geography I studied and mastered English grammar. I began with "Murray's Primary Grammar," and committed the entire book to memory, but did not understand it; so I reviewed it. Then light sprung up; still I felt like one in a dungeon who beheld a glimmer of light at a distance, and with steady but cautious footsteps moved toward it, inspired by the hope that I would soon find its source and come out into the full blaze of animated day. I then made a second review of it, and felt conscious of my power to teach it. I therefore added that to my curriculum.

Having now the groundwork, I began to build the superstructure. I commenced with "Playfair's Euclid,"[20] and proceeded as far as the first five books. The next thing which arrested my attention was botany. The author and her specimens enchanted me; my progress was rapid, and the study became to me a source of great happiness and an instrument of great usefulness. Descriptive chemistry, natural philosophy, and descriptive astronomy followed in rapid succession.

"Burret's Geography of the Heavens"[21] was my text-book in the last-named science. Stimulated by this interesting guide, I watched the total eclipse of 1832 from its commencement to its completion with my *naked eye;* but I paid dear for my rash experiment. The immediate result was a partial loss of sight. No book could be read for about three weeks. Whenever I opened a book the pages had the appearance of *black sheets.* From this injury I have never fully recovered. Up to that time my eyes were like those of the eagle; ever since they have been growing weaker and weaker.

Then, on a Thursday morning, I bought a Greek grammar, a lexicon, and a Greek Testament. On the same day I mastered the Greek alphabet; on Friday I learned to write them; on Saturday morning I translated the first chapter of Matthew's Gospel from Greek into English. My very soul rejoiced and exulted in this glorious triumph. Next came the Latin and the French. Meanwhile I was pushing my studies in drawing and coloring till I was able to produce a respectable flower, fruit, or animal on paper and on velvet.

My researches in botany gave me a relish for zoology; but as I could never get hold of any work on this science I had to *make books* for myself. This I did by killing such insects, toads, snakes, young alligators, fishes, and young sharks as I could catch. I then cleaned and stuffed those that I could, and hung them upon the walls of my school-room. The following fact will give the index of my methods. I bought a live alligator, made one of my pupils provoke him to bite, and whenever he opened his mouth I discharged a load of shot from a small pistol down his throat. As soon as he was stunned

I threw him on his back, cut his throat, ripped open his chest, hung him up and studied his viscera till they ceased to move. The flesh of all that I killed I cooked and tasted. I excepted nothing but the toad and snake. My detestation for these was too intense to allow me to put their flesh into my mouth.

My enthusiasm was the inspiration of my pupils. I used to take my first class of boys into the woods every Saturday in search of insects, reptiles, and plants, and at the end of five years I had accumulated some fine specimens of each of these. I had also taken a fatherless boy to educate gratuitously. This lad's sister one day found a large caterpillar on an elderberry-tree. This worm she sent to me. It was the length and thickness of a large laboring-man's middle finger. Its color was that of gold blended with azure. It had four rows of horns running the whole length of its body; these horns were made up of golden and ebony-like points; its head was also encircled with a crown of these horns.

Not being able to determine the species or genus of this worm, I took it to Mrs. Ferguson, the sister of Judge Colcox who was unable to give me any information in regard to it; but she advised me to take it to Dr. Bachman,[22] who was then the most distinguished naturalist in South Carolina. I little knew what that visit was to bring about ultimately.

The Doctor received me kindly, and gave its classification. He also instructed me in its nature and habits, and how to carry it through its different stages of existence. This, however, I preferred him to do, allowing me at the same time to visit his studio and observe the transformations. This request was kindly complied with by the learned divine and naturalist. On my second visit he took me into his garden and showed me his fine collections of flowers. He also exhibited to me his herbarium and his valuable collection of insects from different parts of the world. On my last visit he took me into his parlor and introduced me to his wife and daughters as "the young philosopher." There I sat and conversed with his family as freely as though all were of the same color and equal rank; and by my request his daughter skillfully performed several pieces upon the piano. A remark of his at that visit has occurred to me many times through life. There was upon the center-table, protected by a large glass globe, an artificial tree bearing a collection of beautifully-mounted birds. My attention was drawn to them, and I expressed myself to the effect that he had about him every thing to make his home pleasant. His reply was substantially this: "Yes; I feel it my duty to throw around my home every possible attraction for my daughters, so that they may never have occasion to seek elsewhere for forbidden pleasures."

My school increased in popularity, and became the most popular of five which then existed. It numbered about sixty children from most of the leading families of Charleston. But I was not without enemies who endeavored to arrest the progress of my school and destroy my usefulness by such remarks as these: "He is an impostor." "Who ever heard of any one learning such things—such things as he teaches—but men trained in a college." "He must deal with the devil."

Such imputations and slanders availed nothing. They seemed to render me more popular, and at last two of the other school-masters came to me to be taught such sciences as they knew not. It was a happiness for me to assist them, which I did, directing them to the authors and the methods which I had employed. It was also one of my methods in order to interest my pupils to erect several gymnastic instruments, that they might develop their muscular systems and find amusement to break the monotony of the school-room; but in all their sports I led them in person. The children and youths were developing rapidly in their studies, but the hour of the Prince of Darkness came upon the school in the following way:

In the prosecution of my studies in zoology I desired to obtain a highland moccasin, which was then considered a species of rattlesnake, and whose bite was deadly. Therefore I engaged the services of a slave of lawyer Lionel Kennedy,[23] who was at that time an alderman of the city of Charleston. The plantation of this gentleman was about one mile distant from the city. On the appointed Saturday I dispatched three of my advanced class (John Lee, Robert Wishan, and Michael Eggart) with a large glass bottle, in order that they might bring me the viper alive. On their arrival at the plantation they found Lawyer Kennedy and his son, Dr. Kennedy, overlooking the work of the slaves. They knew me and knew the boys' parents. Calling the lads to them, they demanded the reason of their appearance on the plantation. A direct answer was given. They then inquired after my motives for buying this serpent from their slaves; to which a direct answer was also given. Then they asked the lads to tell them what were the different things taught them, and they also examined them in their studies. The boys answered every question put to them except one. Then said the young doctor: "Why, pa, Payne is playing hell in Charleston." This occurred about the middle of the summer of 1834.

⸰⸰ "Slavery Brutalizes Man"

MR. PRESIDENT: I move the adoption of the Report, because it is based upon the following propositions:

American Slavery brutalizes man—destroys his moral agency, and subverts the moral government of God.

Sir, I am opposed to slavery, not because it enslaves the black man, but because it enslaves *man.* And were all the slaveholders in this land men of color, and the slaves white men, I would be as thorough and uncompromising an abolitionist as I now am; for whatever and whenever I may see a being in the form of a man, enslaved by his fellow man, without respect to his complexion, I shall lift up my voice to plead his cause, against all the claims of his proud oppressor; and I shall do it not merely from the sympathy which man feels towards suffering man, but because God, *the living God,* whom I dare not disobey, has commanded me to open my mouth for the dumb, and to plead the cause of the oppressed.

Slavery brutalizes man. We know that the word *man,* in its primitive sense, signifies —.* But the intellectual and moral structure of man, and the august relations which he sustains to the Deity, have thrown around the name, and being designated by it, a halo of glory, brightened by all the ideas, that are ennobling on earth, and blessed in eternity. This being God created but a little lower than the angels, and crowned him with glory and honor; but slavery hurls him down from his elevated position, to the level of brutes, strikes this crown of glory from his head and fastens upon his neck the galling yoke, and compels him to labor like an ox, through summer's sun and winter's snow, without remuneration. Does a man take the calf from the cow and sell it to the butcher? So slavery tears the child from the arms of the reluctant mother, and barters it to the soul trader for a young colt, or some other commodity! Does the bird catcher tear away the dove from his mate? So slavery separates the groaning husband from the embraces of his distracted and weeping wife! And are the beasts of the forest hunted, tortured and slain at the pleasure of the cruel hunter? So are the slaves hunted, tortured and slain by the cruel monster slavery! To treat a man like a brute is to brutalize him. We have seen that slavery treats man like a brute, therefore slavery brutalizes man! But does slavery stop here? Is it content with merely treating the external man like a brute? No, sir, it goes further, and with a heart as brazen as that of Belshazzar and hands still more sacrilegious, it lays hold of the *immortal mind, seizes the will, and binds that which Jehovah did not bind—fetters that which the Eternal made as free to move and act as the breath of Heaven. "It destroys moral agency!"* To destroy moral agency is to fetter or obstruct the will of man. Now let us see if slavery is innocent of this. The very moment that a man conceives the diabolic design of enslaving his brother's body, that very moment does he also conceive the still more heinous design of fettering his will, for well does he know that in order to make his dominion supreme over the body, he must fetter the living spring of all its motions. Hence, the first lesson the slave is taught is to yield his will unreservedly and exclusively to the dictates of his master. And if a slave desire to educate himself or his children, in obedience to the dictates of reason or the laws of God, he does not, he cannot do it without the consent of his master. Does reason and circumstances and the Bible command a slave to preach

---

*The blank space is the original report of the speech.

the gospel of his brethren? Slavery arises, and with a frown, an oath and a whip, fetters or obstructs the holy volition of his soul! I knew a pious slave in Charleston who was a licensed exhorter in the Methodist Episcopal Church; this good man was in the habit of spending his Saturday nights on the surrounding plantations, preaching to the slaves. One night, as usual, he got into a canoe, sailed upon James' Island. While in the very act of preaching the unsearchable riches of Christ to dying men, the patrols seized him and whipped him in the most cruel manner, and compelled him to promise that he would never return to preach again to those slaves. In the year 1834, several colored brethren, who were also exhorters in the Methodist Episcopal Church commenced preaching to several *destitute white families,* who gained a subsistence by cultivating some poor lands about three or four miles from Charleston. The first Sunday I was present; the house was nearly filled with these poor white farmers. The master of the house was awakened to a sense of his lost condition. During the following week he was converted. On the third Sunday from the day he was convinced of sin he died in the triumphs of faith, and went to heaven. On the fourth Sunday from the time the dear brethren began to preach, the patrols scented their tract, and put them to chase. Thus, an end was put to their labors. Their willing souls were fettered, and the poor whites constrained to go without the preaching of the gospel. In a word, it is in view of man's moral agency that God commands him to shun vice, and practice virtue. But what female slave can do this? I lived twenty-four years in the midst of slavery and never knew but six female slaves who were reputedly virtuous! What profit is to the female slave that she is disposed to be virtuous? Her will, like her body, is not her own; they are both at the pleasure of her master; and he brands them at his will. *So it subverts the moral government of God.*

In view of the moral agency of man, God hath most wisely and graciously given him a code of laws, and certain positive precepts, to control and regulate moral actions. This code of laws, and these positive precepts, with the divine influence which they are naturally calculated to exert on the mind of man, constitutes his moral government.

Now, to nullify these laws—to weaken or destroy their legitimate influence on the human mind, or to hinder man from yielding universal and entire obedience to them is to subvert the moral government of God.

Now, slavery nullifies these laws and precepts—weakens and destroys their influence over the human mind, and hinders men from yielding universal and entire obedience to them; therefore slavery subverts the moral government of God. This is the climax of the sin of slavery! This is the blackest, foulest, and most horrid feature of the heaven-daring *Monster!* He stretcheth out his hand against God, and strengtheneth himself against the Almighty— he runneth on him, even on his neck, upon the thick bosses of his buckler.

Thus saith the Lord, "Thou shalt not commit adultery." But does the man who owns a hundred females obey the law? Does he not nullify it and compel the helpless woman to disobey God? Concerning the religious instruction of children, thus saith the Lord, "Bring them up in the nurture and admonition of the Lord." But what saith slavery? "They are my property, and shall be brought up to serve me." They shall not *even learn to read his word,* in order that they may be brought up in his nurture and admonition. If any man doubts this, let him read the slave code of Louisiana and see if it is not death to teach slaves. Thus saith the Lord, "Remember the Sabbath day, to keep it holy." Does not slavery nullify this law, and compel the slave to work on the Sabbath? Thus saith the Lord, "Obey thy father and thy mother." Can the slave children obey this command of God? Does not slavery command the children to obey the master and let him alone? Thus saith the Son of God, "What God hath joined together let no man put asunder." Does not slavery nullify this law, by breaking the sacred bands of wedlock, and separating the husband and wife forever? Thus saith the Son of God, "Search the Scriptures." Does not slavery seal up the word of God and make it criminal for the slave to read it? In 1834, the legislature of South Carolina enacted a law prohibiting the instruction of any slave; and Mr. Lawrence in a pamphlet which he published in 1835, to defend this law, declared that if the slaves were permitted to read the Bible, ninety of them would become infidels, like Voltaire, where ten would become Christians.[24] "Go ye into all the world, and preach the Gospel unto every creature," saith the Son of God. Does slavery permit it? In 1835, a minister of the Episcopal Church, in the city of Charleston, appealed to the civil authority for permission to preach to the free population of an evening, but they would not permit him.

The objector may reply, that at the present moment there are four Methodist missionaries, and one Lutheran, laboring among the slave population of South Carolina. We answer, that this is true, and we are glad of it; but this fact does not overthrow our proposition, nor falsify what we have stated, for although a few planters have permitted the Gospel to be preached to their slaves, the majority of them prohibit it, and this permission is extraneous to slavery and is no part of its creed or code. Slavery never legislates for the religious instruction of slaves, but, on the contrary, legislates to perpetuate their ignorance; and there are laws this very moment in the statute books of South Carolina and other states, prohibiting the religious instruction of slaves. But this is not all that slavery does to subvert the moral government of God. The slaves are sensible of the oppression exercised by their masters; and they see these masters on the Lord's day worshiping in his holy Sanctuary. They hear their masters professing Christianity; they see their masters preaching the Gospel; they hear these masters praying in their families, and they know that oppression and slavery are inconsistent with the Christian religion; therefore they scoff at religion itself—mock their masters, and distrust both the goodness and justice of God. Yes, I have known them even to question His existence. I speak not of what others have told me, but of what *I have both seen and heard from the slaves themselves.* I have heard the mistress ring the bell for family prayer, and I have seen the servants immediately begin to sneer and laugh; and have heard them declare they would not go in to prayers, adding, if I go in she will only just read, "Servants obey your masters"; but she will not read, "Break every yoke, and let the oppressed go free." I have seen colored men at the church door, *scoffing at the ministers,* while they were preaching, and saying, you had better go home, and set your slaves free. A few nights ago between ten and eleven o'clock a runaway slave came to the house where I live for safety and succor. I asked him if he was a Christian. "No sir," said he, "white men treat us so bad in Mississippi that we can't be Christians."

Sir, I taught school in Charleston five years. In 1834 the legislature of our state enacted a law to prohibit colored teachers.[25] My school was filled with children and youth of the most promising talents; and when I looked upon them and remembered that in a few more weeks this school shall be closed and I be permitted no more to teach them, notwithstanding I had been a professor seven years, I began to question the existence of the Almighty and to say, if indeed there is a God, does he deal justly? Is he a just God? Is he a holy Being? If so, why does he permit a handful of dying men thus to oppress us? Why does he permit them to hinder me from teaching these children, when nature, reason and Revelation command me to teach them? Thus I began to question the divine government and to murmur at the administration of His providence. And could I do otherwise, while slavery's cruelties were pressing and grinding my soul in the dust, and robbing me and my people of those privileges which it was hugging to its breast, and giving thousands to perpetuate the blessing which it was tearing away from us? Sir, the very man who made the law alluded to, did that very year, increase the property of South Carolina College.

In a word, slavery tramples the laws of the living God under its unhallowed feet—weakens and destroys the influence which those laws are calculated to exert over the mind of man, and constrains the oppressed to blaspheme the name of the Almighty. For I have often heard them sneeringly say, that *"The Almighty made Charleston on Saturday night, when he was weary, and in a great hurry." O, Brethren of the Franckean Synod! awake! Awake to the battle and hurl the hottest thunders of divine truth at the head of this cruel monster, until he shall fall to rise no more, and the groans of the enslaved are converted into the songs of the free!!*

NOTES

1. Established in 1803, the Minor's Moralist Society was one of several black benevolent societies that emerged in antebellum Charleston. The societies offered various services to the black community, including burial assistance, loans, education, and charity for the poor. Drago, *Charleston's Avery Center,* 34.

2. Payne, "The Past, Present and Future of the A.M.E. Church."

3. Steward, "Prefatory Note" in Smith, *A History,* 504.

4. Dickerson, "About Us." The current motto, "God Our Father, Christ Our Redeemer, Holy Spirit Our Comforter, Humankind Our Family," was officially adopted during the AMEC's 2008 General Conference.

5. Francis Grimké, "Introduction," in Payne, *Recollections of Seventy Years,* 5.

6. Lionel Kennedy had been a judge on the Denmark Vesey case in 1822 that saw sixty-seven men convicted and thirty-five men put to death for attempting to raise a slave insurrection in Charleston. In sending his students near the Kennedy plantation, Payne erred in attracting the attention of a man whose career had been thrust into prominence by a slave rebellion and whose influence in the legislature allowed him to later help compose the legal prohibition against teaching any black person to read or write.

7. In the Methodist Episcopal Church and other Methodist denominations, a "seeker" is one who attends church but has not been officially converted to the religion. A "member" is a person who has been baptized and has entered into the covenant of being received into the fellowship of the church.

8. Several cities celebrated the end of the War of 1812 by having residents place candles in their windows. Payne may be referring to this occurrence in the city of Charleston.

9. The Catawba Indians have traditionally resided in the Piedmont regions of North and South Carolina. They first made contact with Europeans via the Spanish explorer Hernando de Soto in 1540. Many descendants of the Catawba today live on a reservation located in York County, South Carolina.

10. The Cumberland Street Church, built in 1787, was the first Methodist church in Charleston.

11. The Rule of Three was a popular method of teaching mathematics in the nineteenth century. It involved the use of proportions; to "cipher" using the Rule of Three meant taking three numbers and determining their relationship. For example, to cipher the Rule of Three for the numbers 3, 15, and 2, one would complete the phrase formed by determining that 3 is to 15 as 2 is to ___ (10).

12. *The Columbian Orator* was a collection of political poems, speeches, and dialogues, many of which concerned republican virtues of liberty and individualism. As a young slave, Frederick Douglass famously learned about liberty in part from the inspiring dialogues he encountered in *The Columbian Orator.*

13. *The Self-interpreting Bible* was an annotated Bible containing summary, analysis, and reflection; it first appeared in Edinburgh in 1778 and was reprinted several times in both Scotland and the United States.

14. *Scottish Chiefs* is a novel written about the War for Scottish Independence (1296–1305). See Porter, *The Scottish Chiefs, a Romance in Five Volumes.*

15. The Reverend John Brown (1722–1787) was the author of *The Self-Interpreting Bible* and other Biblical reference books, including *The Dictionary of the Bible* and *A General History of the Christian Church.*

16. Samuel Weston was a free black tailor in antebellum Charleston. His family was the wealthiest free black family in Charleston prior to the Civil War. A devout Methodist, he taught his class to become "useful and respectable members of society." Drago, *Charleston's Avery Center,* 34.

17. Clothes-horses are frames upon which clothes were hung to dry after being washed. "Corset-bones" are inserted into corsets to stabilize them and give them shape.

18. Located on Church Street, the Planters' Hotel was Charleston's first hotel. It later became the Dock Street Theater.

19. Mercator's projection is a manner of constructing a map in which at all places the degrees of latitude and longitude have the same ratio to one another as to the sphere itself. Globular projection is a manner of constructing a map in which the projection of the surface of a hemisphere is placed upon a plane that is parallel to the base of the hemisphere.

20. In 1785, the Scottish mathematician John Playfair published an alternative formulation of Euclid's Parallel Postulate. It is more commonly known as Playfair's Axiom.

21. Burret's Geography of the Heavens is a celestial chart created in 1835 by Elijah H. Burritt.

22. John Bachman was a clergyman, naturalist, and social reformer. He worked with John James Audubon to produce *Viviparous Quadrupeds of North America,* published in 1851. He also published several natural history papers and was a frequent contributor to the *South Carolina Medical Journal.* He founded Newberry College in 1856. His scientific collections and library, meant to be donated to Newberry, were destroyed by Sherman's army during the Civil War. He died in Charleston in 1874.

23. Drago, *Charleston's Avery Center,* 46. Lionel Kennedy served in the South Carolina House of Representatives and was one of the examining magistrates in the Demark Vesey trials. The Kennedy family supported passage of the Act of 1834, which tightened restrictions on free black schools.

24. Payne was likely referring here to Edward Laurens, who in 1835 published a pamphlet defending the legislation and arguing that "where one would draw the pure waters of life from the fountain of inspiration, hundreds would follow after false prophets, to their disquiet here, and perdition hereafter." See Laurens, *Letter to Seabrook,* 9.

25. Section 1 of the 1834 law forbidding any slave or free people of color to learn to read also forbade any slave or free person of color "to keep any school or other place of instruction." See McCord, "Act to Amend," 468.

Martin Robison Delany
(1812–1885)

⅔ AUTHOR, BLACK NATIONALIST

In this review I intend to speak plainly, call things by their right names,
and look those of whom I speak directly in the face.

U nlike many other individuals profiled in this collection, Martin Robison Delany was not born in South Carolina. Nonetheless, his spectacular life is closely identified with nineteen pivotal years in South Carolina. In the words of his biographer Robert Levine, "South Carolina was not a distant outpost; [for Delany] it was the *key* testing ground for the possibilities of a reconstructed United States in which blacks would be accorded citizenship and equal rights, and together with the whites of the state would figure out how to live together amicably and productively in a multiracial United States."[1] For Delany, who had an incredible career on the national and international stage long before he moved to South Carolina, his work and writing during his South Carolina sojourn came to signify how politics on a local level could play out the possibilities for black citizenship nationally.

Martin R. Delany is commonly identified as the one of the great early black nationalists in American history. Today he is also remembered as the author of one of the earliest novels published by a black writer in the United States, *Blake; or, the Huts of America: A Tale of the Mississippi Valley, the*

Southern United States, and Cuba.[2] Delany's achievements, however, far exceed these two categories of exceptionalism. Born in 1812 to a slave father, Samuel, and a free black seamstress, Pati, in Charles Town, Virginia (now part of West Virginia), he fled the state with his family when it was discovered that his mother had violated Virginia's prohibition against teaching black people to read by using a spelling book to instruct her five children. The family took refuge in Chambersburg, Pennsylvania, where Delany continued to study. At the age of nineteen, Delany moved to Pittsburgh, then a city with an active and influential African American population. There, Delany briefly studied Latin and Greek at Jefferson College.[3] During the cholera epidemic of 1833 he apprenticed with a Pittsburgh physician, learning to be a "cupper" and to apply leeches. It was while he was in Pittsburgh that he first became involved in smuggling fugitive slaves to freedom. He also during this period met and married Catherine A. Richards, with whom he was to eventually have eleven children, seven of whom survived into adulthood. In 1843 he founded a short-lived newspaper, the *Mystery,* but closed it in 1847 when he joined forces with Frederick Douglass to found the *North Star,* an abolitionist paper based in Rochester, New York. Delany traveled across Ohio, Pennsylvania, and Kentucky to lecture, report, and obtain subscriptions while Douglass attended to business and editorial matters in New York. Delany didn't collect enough subscriptions to support the paper, and he ended his relationship with the faltering enterprise by June 1849. Nonetheless, traveling and writing for the paper brought him into contact with an influential activist class of both black and white individuals outside Pittsburgh.

Seeking an entirely different career and perhaps a more stable means of support, Delany applied to and was rejected by several medical schools. He was eventually accepted at Harvard and began his studies in 1850 as one of three black men, who were the first to be accepted to the medical school. The uproar from white medical students at the thought of studying alongside black students as equals led Harvard dean Oliver Wendell Holmes Sr. to dismiss Delany and the others from the school after only one semester. Deeply scarred by this event and now skeptical that reason might ever sway power from prejudice, Delany went on in 1852 to publish "The Condition, Elevation, Emigration, and Destiny of the Colored People of the United States, Politically Considered." This work put forth the argument that black Americans should emigrate to Central or South America because the hope of integrated justice and acceptance in mainstream U.S. culture was dead. Indeed, following upon this notion, Delany and his family moved to Canada in 1856 and lived there for several years. He continued to publish and advocate emigration as a solution to racial problems in the United States, becoming the nineteenth century's best-known advocate of black nationalism. It was at this point that he began work on his novel, *Blake; or the Huts of America,* as a response to Harriet Beecher Stowe's *Uncle Tom's Cabin*, which he felt misrepresented enslaved people as passive.

Delany traveled to Africa and continued to advocate for emigration, supporting a number of different schemes, until the start of the Civil War forced him to turn from international to national issues. He met with President Lincoln and so impressed him that he was commissioned as the first black line field officer in the U.S. Army; as a major he received the highest rank granted any African American during the Civil War. At the end of the war Delany was assigned to the Freedman's Bureau at Beaufort, South Carolina, and took on increasing leadership positions as he worked, studied, and came to identify with the population of newly freed African Americans who were seeking to reshape and redefine their lives. Many of his important writings on this topic advocated what he imagined as a "triple alliance" linking northern capital, southern white landowners, and black labor.

Delany's politics, never consistent or simple enough to fit easy labels, became increasingly marked by surprising positions that often put him at odds with other black leaders and made him enemies and allies in unexpected places. In 1867 he took a public stance opposing the notion of a black vice-presidential candidate for the Republican Party. After an unsuccessful attempt to secure the post of Minister Resident and Consul General to Liberia in 1869, he returned to his activities in South Carolina politics. He supported many black officeholders in the Republican Party and fervently encouraged participatory citizenship by the newly free black population of South Carolina. Nonetheless he ran for lieutenant governor on an independent ticket in 1874 and closely lost to a black Republican rival. He then returned to the Republican Party and was appointed a trial justice in Charleston County. After a series of tussles over politically motivated accusations and local scandals, he turned to the Democratic Party and supported the candidacy of Wade Hampton III, a Democrat, for governor, seeing him as a moderate who would support black education. Delany's advocacy was no tacit nod or quiet editorial; rather, it took the form of traveling speeches and endorsements. His position so shocked and alienated many black freemen that in 1876 a rally for Hampton in Cainhoy, South Carolina, at which Delany spoke and which was attended by a number of heckling black Republicans dissolved into a violent riot between white and black Democrats and Republicans. Delany escaped, but several people were killed.

In the letter featured here Delany writes to his longtime friend and rival Frederick Douglass. This open letter was first published as a public document in the Charleston *Daily Republican* in 1871. It was later republished on August 31, 1871, with a response by Frederick Douglass in his own paper, the *New National Era*. Delany's candor is startling. He addresses color prejudice within the black community against dark-skinned people such as himself.

He lays out in no uncertain terms how the Republican Party has sullied its name in just a few short years through corruption and mismanagement. And he addresses the ways in which corrupt northerners and disingenuous white southerners have hijacked the Republican Party at the expense of the naïve population of freemen.

Delany's arguments echo with the claims of postracial rhetoric that one can hear in many twenty-first-century discussions. Yet such arguments were shocking to hear only a few years after the Emancipation Proclamation. Delany accuses the demagogues of South Carolina (both northern carpet-baggers and southern scalawags) of manipulation and of "rioting on the people's rights":

> Among other things, they taught the simple-minded people that suffrage was inviolably secure, the blacks being in the majority, would always control the affairs of State in the South; and that the fifteenth amendment had abolished color and complexion in the United States, and the people were now all of one race. This barefaced deception was so instilled in them that it became dangerous in many instances to go into the country and speak of color in any manner whatever without the angry rejoinder: "We don't want to hear that; we are all one color now!"

Delany's prescient analysis of how the rhetoric of ironic and malicious inclusivity could be harnessed to exclude blacks from meaningful and pro-portional representation was a remarkable instance of political courage. And, as mentioned earlier in the case of the riot at Cainhoy in 1876, it was the kind of bold and controversial position that fueled the attacks he later faced from both black and white Republican sympathizers.

His arguments about how token appointments of blacks to government positions actually hurt the cause of significant or meaningful black represen-tation (a point that could have been read only as an unsubtle jab at Douglass, who had recently been appointed assistant secretary to the Commission of Inquiry to Santo Domingo), are notable for how they embody a high-minded and almost utopian dream, not dissimilar to the kind of hope he had had for settling American-born blacks in Africa. (And Douglass responded: "The idea is equal and admirable in theory; but does it not already seem to you a little absurd as a matter of practice?")[4]

Douglass had a compelling point, but Delany's arguments about pro-portional representation echo with a poignancy specific to the era. After all, it had been only a few short years earlier that a war had been fought in part over the injustice of what has come to be known as the Three-Fifths Compro-mise, a provision in the Constitution that allowed enslaved black people in southern states to be considered three-fifths of a person for the purposes of enumeration when it came to issues of apportionment in the House of Representatives but not people at all inasmuch as they had no rights as citizens. Thus Delany's arguments might not have been seen as practical, but surely Douglass would have been aware that they resonated with a righteous anger particularly raw among the recently freed population.

It came as no surprise to anyone when, in 1876, Martin Delany was removed from his appointed post as a trial justice as part of the strategic rollback of Reconstruction gains by the conservative political parties under the leadership of Benjamin Tillman. Delany, with characteristic resilience, renewed his focus upon African settlement and chaired a finance committee for the Liberia Exodus Joint Stock Steamship Company, later serving as its president. He continued to write about race and politics but did not himself settle in Africa. Rather, he continued to practice medicine in South Carolina for a few more years. In 1884 he died in Xenia, Ohio.

?◕ Letter from Major Delany to Frederick Douglass

Hon. Frederick Douglass:[5]

My Dear Sir: It has been ten years since last we met (in your library at Rochester) to discuss and reconcile ourselves to President Lincoln's war policy. Since then slavery has been overthrown, and no "reunion" of what were, for twenty years or more, the leading colored men of the country, who shaped the policy and course of our race, which led to disenthrallment, having taken place, and consequently no interchange of ideas by counsel; I therefore deem it of importance at this time to take a political review of South Carolina, which I think will apply justly to nearly, if not the whole, of the "reconstructed States" of the South as well as the National Government.

When the war ended the colored people of the South had little knowledge of social and political affairs, and had of necessity to accept such leaders as presented themselves. The first of these were in the persons of various agencies; as school teachers (mostly women,) the Christian Commission, colporteurs and agents of the "Freedmen's Affairs," (not the Bureau,) who aided in directing their social and domestic relations.[6]

When reconstruction commenced, political leaders were greatly required, but few to be had. Southerners (the old masters) studiously opposed and refused to countenance reconstruction, and the freemen were fearful and would not have trusted them if they could have obtained their aid.

Those who came with or followed the army, with a very few native whites, were the only available political element to be had to carry out the measures of reconstruction.

These were readily accepted by the blacks (by this I include the entire colored people) and the fullest confidence reposed in them. Some were or had been officers in the army, some privates, some sutlers, others peddlers, and various tradesmen, others gamblers, and even pick-pockets, "hangers on" and "bummers."[7] I am particularly speaking of the whites. Among these were men of refinement, educated gentlemen, and some very good men; but a large part of those most active were of the lowest grade of Northern society, negro-haters at home, who could not have been elected to any position of honor or trust. Just such men as burnt down negro orphan asylums, and hung negro men to lamp-posts in the New York riot of 1863.[8] In this review I intend to speak plainly, call things by their right names, and look those of whom I speak directly in the face.

The best and most competent men were chosen to fill the most important positions in State and local governments, while the others readily obtained such places as required incumbents. Indeed, there were scarcely one so incompetent as not to have been assigned some position of trust.

Positioned in places of power, profit and trust, they soon sought by that guile and deception, known only to demagogues, under the acceptable appellations of Yankee, Republican, and Radical, to intrude themselves into the confidence of the blacks, and place themselves at their head as leaders. So insidiously did they do this that it was not discovered by the few colored men of intelligence who held places among them till too late to remedy the fatal evil.

These demagogues laid the foundation of their career upon a basis of the most dangerous political heresy. Deception, lying cheating, stealing, "whatever can be done in politics is fair," and to "beat is the duty in a political contest, no matter what means are used to effect it," are among the pernicious precepts of this moral infidelity.

Jealous of the few intelligent colored men among them, they studiously sought to divide the blacks, by sowing the seed of discord among them. This was facilitated by prejudicing the ignorant against the intelligent. These men strove and vied each with the other, regardless of consequences, to place himself in the lead of a community of blacks in both town and country, which in time was reduced to little else than a rabble mob of disorder and confusion. Trained in the leagues as serfs to their masters, it became dangerous to oppose these men of mischief. Because, having been recommended to their confidence at the commencement of reconstruction, their experience and knowledge in public men and matters were too limited to believe anything against them.

A knowledge of this emboldened these men to a persistence in their course of crime and corruption. Hence, many otherwise good men, both white and black, from age, inexperience, or weakness, were induced to accept the monstrous teachings and join with or follow the lead of these wretched impostors. Their sole object being personal gain, they cared little or nothing for public weal, the interest of the State or people, black or white, nor the Republican cause, upon which they had indecently imposed themselves. This is that which controlled Charleston politics and brought deserved defeat to the Republicans in the recent municipal election. It was just retribution to a set of unprincipled miscreants, rioting on the peoples' rights under the name of "Republicans." Honest, upright men of all parties, white and black, no longer able to bear it, determined to put down the abominable thing; leading Republicans, who had been standing aloof, taking an active part.

Among other things they taught the simple-minded people that suffrage was inviolably secure, the blacks being in the majority, would always control the affairs of State in the South; that the fifteenth amendment had abolished color and complexion in the United States, and the people were now all of one race.[9] This barefaced deception was so instilled into them that it became dangerous in many instances to go into the country and speak of color in any manner whatever, without the angry rejoinder: "We don't want to hear that; we are all one color now!"

These ridiculous absurdities were fostered by the demagogues the better to conceal their own perfidy and keep themselves in the best positions, as "Republicanism knows no race," they taught.

Another imposition was that colored people did not require intelligent colored leaders; that the Constitution had been purged of color by a Radical Congress, and to be a Republican was all that was required to make a true representative. That mental culture and qualifications were only required by the proud and arrogant; that all who requested those accomplishments were enemies to both black and white; that race representation was making distinctions on account of race and color. By this means they opposed the qualified men among the blacks, encouraged the ignorant and less qualified that they might of necessity take the lead and occupy the best places in the party. These are plain, indisputable truths, which will not be denied by any upright, intelligent Republican, black or white.

Before the introduction of these men among them, there never was a better population, rural or town, out of which to shape a useful political element. Good-hearted, simple-minded, uneducated, they were ready and willing to receive any instruction supposed for their own good, which they anxiously awaited and as eagerly sought. And could they have had the advice of the maturely intelligent, good and virtuous friends of humanity, such as was received and given by us during more than thirty years, of toilsome battle for liberty and right, there never could have been the cause for complaint against us as a race now in a measure justifiable.

One most fruitful cause of mischief in the party arose from the age and want of experience on the part of the good white men who assumed to lead in politics—as well as ignorance in the most of them—and the same may be said of their colored colleagues. For the most part young men, where they possessed the cultivated qualification, they were deficient in experience and knowledge in politics.

To such an extent were they misled that they regularly trained themselves with firearms and marched in companies to political meetings, frequently led by miserable white men. Menacing, threatening, abusing, quarreling, confusion, and frequently rioting are common results of this most disgraceful state of affairs under which we live, all in the name of Republicanism.

The effect upon the people is wonderful. From a polite, pleasant, agreeable, kindly common people, ever ready and obliging, there is now to be met with an ill-mannerly, sullen, disagreeable, unkind, disobliging populace, seemingly filled with hatred and ready for resentment. These changes in the character of the people must have been noticed by every intelligent observer, in contradistinction to their former excellent reputation. Formerly they were proverbial for their politeness, latterly they are noticed for their absence of it. These people are despoiled of their natural characteristics, and shamefully demoralized by renegade intruders.

These strictures have no reference whatever to the intelligent, high-minded, upright gentlemen among the white Republicans, whose examples and precepts have aided in building up society and contributing to the public good; but especially to that class who almost live in the quarters of the country people and hamlets of the towns, among the black population, keeping them distracted with excitement, who are a curse to the community at large, and a blight in the body-politic.

The social relations of the colored people is another shameful evil, which does more to weaken their strength, neutralize their efforts, and divide them in politics than even the graceless intrusion and imposition of white demagogues, because being of their own household. Still adhering to an absurdity, a relic of the degraded past, they cling to the assumption of superiority of white blood and brown complexion. And to such an extent is this carried, I am told, that old societies have been revived and revised, and absolute provisions made against the admission among them of a pure blooded black. Fire, military companies, and even churches and graveyards, it is said, are permanently established on this basis. In one church, at least, no blacks are to be seen, and in another there is a division line between the blacks and browns by different seats.

These distinctions naturally sour the blacks and widen the breach which should never have existed. What a commentary is this on the condition of the race! Cultivated intelligence and enlightened civilization will alone remedy a humiliating condition of a people now receiving the commiseration of the educated world. This canker, this leprosy, must be at once healed, and by a permanent purification purged from the social system of our people whose vitals it has entered, threatening death to its emaciated victims, now the scoff and derision of the Caucasian race.

Of a piece with this, is the ridiculous aping objection raised on account of nativity. Do they not know that (unlike the white race which has various established nationalities of the highest civilization throughout the world) we cannot, as a race, afford to be divided? That instead of objections, we should welcome with pride the coming among us of people of our own race, of intelligence, culture, and respectability, from withersoever they might come?

This anomalous imitation, not original, but borrowed from the other race, is not confined to class among us, but equally indulged in by many blacks and browns of every social position. Let the colored people learn this simple, though important, lesson: That the rejection of people because of their birthplace is social and political death to their race. That without intercourse and accession from abroad, intelligence, like wealth, must be limited and impotent. That the power and glory of the white race consists in their universal intercourse and unlimited recognition.

But among these are excellent ladies and gentlemen, who, though by affinity and predilection, may belong to such associations, yet they have no sympathy with the motives that induced their formation, and, therefore, discard them as humiliating, and will not be bound by their provisions. And to the credit of the greater part of those known as the "common people" among the mixed race, they entirely ignore these ridiculous distinctions, studiously refusing to recognize them—the distinction of color being propagated alone by that part known as the "higher class" among them.

To another important point I would invite your attention—that of the course of the National Government. While distinction in the rights of citizens on account of "race or color" is most pointedly prohibited, distinction on account of color is most definitely made by the Government at Washington.

It is a fact most noticeable in executive appointments of colored men; there are none of pure black men, the pure negro race, but all have been most carefully selected from those having an admixture of white blood. In neither of the Departments in Washington is there a single black holding a position above that of porter or lacquey,[10] while in many, if not all of them— except the army and navy—there are those of mixed blood holding positions of clerkships—as is just and right—and other equally respectable places. Nor in no appointment requiring qualification by culture, in and out of Washington, is there a pure black man or woman to be found, while many such applications have been made, but always rejected. This is no fault of our brown brother, but that of the Government, and the misfortune of the blacks.

There may be these two exceptions: An ordinary black man, the keeper of a grog-shop, received the appointment of postmaster across the James river, opposite to Richmond, Virginia—obtained, it is said, at the request of a Democratic community. Also, it is said, that a black man has received the appointment of Consul General and Minister Resident to the Republic of Liberia, Africa, which required a recommendation from nearly the whole of the Republican members of the Senate to obtain the notice of Mr. Secretary of State, Hamilton Fish! This minister, I am told, persistently refuses to recognize the application of a *black* for any position. And, indeed, I am further informed refer that his prejudice to color caused the removal of the accomplished Haitian Minister, Colonel Romain, from Washington to New York city. Other members of the Cabinet, it is said, largely share these feelings against the pure negro race.

Nor, out of the six hundred thousand colored people [in the] North, have there been any Federal appointments in the Northern States to any position above that of messenger or the merest subordinate, except a post office clerkship in Boston and Chicago, one each, I believe.

And what is said of Executive appointments at Washington in relation to blacks, the same I think may be safely said of the different State governments, the blacks being studiously neglected, except indeed to persistently make appointments of incompetent black men to positions which only bring discredit on them and their race. And in not a single instance does it occur to my mind in which a competent black man has received an appointment from a State executive, with a single exception; that of the Governor of a far Southern State, who appointed black man (a special favorite of his) as one of four harbor masters—the others being white—he having to employ a white man at one hundred dollars a month to do his duties for him; when in the same city there were a number of well qualified black men, not one of whom ever received an office of equal significance. The fact is not ignored of the Governor of South Carolina honoring a black man with an appointment of aide-de-camp on his staff, an office purely of honor, yet an honor which any gentleman might accept, and is duly appreciated by the recipient. The entire population of the African race is about five millions; one-eighth of the whole American people.[11] According to the ration of population, they are entitled to thirty-two (32) representatives in Congress, and a corresponding ratio of official appointments. Allowing one and a half million to be mixed blood, leaves three and a half millions of pure-blooded blacks. These, by the foregoing estimate, are entitled to about twenty-six (26) representatives, with their ratio of Federal offices. And yet these three and a half millions of people, with their political claims, have been persistently neglected and almost ignored, by both general and State governments (except in cases of incompetent blacks for mere political purposes, to conciliate the ignorant blacks), while their more favored brethren of mixed blood have received all the places of honor, profit, and trust, intended to represent the race.

In the name of a common race, for whose liberty and equal rights you and I for years have struggled, I now for the first time expose this disparaging injustice, and call upon you to aid in righting the wrong. A wrong which seems to be studied and determinedly persisted in. A wrong which longer to endure in silence would be an evidence of conscious inferiority and unworthiness.

Republicanism is simply the claims to equal rights established by our fathers in Philadelphia, 1816; by them renewed in 1829, in Cincinnati, Ohio; continued 1830–31–32 in Philadelphia; endorsed by their white brethren in 1833 in Boston as the "anti-slavery" and "abolition" of the country; the free soil of the Buffalo Convention, 1848, and Pittsburgh Convention, 1852; when it was engrafted into politics as Republicanism, at the nomination of Fremont at Rochester, N.Y., 1856, and Lincoln at Chicago, 1860.[12]

Anti-slavery, as established by our fathers, and propagated by us and our white friends, had for its basis "justice and equal rights to all men;" and for its motto: "Whatsoever ye would that others do unto you, do ye even so to them."[13] This is "anti-slavery" as originally propagated by our brethren, aided by their white friends, continued by us, aided by our white friends, and engrafted into politics. This should be Republicanism. Have these principles been adhered to under the dispensation of Republican rule? Have they not been shamefully perverted?

Both of the old parties—Democrat and Whig—favored slavery, having as their basis the inferiority of the negro and the right to oppress him and hold him perpetually in bondage, denied of every right but that at the option of the master. Republicanism was intended to supersede these and accord to him the enjoyment of all the rights and privileges of American citizenship.

Under the rallying-cry of acting for and representing the "negro," men of every shade of complexion have attained to places of honor, profit, trust, and power in the party, except the real negro himself—save such places as he had the power with which to elect himself—who remains to-day as before emancipation, a political nonentity before the governments of the country.

You have now seen the elements of which the party is composed in South Carolina, and its material through the nation. Are these harmonious elements? Does the structure consist of solid material? Can it stand the storms of political attacks from without, and the strife and struggles from within? Is there no repair to be made to the structure, or is it to be left to tumble to pieces by decay and damage from ill usage? These are questions worthy of the attention of the publicist and statesman.

There must be to make it effective a renovating reorganization in this State, based upon intelligence, respectability, and honesty. The discordant elements must become harmonized. One class or race must not be permitted to enjoy privileges of which another is debarred. If this be continued as heretofore, devastation and ruin will come upon the party, when it will cease to exist, as it would deserve to do; as no party, by whatever name, should exist a single day, which does not accord and practically extend equal rights and their enjoyments to all citizens, without distinction of race or color.

You and I have spent the best of our lives in the cause of humanity, living to see the overthrow and death of slavery, and universal liberty proclaimed in the land; and it now becomes equally our duty to crush, in infancy, the offspring of the monster wherever found.

Preparatory to any action on their part with the other race as a party, the colored people must first become reconciled to themselves as a race, and respect each other as do the whites, regardless of complexion and nativity, making merit only the mark of distinction, as they cannot afford to be divided.

Having settled the above "preparatory," I would lay down the following principles as a basis of all future party action, by whatever name it may be called, whether Republican or otherwise:

1. Equality before the law to every person of whatever race or color, and strict adherence to the reconstruction acts bearing upon the same.
2. Colored people must have intelligent leaders of their own race, and white people intelligent leaders of theirs; the two combined to compose the leaders of the party. This must be accepted and acknowledged as the basis of all future political action and necessary to the harmony and safety of both races.
3. All measures in the party must emanate from consultation of the leaders; otherwise such measures may not be respected.
4. Demagogues and disreputable men must be discarded as leaders, and never more be given opportunity to betray their trust and abuse the interests of the people whom they assumed to represent.

I am no candidate nor aspirant for office. I would accept nothing that made me depend upon the position for my support, or cause me to relinquish my personal business. I have spoken simply as an humble citizen, interested in the welfare of the community at large.

With the above platform to guide my future action, I close my review of the political situation.

Thanking the editor of the Charleston *Republican* for the liberal use of his columns in granting this publication, I beg to remain, distinguished sir, as ever, your friend and co-laborer in the cause of humanity,

M. R. Delany

NOTES

1. Levine, *Martin R. Delany*, 377.

2. The first part of the novel was mostly serialized in the *Anglo-African Magazine* in 1859, and the first and second part were then serialized together in the *Weekly Anglo-African* from 1861 to 1862.

3. Jefferson College was originally founded in Canonsburg, Pennsylvania, as a "log cabin" college in the 1780s and received an official charter as Canonsburg Academy in 1794. It later merged with Washington College in 1865 and become part of Washington and Jefferson College. For more information see Coleman, *Banners in the Wilderness.*

4. Levine, *Martin R. Delany*, 440.

5. The notes here provide information that is more fully fleshed out in Robert Levine's careful glossing of Martin Delany's work and, in particular, in the precise notes and references he lists. There is some overlap of our information, of course, but for a broader presentation of the context of Delany's work and the significance of this particular letter we direct readers to Levine's work. *Martin R. Delany: A Documentary Reader,* ed. Robert Levine (Chapel Hill: University of North Carolina Press, 2003).

6. Delany refers to book distributors as "colporteurs." The Freedmen's Bureau is a shortened name for the Bureau of Refugees, Freedmen, and Abandoned Lands, organized by Congress in 1865. It was charged with organizing a free labor system, securing justice for blacks in southern courts, overseeing thousands of schools, and generally assisting black people's transition from a state of slavery to a position as free in a free society.

7. A sutler provides equipment or merchandise to an army. "Bummers" was a term used to refer to marauding or pillaging soldiers.

8. The New York City draft riots in July of 1863 saw a white working-class uprising against conscription take the form of violence and destruction, directed particularly against black people. An African American orphanage was set afire along with many other buildings and institutions, and there are many accounts of black men murdered and strung up on lampposts. Reports vary considerably on the numbers of civilians injured and murdered. See McPherson, *Ordeal by Fire,* 399.

9. Ratified on February 3, 1870, the Fifteenth Amendment to the Constitution prohibited the denial of a citizen's right to vote on the basis of the person's "race, color or previous condition of servitude."

10. A variant of *lackey, lacquey* denotes "uniformed manservant" in this context.

11. According to the 1870 census, Delany's figures weren't far off. The 1870 census reported that approximately 12.7 percent of the U.S. population was of African descent and that approximately 4.8 million people out of 39 million could be identified as black.

12. Robert Levine, in his authoritative edition of Martin Delany's works, edited this letter and glossed the following paragraph thoroughly by explaining here: "Delany refers to Philadelphia blacks' opposition to the American Colonization

Society ("A Voice from Philadelphia," published in January 1817, reprinted in William Lloyd Garrison, *Thoughts on African Colonization*, vol. 2 [Boston: Garrison and Knapp, 1832], pp. 9–13); black protest in Cincinnati in 1829 against Ohio's racist Black Codes; the emergence of the black convention movement in the early 1830s; the founding of William Lloyd Garrison's American Anti-Slavery Society in 1833; and the series of political conventions culminating in the rise of the Republican party." Levine, *Martin R. Delany,* 438.

13. Matthew 7:12.

John Andrew Jackson
(c. 1825–c. 1896)

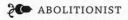 ABOLITIONIST

I, John Andrew Jackson, once a slave in the United States, have seen and heard all this, therefore I publish it.

John Andrew Jackson, The Experience of a Slave in South Carolina

In 1862 John Andrew Jackson, a fugitive slave from South Carolina, published his life story from London. He had come a long way from his brutal upbringing on a Sumter Country plantation, where he had witnessed tremendous violence and cruelty. When his wife and child were taken away to Georgia, his despair led him to conceive a plan that was reckless and foolhardy in the extreme; he planned to escape during the Christmas holidays on a hidden pony he had acquired, make his way to Charleston (easily more than one hundred miles away), and hide himself on a boat bound for the north. Improbably, he succeeded and built for himself a life as an important black activist of the nineteenth century.

After his escape he established himself first in Boston and soon thereafter in Salem, Massachusetts, where he worked for some years as a tanner and as a laborer at a sawmill. Salem was a sensible place for a fugitive to land. It was a large community outside Boston with an influential society of African American abolitionists in residence.

Jackson may have received some education while in the liberal and comparatively safe atmosphere of Salem. He may even have learned to read or write there, possibly with the assistance of the Colored Mission of Salem, which was active in that sort of outreach activity during the 1840s and 1850s. It certainly seems unlikely that he would have known how to write before arriving in Massachusetts. An 1850 letter now held by the American Antiquarian Society and signed by Jackson with a practiced and perfectly casual hand certainly looks like the writing of a man who wrote with ease—an observation that is difficult to reconcile with the fact that another sympathetic abolitionist described him as "extremely ignorant."[1] Much of this is speculation, of course, for in his memoir Jackson does not discuss how or whether he learned to read or write. The relatively smooth nature of his 1862 narrative suggests that his memoir was written in, at the very least, close editorial consultation with a highly literate and sympathetic friend. That being said, Jackson's title page states clearly and definitively that the work is by him, and he ends his memoir with the declaration "I, John Andrew Jackson, once a slave in the United States, have seen and heard all this, therefore I publish it"—a sentence that can be understood as claiming full responsibility for the narrative yet not going so far as to attest to its technical composition.

Any discussion of his authorship and education, however, must consider an American broadside that was printed in 1867, only a few years after Jackson's memoir was published. An advertising flyer, really, it offers us a clue not only to his literacy but also to his career after the publication of his story. In this broadside we read that Jackson was scheduled to give several public lectures from a boat moored in Salem Harbor and that there would even be "singing on the occasion."[2] The broadside announced that he had been working as a teacher for the Freedmen's Bureau and was raising funds to erect a schoolhouse in Darlington, South Carolina. Thus we know that by 1867 Jackson was at least sufficiently literate to teach school. It is not, therefore, such a stretch to imagine that he had already learned to read and write with some sophistication by 1862, when his memoir was published after he had been out of slavery for more than a decade.

His sojourn in Salem did not last, however. Even in that refuge, all was not safe. After a year or so of working in Salem, with the help of intermediaries, Jackson contacted his legal owner, hoping to negotiate the sale of various family members. His attempts did not succeed in liberating anyone, but they did succeed in gaining him publicity—some welcome, some troubling. In 1850, for example, a northern newspaper, likely from Northampton, Massachusetts, published a disdainful open missive from one H. Haynsworth, who was somehow intimately familiar with the inquiries that had been made on Jackson's behalf. Haynsworth wrote that the inquiries about Jackson's family had been received by interested parties and that well over $800 would need to be raised for the purchase of his wife and child. The open

letter then proceeded to rail against the hypocrisy of northerners and abolitionists in general and to mock the premises of their liberation ideology. The
newspaper that carried this letter, however, framed it with an announcement
that Jackson would be speaking at a Northampton, Massachusetts, town hall
in the near future to share his side of the story and to take up a collection
for his family.[3]

The English family, in keeping with this public letter sent by their indig-
nant friend, H. Haynsworth, replied by sending an agent north to Boston to
search for the runaway. Jackson had anticipated this possibility and fortunately eluded capture but nonetheless was considerably frightened.

The Fugitive Slave Act—which Jackson termed the "most atrocious of
all laws"—passed in 1850. Jackson fled Salem, and the United States, about a
year later. Jackson reports that, doubtless thanks to introductions from his
abolitionist friends, he was able to take refuge with Harriet Beecher Stowe
for a night on his way north. Eventually making his way to Canada, Jackson
realized that he might well aid the abolitionist cause with his powerful story.
Jackson thus went overseas to lecture for the movement. By 1857 he was
touring Scotland, giving speeches in Edinburgh, Stirling, and Glasgow.

His public presence and success as a speaker were attested to by at least
one newspaper report in the *Christian News* (Glasgow) that noted: "Mr. J. A.
Jackson, a fugitive slave, delivered a lecture in the Scottish Exhibition Rooms,
Bath Street, illustrative of the evils of slavery, and gave a history of his own
bondage and escape from the horrors of the 'peculiar institution.' . . . Mr.
Jackson is an intelligent looking black i[n] the prime of life; and although
his command of the English language is far from perfect, yet in the peculiar
broken dialect of the negro, he did 'a round, unvarnished tale deliver' of his
captivity and escape and was easily understood" (June 6, 1857).

The newspaper paraphrased his life story as he had told it and then
reported that Jackson told a "thrilling tale about a noble slave named Dred"—
clearly a summary of Harriet Beecher Stowe's novel *Dred: Or a Tale of the
Great Dismal Swamp*, which would have appeared in print only a year earlier. Whether Jackson presented the story as a true account he was familiar
with personally or whether he openly acknowledged that he was retelling
Stowe's tale is unclear in the newspaper summary. It does give us insight,
at least, into the careful way in which Jackson managed his audiences: he
shared personal testimony but also expressed perhaps broader emotional
truths with fictive but equally compelling tales from Stowe.

In our collection we have thus identified from his memoir passages
that deal with his escape. These selections are representative of the ways in
which fugitive slaves understood their testimony as important cultural narratives with both entertainment and shock value in conveying the horror of

bondage. Jackson's account here, with its careful step-by-step recollection of how he got aboard a vessel, what he brought with him, and how moment-by-moment his own emotions and fears preyed upon him, illustrate the kind of powerful storytelling necessary to sway large public audiences and venues.

Jackson's later years after his memoir was published are a bit less documented, and there is still much to be discovered. As was noted in the broadside mentioned earlier, he had been a teacher for the Freedmen's Bureau and had raised money for freedmen's schools. There also is one other tantalizing piece of information about his life that appeared decades later. In 1893 Jackson was interviewed by a newspaper reporter in Rochester, New York. Jackson, who was probably in his sixties by that time, stated that he was interested in raising money for an orphan's home and school in Magnolia, Sumter County, South Carolina, but also had plans for himself: "I came back to this country after the war. I'm getting old and feeble and I only want to live till I get the money for the Home, and then I will go down to Old Carliny and there is where I want to die, down in my old cabin home" (Rochester *Union and Advertiser,* August 9, 1893).[4]

Whether or not he ever made it back to South Carolina and raised enough money for the orphanage he spoke of is unknown. But with his track record of enacting change and achieving seemingly impossible goals, this world-traveled, educated, and well-connected former slave could certainly have returned to South Carolina in humble triumph, knowing he had helped awaken his state to its fuller possibilities—and his resolution to return to his cabin home is remarkable but should not be surprising for a man who perhaps became a South Carolinian only when he was free to come and go there at will.

ᴣᴇ Excerpt from *The Experience of a Slave in South Carolina:* "My Escape"

A slave on a neighboring plantation had a pony; it being discovered by his mistress, she ordered the overseer, the Rev. P. Huggin, to kill it. Meanwhile, I went in the night and purchased it of the slave with some fowls. As my master had just then gone out of his mind I could keep it with greater impunity, so that at length I went to a camp meeting on it. My mistress' grandson saw me on it, and told Ransom Player, the overseer, and my mistress ordered him to give me one hundred lashes, and to kill the pony. When he attempted to tie me I resisted and fled, and swam across a mill pond, which was full of alligators, and so escaped the whipping. I went to work next day, and kept a look out for them. My mistress hearing of it, said to the overseer, Mr. Player, "You can't whip that nigger yourself, wait till Rev. T. English, and Mr. M'Farden, and Mr. Cooper, are here, and then you can catch him in the barn." The last two were her sons-in-law. I kept the pony hid in the woods till Christmas.

We all had three days' holiday at Christmas, and I, therefore, fixed upon that time as most appropriate for my escape. I may as well relate here, how I became acquainted with the fact of there being a Free State. The "Yankees," or Northerners, when they visited our plantations, used to tell the negroes that there was a country called England, where there were no slaves, and that the city of Boston was free; and we used to wish we knew which way to travel to find those places. When we were picking cotton, we used to see the wild geese flying over our heads to some distant land, and we often used to say to each other, "O that we had wings like those geese, then we could fly over the heads of our masters to the 'Land of the free.'" I had often been to Charleston—which was 150 miles distant from our plantation—to drive my master's cattle to market, and it struck me that if I could hide in one of the vessels I saw landing at the wharfs, I should be able to get to the "Free country," wherever that was. I fixed, as I said before, on our three days' holiday at Christmas, as my best time for escape. The first day I devoted to bidding a sad, though silent farewell to my people; for I did not even dare to tell my father or mother that I was going, lest for joy they should tell some one else. Early next morning, I left them playing their "fandango" play.[5] I wept as I looked at them enjoying their innocent play, and thought it was the last time I should ever see them, for I was determined never to return alive. However, I hastened to the woods and started on my pony. I met many white persons, and was hailed, "You nigger, how far are you going?" To which I would answer, "To the next plantation, mas're;" but I took good care not to stop at the next plantation. The first night I stopped at G. Nelson's plantation. I stopped with the negroes, who thought I had got leave during Christmas. Next morning, before day, I started on for the Santé River.[6] The negro who kept that ferry, was allowed to keep for himself all the money he took on Christmas day, and as this was Christmas day, he was only too glad to get my money and ask no questions; so I paid twenty cents, and he put me and my pony across the main gulf of the river, but he would not put me across to the "Bob Landing;" so that I had to wade on my pony through a place called "Sandy Pond" and "Boat Creek." The current was so strong there, that I and my pony were nearly washed down the stream; but after hard struggling, we succeeded in getting across. I went eight miles further, to Mr. Shipman's hotel, where one Jessie Brown, who hired me of my master, had often stopped. I stayed there until midnight, when I got my pony and prepared to start. This roused Mr. Shipman's suspicions, so he asked me where I belonged to. I was scared, but at length, I said, "Have you not seen me here with Jesse Brown, driving cattle?" He said, "Yes, I know Jesse Brown well. Where are you going?" I answered, "I am going on my Christmas holiday." This satisfied him.

I was going to take a longer holiday than he thought for. I reached Charleston by the next evening. There I met a negro, who allowed me to put my pony in his master's yard, his master being out of town at the time. It is the custom there, for the masters to send their slaves out in the morning to earn as much money as they can, how they like. So I joined a gang of negroes working on the wharfs, and received a dollar-and-a-quarter per day, without arousing any suspicion. Those negroes have to maintain themselves, and clothe themselves, and pay their masters two-and-a-half dollars per week out of this, which, if they fail to do, they receive a severe castigation with a cat-o'-nine-tails. One morning, as I was going to join a gang of negroes working on board a vessel, one of them asked me if I had my badge?[7] Every negro is expected to have a badge with his master's name and address inscribed on it. Every negro unable to produce such badge when asked for, is liable to be put in jail. When I heard that, I was so frightened that I hid myself with my pony, which I sold that night for seven-and-a-half dollars, to a negro. I then bought a cloak from a Jewish lady, who cheated me, and gave me a lady's cloak instead of a man's, which, however, answered my purpose equally well. I then got seven biscuit-loaves of bread, and a bottle of water which I put in my pocket, and I also bought a large gimlet and two knives.[8] I then found I had over ten dollars left of what I had earned. I then went to the wharf early in the morning with my cloak on, and underneath all my rattle-traps. A few days previously, I had enquired of a mulatto negro, for a vessel bound for Boston. I then went on board and asked the cook, a free negro, if his vessel was bound for Boston? To which he replied, "Yes." "Can't you stow me away?" said I. "Yes," said he, "but don't you betray me! Did not some white man send you here to ask me this?" "No." "Well," answered he, "don't you betray me! for we black men have been in jail ever since the vessel has been here; the captain stood bond for us yesterday and took us out." "What did they put you in jail for?" said I. "They put every free negro in jail that comes here, to keep them from going among the slaves.[9] Well, I will look out a place to stow you away, if you are sure no white man has sent you here." So I went the next morning to ask him to redeem his promise. I went on board, and saw him lighting a fire in his galley, so I said to him, "Now I am ready for you to stow me away." "Walk ashore, I will have nothing to do with you; I am sure some white person sent you here." I said, "No, no one knows it but me and you." "I don't believe it," said he, "so you walk ashore;" which I did. But as I looked back, I saw him go into the galley again and shut the door, so I went on board the vessel again, and crept stealthily on tiptoe to the hatch. I stood there fearing and hoping—fearing lest the cook should come out of the galley, and hoping that the mate or captain would come from the cabin, and order me to take off the hatch. Presently the mate came out of the cabin, and I asked him if I should take off the hatch. He, thinking that I was one of the gang coming to work there, told me I might. So I immediately took off the hatch, and descended. The gang soon came down; they asked me, "Are you going to work here this morning?" I said, "No." "Aren't you a stevedore?" I said, "No." "I know better, I know by that cloak you wear. Who do you belong to?" I answered, "I belong to South Carolina." It was none of their business whom I belonged to; I was trying to belong to myself. Just then they were all ordered on deck, and as soon as I was left, I slipped myself between two bales of cotton, with the deck above me, in a space not large enough for a bale of cotton to go; and just then a bale was placed at the mouth of my crevice, and shut me in a space about 4-ft. by 3-ft., or thereabouts. I then heard them gradually filling up the hold; and at last the hatch was placed on, and I was left in total darkness. I should have been stifled for want of air, but by the providence of God, a board in the partition between the sailors' sleeping place and the hold where I was, was broken out, so that the air came through there. Next morning, I heard the sailors singing their farewell songs, and soon after, the vessel began to rock from side to side. I then began to feel that I was indeed, now upon my journey from slavery to freedom, and that I soon should be able to call myself FREE, and I felt so happy, and rejoiced so in my heart; but all these feelings were rudely stopped by a feeling of sickness, and the more the vessel went, the sicker I got, till I felt as miserable as I was happy before. I then began to bore with my gimlet, and after a long time, I was able to bore two holes in the deck with great labor, through which I could see the sailors passing and re-passing overhead. By this time I found that my water was exhausted, and I began to feel all the horrors of thirst. I felt that I could with pleasure have drunk the filthiest water in my native swamps. I cast my eyes up through the gimlet holes and saw the stars, and I thought that God would provide for me, and the stars seemed to be put there by Him to tell me so; and then I felt that He would care for me as He did for Jonah in the whale's belly, and I was refreshed. Next morning I saw through the holes, a man standing over them with his arms folded, apparently in deep thought, so I called out, "Pour me some water down, I am most dead for water." He, however, looked up instead, and persisted in examining the rigging, apparently thinking the voice came from there, so I cut a splinter and pushed it through the hole to attract his attention; as soon as he caught sight of it, he ran away and called to the captain, "Run here, cap'n, there is a ghost aboard!" The captain came and knelt down and examined the holes, and asked me how I came there? I said, "I got stowed away." He asked me if some white man did not stow him away to get him in trouble? I assured him he was mistaken, as I stowed myself away. The cook said, "Cap'n, there was one wanted me to stow him away at Charleston, but I would not." "Cook, you should have told me that," said the captain. "Boys, get the chisel and cut him out." As soon as I was out, I saw the cook preparing to wash his hands, and I seized upon the water and drained it to the last drop. It was nearly half-a-gallon.

The vessel continued her journey to Boston. The captain persisted that some white man had placed me there to get him into trouble; and said he would put me into the first vessel he met, and send me back; however, he met no vessel, and we gradually approached Boston. At last the pilot come on board, and I was sent into the forecastle to prevent his seeing me, and we soon arrived at Boston.[10] At nine o'clock on the evening of the 10th of February, 1847, I landed at Boston, and then indeed I thanked God that I had escaped from hell to heaven, for I felt as I had never felt before—that is, *master of myself,* and in my joy I was as a bouncing sparrow. Three sailors named Jim Jones, Frank, and Dennis, took me to the sailor's boarding-house, kept by one Henry Forman, Richmond-street, and I became his servant, and worked for him, and received my board as payment. About June I left him, and went to Salem, and worked for James Brayton, Samuel Pittman, and many others, in the tan yards. I received a dollar-and-a-half per day, out of which I saved one hundred dollars in the course of a year, which I put in the savings bank. I used often to work at sawing wood during the night, and it did not seem such a hardship as when I did the same in South Carolina. Why? Because I felt that I was free, and that I worked because I wished; whilst in South Carolina I worked because my master compelled me. This *fact* is, in my mind, more satisfactory than twenty theories, as to the superiority of free labor over slave labor. When I was a slave we were employed the whole of the day in breaking and hauling home the corn, and then when night came on we were not allowed to snatch an instant's sleep until we had shucked the whole of the corn brought in during the day; so that it was generally between one and two o'clock in the morning before we were allowed to rest our weary bodies. As soon as dawn appeared we were roused by the overseer's whip, for we were so exhausted that the horn failed to rouse us as usual; and then we would discover that the rats had actually eaten a part of our feet. As the slaves are not allowed boots or shoes (except for a short time in the winter), the combined action of the frost at night, and the heat during the day, harden the feet; so that the outside skin at last cracks, and is very painful to the negroes. This outside skin is called "dead skin," as the slaves cannot *feel* the rats eating it until their teeth touch the more tender part of the feet. During the day, that part of the foot which has been skinned by the rats is very tender and causes great pain. The presence of rats in our houses brought venomous snakes, who frequented them for the purpose of swallowing the rats, and who sometimes bit the negroes, and then my father's power of curing snakebites was called into play. . . .

. . . But I am wandering. While I was at Salem, I heard from Mr. Forman, that Anderson, my old slave-driver, had called for me. I will give some incidents that will illustrate his character. He was brought up among the negroes, and was so familiar with negro habits, that he possessed unusual facilities for getting them into trouble. He was hired for the purpose of subduing me and another slave named Isaac, but fortunately my escape saved me from experiencing his tender mercies. . . .

. . . Had I sufficient space I could fill a volume with instances of his wickedness and cruelty. But, to proceed—he was so anxious to catch me that he followed me to Boston—at least, I believe, from the description given by Mr. Forman, that it was he; but fortunately I had gone to Salem, which is 15 miles from Boston. Mr. Forman did not tell Anderson where I was, but merely told him that there was no such person as Jackson there. Anderson said, "I know better, here is the letter he wrote home, wishing to know what he can buy his father and mother for, and I now want to see him." This incensed the sailors, who said, "Here are the slave-hunters, hunting for niggers," and drove them from the house. Mr. Forman wrote to me at Salem, to warn me not to come to Boston, as they were hunting for me there. I remained at Salem, and worked in the tan yard there, turning the splitting machine, until I had saved one hundred dollars. Since my escape I have saved about one thousand dollars of my own earnings, for the purpose of purchasing my relatives. I was in correspondence with some gentlemen in America, through my friend the Rev. C. H. Spurgeon, for that purpose, when the present war interrupted and broke up my hopes and plans. If this war obviates the necessity of buying my people, by freeing the negroes, (as I hope and pray to God it will, and as I believe it will) I shall then, if God pleases, devote my money in building a Chapel in Canada, for escaped slaves; or wherever my old fellow-laborers are located. Though "absent in the body," my whole heart is with my fellow-sufferers in that horrible bondage; and I will exert myself until the last of my relatives is released.

NOTES

1. Samuel Osgood to Lucy Chase about John (Andrew) Jackson, April 1, 1850, *Through a Glass Darkly: Images of Race, Region, and Reform,* online exhibition, American Antiquarian Society, 2006, curated by Lucia Z. Knoles, an English professor at Assumption College. The exhibition included Jackson's letter, along with other documents discussed in this introduction. See American Antiquarian Society, http://faculty.assumption.edu/aas/intros/chasejackson.html.

2. "John Andrew Jackson's Later Career as a Public Speaker and Activist," *Through a Glass Darkly: Images of Race, Region, and Reform.*

3. "A Slaveholder's Letter," *Through a Glass Darkly: Images of Race, Region, and Reform.*

4. Blassingame, *Slave Testimony,* 513.

5. "Fandango" here means foolish or lighthearted play.

6. Jackson is likely referring to the Santee River, which runs through South Carolina from its border with North Carolina to the Atlantic Ocean. Assuming Jackson was traveling south to Charleston, he would have had to cross the Santee.

7. A badge was usually a metal tag issued by the local authorities to be worn by the enslaved people leasing out their labor for short term hire. Used primarily in urban centers in the South, they are most commonly associated with men enslaved in Charleston, South Carolina, where the practice was tightly regulated and metal badges have more easily survived.

8. The gimlet to which Jackson refers is a small hand tool used for drilling holes.

9. Laws regulating the freedom of "free" negroes were common in several states, as free negroes were thought to provoke slave rebellions. Examples of such laws include one passed in Virginia in the early 1800s that required all newly freed slaves to leave the state and one passed in South Carolina in the 1820s that prohibited free blacks from entering the state. The law referred to here is the 1822 Negro Seaman's Act. It required that all free black seamen be imprisoned while their ships were in harbor; if this procedure was not followed, the state could confiscate the seamen as slaves and put them up for auction. The Negro Seaman's Act was passed in response to the discovery of the Denmark Vesey conspiracy.

10. A ship's forecastle is a section of the upper deck located near the ship's bow, normally used as the crew's living quarters.

Robert Smalls
(1839–1915)

❧● UNION ARMY VETERAN, STATE LEGISLATOR,
U.S. CONGRESSMAN, CIVIL SERVANT

My race needs no special defense, for the past history of them in this
country proves them to be equal of any people anywhere. . . . I stand
here the equal of any man.

With these words, Robert Smalls defiantly dismissed questionable charges of fraud and corruption that white Democrats hurled against him during the 1895 South Carolina constitutional convention to thwart his efforts to secure suffrage for African Americans. Twenty-seven years earlier, Smalls had triumphed with a majority-black delegation in ratifying a new state constitution required by Congress to protect the rights of a post–Civil War integrated populace. Soon after federal troops were withdrawn from the South in 1876, however, South Carolina's Democratic Party, spurred on by Benjamin R. "Pitchfork Ben" Tillman and bands of red-shirted paramilitary groups on horseback, initiated a terror campaign that sparked an exodus of African Americans from the state and prevented most black Republicans who remained from participating in elections. Smalls faced off frequently with Tillman, often winning on principle despite being overcome by adversarial politics. At the 1895 convention initiated by Tillman, for example, Smalls refused to sign the new state constitution. When a delegate introduced a resolution to withhold honorariums for those who would not affix their signature to the document, Smalls vowed to walk the 137 miles from the State House in Columbia to his home in Beaufort. Smalls won the skirmish but lost the battle. The majority-white Democratic delegation overwhelmingly supported the new constitution that ushered in the Jim Crow era in South Carolina.

Smalls's improbable journey to the South Carolina State House began on John McKee's Ashdale Plantation in Ladies' Island (now Lady's Island), South Carolina, where he was born and where he and his mother, Lydia Polite, labored as house slaves. The identity of Smalls's father is unknown. As a favored slave in the McKee household, Smalls escaped the backbreaking work of cotton, rice, and indigo production that other enslaved African Americans in the lowcountry began at ages as young as five years. Smalls's mother, concerned that the favor her son received might lead him to misunderstand the true nature of servitude, took him on a tour of Beaufort, where he witnessed enslaved African Americans being sold at the market and an enslaved friend receiving a whipping. When the time came for Smalls to begin fieldwork at age twelve, his mother convinced John McKee that her son was better suited for hiring out in Charleston, where he would have opportunities to learn a trade and earn limited wages. Smalls was required to give his master all but one dollar of his pay from a variety of jobs, including pilot on a steamer named the *Planter,* where he mastered the navigation of South Carolina and Georgia coastal waterways. Smalls increased his meager earnings by purchasing fruits and vegetables and selling them for profit to wharf workers. When he turned eighteen, Smalls persuaded McKee to allow him to pay fifteen dollars per month in exchange for the opportunity to find his own work. About a year later, Smalls married thirty-two-year-old Hannah Jones, an enslaved African American domestic. He gained permission from their masters to rent an apartment in Charleston and later negotiated a complex business agreement to purchase and assume ownership of his wife and their firstborn daughter, Elizabeth Lydia, for $800, thereby circumventing laws that prohibited enslaved African American from becoming slaveholders.

While toiling to emancipate his family as an enslaved pilot for the *Planter,* Smalls conceived a more daring means of escape. After the firing on Fort Sumter that commenced the Civil War, on April 12, 1861, Smalls and his crew of enslaved African Americans began transporting supplies, soldiers, and munitions for the Confederate Army. At 3:00 A.M. on May 13, 1862, while the white officers were ashore visiting their families, the enslaved crew members commandeered the *Planter,* picked up their family members, and sailed past six Confederate forts to the Union blockade ship *Onward.* The North feted the "boat thief" as a hero. Smalls soon met with President Lincoln, obtaining permission for General David Hunter to establish a regiment of

African American soldiers in South Carolina.[1] Between 1863 and 1866 he was inducted into the U.S. Army, served as pilot for the Union Navy, recruited black troops, functioned as a liaison between Gullah freedmen and Union forces, acquired basic literacy, and joined the lecture circuit to raise funds for the Union Army.

After the war, Smalls returned to his hometown of Beaufort and engaged in a variety of business, religious, educational, and political enterprises. He purchased the house where he and his mother had been enslaved and where his mother had lived and worked as a housekeeper for Union troops during the Civil War. When his former mistress, Jane McKee, became ill, Smalls invited her into his home and cared for her until she died. He joined and generously supported the First African Baptist Church and also invested in the community, increasing his wealth by opening a general store, purchasing real estate, and establishing the Enterprise Railroad, a black-owned passenger and freight company in Charleston. In 1867 he was appointed to the Beaufort County school board and raised funds to open the first public school for African Americans in Beaufort. He soon entered into a business venture with thirty-five African American men and three white men in forming the Beaufort County Republican Club, which helped transform the majority-black district into a powerful constituency. The increasingly influential Smalls was dubbed "King of Beaufort County."[2]

Using Beaufort County as his base, Smalls embarked upon a remarkable forty-year political career while continuing his military service. As one of seventy-six African American delegates to the 1868 South Carolina constitutional convention, which barred participants who had supported the Confederacy, he helped initiate a revolution that transformed South Carolina from a slave society into a democratic state. Smalls's greatest achievement was the ratification of legislation that established a public school system for all children. Within a year, he was elected to the South Carolina House of Representatives. By 1870, Smalls won a seat in the South Carolina Senate to serve out the unexpired term of Jonathan J. Wright, who had vacated his seat after being appointed to the state supreme court. Smalls was subsequently elected to a four-year term, enabling him to continue advocating public education, voting rights, and government accountability. Success in local politics won him recognition from the national Republican Party. Smalls served as a delegate to the 1872 presidential convention in Philadelphia and the 1876 convention in Cincinnati. While becoming more engaged in local and national politics, Smalls joined the South Carolina State Militia, was commissioned as a lieutenant colonel and ultimately promoted to major general.

In 1875 Smalls parlayed his success as a South Carolina legislator into a victorious campaign for U.S. representative. In Congress, he introduced federal bills that provided enormous economic resources for South Carolina, including a naval base in Port Royal. By the time he sought reelection, however, the Democratic Party had reinstituted intimidation and violence as tactics to disenfranchise African Americans. In 1877, during a campaign visit to the state with South Carolina governor Daniel H. Chamberlain, Smalls barely escaped lynching as an angry crowd chanted, "Kill the nigger!" He later described the atmosphere as "a carnival of bloodshed and violence." Smalls regained his seat, but his political career was nearly derailed by the "Redeemers," white Democrats who accused him of taking a $5,000 bribe while he was a state senator. He was forced to return to South Carolina to stand trial. Despite conflicting, unsubstantiated evidence, he was convicted and sentenced to three years' hard labor. Rather than concede defeat or accept a $10,000 bribe from Democrats to vacate his office, Smalls fought back and eventually overcame his adversaries. After losing his appeal to the state supreme court, he was outmaneuvered by political opponents who secretly arranged for him to receive a pardon, thwarting his plans to submit his case to the U.S. Supreme Court. Smalls returned to Congress, however, and completed his term.

Over the next twelve years, Smalls clashed repeatedly with white South Carolina Democrats, who eventually forced him out of office. In 1878 he faced a temporary setback when he lost his congressional seat to a white Democrat, George D. Tillman, in the first major election held after federal troops withdrew from the state. Smalls returned to Beaufort to resume his community and business ventures and to prepare for the next political campaign. After losing to Tillman a second time, in 1880, Smalls requested an investigation into voter intimidation, confident that the majority-Republican Congress would provide a favorable hearing. He was eventually reappointed late in the term. Smalls lost his reelection bid in 1882 but regained his seat in a special election to fill the vacancy created by the death of Representative Edmund W. M. Mackey. During his term, Smalls introduced a bill to add $50 per month to a pension for Maria Hunter, widow of General David Hunter, who had issued orders to liberate slaves in South Carolina, Georgia, and Florida before the issuance of Lincoln's Emancipation Proclamation. Years later Smalls sought to ensure that Hunter's widow received the pension that Congress routinely authorized for Civil War veterans and their families. When Democratic president Grover Cleveland vetoed the measure, Smalls severely criticized him in a speech delivered on the House floor. Reportedly, President Cleveland was so angered by Smalls's public attack that he lent his support to the Democrats, who defeated Smalls in the 1886 election. Within two years, President Benjamin Harrison, a Republican, restored Smalls to his position as political power broker for the Sea Island district through an appointment as customs collector for the Port of Beaufort.

As Smalls took up his customs duties, he played an influential role in the suffrage debate that raged in South Carolina, stoked by continuing terror tactics perpetrated by white Democrats, Red Shirt militias, and the Ku Klux Klan to intimidate and disenfranchise African American voters. In the first selection presented here, the article "Election Methods in the South," published in the influential Boston-based literary magazine the *North American Review,* Smalls decries South Carolina's failure to protect the voting rights of black citizens and urges northerners to support the Lodge Election Bill, introduced by Massachusetts Republican representative Henry Cabot Lodge to provide federal protection for southern voters. Rather than give Smalls a traditional byline, the periodical identifies him as "Hon. Robert Smalls, Formerly Representative in Congress from South Carolina," affirming him as a credible voice in the debate, both as a nationally elected official and as a representative of the state in which African American men were losing suffrage rights. Indeed, Smalls had investigated voting irregularities during his tenure in the South Carolina State House and had experienced the effects of disenfranchisement of black voters in his own campaigns. In the article, he details the increasingly violent atmosphere that has developed in state elections since 1874 and the progressively more sophisticated tactics Democrats have crafted to disenfranchise African American voters. Smalls meticulously recounts how fraud has corrupted the election process, with outnumbered Democrats craftily inventing means to sway vote counts in their favor, including the eight-box ballot, which required voters to correctly cast their ballots into eight different boxes. By exposing South Carolina's fradulent election process in the *North American Review* and linking it to the Lodge Election Bill, Smalls transforms a state issue into a national concern, revealing how trampling upon the rights of African American South Carolinians undermines the integrity of national elections and thereby weakens the strength of the democracy.

The filibustering and defeat of the Lodge Election Bill in 1890 reflected the setbacks African Americans were experiencing at the state level. In 1895 Smalls and five other African Americans were appointed to the South Carolina constitutional convention, which U.S. Senator Benjamin Tillman had advocated to rewrite the 1868 state constitution. Smalls presented a suffrage plan that several black delegates, notably state legislators Thomas E. Miller and James Wigg and attorney Isaiah R. Reed, supported in eloquent speeches to the convention, accusing white delegates of disenfranchising African Americans, preserving white supremacy, and blocking access to liberty. Benjamin Tillman, chairman of the Committee on the Right to Suffrage, responded by denouncing Reconstruction, the 1865 state constitution, and black Republicans, particularly Smalls.

In the second featured reading, Smalls responds to Benjamin Tillman's accusations, transforming the South Carolina State House into a courtroom and giving himself the public hearing that his adversaries had denied him when they blocked his appeal with a pardon. Speaking like a defense lawyer on his own behalf, Smalls refutes the charge of bribery with evidence that contradicts the claims of his adversaries by detailing discrepancies in their timeline, casting doubt on the credibility of their witnesses, revealing the erroneous nature of their testimony, and questioning the validity of reinstating the charges during the constitutional convention proceedings. He contrasts his noble act of protecting his "name and honor" with the craftiness of state officials who secretly offered him a bribe in exchange for his congressional seat. In facing the charges a second time, Smalls publicly clears his name and leaves a permanent record of his defense in the convention proceedings.

Smalls continued serving at the Custom House, except for a four-year break during Democratic president William McKinley's tenure, until his political nemesis Benjamin Tillman, who had been elected to the U.S. Senate in 1894, joined Senator Ellison D. Smith in successfully blocking his reappointment in 1912. Within three years of losing his position as customs collector, Smalls died at home and was buried in the Tabernacle Baptist Church Cemetery. In 1974 the Robert Smalls Home was added to the National Historic Register and identified as a National Historic Landmark. Since 1976, South Carolinians have celebrated Robert Smalls Day annually on February 22. Schools and streets in Beaufort and throughout the nation are named in his honor, as is the U.S. Army vessel *Major General Robert Smalls.*

?**❧** "Election Methods in the South"

*By the Hon. Robert Smalls, Formerly Representative
in Congress from South Carolina*

The highest right of a citizen, and by far the most important for the protection of all citizens, is the right to vote for the candidates of his choice and to have his vote counted as cast. The Constitution of the United States and the constitutions of all the States guarantee this right to all citizens who have not forfeited the same by the commission of certain crimes and conviction therefor. It is not a question of fitness, intelligence, wealth, color, or previous condition of servitude, but a right secured by the organic law of the country and bestowed upon all.

In South Carolina there is neither a free ballot nor an honest count, and since the election in 1874 the history of elections in the State is the history of a continued series of murders, outrages, perjury, and fraud. The brutality and fraud of the Democracy in the campaign and election of 1876[3] and the determination of its result were only equaled, but not excelled, by the Kuklux outrages[4] which aroused the just indignation of the entire North. Republicanism was in that year overthrown by murderous gangs called "rifle clubs,"[5] who, acting in concert, terrorized nearly the entire State, overawing election officers and defying the courts. The elections in 1878 and 1880[6] were repetitions of the outrages of 1876. The shot-gun and rifle were the factors that prevented a thorough canvass, and a false count in those counties where Republicans made contests completed the work. Having perfect immunity from punishment, the encouragement, if not the active participation, of the State government, and the protection of the courts of the State, the rifle clubs committed their outrages without restraint, and the election officers their frauds without even the thin veneer of attempted concealment. Elections since then have been carried by perjury and fraud—two things worshipped and adored by the South Carolina Democracy.

Many apologists for the rule of the minority in South Carolina assert that the negro votes the Democratic ticket, and that to form a majority from the census giving the entire vote to the Republican party is erroneous. There are colored men who vote the Democratic ticket, and I suppose that there are Irishmen in Ireland who act with the Tories of England. There are, however, more white Republicans in the State who vote the Republican ticket than negroes who vote the Democratic ticket; and what better authority for the statement that a minority rules in South Carolina could be asked than the following from the lips of the present Governor of the State,[7] who is also a member of the Board of State Canvassers,[8] in a speech delivered at Chester, S.C., July 30, 1888, and repeated at Charleston, August 10, 1888?—

"We have now the rule of a minority of 400,000 over a majority of 600,000. No army at Austerlitz, Waterloo, or Gettysburg[9] could ever be wielded like that mass of 600,000 people. The only thing that stands to-day between us and their rule is a flimsy statute—the Eight-Box Law[10]—which depends for its effectiveness upon the unity of the white people."

The statement is true as far as it goes, but it is not complete. In the manner of enforcing the election statutes lies the strength of minority rule, for even if the election laws which impose an educational qualification and otherwise restrict suffrage were properly administered, Republicans would still have a majority of the legal voters in the State.

The Election Law places in the hands of the Governor the appointment of the supervisors of registration and their assistants, the commissioners of election for the election of Presidential electors and Members of Congress, and the commissioners of election for the election of State and county officers. The commissioners appoint three managers at each poll, who conduct the election, canvass the return of the managers, and determine all controversies in relation to the election. The manner of their appointment will give a better indication of how the officers act, and of their motives, than any partial discussion of their character, and for it to be understood properly some idea of the political organization of the Democracy is necessary. There is a State Executive Committee, the centre of control, with more power in the State than the President of the United States and all the laws of the country and State. Each county has an executive committee and a county chairman; the former is elected by the State convention and the latter by the county conventions. The rifle and other clubs exist, although murder has given way to theft, and delegates from them compose the county conventions—the basis of political action.

The governor of the State receives his orders, called recommendations, from those political committees, and they in turn receive their orders from the rifle clubs. The supervisor of registration and the commissioners of election, both State and Federal, are appointed upon the recommendation of the Democratic county chairman and county executive committee, and the managers are selected from the rifle clubs in each precinct on their recommendation. It will therefore be seen that the entire machinery of the State is in the hands of the active politicians and partisans of a single party, without the presence of a single representative of any other party to secure even the appearance of justice.

With one or possibly two exceptions, the policy of the supervisors is inaction so far as Republicans are concerned, and in nearly every county in the State it is almost as easy to earn at once a competency from a basis of zero as it is for a Republican to secure a registration ticket or correct any change of residence or irregularity; and frequently when everything appears to be in shape, the registration-book on the day of election shows different initials, residence, or some technical objection that deprives him of his vote. The officer seldom appears on the day fixed by law,* and when he does, he manages to create so many delays that the few hours he remains are not sufficient for anything like the proper transaction of his business. Thousands of voters, after traveling fifty and often one hundred miles to the county-seat, the only place for registration, have to return home after a fruitless search for the register on the days that the law requires him to be present, and as these journeys cannot be made often, the voters are disfranchised and the votes lost. All persons desiring to vote the Democratic ticket are registered without personal application, and certificates are furnished them either before or on the day of election without even the formality of an oath as to eligibility. Registration, the fountain-source of election, curtails Republican suffrage

---

* Which is the first Monday in each month commencing in January and closing on the first Monday in July of each year in which elections are held.

by the expense and inconvenience it entails upon persons not living at the county-seat, by refusal through willful neglect to register Republicans, and by fraud of the supervisor in making false entries; it adds to the Democratic vote through his fraud in unlawfully adding to the names on the registration-books those of all persons who are expected to vote the Democratic ticket.

If fortunate enough to obtain a certificate and he is in the low country or the Seventh Congressional District, which strikes nearly every Republican centre, the Republican goes to the polls, if he can find them, early in the morning, as he is more or less acquainted with the delays there, especially if there is a promise of a large Republican vote. The hour for the opening of the polls comes and goes, and neither managers nor boxes make their appearance. The crowd grows larger and soon there are four or five hundred Republicans. Anxious inquiries are made for the managers. It is learned later that, of the managers, Colonel Jones has gone to town, Mr. Brown has gone hunting, and Mr. Smith says he does not intend to serve, as there is no pay in it. Four or five hundred Republicans are disfranchised by the neglect of the managers, and not even the letter or spirit of the law is violated by the poll not being opened.

At a neighboring poll another scene is enacted. The polls are open, the boxes shown, the voters deposit their ballots, there is general levity, and everything appears to be fair. There are three hundred Republican voters; the Democrats have secured forty or fifty votes, and the polls close. The votes are counted; there are two or three hundred more ballots than names on the poll-list; instead of fifty Democratic ballots there are three hundred and fifty. The ballots are of regulation size, nobody has had access to the boxes but the managers, and the opening is too small for the introduction of any quantity of ballots without detection. Who put them in the box? The managers. The law for legalizing fraud is invoked. It requires the managers to draw ballots from the box until the number in the box tallies with the total number of votes cast. The box is shaken, for there is nothing for the Democracy to lose, being a case of "tail I win, head you lose"; the drawing is made; the votes are again counted. Result: the Democracy have a majority of fifty votes, more or less, at an overwhelming Republican precinct. The law has been obeyed and the rights of all protected.

"The ballot shall be without ornament, designation, mutilation, symbol, or mark of any kind whatsoever, except the name or names of the person or persons voted for, and the office to which such person or persons are intended to be chosen." Advantage is taken of the law by Democratic managers to perpetrate a fraud of their own. The opening in the ballot-box being small, a ticket inserted does not fall to the bottom of the box. The obliging and attentive manager pushes it down with his lead-pencil, managing to leave a mark on the ballot. At the count the marked ballots are thrown out as mutilated, and are not included in the vote. At an election in Beaufort County, a dishonest manager was caught performing the trick. The people at the polls prevented the ballots from being destroyed, but one of the commissioners of election, when the box reached Beaufort, obtained and destroyed them to prevent me from using them as part of my evidence.

Other Republican precincts with large majorities are disfranchised by the managers of the election willfully neglecting to take the oath required by law, failing to sign the returns or seal the boxes, or taking advantage of any other possible omission or violation of the numerous requirements of the election statute. These matters form the basis of protests from Democratic candidates, and are parts of the scheme of fraud that are seized upon by the Democratic commissioners of election as pretexts for refusing to count the votes of protested precincts.

A little explanation as to the mode of procedure in deciding protests will at once show the injustice, amounting to fraud, that is practiced. The commissioners meet. The boxes are in their custody, and the canvass of the votes goes on. All of the precincts where there is a considerable Democratic vote are counted at once. When the Republican precincts are reached, there is a protest filed by one of the conspirators. It charges an array of irregularities, and, incredible as it may appear in fraud-ridden and bulldozed South Carolina, it often contains a charge of Republican intimidation. The protest is general in its wording. No testimony is taken; the controversy is settled by affidavits; and as Republicans are not allowed by the commissioners to have any knowledge of the contents of the affidavits supporting the protests until the final hearing, when charges like intimidation, bribery, etc., are made, they have to make their fight in the dark, and their affidavits can contain little except general denials of the charges. The commissioners hear the affidavits and arguments, if there are any, and by their decision reject sufficient Republican precincts to give the Democracy a majority in the county or Congressional district. The dirty work required of the commissioners where contests are made makes the office an undesirable one for honest men, and there are many honest Democrats who have no sympathy with the schemes of fraud and acts of violence practiced by their political associates; but they are powerless in the face of the Democratic political machine that rules Democrat and Republican alike with its iron hand. Men are generally appointed who have little or no character and are violent persons.

I have given as fully as limited space will permit the most prominent frauds and acts of injustice that occur in the registration of voters and after the gantlet of the eight boxes has been passed, and it will be seen that considerable more is necessary for the continuance of minority rule than eight ballot-boxes. The eight-box section, from which by common consent the statute takes its name, depends upon the unfair methods of its enforcement for its effectiveness. The poor whites who form the bulk of the Democratic voters could no more vote intelligently under its provisions than the ignorant colored voter. The mode of making the law one-sided is as follows: The managers have the custody of the Democratic ballots. They place a package for each box alongside or generally upon it, and the Democratic voter has nothing to do but fold and put it in. The boxes are often shifted to prevent intelligent Republicans from indicating to their more ignorant brethren the location of the boxes. The law requires the managers to read the names on the boxes when requested, but as this would be of no value to a man who could not read the ticket in his hand, and as managers have been caught lying so often when they pretended to read the names, the apparent protection is only a further abuse of a free ballot. As no ignorant man can place in the proper boxes eight or more distinct ballots with no other guidance than the names upon them, it can be readily seen that the section imposes an educational qualification upon voters contrary to the constitution of the State; and it is this flagrant violation of the organic law that has given this section so much prominence. Democratic majorities in South Carolina are due, not to obedience to the law, but to its flagrant violation. If through mistake a ballot is placed in the wrong box, it is not counted, for this reason: the ballot-boxes are shifted, and only one voter at a time is allowed in the room where the votes are deposited. He is compelled by law to deposit his own ballots in the boxes.

In view of all these frauds and outrages I call upon the true Representatives who are in favor of honest elections and a fair count to give their undivided support to the Lodge Election Bill.[11]

The State Republican Convention, when it adjourned on September 18, referred the matter of nominating a State ticket to its Executive committee. This committee, of which I am a member, at its meeting in Columbia on October 6, owing to the above-stated facts, decided that it was inexpedient to nominate a State ticket.

Since the adjournment of the committee the straight-out Democrats of this State have nominated a ticket, which brings about a split in the Democratic ranks. That ticket, I think, is 90 per cent better than the ticket nominated in Columbia, headed by B. R. Tillman,[12] who is the personification of red-shirt Democracy.[13] He bases his claims and qualifications for the office on the fact that he organized the first red-shirt club in South Carolina, and led it in the bloody massacres at Hamburg and Ellenton,[14] and that the trusty rifle which did such deadly execution now occupies a prominent position in his parlor, and is one of the most cherished of all of its ornaments. He also opposes the levying of the two-mills school-tax, which is required by the constitution of the State. He is in favor of calling a constitutional convention, should he be elected governor, for the purpose of framing a new constitution. The nominee for lieutenant-governor[15] on the same ticket said, in a public speech at Florence, that "it made his blood boil in his veins to see a negro woman occupy a seat in the same car with white people."

While it is repugnant to my feelings as a Republican to advise my people to vote for any Democrat, yet in this emergency I must advise them to do anything that is legitimate to bring about the defeat of this arch-enemy of my race. The ticket headed by Mr. Haskell[16] represents the better element of the Democracy of South Carolina, who, in my opinion, are opposed to the frauds perpetrated against a free ballot, while the election of the ticket headed by Tillman means a perpetuation of all of the evils mentioned in this article, *and more.*

I desire to state in the most positive and emphatic manner that the number of negroes in South Carolina who have voted the Democratic ticket from compulsion of other causes from 1867 to the present time would not exceed five hundred. The entire white vote of the State (census of 1880) is only 86,900, while the total colored vote is 118,889, and yet at no election held in the State, except the election of 1876, when the gigantic steal was perpetrated by the Democrats, has the Democratic vote ever exceeded 70,000. At any election in South Carolina when the votes shall be counted as cast, it will be found that the negroes of the south are as true and as loyal to the principles of Republicanism as they were to the flag of this great country when treason sought to blot it out.

There are men now in Congress who are willing to vote for an appropriation out of the treasury to have us sent out of the country. As long as there was a Democratic government at Washington, and the South could get false representation in Congress, they were opposed to our leaving. But now with that lover of constitutional liberty, Benjamin Harrison, in the White House, they certainly know that the rights of all the citizens of this great country will be protected alike, and that South Carolina, like Massachusetts, will have an honest election law, under which there will be free elections and fair counts. These men forget that the negroes of the country gave 186,000 men who fought in two hundred and fifty-two battles for the perpetuity of this great nation.[17] We do not intend to go anywhere, but will remain right here and help make this the most powerful of all governments.

ᘰ Hon. Robert Smalls's Speech to the 1895 South Carolina Constitution Convention

Mr. Smalls spoke as follows:

Mr. President: I had thought that I would not find it necessary to have a word to say in regard to this contest for the right of freemen, for the question had been ably presented by others; but to my surprise I find the distinguished gentlemen from Edgefield, Mr. B. Tillman[18] and Mr. J. C. Sheppard,[19] going away from the all-important question, the right to let free Americans cast an honest ballot for honest men.

By those gentlemen I am arraigned here and placed on trial for an act said to have been committed in 1873 in South Carolina. It is true, sir, that I was arrested in the State in 1877, charged by the Democrats of the State with receiving a bribe in 1873. This was done after the Democratic party had taken charge of State affairs; but the evidence upon which this trumped-up charge was brought was that of one Josephus Woodruff,[20] who was Clerk of the Senate and also Public Printer of the State, and who had acknowledged that he had robbed the State out of over $250,000, and had run away and was brought back from Pennsylvania by a writ issued on the Governor of that State.

This man Woodruff testified that of twenty checks which he had given to "cash" or to "bearer" one was given to Robert Smalls. Why so?

Simply because they found that I had deposited in the Banking and Trust Company of the State $5,000 on the 18th day of January, 1873. But when they went to examine the record they found that the check in question was drawn on the 19th day of said month. On examining the calendar they found that the 19th day of January was Sunday, and that if the check was given to me on that day I could not have deposited until the 20th.

The gentleman, Mr. Sheppard, a few moments ago said that I was convicted, the testimony being corroborated by the Cashier of the bank. That gentleman was a member of the Committee: but, sir, he could not have read the record in this case. The Cashier of that bank was a man named Jacobs, who had been charged, as the record shows, under four indictments for perjury, and had fled the State, and a man by the name of Zealy[21] brought in a little slip of paper, written in pencil, and said it was the handwriting of Mr. Jacobs,[22] the Cashier of the bank. Mr. Woodruff himself testified that he had made arrangements to borrow money, or had been trying to do so, and asked me to loan him $5,000, and that when I brought the money to him he had already made the arrangements to get $20,000 from Dr. Neagle.[23] I am as innocent of that charge as you are.

But, sir, that matter is brought in here. The State of South Carolina was in the hands of the Democratic party. It has been said that Judge Townsend[24] was a Republican. This is the first I have ever known of it. He was not elected as a Republican, but as a Democrat, from Marlboro County, and to-day stands here as a Democrat. No one ever heard of Judge Townsend in the Republican ranks anywhere or at any time until now it seems convenient to serve a Democratic purpose.

The gentleman said that I was convicted by a jury of colored men or Republicans. Mr. Speaker, there were two colored men that might have been Republicans on that jury; but every man on that jury had been a Democrat, and had worked and voted for Wade Hampton.[25] There is Joe Taylor.[26] Where is he to-day? Somewhere in Canada. He is a good Democrat, but he stole twenty bales of cotton the other day and has now gone somewhere else. I stand here to-day, and am just as innocent of the charge as either of the gentlemen from Edgefield, who have gone out of the way to make this personal onslaught.

Now, let me say that after that trial and after I was arrested I appealed to the Supreme Court of the State. The Supreme Court held that opinion off over one year, as the record will show. After I had run for Congress a second time the Supreme Court rendered a decision sustaining the action of the lower Court. After that was done, under Section 641 of the Revised Statutes,[27] I took an appeal to the Supreme Court of the United States. I went to Washington and appeared before that Court. The record shows it. I went before Chief Justice Waite,[28] and he granted the appeal and docketed the case.

No sooner was this done, and no sooner had I returned to South Carolina, than, without a single word from me, or friend of mine, directly or indirectly, Governor Simpson,[29] of South Carolina, issued and sent to me in Beaufort a pardon which I have here in this paper.

Mr. President, my acts in defense of my name and honor are such as are entitled to the respect of every freeman. I did all that man could do; but without my knowledge, against my will, the Attorney General of South Carolina, Mr. Youmans,[30] went before the United States Supreme Court and asked that the case be stricken from the docket, on the ground that it had been adjudicated in the State. I knew nothing of this at all until I happened to see a sketch of it in the News and Courier, published in Charleston, saying that Mr. Youmans was in Washington and had made such a motion.

But while I was in Columbia, before the trial came off, Mr. Cochran,[31] the Chairman of that great investigating committee appointed by the Legislature of South Carolina,[32] said to me, "Smalls, you had better resign." "Resign what?" "Resign your seat in Congress." "What," said I, "the seat the people elected me to!" "Yes; you had better resign, because if you don't they are going to convict you." Said I: "I don't believe that, sir. I am innocent and they cannot do it." "Well," said he, "bear in mind that these men have got the Court, they have got the jury, and an indictment is a conviction." I did not believe it, but I tell you those gentlemen taught me it was so. And it was so. I was sought by another gentleman, a gentleman from Aiken County, Mr. Drayton,[33] the editor of a paper there. He came to me and said: "Smalls, we don't want to harm you. Get out of the way. We know you were kind to our people just after the surrender, and Governor Hampton says he doesn't want to injure you. We want this government, and we must have it. If you will vacate your office we will pay you $10,000 for your two years' salary." Said I, "Mr. Drayton, where did you get this money to give me?" Said he,

"Smalls, don't you ask that. We have got the money. The people of South Carolina have paid in 10 percent on their taxes to perpetuate the Hampton government and we intend to have it." Said I: "Sir, if you want me to resign my position you must call meetings all over the Congressional District and get those people who elected me to pass resolutions requiring me to resign, and then you can have the office without a penny. Otherwise I would suffer myself to go into the Penitentiary and rot before I would resign an office that I was elected to on a trumped-up charge against me for the purpose of making me resign."

Make me resign when I am innocent; make me resign when the only testimony against me is that of a self-confessed thief. And, Mr. President, this self-confessed thief at my trial admitted, under oath, that he had been granted immunity from trial because he had promised the prosecution to testify against me. And, Mr. President, this man Woodruff has never been tried.

Why should this matter be dragged into this debate? Why, sir, it is to inflame the passions of delegates against Republicans and force them to vote for this most infamous Suffrage Bill, which seeks to take away the right to vote from two-thirds of the qualified voters of the State.

It has been claimed that there has been a compromise in my case, but this is not true. I refused all offers of compromise, but there were compromises made but I was not included; I received no advantage therefrom. I have here a copy of a compromise entered into by the State of South Carolina and the United States District Attorney for South Carolina, which I send to the desk and ask that it be read, which speaks for itself: "EXECUTIVE DEPARTMENT,"

OFFICE OF THE ATTORNEY-GENERAL,
COLUMBIA, S.C., April 22, 1879.
Hon. L. C. Northrop,[34] *U.S. District Attorney*
for the District of South Carolina,
Charleston, S.C.

Dear Sir: After seeing in writing the views of the Governor and the State delegations in both branches of Congress, and after consultation with the State officers and others, I have deemed it proper, in the interests of peace and quiet in the State, to address you this letter in regard to the action thought to be the most conducive to that end, and most practicable under the circumstances, as to certain prosecutions which have been, or may be, brought by the United States and State governments respectively.

That action is that the United States government shall continue the cases against all persons charged with violations of law by the commission of any acts whatever in connection with, or growing out of, past canvasses or elections, and at the next term, or as soon thereafter as practicable, *nol pros.*[35] them, and that no more prosecutions shall be had.

That upon this continuance by the United States, the State shall continue the pending cases against D. H. Chamberlain[36] and others, brought under the resolution of the General Assembly, and all cases against persons charged with violations of law by the commission of any acts whatever in connection with, or growing out of, past canvasses or elections, and all cases of criminal malfeasance on the part of any public officers of the State, or of bribery or corruption of the public officers of the State, prior to January 1, 1877, and *nol pros.* the same, upon the United States *nol prossing* the prosecutions aforesaid brought by the United States government, and that no more such prosecutions shall be had by the State.

If you will do what is necessary to carry this out, as United States Attorney, I will do what is necessary to carry it out as Attorney-General.

Very respectfully,
(Signed) LeRoy F. Youmans,
Attorney-General South Carolina.
Charleston, S.C., April 29, 1879.

I certify that the above is a true and exact copy of a letter handed to me to-day after the cases alluded to were continued in the United States Court. (Signed) L. C. Northrop.
True copy of the certified copy as above in L. C. Northrop's handwriting. Warren R. Marshall.[37]
April 30, 1879.

Mr. President, I am through with this matter. It should not have been brought in here. All the thieves are gone; they are scattered over the nation, but I have remained here. My race has honored me with a seat on this floor, and I shall serve them to the best of my ability. My race needs no special defense, for the past history of them in this country proves them to be the equal of any people anywhere. All they need is an equal chance in the battle of life. I am proud of them, and by their acts toward me I know that they are not ashamed of me, for they have at all times honored me with their votes.

I stand here the equal of any man. I started out in the war with the Confederates; they threatened to punish me and I left them. I went to the Union army. I fought in seventeen battles to make glorious and perpetuate the flag that some of you trampled under your feet.

Innocent of every charge attempted to be made here to-day against me, no act or word of yours can in any way blur the record that I have made at home and abroad.

Mr. President, I am through, and shall not hereafter notice any personal remark. You have the facts in the case; by them I ask to be judged.

NOTES

1. David Hunter (1802–1886), a graduate of the United States Military Academy and a general in the Union Army, stirred up controversy in April 1862 by issuing General Order No. 11, which emancipated slaves in Georgia, Florida, and South Carolina without federal authorization and by recruiting African Americans for a black military unit. Lincoln rescinded the order out of concern that it would inflame tensions in border states. Hunter later served in the honor guard at Lincoln's funeral and was appointed president of the commission that tried Confederate conspirators.

2. Quoted in the *Beaufort Tribune,* May 12, 1875, n.p.

3. The election of 1876 ended Republicans' domination of politics in South Carolina when a white Democrat, Wade Hampton III, won a contest marred by violence against the white Republican governor, Daniel Chamberlain. Both parties initially claimed victory and established separate governments to rule the state. After President Rutherford B. Hayes withdrew troops from South Carolina, however, Chamberlain conceded the election.

4. White conservatives organized the Ku Klux Klan in South Carolina during Reconstruction to wrest power from the Republican Party after the majority-black delegation to the state constitutional convention of 1868 enacted legislation to protect civil rights and affirm the equality of black and white citizens. The Klan often employed violent tactics to intimidate and disenfranchise African American Republicans as it sought to restore Democratic rule and enforce white-supremacist ideology in South Carolina.

5. During Reconstruction, white South Carolina conservatives organized Rifle Clubs, ostensibly for sporting and military drills; however, members often engaged in night-riding and voter intimidation to overthrow radical Republicanism.

6. Although Governor Hampton ran unopposed for governor and the Republican Party did not offer a slate of candidates for other offices in the 1878 election, the contest was marred by violence and voter fraud. In the 1880 election, the Republicans adopted the same strategy, offering no slate of candidates and hoping internal dissension would eventually weaken the Democratic Party.

7. Benjamin Ryan "Pitchfork Ben" Tillman (1847–1918), a white segregationist who was elected governor on November 4, 1890, spearheaded the drive to institute Black Codes and to disenfranchise African American voters.

8. The South Carolina Board of State Canvassers (composed of at least four of the following officials: secretary of state, comptroller general, attorney general, state treasurer, adjutant and inspector general, and chairman of the Committee on Privileges and Elections of the House of Representatives) counted votes and declared winners in state elections.

9. Smalls is referencing three pivotal battles: Napoleon's victory over the Russo-Austrian army at Austerlitz in 1805, Napoleon's defeat at Waterloo in 1815, and the Union Army's decisive victory at Gettysburg in 1863, during the Civil War.

10. The Eight-Box Law required electors to correctly insert ballots into eight different boxes identified by the name of a specific office such as "governor" or "senator" in order for their vote to be valid. Illiterate white voters often received assistance from white poll workers, who did not similarly assist illiterate African American voters, effectively disenfranchising them.

11. A white U.S. representative, Henry C. Lodge (1850–1924), introduced the Lodge Election Bill or Federal Election Bill of 1890 to empower the federal government to guarantee fair elections, particularly for African American Republicans in the South who were being disenfranchised by Democratic-controlled state legislatures.

12. Smalls is referring to Benjamin R. Tillman.

13. Red-shirt democracy characterizes politics in South Carolina during the 1870s advanced by a paramilitary group of Democrats known as the Red Shirts, who ensured Tillman's election as governor through intimidation of African American Republican voters.

14. The "bloody massacres at Hamburg and Ellenton" refer to two incidents that led up to the election of 1876 and Republicans' regaining control of the South Carolina State House. On July 4, 1876, a hostile encounter near Hamburg, South Carolina, between two white men and African American members of the South Carolina National Guard escalated into violence that left at least six African Americans dead. In September 1876, African Americans and whites clashed in Ellenton after two African Americans were accused of robbing a white couple. White militia members killed one of the suspects, but armed African American citizens refused to turn over the second man. A violent confrontation ensued, leaving nearly forty African Americans and two white men dead.

15. The nominee for lieutenant governor was E. B. Gary, a former associate of the South Carolina Supreme Court.

16. Attorney Alexander C. Haskell (1839–1910), a former Confederate soldier, served as chairman of the Democratic Party executive committee, president of the Columbia and Greenville Railroad, and vice president of the National Loan and Exchange Bank of Columbia and was a justice on the state supreme court. He opposed Tillman's gubernatorial run in 1890 but failed to garner enough support to derail Tillman's nomination or defeat him on the ballot during the general election.

17. Smalls is likely referencing battles African American soldiers fought in during the Civil War.

18. Tillman, who served as South Carolina's governor from 1890 to 1894 and as a U.S. senator from 1895 to 1918, organized the Red Shirts, a paramilitary group, to

terrorize African American Republicans and orchestrated the resurgence of the Democratic Party to advance white-supremacist ideologies, disenfranchise black citizens, and enact Jim Crow laws.

19. John C. Sheppard (1850–1931), a white attorney, served as speaker of the South Carolina House of Representatives, state senator, lieutenant governor, governor, president of the Edgefield Bank of South Carolina, and president of the South Carolina Bar Association.

20. During Reconstruction, stenographic reporter Josephus Woodruff (1828?–1892), a white man, served as clerk of the South Carolina Senate and was co-owner of the Republican Printing Company.

21. Lawrence W. Zealy (1849–?), a white businessman, was the assistant bookkeeper for the South Carolina Bank and Trust Company.

22. S. F. Jacobs, a white businessman, was an officer of the South Carolina Bank and Trust Company.

23. Dr. J. L. Neagle (1838–?) was comptroller general and had served as a delegate from York, S.C., to the 1868 South Carolina Constitutional Convention.

24. Judge Charles Pinckney Townsend (1835–?) was a circuit court judge from 1872 to 1878 and served as a South Carolina state representative for three terms. Smalls's defense attorney petitioned to move the trial to the federal circuit court, citing Judge Townsend's racial prejudice.

25. Wade Hampton III (1818–1902), a white Democrat, was a staunch opponent of Republican Reconstructionist policies in South Carolina. In the 1876 South Carolina gubernatorial election, one of the bloodiest in the state's history, Hampton finally claimed victory when the South Carolina Supreme Court named him governor of after six months of political wrangling.

26. Joseph D. Taylor (1830–1899), a white attorney and a Civil War veteran, served two terms as a U.S. representative from Ohio from 1883 to 1885 and from 1887 to 1893.

27. Section 641 of the Revised Statutes of the United States allowed for the transference of any state civil suit or criminal prosecution to the U.S. Supreme Court.

28. After a successful career as an attorney and an Ohio state senator, Morrison Waite (1816–1888), a white Republican, served from 1874 to 1888 as the seventh chief justice of the U.S. Supreme Court.

29. William Simpson (1823–1890), a white Democrat, was the seventy-eighth governor of South Carolina, serving from 1879 to 1880, when he became chief justice of the state Supreme Court.

30. Confederate Army veteran Leroy F. Youmans (1834–1906) served as solicitor of the Southern Circuit from 1866 to 1888, lead counsel for Wade Hampton III during the disputed 1876 election, and attorney general of South Carolina from 1877 to 1882.

31. In 1877, John R. Cochran (1842–1923), a white Republican, was appointed chairman of the Joint Investigating Committee on Public Frauds by the Democratic-controlled state legislature of South Carolina and initiated a two-year investigation that presented criminal charges against Republicans prior to the 1877 election. See Rubin, *South Carolina Scalawags,* 112–13.

32. Cochran issued the committee's report in 1878. See Cochran, *Report of the Joint Investigating Committee.*

33. Charles E. Drayton, a white businessman, was a member of the Red Shirts and the owner and editor of the *Aiken Recorder,* a weekly newspaper.

34. Lucius C. Northrop (1838–1894?), a white Republican, practiced law, edited a Republican newspaper, and served as a circuit judge before he was appointed South Carolina's U.S. district attorney by President Rutherford B. Hayes in 1877.

35. *Nol pros* is an abbreviation for the legal term *nolle prosequi,* an entry inserted into the court record to indicate that the plaintiff or prosecutor will not proceed.

36. Daniel Henry Chamberlain (1835–1907), a white Republican, served as South Carolina's attorney general from 1868 to 1872 and as its governor from 1874 to 1876.

37. Warren R. Marshall (1842–?), a white Republican, served as South Carolina's assistant U.S. district attorney and was elected reading clerk for the South Carolina House of Representatives in 1876.

Archibald Grimké
(1849–1930)

🙰 LAWYER, DIPLOMAT, AUTHOR, CIVIL RIGHTS ACTIVIST

*Oppression is a powder magazine exposed always to
the danger of explosion from spontaneous combustion.*

As the nadir ended and racial tensions simmered in early twentieth-century America, Archibald Grimké published "Right on the Scaffold; or The Martyrs of 1822," his powerful elegiac essay that reconfigures the insurrectionist Denmark Vesey and his coconspirators as revered revolutionaries.[1] Grimké's characterization of favored slaves as cunning dissemblers encouraged black activists and white racists to reconsider their misgivings about accommodationists like Booker T. Washington and to imagine him as a potential powder keg who was plotting to ignite a black revolution.

Archibald Grimké stood out from other enslaved African American boys at Cane Acre, the rice plantation near Charleston where he spent the first twelve years of his life. His father, the white planter and lawyer Henry Grimké, who was the brother of the prominent abolitionists Angelina Grimké Weld and Sarah Grimké, owned the estate and gave his son the name "Archibald" to distinguish him from the majority of enslaved boys, whom he called "James." His mother, Nancy Weston, had labored as a slave nurse for Henry and his wife Selina's three children. After Selina died, in

1843, Henry Grimké moved from Charleston to the relative isolation of Cane Acres, where he established a relationship with Nancy Weston, which was constrained by South Carolina laws that forbade interracial marriages and manumissions within the state.[2]

In 1852 life changed dramatically for Archibald and his family after his father died of typhoid fever. Henry Grimké had designated his sister Eliza Grimké as executor of his estate and his eldest son, Montague, as the new owner of Archibald, Archibald's younger brother, Francis, and their mother, who was expecting a third child, whom she would name John. Eliza Grimké auctioned off all of her brother's property except Nancy Weston and her sons, whom she relocated to Charleston. Nancy Weston labored as a domestic to support her boys and depended on the kindness of family and friends within the black community to supplement her meager income. She also hired a tutor for her sons and occasionally sent them to illegal "home schools" for black children.

Within five years of relocating to Charleston, Archibald experienced a second significant shift in his quasi-free status when Montague married and forced his half brother to work for him and his bride as an enslaved house servant. Archibald rebelled repeatedly, refusing to complete even simple tasks such as setting the table. After he failed to light a fire properly, Montague flogged him and then sent him to a workhouse for additional punishment. Instead of complying, Archibald became a fugitive slave, hiding with the Coles, a free black family in Charleston, for nearly two years. He devoted most of his time to reading newspapers and novels, including Harriet Beecher Stowe's *Uncle Tom's Cabin* and Hinton Rowan Helper's *The Impending Crisis of the South: How to Meet It.*[3] Archibald gained his freedom when Union forces occupied Charleston during the Civil War. He worked as an officer's boy for Northern troops and reunited with his brothers when he enrolled in the Morris Street School, established by the Freedmen's Bureau.[4] School administrators and the influential white abolitionists Gilbert and Frances Pillsbury quickly recognized Archibald's and his brother Francis's academic potential and arranged for them to work for New England families in exchange for housing, board, and education. Archibald was promised placement with a Boston attorney, Samuel Sewall, but ended up boarding with a family in Rhode Island. His mother soon arranged for him to relocate to Lincoln University, a historically black institution in Pennsylvania. He graduated second in his class, next to his brother, Francis, earning a bachelor's degree in 1870 and a master's degree in 1872. While at Lincoln, he met his father's sisters, Angelina Grimké Weld and Sarah Grimké, who had learned about him when Sarah read an article in the *National Anti-Slavery Standard* about two former slaves named "Grimkie" who were excelling at Lincoln. The sisters embraced the brothers as family, providing financial support for

Archibald's education at Lincoln and at Harvard Law School and welcoming him into their close-knit circle of reformers and former abolitionists.

Archibald Grimké began his legal career at William Bowditch's Boston law firm in 1874 and passed the Suffolk County bar in Massachusetts a year later. While establishing himself as an attorney for a predominately black clientele, he cultivated an expansive social circle almost exclusively composed of members of prominent white families, including the Garrisons,[5] Wymans,[6] and Bradfords.[7] In 1879 Archibald Grimké married Sarah Stanley, a young white student attending Boston University, despite her father's objections. Their daughter, Angelina Weld Grimké, named after Archibald Grimké's influential aunt, was born about a year later. Archibald and Sarah Grimké's marriage was short-lived, however, troubled by Sarah's concerns about interracial union, suspicions of infidelity, and problems with poor health. Eventually they separated. In 1898 Sarah's life came to a tragic end when she committed suicide by poisoning herself in San Diego, California.

Angelina reunited with her father just as he was accelerating his political career. From 1883 to 1885, Archibald Grimké edited the *Hub,* a Republican Party–affiliated African American newspaper in Boston, which enhanced his visibility and influence as an activist and provided strong connections to the black community. In the *Hub* he aggressively addressed varied local and national issues, including universal suffrage, racial equality, and women's rights, offering fresh perspectives on persistent social problems. He also published his own lectures and the writings of fellow activists, including John Cromwell[8] and Albert Pillsbury.[9] Although Boston Republicans promised to provide financial support for the paper, their interest waned after Archibald Grimké's militant, critical editorials helped defeat Democratic Massachusetts governor Benjamin F. Butler in the 1883 election. Undaunted, Archibald Grimké invested his own money in the newspaper and organized fund-raisers to keep it afloat.

Archibald Grimké's work at the *Hub* brought him to the attention of Boston activists and politicians, who increasingly tapped him to publish essays, present lectures, endorse causes, or perform public service. In 1884 he delivered a powerful speech at the memorial service for Wendell Phillips, exhibiting a keen sense of the abolitionist tradition as well as Phillips's contributions and legacy.[10] That same year, Massachusetts governor George Robinson appointed him as a trustee for the Westborough State Hospital, which offered care for the mentally impaired. By the final decade of the nineteenth century, he affirmed his role as an influential voice among African American activists through the publication of two well-received biographies, *William Lloyd Garrison* and *The Life of Charles Sumner: The Scholar in Politics.* Like Garrison and Sumner, Archibald Grimké had come of age during a tumultuous period in American history that required reformers to deftly navigate the publishing, political, activist, and academic arenas in addressing the needs of the day.

As Archibald Grimké established himself as a public man, he broke with the Republican Party, convinced that it had abandoned its commitment to African Americans. He was particularly unsettled after the Compromise of 1877, when the Republican presidential candidate Rutherford Hayes agreed to withdraw troops from the South in exchange for delegates who tipped the 1876 presidential election in his favor. Archibald Grimké identified himself as an Independent and campaigned for Democrats. Two years later, he supported Grover Cleveland's run for president and was narrowly defeated when he ran as a Democrat for state representative. Near the end of Cleveland's administration, his friend Charles R. Codman sent a letter to the president recommending him as U.S. consul to Santo Domingo.[11] Congress delayed the confirmation, however, forcing him to wait until Cleveland was reelected to gain the post. In 1894 the Senate approved Archibald Grimké's long-awaited appointment. He was a highly effective diplomat, negotiating mutually beneficial treaties that revealed the potential for strong relationships between America and nations governed by people of African descent. Although Archibald Grimké and his friends lobbied for his reappointment, he lost his post to a Republican nominee when William McKinley was elected president in 1896. Archibald Grimké returned to the United States and immediately resumed his activist work, joining his brother, Francis, at the American Negro Academy, a public forum in Washington, D.C., that provided black intellectuals opportunities to discuss diasporic concerns.

In 1901 the American Negro Academy published the selection that appears in this volume, "Right on the Scaffold; or The Martyrs of 1822," which examines a conspiracy led by Denmark Vesey that sought to incite a slave insurrection in Charleston. Archibald Grimké begins with an allusion to the Song of Solomon, "He was black but comely," but quickly signals that his narrative will deviate from the sensuous love story to a tale about how a man's love of freedom compels him to convince a large group of people to undertake the seemingly impossible task of revolting against slaveholders.[12] Unlike W. W. Brown and other historians who include portions of the Official Reports in their histories, Grimké, in effect, issues a revised and enlarged Official Report that posits Vesey as an extraordinary, noble, well-spoken, intelligent, passionate, and courageous man who was born a slave but learned to feign his way into the favor of his masters. Grimké delineates the strategy that the slave subtly implements against his oppressor, deceiving him into believing he is loyal and content while quietly inspiring a community of slaves and free blacks to rebel. The restrictions of slavery and freedom stoke Vesey's ire, impelling him to proceed with his plans. Winning the East Bay Street lottery enables him to purchase his freedom but does not give him the right to liberate his enslaved wife and children. In positioning Vesey as an artful dissembler, Grimké suggests that slavery compelled African Americans to become more cunning than their masters. The widening disparity between white Americans' prosperity and African Americans' oppression stoked fires of rebellion within the enslaved and free black communities. Vesey's conspiracy was uncovered; he and his coconspirators died courageously. Archibald Grimké conveys a dual message. Like Vesey, contemporary African American activists who seemingly kowtow to whites may actually be appropriating the art of dissimulation as they develop more radical plans. Additionally, African American activists must be willing to die for the cause of freedom, advice some well-heeled, middle-class black activists may have been loath to follow.

Archibald Grimké became involved in the American Negro Academy just as black activists were splitting into pro– and anti–Booker T. Washington factions following Washington's Atlanta Compromise speech, which advocated industrial education as the solution to the race problem. Although he critiqued Washington's philosophy, Archibald Grimké maintained ties with the young race leader, perhaps hoping that he might be a Vesey who maintained an accommodationist façade while quietly advancing a more radical agenda. Despite their public denunciations of Washington's views, Archibald Grimké and other activists were accused of maintaining a cowardly silence regarding Washington's positions on suffrage, equality, and education, notably by W. E. B. Du Bois (1868–1963) in *The Souls of Black Folk* (1903). Archibald Grimké continued to circulate and refine his views on racial advancement by accepting Thomas Fortune's invitation to be the Washington, D.C., correspondent for the *New York Age,* a leading African American newspaper affiliated with Booker T. Washington. His eventual alienation from Washington can be traced in part to Washington's failure to speak out against the 1906 Brownsville Incident, which occurred when members of the black Twenty-Fifth Infantry Regiment were falsely accused of shooting white Americans in a small Texas town. Despite the absence of a trial or hearing, President Theodore Roosevelt ordered 167 of the 170-member company dishonorably discharged. Many black leaders believed the soldiers' punishment was unjustified. Archibald Grimké publicly condemned President's Roosevelt's decision and Washington's silence on the issue in editorials published in the *Age.* Within a year of the Brownsville Incident, Archibald Grimké left the newspaper due to intense pressure from Washington's supporters to stop criticizing their leader and President Roosevelt. He refused to relent, however, and continued to write and speak on the soldiers' behalf until some of them were exonerated several years later.

The Brownsville Incident was one of several racial events that compelled activists and reformers to develop an interracial organization to bridge the chasm between the Du Bois and the Washington camps in order to present a united front against racism in America. In 1909 an interracial group founded the National Negro Conference, renamed the National Committee for the Advancement of the Negro, and appointed a Committee of Forty to establish the group's rules and objectives. By 1911 the organization became known as the National Association for the Advancement of Colored People (NAACP). Although Archibald Grimké did not play a major role in the founding of the NAACP, he soon became an influential leader within the organization. He first joined the Boston chapter and worked to combat southern Democrats' efforts, under the guidance of President Woodrow Wilson, to enact legislation that codified segregation. In 1913 Archibald Grimké wrote letters to support the NAACP's unsuccessful campaign to stop legislation that outlawed interracial marriages. By the end of that year, the NAACP's national leaders elected Archibald Grimké president of the Washington, D.C., branch, which he transformed into the most effective and influential division of the NAACP. He eventually served as the organization's national vice president.

In 1919 Archibald's Grimké began to take more militant stances, particularly after black soldiers were convicted and condemned to death for their role in a racial incident in Houston. Grimké fired off a complaint to President Wilson and commemorated the tragedy in a poem, "Her Thirteen Black Soldiers," which was published in the *Messenger,* a black socialist journal founded by A. Philip Randolph[13] and Chandler Owen.[14] That same year, the NAACP honored him with its Spingarn Medal, its highest award for a lifetime of service to the race.

In the mid-1920s, Archibald Grimké stepped aside as a new generation of race leaders began to exert their influence in the NAACP and other civil rights organizations. By 1928 his health had deteriorated, and he moved into his brother Francis's home, where he died on February 25, 1930.

❧ "Right on the Scaffold; or The Martyrs of 1822"

He was black but comely.[15] Nature gave him a royal body, nobly planned and proportioned, and noted for its great strength. There was that in his countenance, which bespoke a mind within to match that body, a mind of uncommon native intelligence, force of will, and capacity to dominate others. His manners were at once abrupt and crafty, his temper was imperious, his passions and impulses were those of a primitive ruler, and his heart was the heart of a lion. He was often referred to as an old man, but he was not an old man, when he died on a gallows at Charleston, S.C., July 2, 1822. No, he was by no means an old man, whether judged by length of years or strength of body, for he was on that memorable July day, seventy-eight years ago, not more than fifty-six years old, although the hair on his head and face was then probably white. This circumstance and the pre-eminence accorded him by his race neighbors, might account for the references to him, as to that of an old man.

All things considered, he was truly an extraordinary man. It is impossible to say where he was born, or who were his parents. He was, alas! as far as my knowledge of his personal history goes, a man without a past. He might have been born of slave parentage in the West Indies, or of royal ones in Africa, where, in that case, he was kidnapped and sold subsequently into slavery in America. I had almost said that he was a man without a name. He is certainly a man without ancestral name. For the name to which he answered up to the age of fourteen, has been lost forever. After that time he has been known as Denmark Vesey.[16] Denmark is a corruption of Telemaque, the praenomen bestowed upon him at that age by a new master, and Vesey was the cognomen of that master who was captain of an American vessel, engaged in the African slave trade between the islands of St. Thomas and Sto. Domingo. It is on board of Captain Vesey's[17] slave vessel that we catch the earliest glimpse of our hero. Deeply interesting moment is that, which revealed thus to us the Negro lad, deeply interesting and tragical for one and the same cause.

This first appearance of him upon the stage of history occurred in the year which ended virtually the war for American Independence, 1787, during the passage between St. Thomas and Cap Francais, of Captain Vesey's slave bark with a cargo of 390 slaves. The lad, Telemaque, was a part of that sad cargo, undistinguished at the outset of the voyage from the rest of the human freight. Of the 389 others, we know absolutely nothing. Not an incident, nor a token, not even a name has floated to us across the intervening years, from all that multitudinous misery, from such an unspeakable tragedy, except that the ship reached its destination, and the slaves were sold. Like boats that pass at sea, that slave vessel loomed for a lurid instant on the horizon, and was gone for ever—all but Denmark Vesey. How it happened that he did not vanish with the rest of his ill-fated fellows, will be set down in this paper, which has essayed to describe the slave plot which he planned, with which his name is identified, and by which it ought to be, for all time, hallowed in, the memory of every man, woman and child of Negro descent in America.

On that voyage Captain Vesey was strongly attracted by the "beauty, intelligence, and alertness" of one of the slaves on board. So were the ship's officers. This particular object of interest, on the part of the slave-traders, was a black boy of fourteen summers. He was quickly made a sort of ship's pet and plaything, receiving new garments from his admirers, and the high sounding name, as I have already mentioned, of Telemaque, which in slave lingo was subsequently metamorphosed into Denmark. The lad found himself in sudden, favor, and lifted above his companions in bondage by the brief and idle regard of that ship's company. Brief and idle, indeed, was the interest which he had aroused in the breasts of those men, as the sequel showed. But while it lasted it seemed doubtless very genuine to the boy, as such evidences of human regard must have afforded him, in his forlorn state, the keenest pleasure. Bitter, therefore, must have been his disappointment and grief to find, at the end, that he had, in reality, no hold whatever upon the regard of the slave traders. True he had been separated by captain and officers from the other slaves during the voyage, but this ephemeral distinction was speedily lost upon the arrival of the vessel at Cap Francais,[18] for he was then sold as a part of the human freight. Ah! he had not been to those men so much as even a pet cat or dog, for with a pet cat or dog they would not have so lightly parted, as they had done with him. He had served their purpose, had killed for them the dull days of a dull sail between ports, and he a boy with warm blood in his heart, and hot yearnings for love in his soul.

But the slave youth, so beautiful and attractive, was not to live his life in the island of Sto. Domingo, or to terminate just then his relations with the ship and her officers however much Captain Vesey had intended to do so. For Fate, by an unexpected circumstance, threw, for better or for worse, master and slave together again, after they had apparently parted forever in the slave mart of the Cape. This is how Fate played the unexpected in the boy's life. According to a local law for the regulation of the slave trade in that place, the seller of a slave of unsound health might be compelled by the buyer to take him back, upon the production of a certificate to that effect from the royal physician of the port. The purchaser of Telemaque availed himself of this law to redeliver him to Captain Vesey on his return voyage to Sto. Domingo. For the royal physician of the town had meanwhile certified that the lad was subject to epileptic fits. The act of sale was thereupon cancelled, and the old relations of master and slave between Captain Vesey and Telemaque, were resumed. Thus, without design, perhaps, however passionately he might have desired it, the boy found himself again on board of his old master's slave vessel, where he had been petted and elevated in favor high above his fellow-slaves. I say *perhaps* advisedly, for I confess that it is by no means clear to me whether those epileptic fits were real or whether they were in truth feigned, and therefore the initial *ruse de guerre*[19] of that bright young intelligence in its long battle with slavery.

However, I do not mean to consume space with speculations on this head. Suffice to say that Telemaque's condition was improved by the event. Nor had Captain Vesey any cause to quarrel with the fate which returned to him the beautiful Negro youth. For it is recorded that for twenty years thereafter he proved a faithful servant to the old slave trader, who retiring in due course of time from his black business, took up his abode in Charleston, S.C., where Denmark went to live with him. There in his new home dame fortune again remembered her protege, turning her formidable wheel a second time in his favor. It was then that Denmark, grown to manhood, drew the grand prize of freedom. He was then about thirty-four years old when this immense boon came to him.

It is not known for how many eager and anxious months or even years, Denmark Vesey had patronized East Bay Street Lottery[20] of Charleston prior to 1800, when he was rewarded with a prize of $1,500. With $600 of this money he bought himself of Captain Vesey. He was at last his own master, in possession of a small capital, and of a good trade, carpentry, which he practiced with great industry. He was successful, massed in time considerable wealth, became a solid man of the community in spite of his color, winning the confidence of the whites, and respect from the blacks amounting almost to reverence. He married—was much married it was said, which I see no reason to doubt, in view of the polygamous example set him by many of the respectabilities of the master-race in that remarkably pious old slave town. A plurality of children rose up, in consequence, to him from the plurality of his family ties; rose up to him, but they were not his, for following the condition of the mothers, they were, under the Slave-Code, the chattels of other men.

This cruel wrong eat deep into Vesey's mind. Of course it was most outrageous for him, a black man, to concern himself so much about the human chattels of white men, albeit those human chattels were his own children. What had he, a social pariah in Christian America, to do with such high caste things as a heart and natural affections? But somehow he did have a heart, and it was in the right place, and natural affections for his own flesh and blood, like men with a white skin. 'Twas monstrous in him to be sure, but he could not help it. The slave iron had entered his soul, and the wound which it made rankled in secret there.

Not alone the sad condition of his own children embittered his lot, but the sad condition of other black men's children as well. He yearned to help all to better social conditions—to that freedom which is the gift of God to mankind. He yearned to possess this God-given boon, in its fullness and entirety, for himself before he passed thence to the grave. For he possessed it not. He had indeed bought himself, but he soon learned that the right to himself which he had purchased from his master was not the freedom of a man, but the freedom accorded by the Slave-Code, to a black man, a freedom so restrictive in quantity and mean in quality that no white man, however low, could be made to live contentedly under it for a day.

In judging this black man, oh! ye critics and philosophers, judge him not hastily and harshly before you have at least tried to put yourselves in his place. You may not even then succeed in doing him justice, for while he had his faults, and was sorely tempted, he was, nevertheless, in every inch of him, from the soles of his feet to the crown of his head, a man.

At the period which we have now reached in his history, he was in possession of a fairly good education—was able to read and write, and to speak with fluency the French and English languages. He had traveled extensively over the world in his master's slave vessel, and had thus obtained a stock of valuable experiences, and a wide range of knowledge of men and things of which few inhabitants, whether black or white, in the slave community of Charleston, during the first quarter of the nineteenth century could truthfully have boasted. Yet in spite of these undeniable facts, in spite of his unquestioned ability and economic efficiency as an industrial factor in that city, he was in legal and actual ownership of precious little of that right to "life, liberty, and the pursuit of happiness" which the most ignorant and worthless white man enjoyed as a birthright. Wherever he moved or wished to move he was met and surrounded by the most galling and degrading, social and civil conditions and proscriptions. True he held a bill of sale of his person, had ceased to be the chattel property of an individual, but he still wore chains, which kept him, and which were intended to keep him and such as him, slaves of the community forever, deprived of every civil right which white men, their neighbors, were bound to respect. For instance, were he wronged in his person or property by any member of the dominant race, be the offender man, woman, or child, Vesey could have had no redress in the courts,[21] in case, the proof of his complaint or the enforcement of his claim depended exclusively upon the testimony of himself and of that of black witnesses, however respectable.

Such a man, we may be sure, was conscious of the possession, notwithstanding his black skin and blacker social and civil condition, of longings, aspirations, which the Slave-Code made it a crime for him to satisfy. He must have felt the stir of forces and faculties within him, which, under the heaviest pains and penalties, he was forbidden to exercise. Thus robbed of freedom, ravished of manhood, what was he to do? Ay, what ought he to have done under the circumstances? Ought he to have done what multitudes had done before him, meek and submissive folk, generations and generations of them, borne tamely like them his chains, without an effort to break them, and break instead his lion's spirit? Ought he to have contented himself with such a woeful existence, and to have been willing at its end to mingle his ashes, with the miserable dust of all those countless masses of forgotten and unresisting slaves? "Never!" replied what was bravest and worthiest of respect in the breast of this truly great-hearted man. The burning wrong which he felt against slavery had sunk in his mind below the reach of the grappling tongs of reason. It lay like a charge of giant powder, with its slow match attachment in the unplumbed depths of a soul which knew not fear; of a soul which was as hot with smouldering hate and rage as is a live volcano with its unvomited flame and lava. As well, under the circumstances, have tried to subdue the profound fury of the one with argument, as to quench the hidden fires of the other with water.

He knew, none better, that his oppressors were strong and that he was weak; that he had but one slender chance in a hundred of redressing by force the wrongs of himself and race. He knew too, that failure in such a desperate enterprise could have for himself but a single issue, viz.: certain death. But he believed that success on the other hand meant for him and his the gain of that which alone was able to make their lives worth the living, to wit.: a free man's portion, his opportunity for the full development and free play of all of his powers amid that society in which was cast his lot. And for that portion, so precious, he was ready to take the one chance with all of its tremendous risks, to stake that miserable modicum of freedom which he possessed, the wealth laboriously accumulated by him, and life itself.

It is impossible to fix exactly the time when the bold idea of resistance entered his brains, or to say when he began to plan for its realization, and after that to prepare the blacks for its reception. Before embarking on his perilous enterprise he must have carefully reckoned on time, long and indefinite, as an essential factor in its successful achievement. For, certain it is, he took it, years in fact, made haste slowly and with supreme discretion and self-control. He appeared to have thoroughly acquainted himself with the immense difficulties which beset an uprising of the blacks. Not once, I think, did he underestimate the strength of his foes. A past grand master in the art of intrigue among the servile population, he was equally adept in knowledge of the weak spots for attack in the defences of the slave system, knew perfectly where the masters could best be taken at a disadvantage. All the facts of his history combine to give him a character for profound acting. In the underground agitation, which during a period of three or four years he conducted in the city of Charleston and over a hundred miles of the adjacent country, he seemed to have been gifted with a sort of Protean[22] ability. His capacity for practicing secrecy and dissimulation where they were deemed necessary to his end, must have been prodigious, when it is considered that during the years covered by his underground agitation, it is not recorded that he made a single false note, or took a single false step to attract attention to himself and movement, or to arouse over all that territory included in that agitation and among all those white people involved in its terrific consequences, the slightest suspicion of danger.

In his underground agitation, Vesey, with an instinct akin to genius, seemed to have excluded from his preliminary action everything like conscious combination or organization among his disciples, and to have confined himself strictly to the immediate business in hand at that stage of his plot, which was the sowing of seeds of discontent, the fomenting of hatred among the blacks, bond and free alike, toward the whites. And steadily with that patience which Lowell calls the "passion of great hearts,"[23] he pushed deeper and deeper into the slave lump the explosive principles of inalienable human rights. He did not flinch from kindling in the bosoms of the slaves a hostility toward the masters as burning as that which he felt toward them in his own breast. He had, indeed, reached such a pitch of race enmity that, as he was often heard to declare, "he would not like to have a white man in his presence."

And so, devoured by a supreme passion, mastered by a single predominant idea, Vesey looked for occasions, and when they were wanting he created them, to preach his new and terrible gospel of liberty and hate. Thus only could he hope to render their condition intolerable to the slaves, the production of which was the indispensable first step in the consummation of his design. Otherwise what possibility of final success could a contented slave population have offered him? He needed a fulcrum on which to plant his lever. He had nowhere in such an enterprise to place it, but in the discontent and hatred of the slaves toward their masters. Therefore on the fulcrum of race hatred he rested his lever of freedom for his people.

As the discontented bondsmen heard afresh with Vesey's ears the hateful clank of their chains, they would, in time, learn to think of Vesey and to turn, perhaps, to him for leadership and deliverance. Brooding over their lot as Vesey had revealed it to them, they might move of themselves to improve or end it altogether, by adopting some such bold plan as Vesey's. Meantime he would continue to wait and prepare for that moment, while they would be training in habits of deceit, of deep dissimulation, that formidable weapon of the weak in conflict with the strong, that *ars artium*[24] of slaves in their attempts to break their chains—a habit of smiling and fawning on unjust and cruel power, while bleeds in secret their fiery wound, rages and plots there also their passionate hate, and glows there too their no less passionate hope for freedom.

Everywhere through the dark subterranean world of the slave, in Charleston and the neighboring country, went with his great passion of hate and his great purpose of freedom, this untiring breeder of sedition. And where he moved beneath the thin crust of that upper world of the master-race, there broke in his wake whirling and shooting currents of new and wild sensations in the abysses of that under world of the slave-race. Down deep below the ken of the masters was toiling this volcanic man, forming the lava-floods, the flaming furies, and the awful horrors of a slave uprising.

Nowhere idle was that underground plotter against the whites. Even on the street where he happened to meet two or three blacks, he would bring the conversation to his one consuming subject, and preach to them his one unending sermon of freedom and hate. It was then as if his stern voice, with its deep organ chords of passion, was saying to those men: "Forget not, oh my brothers your misery. Remember how ye are wronged every day and hour, ye and your mothers and sisters, your wives and children. Remember the generations gone weeping and clanking heavy chains from the cradle to the grave. Remember the oppression of the living, who with heart-break and death-wounds, are treading their mournful way in bitter anguish and despair across burning desert sands, with parched soul and shriveled minds, with piteous thirsts, and terrible tortures of body and spirit. Weep for them, weep for yourselves too, if ye will, but learn to hate, ay, to hate with such hatred as blazes within me, the wicked slave-system and the wickeder white men who oppress and wrong us thus."

Ever on the alert was he for a text or a pretext to advance his underground movement. Did he and fellow blacks for example, encounter a white person on the street, and did Vesey's companions make the customary bow, which blacks were wont to make to whites, a form of salutation born of generations of slave-blood, meanly and humble and cringingly self-effacing, rebuking such an exhibition of sheer and shameless servility and lack of proper self-respect, he would thereupon declare to them the self-evident truth that all men were born free and equal, that the master, with his white skin, was in the sight of God no whit better than his black slaves, and that for himself he would not cringe like that to any man.

Should the sorry wretches, bewildered by Vesey's boldness and dazed by his terrifying doctrines, reply defensively "we are slaves," the harsh retort "you deserve to remain so," was, without doubt, intended to sting if possible, their abject natures into sensibility on the subject of their wrongs, to galvanize their rotting souls back to manhood, and to make their base and sieve-like minds capable of receiving and retaining, at least, a single fermenting idea. And when Vesey was thereupon asked "What can we do?" he knew by the token that the sharp point of his spear had pierced the slavish apathy of ages of oppression, and that thenceforth light would find its red and revolutionary way to the imprisoned minds within. To the query "What can we do?" his invariable response was "Go and buy a spelling book and read the fable of Hercules and the Wagoner."[25] They were to look for Hercules in their own stout arms and backs, and not in the clouds, to brace their iron shoulders against the wheels of adversity and oppression, and to learn that self-help was ever the best prayer.

At other times, in order to familiarize the blacks, I suppose, with the notion of equality, and to heighten probably at the same time his influence over them, he would select a moment when some of them were within earshot, to enter into conversation with certain white men, whose characters he had studied for his purpose, and during the shuttle-cock and battledore of words

which was sure to follow, would deftly let fly some bold remark on the subject of slavery. "He would go so far," on such occasions it was said, "that
had not his declarations in such situations been clearly proved, they would
scarcely have been credited." Such action was daring almost to rashness, but
in it is also apparent the deep method of a clever and calculating mind.

The sundry religious classes or congregations with Negro leaders or
local preachers, into which were formed the Negro members of the various churches of Charleston, furnished Vesey with the first rudiments of an
organization, and at the same time with a singularly safe medium for conducting his underground agitation. It was customary, at that time, for these
Negro congregations to meet for purposes of worship entirely free from the
presence of the whites. Such meetings were afterward forbidden to be held
except in the presence of at least one representative of the dominant race.[26]
But during the three or four years prior to the year 1822, they certainly offered Denmark Vesey regular, easy and safe opportunities for preaching his
gospel of liberty and hate. And we are left in no doubt whatever in regard to
the uses to which he put those gatherings of blacks.

Like many of his race he possessed the gift of gab, as the silver in the
tongue and the gold in the full or thick-lipped mouth, are oftentimes con-
temptuously characterized. And like many of his race he was a devoted student of the Bible to whose interpretation he brought like many other Bible
students, not confined to the Negro race, a good deal of imagination, and not
a little of superstition, which with some natures is perhaps but another name
for the desires of the heart. Thus equipped it is no wonder that Vesey, as he
pored over the Old Testament Scriptures, found many points of similitude
in the history of the Jews and that of the slaves in the United States.[27] They
were both peculiar peoples. They were both Jehovah's peculiar peoples, one
in the past, the other in the present. And it seemed to him that as Jehovah
bent his ear, and bared his arm once in behalf of the one, so would he do the
same for the other. It was all vividly real to his thought, I believe, for to his
mind thus had said the Lord.

He ransacked the Bible for apposite and terrible texts, whose commands
in the olden times, to the olden people, were no less imperative upon the new
times and the new people. This new people was also commanded to arise
and destroy their enemies and the city in which they dwelt, "both man and
woman, young and old, & & & with the edge of the sword."[28] Believing super-
stitiously, as he did, in the stern and Nemesis-like God of the Old Testament,
he looked confidently for a day of vengeance and retribution for the blacks.
He felt, I doubt not, something peculiarly applicable to his enterprise, and intensely personal to himself in the stern and exultant prophecy of Zachariah,
fierce and sanguinary words which were constantly in his mouth: "Then

shall the Lord go forth, and fight against those nations, as when he fought in the day of battle."[29] According to Vesey's lurid exegesis "those nations" in the text meant, beyond a peradventure, the cruel masters, and Jehovah was to go forth to fight against them for the poor slaves, and on which ever side fought that day the Almighty God, on that side would assuredly rest victory and deliverance.

It will not be denied that Vesey's plan contemplated the total annihilation of the white population of Charleston. Nursing for many dark years the bitter wrongs of himself and race had filled him, without doubt, with a mad spirit of revenge, and had so given him a decided predilection for shedding the blood of his oppressors. But if he intended to kill them to satisfy a desire for vengeance, he intended to do so also on broader ground. The conspirators, he argued, had no choice in the matter, but were compelled to adopt a policy of extermination by the necessity of their position. The liberty of the blacks was in the balance of fate against the lives of the whites. He could strike that balance in favor of the blacks only by the total destruction of the whites. Therefore, the whites, men, women and children, were doomed to death. "What is the use of killing the louse and leaving the nit?" he asked coarsely and grimly on an occasion when the matter was under consideration. And again he was reported to have, with unrelenting temper, represented to his friends in secret council, that, "It was for our safety not to spare one white skin alive." And so it was unmistakably in his purpose to leave not a single egg lying about Charleston, when he was done with it, out of which might possibly be hatched another future slave-holder and oppressor of his people. "Thorough" was in truth, the merciless motto of that terrible man.

All roads, on the red map of his plot, led to Rome. Every available instrument which fell in his way, he utilized to deepen and extend his underground agitation among the blacks. Wherefore it was that he seized upon the sectional struggle which was going on in Congress over the admission of Missouri,[30] and pressed it to do service for his cause. The passionate wish, unconsciously perhaps, colored if it did not create the belief on his part, that the real cause of that great debate in Washington, and excitement in the country at large was a movement for general emancipation of the slaves. It was said that he went so far in this direction as to put it into the heads of the blacks that Congress had actually enacted an emancipation law, and that therefore their continued enslavement was illegal. Such preaching must have certainly added fresh fuel to the deep sense of injury, then burning in the breasts of many of the slaves, and must have operated also to prepare them for the next step which Vesey's plan of campaign contemplated, viz.: a resort to force to wrest from the whites the freedom which was theirs, not only by the will of Heaven, but as well by the supreme law of the land.

A period of underground agitation, such as Vesey had carried on for about three or four years will, unless arrested, pass naturally into one of organized action. Vesey's movement reached, in the winter of 1821–22, such a stage. As far as it is known, he had up to this time done the work of agitator singlehanded and alone. Singlehanded and alone he had gone to and fro through that under world of the slave, preaching his gospel of liberty and hate. But about Christmas of 1821, the long lane of his labors made a sharp turn. This circumstance tended necessarily to throw other actors upon the scene, as shall presently appear.

The first step taken at the turn of his long and laborious lane was calculated to put to the utmost test his ability as a leader, as an arch plotter. For it was nothing less momentous than the choice by him of fit associates. On the wisdom with which such a choice was made, would depend his own life and the success of his undertaking. Among thousands of disciples he had to find the right men to whom to entrust his secret purpose and its execution in co-operation with himself. The step was indeed crucial and in taking it he needed not alone the mental qualities which he had exhibited in his role of underground agitator, viz: serpent-like cunning and intelligence under the direction of the most alert and flexible discretion, but as well a practical and profound knowledge of the human nature with which he had to deal, a keen and infallible insight into individual character.

It is not too much to claim for Denmark Vesey, that his genius rose to the emergency, and proved itself equal to a surpassingly difficult situation, in the singular fitness of the five principal men on whom fell his election to associate leadership, with himself, and to the work of organizing the blacks for resistance. These five men, who became his ablest and most efficient lieutenants, were Peter Poyas,[31] Rolla and Ned Bennett,[32] Monday Gell[33] and Gullah Jack.[34] They were all slaves and, I believe, full-blooded Negroes. They constituted a remarkable quintet of slave leaders, combined the very qualities of head and heart which Vesey most needed at the stage then reached by his unfolding plot. For fear lest some of their critics might sneer at the sketch of them which I am tempted to give, as lacking in probability and truth, I will insert instead the careful estimate placed upon them severally by their slave judges. And here it is: "In the selection of his leaders, Vesey showed great penetration and sound judgment. Rolla was plausible and possessed uncommon self-possession; bold and ardent, he was not to be deterred from his purpose by danger. Ned's appearance indicated that he was a man of firm nerves and desperate courage. Peter was intrepid and resolute, true to his engagements, and cautious in observing secrecy where it was necessary; he was not to be daunted nor impeded by difficulties, and though confident of success, was careful against any obstacles or casualties which might arise, and intent upon discovering every means which might be in their favor if thought of beforehand. Gullah Jack was regarded as a sorcerer, and as such feared by the natives of Africa, who believe in witchcraft. He was not only considered invulnerable, but that he could make others so by his charms; and that he could and certainly would provide all his followers with arms. He was artful, cruel, bloody; his disposition in short was diabolical. His influence among the Africans was inconceivable. Monday was firm, resolute, discreet and intelligent."

From this picture, painted by bitter enemies, who were also their executioners, could any person, ignorant of the circumstances and the history of those men, possibly guess, with the exception of Gullah Jack, to what race the originals belonged, or think you, that such a person would so much as dream that they were in fact, as they were in the eye of the law under which they lived, nothing more than so many human chattels, subject like cattle to the caprice and the cruelty of their owners?

Such nevertheless was the remarkable group of blacks on whom had fallen Vesey's choice. And did they not present an assemblage of high and striking qualities? Here were coolness in action, calculation, foresight, plausibility in address, fidelity to engagements, secretiveness, intrepid courage, nerves of iron in the presence of danger, inflexible purpose, unbending will, and last though not least in its relations to the whole, superstition incarnate in the character of the Negro conjurer.[35] Masterly was indeed the combination, and he had no ordinary gift for leadership, who was able to hit it off at one surprising stroke.

As the work of organized preparation for the uprising advanced, Vesey added presently to his staff two principal and several minor recruiting agents, who operated in Charleston and in the country to the North of the city as far as the Santee, the Combahee,[36] and Georgetown.[37] Their exploitation in the interest of the plot extended to the South into the two large islands of James and John's,[38] as well as to plantations across the Ashley River.[39] Vesey himself, it was said, traveled south-wardly from Charleston between seventy and eighty miles, and it was presumed by the writers that he did so on business connected with the conspiracy, which I consider altogether probable. He had certainly thrown himself into the movement with might and main. We know, that its direction absorbed finally his whole time and energy. "He ceased working himself at his trade," so ran the testimony of a witness at his trial, "and employed himself exclusively in enlisting men."

The number of blacks engaged in the enterprise was undoubtedly large. It is a sufficiently conservative estimate to place this number, I think, at two or three thousand, at least. One recruiting officer alone, Frank Ferguson, enlisted in the undertaking the slaves of four plantations within forty miles of the city; and in the city itself, it was said that the personal roll of Peter Poyas embraced a membership of six hundred names. More than one witness placed the conjectural strength of Vesey's forces as high as 9,000, but I am inclined to write this down as a gross overestimate of the people actually enrolled as members of the conspiracy.

Here is an example of the nice calculation and discretion of the man who was the soul of the conspiracy. It is contained in the testimony of an intensely hostile witness, a slave planter, whose slaves were suspected of complicity in the intended uprising.

"The orderly conduct of the Negroes in any district of country within forty miles of Charleston," wrote this witness, "is no evidence that they were ignorant of the intended attempt. A more orderly gang than my own is not to be found in this state, and one of Denmark Vesey's directions was, that they should assume the most implicit obedience."

Take another instance of the extraordinary aptitude of the slave leaders for the conduct of their dangerous enterprise. It illustrates Peter's remarkable foresight and his faculty for scenting danger, and making at the same time provision for meeting it. In giving an order to one of his assistants, said he, "Take care and, don't mention it [the plot] to those waiting men who receive presents of old coats, &c., from their masters or they'll betray us." And then as if to provide doubly against betrayal at their hands, he added "I'll speak to them." His apprehension of disaster to the cause from this class was great, but it was not greater than the reality, as the sequel abundantly proved. Let me not, however, anticipate.

If there were immense difficulties in the way of recruiting, there were even greater ones in the way of supplying the recruits with proper arms, or with any arms at all for that matter. But vast as were the difficulties, the leaders fronted them with buoyant and unquailing spirit, and rose, where other men of less faith and courage would have given up in despair, to the level of seeming impossibilities, and to the top of a truly appalling situation. Where were they, indeed, to procure arms? There was a blacksmith among them, who was set to manufacturing pike-heads and bayonets, and to turning long knives into daggers and dirks. Arms in the houses of the white folks they designed to borrow after the manner of the Jews from the Egyptians.[40] But for their main supply they counted confidently upon the successful seizure, by means of preconcerted movements, of the principal places of deposit of arms within the limits of the city, of which there were several. The capture of these magazines and storehouses was quite within the range of probability, for every one of them was at the time in a comparatively unprotected state. Two large gun and powder stores, situated about three and a half miles beyond the Lines, and containing nearly eight hundred muskets and bayonets, were, by arrangement with Negro employees connected with them, at the mercy of the insurgents whenever they were ready to move upon them. The large building in the city, where was deposited the greater portion of the arms of the State, was strangely neglected in the same regard. Its main entrance, opening on the street, consisted of ordinary wooden doors, without the interposition between them and the public of even a brick wall.

In the general plan of attack, the capture of this building, which held tactically the key to the defense of Charleston, in the event of a slave uprising, was assigned to Peter Poyas, the ablest of Vesey's lieutenants. Peter, probably disguised by means of false hair and whiskers, was at a given signal at midnight of the appointed day, to move suddenly with his band upon this important post. The difficulty of the undertaking lay in the vigilance of the sentinels doing a duty before this building, and its success depended upon Peter's ability to surprise and slay this man before he could sound the alarm. Peter was confident of his ability to kill the sentinel and capture the building, and I think that he had good ground for his confidence. In conversation with an anxious follower, who feared lest the watchfulness of the guard might defeat the attempt, Peter remarked that he "would advance a little distance ahead, and if he could only get a *grip at his throat he was a gone man,* for his sword was very sharp; he had sharpened it, and made it so sharp it had cut his finger." And as if to cast the last lingering doubt out of his disciple in regard to his (Peter's) ability to fix the sentinel, he showed him the bloody cut on his finger.

Other leaders, at the head of their respective bands, were at the same time, and from six different quarters, to attack the city, surprising and seizing all of its strategical points, and the buildings, where were deposited its arms and ammunition. A body of insurgent horse was, meanwhile, to keep the streets clear, cutting down without mercy all white persons, and suspected blacks, whom they might encounter, in order to prevent the whites from concentrating or spreading the alarm through the doomed town. Such was Denmark Vesey's masterly and merciless plan of campaign in bare outline for the capture of Charleston, a plan, which, with such a sagacious head as was Vesey, was entirely feasible, and which would have, undoubtedly, succeeded but for the happening of the unexpected at a critical stage of its execution. Against such an occurrence as was this one, no man in Vesey's situation, however supreme might have been his ability as a leader, could have completely provided. The element of treachery could not by any device have been wholly eliminated from his chapter of accidents and chances. To do what he set out to do, with the means at his disposition, Vesey had of necessity to take the tremendous risk of betrayal at the hand of some black traitor. It was, in reality, sad to relate his greatest risk, and became the one insurmountable barrier in the way of his final success.

Sunday at midnight of July 14, 1822, was fixed upon originally as the time for beginning his attack upon the city. But about the last of May, owing to indications that the plot had been discovered, he shortened the period of its preparation, and appointed instead midnight of Sunday, June 16th of the same year. His reason for selecting the original date illustrates his careful and astute attention to details in making his plans. He had noted that the white population of Charleston was subject, to a certain extent, to regular tidal movements; that at one season of the year this movement was at high tide, and that at another it was at low tide. It was no great difficulty, under the circumstances, for a man like Denmark Vesey to forecast with reasonable accuracy these recurrent movements, and natural enough that he should have planned his attack with reference to them. And this was exactly what he did when he appointed July 14th as the original date for beginning the insurrection. At that time the city was less capable than at an earlier date to cope with a slave uprising, owing to the departure in large numbers from it, for summer resorts, of its wealthier classes.

Again his selection of the first day of the week in both instances was equally the result of careful calculation on his part, as on that day large bodies of slaves from the adjacent plantations and islands were wont to visit the town without molestation, whereas on no other day could this have been done. Thus, without exciting alarm, did Vesey plan to introduce his Trojan horse or country bands into the city, where they were to be concealed until the hour for beginning the attack.

But the attack, carefully planned as it was, did not take place. For the thing which Peter Poyas feared, and had vainly endeavored to provide against, came to pass. One of those very "waiting men," for whom Peter entertained such deep distrust, and against whom he had raised his voice in sharp warning, betrayed to his master the plot, the secret of which had been communicated to him by an overzealous convert, whose discretion was shorter than his tongue. All this happened on the morning of the 30th of May, and by sunset of that day the secret was in possession of the authorities of the city. Precautionary measures were quickly taken by them to guard against surprise, and to discover the full extent of the intended uprising.

Luckily for the conspirators the information given by the traitor was vague and general. Nor was the city able to elicit from the informant of this man, who had been promptly arrested and subjected to examination, any disclosures of a more specific or satisfactory character. He was, in truth, in possession of but few particulars of the plot, and was therefore unable to give any greater definiteness to the government's stock of knowledge relative to the subject. Suspicion, however, lighted on Peter Poyas and Mingo Harth,[41] one of Vesey's minor leaders. They were, thereupon apprehended, and their personal effects searched, but nothing was found to inculpate either, except an enigmatical letter not understood by the authorities at the time. This circumstance, coupled with the coolness and consummate acting of the pair of suspected leaders, perplexed and deceived the authorities to such a degree that they ordered the discharge of the prisoners. But the fright and anxiety of the city were not so readily got rid of. They held Charleston uneasy and apprehensive of danger, and so kept it suspicious and watchful.

Things remained in this state of watchfulness anxiety, on both sides, for about a week. Vesey on his part remitted nothing of his preparations for the coming 16th of June, but pushed them if possible with increased vigor and secrecy. He held the while nocturnal meetings at his house on Bull street, where modified arrangements for the execution of his plans were broached and matured. How he dared at this juncture to incur such extreme hazard of detection, it is difficult to understand. But he and his confederates were men of the most indomitable purpose, and took in the desperate circumstances, in which they were then placed, the most desperate chances. They had to. They could not do otherwise.

The city on its side, was listening during a part of this same week to a second confession of that poor fellow whose tongue had outmeasured his discretion. It was listening with reviving dread to the wild and incoherent disclosures of this man, whom it had flung into the black hole of the workhouse. There, crazed by misery and fear of death, he raved about a plot among the blacks to massacre the whites and to put the town to fire and pillage. This second installment of William Paul's[42] excited disclosures, while it increased the sense of impending peril, did not put the government in better position to avert it. For groping in the dark still, it knew not yet where or whom to strike. But in this period of horrible suspense and uncertainty its suspicion fell on another one of Vesey's principal leaders. This time it was on Ned Bennett that the city's distrustful eye fastened. Like that game which children play where the object of search is hidden, and where the seekers as they approach near and yet nearer to the place of concealment, grow warm and then warmer, so was the city, in its terrible search for the source of its danger, growing hot and hotter. That was, indeed, a frightful moment for the conspirators when Ned Bennett became suspected. The city, as the children say in their game, was beginning to burn, for it seemed as if it must at the next move, thrust its iron hand into that underground world where the plot was hatching, and clutching the heart of the great enterprise, snatch it, conspiracy and conspirators, into the light of day. But it was at such a tremendous moment of danger, that the leaders, unawed by the imminency of discovery, took a step to throw the city off of their scent, so daring, dextrous and unexpected as to knock the breath out of us.

Ned Bennett, whom the city was watching as a cat, before springing, watches a mouse, went voluntarily before the Intendant or Mayor of the city, and asked to be examined, if so be he was an object of suspicion to the authorities. Ned was so surprisingly cool and indifferent, and wore so naturally an air of conscious innocence, that the great man was again deceived, and the city was thus thrown a second time out of the course of its game. Ned's arrest and examination were postponed, as the authorities in their perplexity were afraid to take at the time any decisive action, lest it might prove premature and abortive. And so lying on its arms, the city waited and watched for fresh developments and disclosures, while the insurgent leaders, in their underground world watched warily too, and pushed forward with undiminished confidence their final preparations, when they would, out of the dark, strike suddenly their liberating and annihilating blow. This awful state of suspense, of the most watchful suspicion and anxiety on one side, and of wary and anxious preparations on the other, continued for about five or six days, when it was ended by a second act of treachery emanating from the distrusted class of "waiting men," whose highest aspirations did not seem to reach above their masters' cast off garments.

Unlike the first, the information furnished to the authorities by the second traitor, was not lacking in definiteness. For this fellow knew what he was talking about. He knew almost all of the leaders, and many particulars connected with the plot. The city was thus placed in possession of the secret. It knew now the names of the ringleaders. But confident, apparently, of its ability to throttle the intended insurrection, it allowed two days to pass and the 16th of June, without making any arrests. Cat-like it crouched ready to spring, while it followed the unconscious movements of the principal conspirators. For Vesey and his principal officers were at that time, ignorant of the second betrayal, and therefore of the fact that they were from the 14th of June at the mercy of the police. On Saturday night, June 15th, an incident occurred, however, which warned them that they were betrayed, and that disaster was close at hand. This incident revealed as by a flash of lightning the hopelessness of their position. On that day Vesey had instructed one of his aids, Jesse Blackwood,[43] to go into the country in the evening for the purpose of preparing the plantation slaves to enter the city on the day following, which was Sunday, June 16th, the time fixed for beginning the insurrection. Jesse was unable to discharge this mission, either on Saturday night or Sunday morning, owning to the increased strength and vigilance of the city police and of its patrol guard. He had succeeded on Sunday morning in getting by two of their lines, but at the third line he was halted and turned back into the city. When this ominous fact was reported to the Old Chief, Vesey became very sorrowful. He and the other leaders must have instantly perceived that they were caught, as in a trap, and that the end was near. It was probably on this Sunday that they destroyed their papers, lists of names and other incriminating evidence. The shadow of the approaching catastrophe deepened and spread rapidly around and above them as they watched and waited helplessly under the huge asp of slavery, which enraged and now completely coiled, was about to strike. The stroke fell first on Peter, Rolla, Ned, and Batteau Bennett. The last, although but a boy of eighteen, was one of the most active of the younger leaders of the plot. Vesey was not captured until the fourth day afterward. So secret and profound had been his methods of operations in the underground world, that the early reports of his connection with the conspiracy, were generally discredited among the whites. Jesse Blackwood was taken the next day, and four days later, on June 27th, Monday Gell was arrested. Gullah Jack eluded the search of the police until July 5th, when he too was struck by the huge slave asp.

In all, there were one hundred and thirty-one blacks arrested, sixty-seven convicted, thirty-five executed, and thirty-seven banished beyond the limits of the United States. Five of these last were of the class of suspects, whom it was thought best to get rid of. Of the whole number of convictions, not one belonged to the bands of either Vesey, or Peter, or Rolla, or Ned, and but few to that of Gullah Jack's. Absolutely true did these five leaders prove to their vow of secrecy, and so died without betraying a single associate. This alas! cannot be said of Monday Gell, who brave and loyal as he was throughout the period of his arrest and trial, yet after sentence of death had been passed upon him, and under the influence of a terror-stricken companion, succumbed to temptation, and for the sake of life, consented to betray his followers. Denmark, Peter, Rolla, Ned, Batteau,[44] and Jesse, were hanged together, July 2, 1822. Ten days later Gullah Jack suffered death on the gallows also. Upon an enormous gallows, erected on the lines near Charleston, twenty-two of the black martyrs to freedom were executed on the 22nd day of the same ill-starred month.

A curious circumstance connected with this plot was the high regard in which the insurgents were held by the whites. But instead of my own, I prefer to insert in this place the remarks of the slave judges on this head. In their story of the plot they observed: "The character and condition of most of the insurgents were such as rendered them objects the least liable to suspicion. It is a melancholy truth, that the general good conduct of all the leaders, except Gullah Jack, had secured to them not only the unlimited confidence of their owners, but they had been indulged in every comfort and allowed every privilege compatible with their situation in the community; and although Gullah Jack was not remarkable for the correctness of his deportment, he by no means sustained a bad character. But not only were the leaders of good character and much indulged by their owners, but this was generally the case with all who were convicted, many of them possessed the highest confidence of their owners, and not one of bad character."

Comment on this significant fact is unnecessary. It contains a lesson and a warning which a fool need not err in reading and understanding. Oppression is a powder magazine exposed always to the danger of explosion from spontaneous combustion. *Verbum sat sapienti.*[45]

Another curious circumstance connected with this history, was the trial and conviction of four white men, on indictments for attempting to incite the slaves to insurrection.[46] They were each sentenced to fine and imprisonment, the fines ranging from $100 to $1,000, and the terms of imprisonment, from three to twelve months.

And now for the concluding act of this tragedy, for a final glance at four of its black heroes and martyrs as they appeared to the slave judges who tried them, and to whose hostile pen we are indebted for this last impressive picture of their courage, their fortitude and their greatness of soul. Here it is: "When Vesey was tried, he folded his arms and seemed to pay great attention to the testimony, given against him, but with his eyes fixed on the floor. In this situation he remained immovable, until the witnesses had been examined by the court, and cross-examined by his counsel, when he requested to be allowed to examine the witnesses himself. He at first questioned them in the dictatorial, despotic manner, in which he was probably accustomed to address them; but this not producing the desired effect, he questioned them with affected surprise and concern for bearing false testimony against him; still failing in his purpose, he then examined them strictly as to dates, but could not make them contradict themselves. The evidence being closed, he addressed the court at considerable length * * * When he received his sentence the tears trickled down his cheeks."

I cannot, of course, speak positively respecting the exact nature of the thought or feeling which lay back of those sad tears. But of this I am confident that they were not produced by any weak or momentary fear of death, and I am equally sure that they were not caused by remorse for the part which he had taken, as chief of a plot to give freedom to his race. Perhaps they were wrung from him by the Judas-like ingratitude and treachery, which had brought his well-laid scheme to ruin. He was about to die, and it was Wrong not Right which with streaming eyes he saw triumphant. Perhaps, in that solemn moment, he remembered the time, years before, when he might have sailed for Africa, and there have helped to build, in freedom and security, an asylum for himself and people, where all of the glad dreams of his strenuous and stormy life might have been realized, and also how he had put behind him the temptation, "because" as he expressed it, "he wanted to stay and see what he could do for his fellow creatures in bondage." At the thought of it all, the triumph of slavery, the treachery of black men, the immedicable grief which arises from wasted labors and balked purposes, and widespreading failures, is it surprising that in that supreme moment hot tears gushed from the eyes of that stricken but lion-hearted man?

But to return to the last picture of the martyrs before their judges: "Rolla when arraigned affected not to understand the charge against him, and when it was at his request further explained to him, assumed with wonderful adroitness, astonishment, and surprise. He was remarkable throughout his trial, for great presence of composure of mind. When he was informed he was convicted and was advised to prepare for death, though he had previously (but after his trial) confessed his guilt, he appeared perfectly confounded, but exhibited no signs of fear. In Ned's behavior there was nothing remarkable, but his countenance was stern and immovable, even whilst he was receiving the sentence of death; from his looks it was impossible to discover or conjecture what were his feelings. Not so with Peter, for in his countenance were strongly marked disappointed ambition, revenge, indignation, and an anxiety to know how far the discoveries had extended, and the same emotions were exhibited in his conduct. He did not appear to fear personal consequences, for his whole behavior indicated the reverse; but exhibited an evident anxiety for the success of their plan, in which his whole soul was embarked. His countenance and behavior were the same when he received his sentence, and his only words were on retiring, 'I suppose you'll let me see my wife and family before I die,' and that not in a supplicating tone. When he was asked a day or two after, if it was possible he could wish to see his master and family murdered who had treated him so kindly, he only replied to the question by a smile."

The unquailing courage, the stern fidelity to engagements and the spirit of devotion and self-sacrifice which characterized so signally the leaders of this slave plot, culminated, it seems to me, in the unbending will and grandeur of soul of Peter Poyas during those last, tragic days, in Charleston. I doubt if in six thousand years this world has produced a finer example of fortitude and greatness of mind in presence of death, than did this Negro slave exhibit in the black hole of the Charleston work-house, when conversing with his Chief and Rolla and Ned Bennett, touching their approaching death, and the safety of their faithful and forlorn followers, he uttered thus intrepid injunction: "Do not open your lips! Die silent as you shall see me do." Such words, considering the circumstances under which they were spoken, were worthy of a son of Sparta or of Rome, when Sparta and Rome were at their highest levels as breeders of iron men.

It is verily no light thing for the Negroes of the United States to have produced such a man, such a hero and martyr. It is certainly no light heritage, the knowledge that his brave blood flows in their veins. For history does not record, that any other of its long and shining line of heroes and martyrs, ever met death, anywhere on this globe, in a holier cause or a sublimer mood, than did this Spartan-like slave,[47] more than three quarters of a century ago.

May some future Rembrandt have the courage, as the genius, to paint that tragic and imposing scene, with its deep shadows and high lights as I see it now, the dark and hideous dungeon, the sombre figures and grim faces of the four glorious black martyrs, with Peter in the midst, speaking his death-less words: "Do not open your lips! Die silent as you shall see me do."

> "Right forever on the scaffold,
> Wrong forever on the Throne,
> Yet that scaffold sways the future,
> And, behind the dim unknown,
> Standeth God within the shadow,
> Keeping watch above His own."[48]

NOTES

1. The period between 1877 and 1901 that the historian Rayford W. Logan identi-fies as the "lowest point" in African Americans' quest for equal rights. Logan, *Negro in American Life.*

2. Robinson, *Dangerous Liaisons,* 4; Edgar, *South Carolina,* 308.

3. Helper (1829–1909) argued that slavery should be abolished because it im-peded the South's economic progress. He supported his argument with statistics from the 1850 U.S. Census Bureau and other sources. Helper advocated colonization for African Americans and encouraged nonslaveholding whites to rebel against plantation owners. Helper, *Impending Crisis of the South.*

4. The Morris Street School was the first school established by the Freedmen's Bureau in Charleston after the Civil War. It served both white and black children in segregated classrooms. By 1867, the school had been designated for African Ameri-can students and was supervised by the Democratic-controlled Board of School Commissioners. Powers, "Community Evolution and Race Relations," 214–33.

5. The Garrisons were descendants of the influential white abolitionist William Lloyd Garrison, editor of the antislavery newspaper the *Liberator.*

6. The influential abolitionists and reformers John Crawford Wyman (1822–1900) and Lillie Chance Wyman (1847–1927) and their son Arthur Crawford Wyman (1879–1930).

7. Ellen Bradford, a descendant of William Bradford, a signer of the Mayflower Compact, was a member of a family of prominent abolitionists and reformers.

8. The African American journalist and educator John Wesley Cromwell (1846–1927) founded the weekly newspaper *People's Advocate* in 1876 and was instrumen-tal in developing organizations to preserve and celebrate African American history and achievement.

9. Albert Enoch Pillsbury (1849–1930), a white lawyer, author, activist, and ora-tor, served as the attorney general of Massachusetts from 1891 to 1894, wrote the bylaws for the NAACP, and lectured and published extensively in support of civil rights for African Americans.

10. The prominent white reformer Wendell Phillips (1811–1884) became well known for his persuasive oratory on the antislavery circuit, but he also supported women's suffrage, temperance initiatives, prison reform, and equal rights for Native Americans.

11. Charles R. Codman was originally affiliated with the Republican Party, but by the late 1880s he switched his allegiance to the Democrats. He served as chairman of the Massachusetts Homeopathic Medical Society and was a trustee for the Westborough Insane Hospital.

12. "I am black, but comely, O ye daughters of Jerusalem." Song of Solomon 1:5, KJV.

13. The African American civil rights and labor activist and socialist A. Philip Randolph (1889–1979) established the Brotherhood of Sleeping Car Porters and was an organizing force behind the 1963 March on Washington.

14. Chandler Owen (1889–1967), an African American writer and editor, worked in public relations, for black newspapers, and as a speechwriter for politicians, including presidents Eisenhower and Johnson. In 1917 he and A. Philip Randolph established the *Messenger,* which remained in circulation until 1928. He also supported Randolph's labor initiatives and served as president of the Brotherhood of Sleeping Car Porters in 1929. Owen was affiliated with the Socialist Party and was accused of treason during World War II.

15. Unattributed quotes that appear in the text are from *An official report of the trials of sundry Negroes, charged with an attempt to raise an insurrection in the state of South-Carolina* (1822), unless otherwise indicated.

Since the 1960s, historians have been embroiled in a debate regarding the accuracy of official accounts of Denmark Vesey's Rebellion. See Egerton, "Forgetting Denmark Vesey"; Johnson, "Denmark Vesey and His Co-Conspirators."

Grimké is alluding to the Shulamite woman's assertion that "I am black, but comely, O ye daughters of Jerusalem, as the tents of Kedar, as the curtains of Solomon." Song of Solomon 1:5 (KJV).

Throughout the essay, Grimké includes quotes from the *Official Report of the Trials of Sundry Negroes.* Some are incorporated as quotes; others are integrated seamlessly into the text.

16. Denmark Vesey (1767?–1822) was captured and sold into slavery as a young West African youth in the late eighteenth century. After winning $1,500 in Charleston's East Bay Street lottery, Vesey purchased his freedom for $600 and soon began plotting an ambitious, yet ultimately unsuccessful slave rebellion.

17. Joseph Vesey was born in Bermuda around the middle of the eighteenth century and spent thirteen years as the captain of various slave ships that traveled between slave markets in Barbados, South Carolina, Haiti, and West Africa.

18. Cap-Français or Cap-Haïtien, as it was renamed after the Haitian revolution, is located on the northern coast of Haiti and is that nation's second largest city. During French colonial rule, Cap-Français served as Haiti's capital until it was superseded by Port-au-Prince in 1770.

19. *Ruse de guerre* is a French term that translates literally to "ruse of war." Its use in English refers to an enemy's deception during war.

20. With authorization from the South Carolina state legislature to collect funds for public works, the city of Charleston organized the East Bay Street lottery on October 15, 1798, to raise $6,000 for the paving of East Bay Street, a busy waterfront road.

21. Vesey's status as a free man afforded him little redress in the courts due to restrictions by the Negro Act of 1740, which prohibited free African Americans from testifying except in cases that involved an African American suspect. McCord, "Better Ordering and Governing," 352–65.

22. "Protean" refers to the ability to change shape or take on different roles.

23. This phrase is from the white Romantic poet James Russell Lowell's (1819–1891) work titled "Columbus."

24. *Ars atrium* is a Latin phrase that means logic and is translated literally as "art of arts."

25. "Hercules and the Wagoner" is a fable about a man whose wagon becomes trapped in mud. When he asks the Roman demigod Hercules for assistance, Hercules tells the man not to call on him until he has done everything he can do to help himself.

26. The South Carolina legislature enacted laws restricting the assembly of slaves in 1800 and 1803 but did not heavily enforce the requirement. After Vesey's conspiracy, in 1822, and Nat Turner's revolt, in 1833, however, South Carolina lawmakers further restricted the assembly of slaves for religious purposes in 1834. May, "Holy Rebellion," 253–54.

27. African Americans drew comfort and inspiration from the biblical story of Exodus, which chronicles the Israelites' providential emancipation from slavery in Egypt, their forty-year wilderness journey, and their conquest and settlement of the Promised Land.

28. Vesey is likely alluding to the Israelites' first battle in the Promised Land, the successful battle for Jericho: "And they utterly destroyed all that was in the city, both man and woman, young and old, and ox, and sheep, and ass, with the edge of the sword." Josh. 6:21 (KJV).

29. The prophet Zechariah offered messages of restoration and renewal to the Israelites after their Babylonian captivity: "Then shall the LORD go forth and fight against those nations, as when He fights on a day of battle." Zech. 14:2 (KJV).

30. Grimké is referring to the Missouri Compromise, a congressional bill passed in 1820 that demarcated the 36°30′ parallel, or the latitude of Missouri's southern border, as the northernmost point to which slavery could extend within the Louisiana territory, with the exception of Missouri. See "Act to Authorize," 545–48, and Forbes, *Missouri Compromise*, x–xi.

31. Peter Poyas labored as an enslaved ship's carpenter for James Poyas. Kennedy and Parker, *Official Report*, 183; Robertson, *Denmark Vesey*, 56.

32. Ned Bennett and Rolla Bennett labored as slaves for then governor Thomas Bennett. Robertson, *Denmark Vesey*, 55–56.

33. Monday Gell labored as an enslaved harness maker for John Gell. Ibid.

34. Jack Pritchard, known as Gullah Jack, labored as a slave for Paul Pritchard. He was a native of Angola, spoke Gullah, and was acknowledged as an invincible shaman who could provide protection in warfare. Ibid., 160–61; Kennedy and Parker, *Official Report*, 183.

35. A Negro conjurer was a spiritual leader believed to possess supernatural power in healing diseases and injuries, predicting the future, and casting or removing spells. Some white slave owners feared the Negro conjurer because of his or her supposed supply of poisons and became paranoid at the prospect of being harmed by a slave who consulted with a conjurer.

36. The Santee and Combahee Rivers are located on either side of Charleston, with the Santee to the north flowing east from Columbia and the Combahee to the south flowing east from Beaufort.

37. In the early nineteenth century, Georgetown, South Carolina, was a bustling port town that amassed enormous wealth from exporting rice.

38. James and Johns are two small islands located to the south of Charleston, South Carolina, separated from the mainland by thin stretches of intracoastal rivers that empty into the Atlantic Ocean.

39. The Ashley is a seventeen-mile river that flows from northwest South Carolina into the Charleston Harbor.

40. After the Israelites were emancipated from slavery in Egypt, their former captors gave them gold and silver jewelry and fine clothing to hasten them on their journey to Canaan (See Exo. 12:35–36 [KJV]). Similarly, Vesey instructed his coconspirators to take weapons from white Charlestonians to use during their rebellion.

41. Mingo Harth was a native Mandingo who worked as mechanic, a "skilled or unskilled laborer," for William Harth. Egerton, *He Shall Go Out Free,* 145; Robertson, *Denmark Vesey,* 159.

42. William Paul, who labored as a slave for John Paul, provided testimony that betrayed his coconspirators. He was confined to the workhouse and then transported out of the United States. Kennedy and Parker, *Official Report,* 186.

43. Jesse (or Jessy) Blackwood labored as a slave for Thomas Blackwood. Ibid., 183.

44. Batteau Bennett labored as a slave for former South Carolina governor Thomas Bennett. Ibid.

45. *Verbum sat sapienti* is a Latin phrase meaning "a word to the wise is enough."

46. These four men were convicted primarily on the basis of the fact that they spoke "favorably" about Denmark Vesey and his men to the black population of Charleston. One of the men, a Spanish sailor, drew a large amount of attention from the Charleston authorities when he made a public address to Charleston's slave community, inquiring, "If you had a favor to ask, would you ask it of a white man or a black man?" Robertson, *Denmark Vesey,* 164.

47. Sparta was a city-state of ancient Greece that was renowned for its strict, militaristic social structure. Spartan life required that boys receive military training and that soldiers be ordered to either return from war carrying their shields in victory or be carried on them in death.

48. This stanza is from Lowell's poem "The Present Crisis," which analyzes events that precipitated the Civil War.

Francis Grimké
(1850–1937)

PRESBYTERIAN MINISTER, CIVIL RIGHTS ACTIVIST

*I belong to what may be called the radical wing of the race, on the
race question: I do not believe in compromises; in surrendering, or
acquiescing, even temporarily, in the deprivation of a single right,
out of deference to an unrighteous public sentiment.*

Francis J. Grimké penned these words to repudiate the accomodation-
ist ideology of the African American educator and activist Booker T.
Washington, who admonished African Americans to cast down their
buckets in the field of industrial labor rather than agitate for their civil
rights. Grimké knew firsthand the degradation of slavery, the sting of racism, the empowerment of education, and the hope of citizenship in his rise
from orphaned slave to prominent pastor of the Fifteenth Street Presbyterian
Church in Washington, D.C. As he marked a more radical path to activism,
he aligned himself with those who eschewed compromise, vowing never to
willingly relinquish his rights.

Francis Grimké was the second son born to a white planter and attorney,
Henry Grimké, and an enslaved African American, Nancy Weston, on the
Cane Acres rice plantation near Charleston, South Carolina. When Francis
was two years old, his father died of typhoid fever, leaving him and his family
under the care of his white half brother, Montague. After his family moved to
Charleston, Francis attended "home schools" for free black children with his

brothers, Archibald and John. Within eight years, Montague abruptly forced Francis into slavery as a house servant for him and his bride. After the Civil War began, Francis ran away and hired himself out as a valet to Lieutenant Moore Rhett, a Confederate officer, who assumed he was free. Francis unexpectedly gained the opportunity to return to Charleston when Lieutenant Francis Miller requested his services on an assignment. Upon his arrival in the city, he discovered a fugitive slave advertisement for himself that Montague had placed in the *Charleston Mercury.* Within two months, Francis was caught, punished, starved, and beaten. As he neared death, his mother took him home and nursed him back to health. Montague sold Francis to Lieutenant Miller, for whom Francis worked until the Civil War ended. When Union forces occupied Charleston, Francis sought new adventures as an officer's boy, but he ended up foraging for food while running. After Union soldiers returned to the North, he returned home and reportedly threatened to exact revenge by whipping Montague.

Francis and his brother Archibald soon enrolled in the Morris Street School managed by Frances Pillsbury, a white abolitionist and a Freedman's Bureau agent. There, their lives changed dramatically. Both young men excelled in their studies and were rewarded with the opportunity to board and work with New England families in exchange for further education. Francis's first trip north took a disastrous turn when his host, Dr. John Brown of Stoneham, Massachusetts, forced him to sleep in a barn and reneged on his promise to provide an apprenticeship as a physician's assistant. His prospects brightened, however, when he enrolled in Lincoln University, a historically black college in Chester, Pennsylvania, with the financial support of a philanthropist and earnings from his summer jobs as a teacher and a waiter. Additional funding and guidance came from an unexpected source after the prominent abolitionist and feminist Angelina Grimké Weld learned of the academic success of two young African American men named "Grimkie" from Charleston. She and her sister, Sarah Grimké, acknowledged Francis and Archibald as their nephews and welcomed them into the Grimké family. In 1870 Francis graduated valedictorian of his class and then worked at Lincoln as a financial agent and mathematics teacher.

Francis Grimké initially pursued a legal career at Lincoln and at Howard University Law School, in Washington, D.C., before heeding a call to the ministry in 1875 and entering Princeton's Theological Seminary to complete training as a Presbyterian minister. His first assignment was the Fifteenth Street Presbyterian Church in Washington, D.C., founded in 1841 to address the spiritual needs of black Washingtonians. Soon after his arrival, he married Charlotte Forten, an African American educator and writer and a member of the prominent black activist Forten family of Philadelphia. Charlotte had taught freedmen in the South Carolina Sea Islands during the Civil

War while her future husband labored as a slave nearby in Charleston. They had one daughter, Theodora Cornelia, who lived only a few months. Frances and Charlotte later served as surrogate parents for their niece Angelina Grimké during her father Archibald's appointment as U.S. consul to Santo Domingo.

Francis Grimké devoted most of his ministry to the Fifteenth Street Presbyterian Church in the nation's capital, except for a four-year break, from 1885 to 1889, at the Laura Street Presbyterian Church in Jacksonville, Florida, where he temporarily relocated to regain his health in a more temperate clime. Fifteenth Street attracted a racially mixed audience that was eager to hear the "craftsman of the homiletic art"[1] fearlessly admonish parishioners to apply biblical principles in everyday life, particularly in race relations. Historians have characterized the sermons of his early years as conservative, however, stressing "self-improvement," "self-respect," "self-reliance," and "high moral values."[2] Renowned reformers, congressmen, Supreme Court justices, and African Americans activists, including Anna Julia Cooper, Frederick Douglass, and Elizabeth Keckley, attended services at the Fifteenth Street Church.[3] As membership at the Fifteenth Street Church grew, Francis Grimké gained national prominence. The young pastor decried civil rights violations and presented biblical remedies for societal ills in his sermons and essays, which he published and distributed widely. After receiving a copy of "The Lynching of Negroes in the South; Its Causes and Remedy" (1898), the African American writer and activist Frances E. W. Harper conveyed her interest helping to finance the printing and distribution of the sermon throughout the nation. Even after he retired, Francis Grimké continued sharing his writings with his friends. He also contributed articles to the *New York Independent* and the *New York Evangelist*.

By the late nineteenth century, Francis Grimké began to consider a more radical means to inspire his congregants to become involved in securing social justice. Initially, he supported Washington's accommodationist strategy. He differed from Washington in advocating liberal arts education, however, as is evidenced by his collaboration with the African American Episcopal minister and activist Alexander Crummell in founding the American Negro Academy (ANA), a members-only think tank for black intellectuals. The increasing violence that African Americans faced from lynching and disenfranchisement, coupled with Washington's disdain for black intellectuals, provoked Francis Grimké to preach a series of sermons signaling his break from accommodationist ideology and his adoption of a more militant response to racial injustice, including violence, if necessary, to rouse the nation's conscious. Nevertheless, Francis Grimké's clear positioning of himself in the anti-Washington camp by the early twentieth century did not shield him from criticism from W. E. B. Du Bois in *The Souls of Black Folk* (1903) for refusing to weigh in on three critical issues facing the black community: voting rights, civil rights, and equal access to education opportunity.[4]

The selection presented here, "The Negro and His Citizenship," published in 1905 in the *ANA Occasional Papers,* titled "The Negro and Elective Franchise," represents Francis Grimké's deft appropriation of scripture to spur social activism within the African American community. Writing during the height of the debate between accomodationists and militant activists, Grimké situates himself solidly within the more radical faction that insists that the rights of citizenship be immediately accorded to African Americans. He claims an affinity with the apostle Paul, who relied on his rights as a Roman citizen to demand fair treatment after his arrest for preaching the gospel. Grimké cites critical points in Paul's experience to inspire African Americans to avoid delay in demanding their rights: (1) his birthright as a Roman citizen, (2) his claim to the protections afforded Roman citizens, (3) his standing up for his rights, and (4) his ability to restrain his persecutors on the basis of his knowledge and articulation of his rights. Grimké asserts that Paul's experience provides a model for African Americans who have been guaranteed the rights of citizenship through the Fourteenth Amendment to the Constitution. He admonishes his community to (1) develop into well-rounded, law-abiding, Christian citizens and (2) to contend for their right to "life, liberty, and the pursuit of happiness," equal accommodations in public facilities, a military career, suffrage, and the right to hold political office. In essence, he issues a battle cry, affirming his call to action with two stanzas from the Civil War song "The Battle Hymn of the Republic." In evoking the memory of both John Brown, who gave his life to free enslaved African Americans, and the soldiers who died in the warfare that ended slavery, Grimké reminds his audience that progress has been made but that their struggle is a contentious, protracted battle that will end victoriously, for it is God's gift.

By 1906 Du Bois acknowledged Grimké's anti-Washington stance by inviting him to join the Niagara Movement. Grimké declined but later collaborated with Du Bois and other black activists and white reformers in establishing the National Association for the Advancement of Colored People (NAACP). As Francis Grimké solidified his relationship with black activists, he distanced himself from white Presbyterians who refused to disavow their support of "separate but equal" churches for both black and white congregants. He vigorously opposed the merger of the Northern Presbyterians and the Cumberland General Assembly, fearing that segregationist policies would permeate the religious institution, and he helped establish the Afro-Presbyterian Council to address institutional racism within the Presbyterian Church.

As Francis Grimké settled into his preacher-activist role, his wife, Charlotte Forten Grimké, maintained an active life as a writer and community activist. In 1913 she became seriously ill, however, and she died about a year later.

Three years following the death of Charlotte Grimké, the election of Democrat Woodrow Wilson ushered in an era of new challenges for African Americans. Francis Grimké soon denounced President Wilson's segregationist policies within the federal government. After World War I began, he decried America's complicity with European nations that were more interested in advancing racist ideologies than in ensuring equal rights. In 1923 he focused his attention on Christian churches and social welfare organizations that advanced racist policies in his address "What Is the Trouble with Christianity Today?" at the Howard University School of Religion.

In 1925, after forty years of service to the Fifteenth Street Presbyterian Church, Francis Grimké tried to step down as pastor, but the congregation refused to accept his resignation. They kept him on the pastoral staff and hired another minister to tend to the needs of the congregation. Until the end of his life, Francis Grimké continued to draw on the power of the pulpit to address issues of national concern. In June 1934, he published the article "Segregation" in the *Crisis,* lambasting Du Bois for embracing the legalized separation of races, which Grimké termed "a badge of inferiority." One month later, as the nation celebrated its founding, he denounced Alabama for its handling of the Scottsboro Case, declaring, "I do not see that there is a difference between lynching a Negro by the mob, and treating him in the manner in which these boy[s] have been treated by the state under the cover of law. They were arrested, tried, and condemned, it is true, but on evidence and under circumstances that make it a mere travesty of justice that cannot be upheld under any decent regard for rights guaranteed under the Constitution."[5] Francis Grimké died at home in Washington, D.C., on October 11, 1937.

?⊷ "The Negro and His Citizenship"

ACTS 22:25–29.—*And when they had tied him up with the thongs, Paul said unto the centurion that stood by, Is it lawful for you to scourge a man that is a Roman and uncondemned? And when the centurion heard it, he went to the chief captain and told him, saying, What art thou about to do? for this man is a Roman. And the chief captain came and said unto him, Tell me, art thou a Roman? And he said, Yea. And the chief captain answered, With a great sum obtained I this citizenship. But Paul said, But I am a Roman born. They then that were about to examine him straightway departed from him: and the chief captain also was afraid when he knew that he was a Roman, and because he had bound him.*

In this passage attention is directed to four things: To the fact that Paul was a Roman citizen; to the fact that he was about to be treated in a way that was forbidden by his citizenship; to the fact that he stood up for his rights as a Roman citizen; and to the fact that those who were about to infringe upon his rights were restrained, were overawed.[6]

I. Attention is directed to the fact that Paul was a Roman citizen. Citizenship was a possession that was very highly esteemed, and that was obtained in several ways,—by birth, by purchase, as a reward for distinguished military services, and as a favor. Paul's came to him by inheritance; his father before him had been a Roman citizen: how it came to the father we do not know. At one time the price paid for it was very great. The chief captain, in the narrative of which our text is a part, tells us that he obtained his with a great sum; and therefore he seemed surprised to think that a man in Paul's circumstances should have it. At first he seemed a little incredulous, but it was only for a moment. The penalty for falsely claiming to be a Roman citizen was death; this fact together with the whole bearing of the apostle finally left no doubt in his mind: he accepted his statement.

It was not only a great honor to be a Roman citizen, but it carried with it many rights and privileges that were not enjoyed by others. These rights were either private or public,—*Jus Quiritium,* and *Jus Civitatis.* Among Private Rights, was the Right of Liberty. This secured him against imprisonment without trial; exemption from all degrading punishments, such as scourging and crucifixion; the right of appeal to the emperor after sentence by an inferior magistrate or tribunal, in any part of the empire; and also the right to be sent to Rome for trial before the emperor, if charged with a capital offence.

Among Public Rights belonging to Roman citizens the following may be mentioned: (1) The right of being enrolled in the censor's book, called, *Jus Census.* (2) The right of serving in the army, called, *Jus Militiae.* At first only citizens of the empire were permitted to engage in military operations, to bear arms and fight in its behalf. (3) The right to vote in the different assemblies of the people, called, *Jus Suffragii.* This has always been and is to-day one of the most important functions of citizenship, and one that should be highly prized and sacredly guarded. (4) The right of bearing public offices in the state.

There were many other rights enjoyed by Roman citizens, but I will not take the time to enumerate them: these are sufficient to show us the value, the importance of Roman citizenship; and this citizenship the apostle Paul was invested with, with all the rights and privileges which were involved in it. On one occasion he said, "I am a citizen of no mean city," referring to Tarsus, which was one of the free cities of Asia Minor; but more than that, as he tells us here, he was a citizen of the empire.

II. Attention is called to the fact that Paul was about to be treated in a way that was forbidden by his citizenship; that was contrary to Roman law. He had gone up to Jerusalem to attend the feast of Pentecost.[7] After meeting the brethren and rehearsing to them the wonderful things which God had wrought through his ministry among the Gentiles, they congratulated him upon his success, but said to him: "Thou seest, brother, how many thousands there are among the Jews of them that have believed; and they are all zealous for the law: and they have been informed concerning thee, that thou teachest all the Jews who are among the Gentiles to forsake Moses, telling them not to circumcise their children neither to walk after the customs. What is it therefore? they will certainly hear that thou art come. Do therefore this that we say to thee: We have four men that have a vow on them; these take, and purify thyself with them, and be at charges for them, that they may shave their heads: and all shall know that there is no truth in the things whereof they have been informed concerning thee but that thou thyself walkest orderly, keeping the law."[8] It was in compliance with this request, that Paul went into the temple to do as he was asked to do: and while there was seen by certain Jews of Asia, i.e., the province of Asia, who at once stirred up the multitude and laid hands on him, crying out, "Men of Israel, help: This is the man that teacheth all men everywhere against the people, and the law, and this place; and moreover he brought Greeks also into the temple and hath defiled this holy place."[9] It was like touching a match to a powder magazine. The people were aroused. Instantly there was a response to the call; and dragging the apostle out of the temple they were in the act of beating him to death, when the chief captain, learning of the tumult, rushed down with a squad of soldiers and rescuing him, brought him into the castle. The next day with a view of ascertaining what the trouble was, the real ground of complaint against the apostle, the chief captain proposed to examine him by scourging, and issued orders to that effect. In obedience to this order the apostle was stripped and actually tied up. The process of examination proposed was very severe. The culprit was stripped and tied in a bending posture to a pillar, or stretched on a frame, and the punishment was inflicted with a scourge made of leathern thongs weighted with sharp pieces of bone or lead, the object being to extort from the sufferer a confession of his guilt or the information desired.

If the chief captain had understood the Hebrew language, and could have followed the address of the apostle which was delivered on the steps of the palace, he would have understood what the trouble was, without attempting to resort to this brutal method of finding out; but evidently he did not. Everything indicated, however, that it was something very serious, judging from their treatment of him, and from the intense excitement which his words produced upon them, and hence, he was all the more anxious to find out. If the apostle was guilty of any offence against the law, it was the duty of the chief captain to take cognizance of it, and to punish him accordingly, but if he was innocent, if he had in no way transgressed the law, it was his duty to release him. The law also provided how the guilt or innocence of an accused person was to be ascertained; and it was the duty of the chief captain to have followed the course prescribed by the law; but it is clear from the narrative that he had determined upon another course: the prisoner is ordered to be scourged, instead of calling upon those who had assaulted him to make their charges, and to substantiate them, and then giving the apostle an opportunity of defending himself.

III. Attention is directed in the text to the fact, that the apostle stood up manfully for his rights. After they had tied him up, as if waiting to see just how far they would go, and just as the process of scourging was about to begin, he challenged their right to proceed: he said to the centurion, who was standing by, and who was there as the representative of the chief captain, to see that the scourging was properly done, and to make note of what he confessed,—he said to this man: "Is it lawful for you to scourge a man that is a Roman, and uncondemned?"[10] The law expressly forbade the scourging of Roman citizens; it was an indignity to which no Roman citizen was to be subjected. This was what was known as the Porcian law, and took its name from Porcius, the Tribune through whose influence its adoption was secured. And this is the law to which the apostle here appeals, whose protection he invokes. Paul, as a Roman citizen, not only knew what his rights were, but he stood up for his rights. He insists here upon being treated, as he was entitled to be treated, as a citizen of the empire. They are about to scourge him, contrary to law, and he says to them, Stop; you have no right to treat me in this way, intimating and they evidently understood it, that if they did not desist, they would hear from him; he would bring the matter to the attention of the emperor.

This is not the only place where Paul falls back upon his rights as a Roman citizen. He did the same thing a little later on. He was removed from Jerusalem to Caesarea, as you will remember, where he remained a prisoner for two years. During that time he was frequently placed on trial before various officials,—before Felix, before Festus, before Agrippa.[11] It was during one of these hearings, that Festus the governor, in order to curry favor with the Jews, intimated that he might be sent back to Jerusalem to be tried: and doubtless this was his intention, having entered into a secret arrangement with the enemies of the apostle, who had resolved to kill him at the first opportunity. This they felt that they would have a better chance of doing if they could only induce the governor to return him to Jerusalem. The apostle, of course, knew all this; he knew how intensely they hated him, and what their plans and purposes were, and he was determined not to be entrapped in this way. The record is: "Paul said in his defence, 'Neither against the law of the Jews, nor against the temple, nor against Caesar have I sinned at all.' But Festus, desiring to gain favor with the Jews, answered Paul and said, 'Wilt thou go up to Jerusalem, and there be judged of these things before me?' But

Paul said, 'I am standing before Caesar's judgment-seat, where I ought to be judged: to the Jews have I done no wrong, as thou also very well knowest. If then I am a wrong doer, and have committed anything worthy of death, I refuse not to die; but if none of these things is true whereof these accuse me, no man can give me up to them. I appeal unto Caesar.' Then Festus, when he had conferred with the council, answered, 'Thou hast appealed unto Caesar, unto Caesar thou shalt go.'"[12]

One of the great privileges of a Roman citizen was the right of appeal; the right of being heard directly by the emperor, of taking his case out of the hands of all inferior judicatories, up to the highest: and this is the right which the apostle here avails himself of. It was the only thing that saved him from being turned over by a corrupt official into the hands of his enemies; and it forcibly illustrates the importance of citizenship. Had he not been a Roman citizen clothed with the sacred right of appeal he would have been basely sacrificed to the malice of his enemies; or, though he had been a Roman citizen, if he had cowardly surrendered his right, if he had failed to exercise it, he would have equally perished; but the apostle stood upon his right, and so succeeded in thwarting the purposes of his enemies.

IV. Attention is directed in the text to the fact, that those who were about to scourge this man, were restrained by the knowledge of the fact that he was a Roman citizen. The moment they became aware of this fact; at the mere mention of that sacred name, citizen, everything came to a stand still; the uplifted hand, ready to smite, is arrested, and we find the centurion running off, in great excitement in search of the chief captain, and saying to him, "What are you about? Do you know that this man is a Roman:" and we see the chief captain coming in great haste and saying to the apostle, "What? can it be possible! Are you really a Roman?" "Yes," said the apostle, "I am; and my father before me was." The chief captain is astonished; yea, more, fear takes hold of him; he becomes suddenly alarmed.[13]

There are two things in this incident that are worthy of note: first, this indignity that was offered to the apostle was through ignorance. It was not known that he was a Roman citizen. The law was violated, but it was not purposely done. It was not the intention of the chief captain to ignore the rights involved in citizenship; for he himself was a Roman citizen, and was interested in maintaining those rights. And, second, to trample upon the rights of a Roman citizen was a very grave offense, a very serious matter; and it became a serious matter because back of this citizenship was the whole power of the empire. These rights were carefully guarded, were rigidly enforced, so that the term, Roman citizen, was everywhere respected. No one could infringe those rights with impunity: hence you will notice what is said here, "The chief captain was afraid when he knew that he was a Roman because he had bound him."[14] He recognized at once the gravity of the offense. That was old pagan Rome; but under its rule citizenship meant something; it was a sacred thing; back of it stood the strong arm of the Government to give efficacy, power to it. This man was afraid when he realized what he had done; and that is the feeling which outraged citizenship ought everywhere to inspire. It ought to mean something; and there ought to be power somewhere to enforce its meaning.

But it is not of Roman citizenship that I desire to speak at this time, but rather of American citizenship, and of that citizenship as it pertains to ourselves. In the providence of God we are citizens of this great Republic. The Fourteenth Amendment to the Constitution declares: "All persons born or naturalized in the United States, and subject to the jurisdiction thereof, are citizens of the United States and of the State wherein they reside." Under this provision of the Constitution we are all citizens; and we have earned the right to be citizens. We have lived here as long as any other class in the Republic; we have worked as hard as any other class to develop the country; and we have fought as bravely as any other class in the defense of the Republic. If length of residence, if unstinted toil, if great sacrifices of blood, if the laying of one's self on the country's altar in the hour of peril, of danger, give any claim to citizenship, then our claim is beyond dispute; for all these things are true of us.

We are *citizens* of this great Republic: and citizenship is a sacred thing: I hope we realize it. It is a thing to be prized; to be highly esteemed. It has come to us after 250 years of slavery, of unrequited toil; it has come to us after a sanguinary conflict, in which billions of treasure and rivers of blood were poured out; it has come to us as a boon from the nation at a time when it had reached its loftiest moral development; when its moral sense was quickened as it had never been before, and when it stood as it had never stood before upon the great principles enunciated in the Declaration of Independence, not as glittering generalities, but as great realities: it was at that sublime period in our history, when the national conscience was at work; when the men who were in charge of affairs were men who stood for righteousness; when the great issues before the country were moral issues, issues involving human rights,—that the nation saw fit to abolish slavery and to decree the citizenship of all men, black and white alike. When we think of what this citizenship has cost, in blood and treasure; of the noble men through whose influence it was brought about; and of the fact that it came to us from the Nation when it was at its best, when it was living up to its highest light, and to its noblest conceptions of right and duty,—we ought to prize it, to set a high value upon it.

And we ought to show our appreciation of it: (I). By being good citizens; by doing everything in our power to develop ourselves along right lines, intellectually, morally, spiritually, and also materially: and to do everything in our power to promote the general good; everything that will help to make for municipal, state, and national righteousness. We are to remember that we are part of a great whole, and that the whole will be affected by our conduct, either for good or bad. If we live right, if we fear God and keep his commandments, and train our children to do the same, we ennoble our citizenship; we become a part of the great conservative force of society, a positive blessing to the community, the state, the nation. It is especially important for us, in view of the strong prejudice against us, the disposition to view us with a critical eye, to hold up and magnify our short-comings, that we be particularly concerned to be constantly manifesting, evidencing our good citizenship by allying ourselves only with the things that are true, and just, and pure, and lovely, and of good report.[15] We ought not to lose sight of the fact that the strongest fight that is being made against us to-day is by those who are doing most to discredit us, to array public sentiment against us,—those who are parading our short-comings and imperfections, who are giving the greatest publicity, the widest circulation to them. There are persons in this country, who are determined, and who never lose an opportunity to blacken our good name. Dr. DuBois, in that splendid document of his, "Credo," said among other things, "I believe in the Devil and his angels, who wantonly work to narrow the opportunity of struggling human beings, especially if they be black; who spit in the faces of the fallen, strike them that cannot strike again, believe the worst and work to prove it, hating the image which their Maker stamped on a brother's soul."[16] And this is one of the conditions that confront us in this country, and that we must not lose sight of. The fact that there is this determination on the part of our enemies to prove that we are utterly unworthy of this great boon of citizenship, should have the effect of creating within us a counter determination to show that we are worthy,—to do our level best in every sphere of life. Now I do not mean by this to say that we are not proving ourselves to be good citizens; for we are: a great many of us are; but I have called attention to it because I feel that it ought to be emphasized; that we need to feel more keenly and more widely than is felt, the meaning of this great boon and the demand which it makes upon us. It is a challenge to every man to live a straightforward, upright, worthy life. And what is needed is, not only that *we*, who have had exceptional opportunities, should feel this way, but that the great mass of our people should be educated to feel the same, to be animated by the same spirit. And *we* are to be their educators; it is through *us* that this spirit is to descend upon them, and take possession of them. If this citizenship means anything, it means that we should be concerned about everything which makes for law, for order, for good government, for individual, municipal, state, and national purity and righteousness; it means that each one of us ought to be a living example of the best type of what a citizen ought to be.

But this is not all: if we value our citizenship we will not only seek to make the most of ourselves, to live on the highest plane but we will also stand up manfully for our rights under that citizenship. I have no patience with those who preach civil and political self-effacement. I never have believed in that pernicious doctrine, and never will. When you have effaced a man, civilly and politically, in a government like our own, what is he? What does he amount to? Who cares for him? What rights has he which any other class is bound to respect?[17] He is a mere nonentity, entitled to no consideration, and with no refuge to which he can fly in the hour of his need. To be civilly and politically effaced is to be civilly and politically dead; and to be civilly and politically dead is to be at the mercy of any and every political party or organization, and to be under the iron heel of the worst elements in the community without any means of redress.

We are *citizens* of this Republic: and I want to direct attention to this fact for a moment; and I am glad of the opportunity of doing it at this time, when we are in the midst of celebrating the inauguration of our President.[18] I thank God for the man at the White House; for his courage; for his high sense of righteousness; for the many splendid things which he has said; and for the noble stand which he has taken on human rights; on equality of opportunity; on the open door for every man in the Republic irrespective of race or color. I rejoice in the fact that we have such a President. I commend him heartily for what he has done. I hope he will do more; I hope there are yet larger things in store for this race through him. But whether he does more or not; or whatever may be his future policy, or the future policy of the leaders of either of the great political parties, or the rank and file of those parties, it cannot, it will not affect in the least, our attitude in regard to our rights under the Constitution. We are citizens, clothed with citizenship rights; and, there is no thought or intention on our part of ever surrendering a single one of them. Whatever others may think of it, or desire in regard to it, we do not propose to retreat a single inch, to give up for one moment the struggle. I say, *we* and in this, I believe I speak for those who represent the sentiment that is taking more and more firmly hold of the heart of this race. I belong to what may be called the radical wing of the race, on the race question: I do not believe in compromises; in surrendering, or acquiescing, even temporarily, in the deprivation of a single right, out of deference to an unrighteous public sentiment. I believe with Lowell,

> "They enslave their children's children,
> Who make compromise with sin."[19]

And this, I believe, at heart, is the sentiment of the race; at least, it is the sentiment of some of us. There is where we have taken our stand and there is where we propose to stand to the end. What belongs to us as citizens we want; and we are not going to be satisfied with anything less. We are in this country, and we are here to stay. There is no prospect of our ever leaving it. This is our home, as it has been the home of our ancestors for generations, and will be the home of our children, and of our children's children, for all time. It is of the greatest importance to us, therefore, that our status in it, as it is permanently fixed, should be, not that of a proscribed class, but that of full citizenship with every right, civil and political, accorded to us that is accorded to other citizens of the Republic. This is the thing that we are to insist upon; this is the evil against which we are to guard.

What our enemies are seeking to effect is to make this a white man's government; to fix permanently our status in it, as one of civil and political inferiority. The issue is sharply drawn; and it is for us to say whether we will be thus reduced, whether such shall be our permanent status or not. One thing we may be assured of: such will surely be our fate unless we clearly comprehend the issue, and set ourselves earnestly to work to counteract the movement, by resisting in every legitimate way its consummation, and by using our influence to create a counter public sentiment.

What are some of these citizenship rights for which we should earnestly contend?

(1) The right to life, liberty, and the pursuit of happiness. In one section of this country, at least, and the area is growing, and is fast including others, the life of a Negro isn't worth as much as that of a dog. He may be shot down, murdered, strung up to a tree, burnt to death, by any white ruffian, or band of lawbreakers and murderers with impunity. The color of his skin gives any white man liberty to maltreat him, to trample upon him. He has no rights which white men are bound to respect.[20] If he goes to law, there is no redress; his appeals avail nothing with judge and jury. That is a condition of things that we ought not to rest satisfied under. As long as the life of a black man is not just as sacred as that of a white man, in every section of the Republic; as long as wrongs perpetrated upon him are treated with greater leniency than wrongs perpetrated upon white men, his status is not the same as that of the white man; and as long as it is not the same an injustice is done him, which he ought to resist; against which he ought to protest, and continue to protest.

(2) Another citizenship right is that of receiving equal accommodations on all common carriers and in all hostelries; on railroads, steamboats, in hotels, restaurants, and in all public places. When we travel, whatever we are able to pay for we are entitled to, just as other citizens are. To-day this is largely denied us. The hotels are not open to us; the restaurants are not open to us, even the little ten cent lunch counters, in this the capital city of the nation, are not open to us: we are shut out from all such places, and shut out because of the color of our skin. If we attempt to travel, and turn our faces southward, we must ride in Jim Crow cars;[21] we must be segregated,

shut up in a little compartment by ourselves. The privilege which we once enjoyed without stint of taking a sleeper or Pullman car, even that now is being taken from us. One state has even gone so far as to make it unlawful to sell a ticket to a person of color on a sleeper.[22] That is the state of Georgia; a State that has in it Atlanta University,[23] and Clark University,[24] and the Atlanta Baptist College,[25] and Spelman Seminary,[26] and the Gammon Theological Seminary,[27] and Haines Institute[28] and many other schools of learning; a State that has within its borders some of the very best type of Negroes in this country. The meaning of all this, don't let us misunderstand: it is a part of the general policy, which is being vigorously pushed by our enemies, to fix our status as one of inferiority, by shutting us out from certain privileges. The whole thing is wrong. Such invidious distinctions ought not to be permitted in a republic. It is inconsistent with citizenship. Everything ought to be open to all citizens alike:—railroad cars, hotels, restaurants, steamboats, the schools and colleges of the land: our public schools ought to be open to all the children alike. There ought not be separate schools for the whites, and separate schools for blacks: all the children of the Republic ought to be educated together; and sooner or later it is bound to come to that. Some one has said, "It isn't so much the Jim Crow car, as it is the Jim Crow Negro[29] in the car." The fallacy of this statement, and its attempted mitigation or justification of the Jim Crow car, lies in the fact that the Jim Crow car has nothing whatever to do with the Jim Crow Negro. It was not instituted for him, but for all Negroes, whether Jim Crow or not: in fact, it was designed, particularly, not for the Jim Crow Negro, but for the intelligent, progressive, self-respecting Negro. If there are Jim Crow Negroes among us we owe them a duty; we ought to seek to improve them, to lift them to higher levels; but while we are doing this, don't let us forget that there is a Jim Crow car, and what it stands for. It stands for a hostile public sentiment; it is a part of a concerted plan which seeks to degrade us, to rob us of our rights, to deprive us of privileges enjoyed by other citizens, because of the color of our skin. If there were no Jim Crow Negroes, we would have the Jim Crow car all the same. We should fight the Jim Crow cars, therefore, not only because of the personal discomfort to which we are subjected in travelling, but also because of the general system of which it is a part,—a system which seeks to establish a double citizenship in the Republic, based upon race and color; the one superior to the other, and carrying with it privileges which are denied to the other.

(3) Another citizenship right is that of serving in the Army and Navy; the right to take up arms and to fight in behalf of the country. This is our right, and we have exercised it, and are still exercising it. We have fought in all the wars of the Republic; and are represented to-day in both Army and Navy. We have made a glorious record for ourselves in this respect. There

is no better soldier in the Army of the Republic, than the black soldier. This right has not been denied us, but let us, nevertheless, keep our eyes on it. There are some things even here that need to be looked into. It has been many years since we have had a representative in the great Naval or Military school of the country; and there have been some rumors about limiting the aspirations of Negroes in the Army, of not permitting them to advance beyond a certain point. If there is such a thought or intention on the part of those in authority, it must be resisted. The Negro must be free—in the Army, in the Navy,—in every part of the Army and Navy,—as other citizens are free; to advance according to his merit. His color must not be allowed to operate against him.

(4) Another citizen right is that of suffrage, the right of the ballot; the right to have part in the government; to say who shall make the laws and who shall execute them; and what the laws shall be; the right to have an opinion, and to have that opinion counted in determining what shall be and what shall not be. This is one of the greatest of rights. In a republic citizenship means very little without it. It is this which marks the difference between a representative government, a government of the people, by the people, and for the people, and a despotism, an absolute monarchy. The glory of the age in which we live is the triumph of democracy; and what is the triumph of democracy but the right of the *people* to say who shall rule; and how is the will of the people expressed? Through the ballot; at the polls. The ballot therefore is the symbol of the sovereignty of the people. If we are to be sovereign citizens of the Republic therefore, this right to vote must be preserved. The old despotic idea of government was, that some people were born to rule, and that others were born to be ruled; and the idea that exists in the minds of some people in this country, in democratic America, in face of the affirmation of the Declaration of Independence, that all men are born free and equal, is that in this country, there are some people who are born to rule, and others who are born to be ruled; and that the people who are born to rule are the whites, and those who are born to be ruled are the blacks: hence the effort that is being made to divest us of this symbol of sovereignty,—the ballot. Let us not be deceived; let us give no heed to any teaching, never mind from what source it may come, which seeks to minimize the importance of the ballot. What difference does it make whether we vote or not? I have heard some weak-kneed, time-serving representatives of our own race say; and the thought has been caught up by the men in the South who have been seeking to rob us of our rights, and by those in the North who have been playing into their hands; and they have said, Yes, What difference does it make? Are you not just as well off without it? What difference does it make? It makes all the difference in the world: the difference between a sovereign citizen of the Republic, and one who has been stripped of his sovereignty; between one

who has a say in what is going on, and one who has not; between one who is ruled with his consent, and one who is ruled without it. If we are just as well off without the ballot, how is it that the white man is not just as well off without it? And if he is unwilling to give it up, why should he ask us to give it up? Why should we give it up? If he needs it in order to protect himself, much more do we, for we are weaker than he is, and need all the more the power which comes from the ballot.

(5) Another citizenship right is, that of holding office, the right to be voted for, and of being appointed to positions of honor and trust by the executive power. This is also a right that belongs to us, and that we must contend for. It is one of our rights that is now being especially contested in the South. The Negro must not be appointed to any office, is the demand of Southern white sentiment. I am glad that the President has not yielded wholly to that sentiment. The fight which he made in the Crum case[30] was a notable one, and clearly indicated that he was not willing to shut that door of opportunity to the Negro; that he was not willing to take the position that a man was to be debarred from public office simply because of the color of his skin. That was the right position for him to take, and the only one that was consistent with his oath of office, and his position as President of *all* the people. I hope that he will continue to act upon that principle; and that he will do more than he has done. There is room for improvement in this direction. A few more appointments of colored men in the North, as well as in the South, would be a good thing. It ought to be done. The right of colored men to receive appointments ought to be clearly and distinctly emphasized by multiplying those appointments. There is nothing like an object lesson in impressing the truth. I hope that the President will give us many such object lessons during the next four years.

The right to life, liberty and the pursuit of happiness; the right to receive equal accommodation on railroads, steamboats, in hotels, restaurants, and in all public places of amusement; the right to be represented in the Army and Navy; the right to vote; the right to hold office: these are some of our citizenship rights, for which we should earnestly contend. Sometimes, we are told, that it would be better to say less about our rights, and more about our duties. No one feels more the importance of emphasizing our duties than I do,— I think I have done about as much of it as anybody,—but among the duties that I have always emphasized, and still emphasize, is the duty of standing up squarely and uncompromisingly for our rights. When we are contending for the truth; when we are resisting the encroachments of those who are seeking to despoil us of our birth-right as citizens; when we are keeping up the agitation for equal civil and political privileges in this country, are we not in the line of duty? If not, where is the line? Duties? Yes. Let us have our duties preached to us,—line upon line, and precept upon precept, here a little and there a little;[31] but at the same time don't let us forget that we have also *rights* under the Constitution, and to see to it that we stand up for them; that we resist to the very last ditch those who would rob us of them. And in doing this, let us remember that we are called to it by the stern voice of Duty, which is the voice of God; and that we need not apologize for our action.

And now in conclusion but a word more and then I am done. The fight before us is a long one. You will not live, nor will I live to see the triumph of the principles for which we are contending; let us not become discouraged however. Things look pretty dark at times, but it isn't all dark. Now and then there are gleams of light, which indicate the coming of a better day. There are forces working *for* us, as well as against us; and with what we can do for ourselves, we need not despair.

> "Mine eyes have seen the glory of the coming of the Lord;
> He is trampling out the vintage where the grapes of wrath are
>   stored!
> He has loosed the fateful lightning of his terrible swift sword;
> His truth is marching on.
>
> He has sounded forth the trumpet that shall never call retreat;
> He is sifting out the hearts of men before his judgment seat;
> O, be swift, my soul, to answer him! be jubilant, my feet!
> While God is marching on."[32]

Let us take courage; let us gird up our loins;[33] let us stand at our post; let us be true to duty; let us hold ourselves to the highest; let us have nothing to do with the unfruitful works of darkness;[34] let us be temperate, industrious, thrifty; let us do with our might what our hands find to do;[35] let us trust in God, and do the right: and then, whether the struggle be long or short, there can be no doubt as to the final issue. We shall come out victorious; we shall be accorded every right belonging to us under the Constitution, and every avenue of opportunity will be opened to us, as to other citizens of the Republic. The future is largely in our own hands. If we allow ourselves to be permanently despoiled of our rights; to be reduced to a position of civil and political inferiority, the fault will be, not "in our stars," as Shakespeare has expressed it, "but in ourselves."[36] Others can help us; others will help us, as they have already done; but the final outcome will depend mainly upon what we do *for* ourselves, and *with* ourselves. If we are to grow in the elements that make for a strong, intelligent, virtuous manhood and womanhood, *we* have got to see to it, to be concerned about it; to be more deeply concerned about it than anybody else. And so, if the agitation for equality of rights and opportunities in this country is to be kept up, and it ought to be kept up, *we* are the ones to see to it. As long as there are wrongs to be redressed, from which we are suffering, we ought not to be silent, ought not for our sake as well as for the sake of the nation at large. Whatever can be done to develop ourselves; whatever can be done to create a healthy and righteous public sentiment in our behalf; whatever can be done to check the encroachments of our enemies upon our rights, *we* must do it, whether others do or not. May God help us all to realize this, and to address ourselves earnestly to the work that lies before us.

> "Be strong!
> We are not here to play, to dream, to drift.
> We have hard work to do, and loads to lift.
> Shun not the struggle; face it. 'Tis God's gift."[37]

NOTES

1. Olmstead, "Francis James Grimke," 165.

2. Perry, *Lift Up Thy Voice,* 236.

3. F. Grimké, "Copied from my diary. Francis J. Grimké, Nov. 20, 1935," F. Grimké Papers.

4. In "Of Mr. Booker T. Washington and Others," Du Bois writes, "Nevertheless, the questions involved are so fundamental and serious that it is difficult to see how men like the Grimkés, Kelly Miller, J. W. E. Bowen, and other representatives of this group, can much longer be silent." Du Bois, *Souls of Black Folk,* 53.

5. F. Grimké, "Scottsboro Case," 475, F. Grimké Papers.

6. The Apostle Paul, known as Saul of Tarsus before his conversion, was an influential leader and missionary in the early Christian church. He wrote many of the books of the New Testament.

7. The Feast of Pentecost is a Jewish celebration of the first harvest and takes place on the fiftieth day after Passover, which commemorates the Jews' miraculous deliverance from slavery in Egypt.

8. Acts 21:20–24 (KJV).

9. Acts 21:28 (KJV).

10. Acts 22:25 (KJV).

11. Marcus Antonius Felix and Porcius Festus were Roman governors of Judea. King Herod Agrippa II was the last of the Herodians to be appointed ruler of a province in the Roman Empire.

12. Acts 25:8–12 (KJV).

13. Grimké is paraphrasing Acts 22:25–29 (KJV).

14. Acts 22:29 (ASV).

15. Philippians 4:8.

16. First published in the *Independent* in 1904, "Credo" presents W. E. B. Du Bois's philosophy and vision for the achievement of racial equality.

17. Grimke is alluding to the the majority opinion written by Justice Robert B. Taney in Dred Scott decision that African Americans "had no rights which the white man was bound to respect."

18. Grimké is referencing Theodore Roosevelt, a Republican, who served as U.S. president from 1901 to 1909.

19. This stanza is from the abolition poem "The Present Crisis" (1845) by James Russell Lowell (1819–1891), an influential writer, diplomat, educator, and reformer.

20. Grimké is alluding to Chief Justice Roger B. Taney's opinion in *Dred Scott v. Sanford*, 60 U.S. 393 (1857): "[The Negro] had for more than a century before been regarded as beings of an inferior order, and altogether unfit to associate with the white race, either in social or political relations; and so far inferior, that they had no rights which the white man was bound to respect; and that the negro might justly and lawfully be reduced to slavery."

21. "Separate but equal" railroad accommodations for African Americans were validated by the U.S. Supreme Court ruling in *Plessy v. Ferguson*, 163 U.S. 537 (1896).

22. Grimké seems to be referring to a 1899 statute in Georgia that provided for the separation of black and white passengers on railroad sleeping cars: "nothing in this act shall be construed to compel sleeping-car companies . . . to carry persons of color in sleeping or parlor cars." Stephenson, "Separation of the Races," 193.

23. Atlanta University, founded in 1865 by the American Missionary Association and the Freedmen's Bureau, is the oldest historically black university in the United States.

24. The Methodist Episcopal Church's Freedman's Aid Society founded Clark College in 1869, and it is now known as Clark Atlanta University.

25. The Atlanta Baptist College, originally located in Augusta, Georgia, was founded as the Augusta Institute in 1867. The school was renamed Morehouse College in 1913.

26. In 1881, Harriet E. Giles (1833–1909) and Sophia B. Packard (1824–1891), two white teachers and Baptist missionaries from the Oread Institute of Worcester, Massachusetts, established the nation's first institution of higher education for black females, Atlanta Baptist Female Seminary, which was later renamed Spelman Seminary. Today, the private liberal arts school is known as Spelman College.

27. The Gammon Theological Seminary was originally founded in 1869 as the Gammon School of Theology, a department of religion and philosophy at Clark University.

28. The Haines Institute was first established in 1886 as the Haines Normal and Industrial Institute. It served as a school and as a cultural and community center for African Americans in Augusta, Georgia

29. Grimké is likely referring to African Americans who refused to challenge segregationist practices.

30. Grimké is referring to President Roosevelt's 1903 appointment of the African American physician and Republican Party loyalist William Demos Crum as collector of customs in Charleston, South Carolina, despite Senate opposition initiated by Benjamin Tillman (D–SC) and influential white Charlestonians. Booker T. Washington and other black leaders viewed the appointment as a test of the Republican Party's loyalty to African Americans. Roosevelt seated Crum through recess appointments until the Senate granted approval in 1905. Gatewood, "William D. Crum," 301–16; "Crum Case."

31. "For precept must be upon precept, precept upon precept; line upon line, line upon line; here a little, and there a little." Isa. 28:10 (KJV).

32. These two stanzas are from Julia Howe's (1819–1910) "The Battle Hymn of the Republic," a popular song during the Civil War.

33. To "gird up our loins" is a figurative biblical expression that means to prepare for action, specifically for warfare or debate. The imagery is derived from an ancient military practice of soldiers' securing their tunics around each leg to facilitate greater agility and movement during battle. See Job 40:7 and Jer. 1:17 (KJV).

34. "The night is far spent, the day is at hand: let us therefore cast off the works of darkness, and let us put on the armour of light." Rom. 13:12 (KJV).

35. "Whatsoever thy hand findeth to do, do it with all thy might; for there is no work, nor device, nor knowledge, nor wisdom, in the grave, wither thou goest." Ecc. 9:10 (KJV).

36. Grimké is quoting Cassius's admonition to Brutus in William Shakespeare's tragedy *Julius Caesar* to choose his own fate rather than trust cosmic forces to determine his future.

37. This is the first verse of the poem "Be Strong" by the popular and influential nineteenth-century Presbyterian minister Maltie Davenport Babcourt (1858–1901).

The Talented Tenth

PART II

Kelly Miller
(1863–1939)

❧❦ EDUCATOR, ACTIVIST, COMMENTATOR

The writer was not born in the United States

In 1905 Kelly Miller wrote an open letter to the white supremacist Thomas Dixon Jr., the author of and told him, "You are a white man born in the midst of the civil war, I am a Negro born during the same stirring epoch. You were born with a silver spoon in your mouth, I was born with an iron hoe in my hand."[1] Indeed, Miller never forgot his humble origins in Winnsboro, South Carolina, and during his long career as a preeminent race leader and educator he frequently referred back to how he was born in 1863 to a slave mother. He understood that all he had achieved since then was not despite that handicap but in some ways fueled by that early hardship. He wielded that metaphorical iron hoe with a ferocity that allowed him to quell and moderate as well as inspire and inflame discussions of race and national policy through the first half of the twentieth century as an essayist, educator, and leading intellectual figure for black America.

He was raised in poverty and educated at one of the local schools set up by the Freedman's Bureau. His fortune turned when his mathematical talent was noticed by a white minister from Delaware, the Reverend Willard Richardson, who helped persuade his parents to release him from family farm work and allow him to attend the newly established grade school for black children at Fairfield Institute in Winnsboro, South Carolina, from 1878 to 1880. Miller was thereafter awarded a scholarship from the New England Missionary Society to Howard University in Washington, D.C., and began what was to be a lifelong association with that institute. He completed Hampton's three-year college preparatory program in Latin, Greek, and Mathematics in two years before entering Howard's college program and graduating with a bachelor of science degree in 1886, all the while holding down a clerk's position with the U.S. Pension Office. He managed not only to support himself during these years but also to save enough money to purchase the family farm and give his parents the deed at his graduation ceremony.

He continued to study advanced mathematics independently with Captain Edgar Frisby, a British mathematician at the U.S. Naval Observatory. With Frisby's strong recommendation as well as that of Simon Newcomb, another prominent astronomer and mathematician at the Naval Observatory and at Johns Hopkins, Miller became the first black man to be accepted at Johns Hopkins University. He studied mathematics, physics, and astronomy there from 1887 to 1889 until a tuition increase prevented him from completing his graduate degree. He dropped out and taught high school math for a year before obtaining in 1890 an appointment to teach mathematics at his alma mater, Howard University.

Increasingly fascinated by the social sciences and the solutions that sociological methods offered to confront seemingly intractable national problems, Miller introduced sociology to Howard's curriculum in 1895 and served as a professor of sociology for the next thirty-nine years. He rose quickly through the administrative ranks, becoming dean of the College of Arts and Sciences. He crusaded to broaden and increase the educational offerings at Howard, spearheading an immensely successful recruitment campaign that quadrupled the size of the student body within his first four years as dean. Indeed, Miller's national profile grew to such a degree that Howard University has occasionally been referred to as "Kelly Miller's university."[2]

As essayist, political commentator, and race advocate, Miller published articles syndicated by more than one hundred newspapers, both black and white, usually in his column, "Kelly Miller Speaks. . . ."[3] In addition to his frequent contributions to scholarly journals, he also published books and widely distributed pamphlets on social theory, public policy, and issues of the day.[4] His political positions varied over the years, but he was commonly known as a moderate in the cultural politics of the black intelligentsia of his day—while he commented that whether the system "pushes up from the bottom or pulls up from the top," it was working in the right direction.[5] In 1908 he wrote an essay titled "Radicals and Conservatives," which outlined weaknesses and strengths in Booker T. Washington's approaches to improving the lot of black people. The essay also assessed the comparative weaknesses and strengths of the rising generation of highly educated black leaders, embodied most particularly by men such as William Monroe Trotter and W. E. B. Du Bois, concluding, in a manner that surely pleased no one, that the difference between the founders of the Niagara movement and the acolytes of the Wizard of Tuskegee was "not essentially one of principle or purpose, but point of view."[6]

Miller's essay on South Carolina, which is featured in this collection, was written for the *Messenger,* a Harlem-based magazine, as part of a 1925 series titled "These 'Colored' United States," which featured state-by-state profiles of the nation written by black intellectuals.[7] Both celebratory and critical, Miller deftly sketches out the contradictions inherent in black South Carolinian identity in his essay, "South Carolina," most particularly the problems of simply knowing whether or not he could be South Carolinian in a state that had continually denied the humanity of its black inhabitants. He tracks the enormous fall from power that black political leaders experienced with the radical dismantling of Reconstruction-era policies that had briefly enabled them to fill "all stations in the government." The resulting disenfranchisement demoralized an entire class and generation of black leadership. Indeed, he argues that the diaspora of the black intelligentsia whose members fled the state after Reconstruction illustrates the sense of South Carolina as a separate country and these migrants as essentially expatriates, a theme Miller introduces in the essay's opening salvo: "The writer was not born in the United States; he was born in South Carolina when that state was out of the union." Whether or not that state had ever truly returned to the union was clearly still in question for Miller.

Miller's attention to issues of discrimination and prejudice among dark-skinned and fairer-skinned black people and among the descendants of free and enslaved people is of special note here and perhaps represents a freedom he felt in sharing such analyses with the *Messenger*'s primarily black audience. His analysis of caste and class bears perhaps an acutely salient edge because of his work in the social sciences. Hailing from the midlands of South Carolina himself, he also bluntly addresses the cultural differences between the black cultures of Columbia and Charleston and makes it clear that the aristocratic superiority of the comparatively freer class of black people in Charleston was crushed under the equalizing oppression of practices and policies of the Black Codes, which left the black population of Charleston with "little to do except the outerskirts of the lower and menial pursuits."

Ultimately Miller's essay reflects the rueful reflections of an elderly expatriate. He writes: "The only big chance now left the Negro in the state is on the farm, which he is prone to abandon for the allurements of the North." While Miller was known for advocating agricultural education and for bemoaning the dominance of the great black migration north in capturing the dreams of all black America, leaving the poor rural class behind, here we see a subtle acknowledgment that the future of black farmers in South Carolina was a dim one indeed. After all, he himself had succumbed to big-city dreams.

Other activists and intellectuals, both black and white, had long crusaded against the scourge of lynching, but Miller's national prominence gave him a pulpit and an audience that few others could boast of. His open letter to President Woodrow Wilson is the second featured piece here. Titled "The Disgrace of Democracy," it was published in August 1917 as a pamphlet and may well have been one of the most wide-reaching and influential pieces he ever wrote. It certainly was one of the most impassioned. While the marketing copy may contain some hyperbole, at least one of its 1917 editions bore the claim "over 100,000 copies distributed." And other editions noted that up to a quarter of a million copies had been sold.[8] The pamphlet was even accorded the dubious honor of being banned on military bases because of the supposed danger it posed to the morale of American troops.[9]

After two especially horrifying episodes of racial violence, Miller composed his furious declaration against the nation's hypocrisy in recruiting black soldiers to fight against oppression abroad while they faced unfettered lawlessness and violence at home. In July 1917 there was a riot in East St. Louis in which at least thirty-nine black people were murdered and, in what historian Kenneth Jackson has termed one of the most vicious lynchings in American history, a black prisoner was dragged off a train in Memphis to be burned alive and dismembered by a lynch mob as local officials made little effort to prevent the atrocity.[10] Moreover, it was commonly assumed that the local authorities had specifically aided the mob.[11] In response to the evidence laid out in these and other violent outrages, Miller argued that "a doctrine that breaks down at home is not fit to be propagated abroad. . . . Why democratize the nations of the earth if it leads them to delight in the burning of human beings after the manner of Springfield, Waco, Memphis, and East St. Louis while the nation looks helplessly on?"

To make his case, Miller walks the president through the history of lynching in the United States and points out that such acts are neither specific to the South nor solely directed at the black man but, rather, represent an evil that transcends all delineations of caste and class. He takes Wilson to task for fearfully resorting to shibboleths about the limits of federal jurisdiction. He assures Wilson that the "Negro's patriotism is vicarious and altruistic." As he puts it bluntly, "The Negro, Mr. President, in this emergency, will stand by you and the nation. Will you and the nation stand by the Negro?"

The answer to Kelly Miller's question is unknown, for Wilson, not surprisingly, never replied. Nonetheless, the work by Miller and other activists during the First World War to reframe debates about civil rights and the meaning of international justice had a lasting effect on not only later generations of both black and white intellectuals but also the soldiers who were immediately returning from war. As W. E. B. Du Bois wrote in 1919,

> We *return.*
> We *return from fighting.*
> We *return fighting.*[12]

For Miller, who was, after all, born not in the United States but in the seceded state of South Carolina, it couldn't have been much of a stretch to foresee how the clarity of distance could impel a new generation to activism.

⊱❧ South Carolina

The writer was not born in the United States; he was born in South Carolina when that state was out of the Union. South Carolina is the stormy petrel of the nation. She arouses the nation's wrath, and rides upon the storm. There is not a dull period in her history. Calhoun threatened nullification; the iron resolution of Old Hickory nullified the threat.[13] She was the first to secede from the Union, and the slowest to recede from the secession. Her fiery son, Preston Brooks, struck down Charles Sumner on the floor of the Senate; his defiant constituency returned him in triumph to his seat in the House of Representatives.[14] She was forced to taste of the bitter cup of reconstruction; but was the first to wash the bitter taste out of her mouth. She sent Benjamin Tillman to the Senate, who boastfully denounced and defied the War Amendments to the Constitution; the North connived at his defiance.[15] Governor Cole Blease, in conference of the governors, openly ejaculated, "To hell with the Constitution!"; he is sent to the Senate to enforce that document with the Eighteenth Amendment added.[16] Truly the palmetto state has been a thorn in the flesh of the nation.

A glimpse at her origin will account for her temperament. She was planted as a colony for restless and dissatisfied spirits. The first successful colony was founded at Charleston, 1670. From the beginning it was a protestant proposition. Roundheads and cavaliers came from England, Huguenots came from France; dissatisfied Dutch came from New York; a restless group came from Barbadoes bringing their slaves, the first known to the colony; even a group of Congregationalists came down from New England. They were held together by but one common tie—the bond of protest. When freedom of conscience is carried to extremes, personal freedom counts for more than conscience. Protestantism means more protestants, until each individual follows his own personal philosophy. The Greek mind invented a scheme of democracy that ignored the bulk of the population with the status of the slave. It was wholly unaware of its ethical inconsistency. The South Carolina philosophy was a little more logical. Calhoun, the great apostle of the ideal of South Carolina, and of the South, never defended human slavery, but African slavery, on the ground the African was not human.[17] These are the words of William Simms Gilmore, the solitary singer whom South Carolina has inspired: "If it be admitted that the institution of Negro slavery is a wrong done the Negro, the question is at an end. No people can be justified for continuance in error and injustice. In the South we think otherwise."[18] Herein lay and lies the crux of the whole question. Abraham Lincoln said, "If slavery is not wrong, then nothing is wrong."[19] South Carolina never developed a conscience on the moral evil of slavery. There was then no conscious moral inconsistency in the slaveholder proclaiming the fullest principles of religious freedom and personal liberty. An act to settle a maintenance upon a minister of the Church of England in Charleston in 1698 reads: "That he should enjoy the lands, houses, slaves, cattle and monies appointed to his use, and that a Negro man and woman and four cows and calves should be purchased for his use." All of this was not without complaisant benevolent intent. In a South Carolina publication in 1743, we read: "The Society for the propagation of the Gospel, having long at heart the propagation of the Gospel among the Negroes and Indian races, had resolved to purchase some country Negroes, causing them to be instructed to read the Bible, and in the chief precepts of the Christian religion, and thenceforth employing them as schoolmasters for the same instructions of Negroes and Indian children. It is thought and believed that they would receive instruction from teachers of their own race with more facility and willingness than from white teachers."

In 1746, thirty-five children and fifteen adults were instructed under these auspices. But the experiment was not continued after one of the two teachers died and the other turned profligate.[20]

I am desirous to show that human conduct is the outcome of attitude. Conscience is a pliable faculty and is shaped to our dealings. How did it happen that South Carolina and Massachusetts, made up of the same moral stuff, assumed such diametrically opposite attitudes on the issue of African slavery? Let this historical analyst determine this. I am now chiefly concerned with the gradual approachments of the two attitudes at the present day. When these attitudes become consolidated on the lower level, the cause of the Negro will be hopeless. The nation as a whole does not now believe that the disfranchisement and segregation of the Negro is morally wrong. And therefore no serious attempt is made to remedy the grievances of which the colored race complains. The Negro has but one recourse, and that is to stimulate the conscience to the moral enormity of it all.

The story of the Negro in South Carolina, except as a negative, or rather a passive instrument of production, hinges about two centers, Charleston and Columbia. Early in the nineteenth century, Denmark Vesey, a West Indian Charleston slave, generalled an insurrection involving some nine thousand, as some estimates have it, in the city and surrounding communities.[21] His generalship was superb and his courage unequalled. He failed because all such fatuous efforts were doomed to fail. Denmark Vesey with many of his followers were hanged. White men were fined and sentenced to prison for culpable complicity. The deathless legacy of that tragic episode are the last words of Peter, one of the culprits, to his partners in distress: "Do not open your lips. Die silent as you shall see me do." These are the dying, though deathless, words of a Charleston Negro in 1822.

Julius Caesar, in one of his sweeping generalizations, injected into the dry details of a military record, says, "All men love liberty and hate the condition of slavery." Denmark Vesey verifies the verdict of Caesar eighteen hundred years later.

The story of the free Negroes in Charleston is one that is full of interest and charm. In all of the older established cities there was a small band of free Negroes who lived in self-satisfied complacency in a little world below the whites and above the slaves. They enjoyed existence with a keenness of relish, which freedom has almost wholly destroyed. It is a glorious experience to have a mass of people below you, even if there are others above you. The free colored people had their own churches and schools, and enjoyed a certain area of recognized privileges which gave them an established place in the city's economy. They were assigned the bulk of the industrial and mechanical work as carpenters, painters, bricklayers, tailors and marketmen. The whites encouraged their social separateness from the slaves, as a means of ruling by division. The line of demarcation coincided almost wholly with the color line. As a result, there grew up between the two shades of color an almost impossible barrier. Many of the free Negroes were owners of slaves, and easily assumed the attitude and hauteur of the white master.

The emancipation proclamation, the reconstruction experiment and the opening of free public schools wiped out much of this conceit. In the earlier days of Howard University, two brilliant boys came from Charleston; one was brown and the other was white enough for anything. They were classmates and the most intimate of friends. In the interchange of intimacies, one day, the whiter of the twain said to his swarthier crony: "I am surely glad that we came to Howard University. I should never have been able to meet you in Charleston." The aristocratic conceit of the free Charleston Negroes, complicated with the color scheme, was deep-seated and hard to remove. I have seen the records of "The Brown Fellowship," a semi-social and literary organization of the Charleston elite that runs back over a hundred years.[22] Charleston retained white teachers in the public schools longer than any other city in the union. It was only a few years ago that they were dislodged, and then this was against the earnest protest of many of the old-time aristocrats, who somehow felt the enchantment of white contact, if it be only to touch the hem of their garment. But the old order has practically passed away. The occupations once monopolized by the free blacks have been grasped by the whites. The Negro is left little to do except the outerskirts of the lower and menial pursuits. Many of the oldtimers have moved away. Many of the free colored people inherited not only the name but the blood of the original founders, along with their proud and dignified spirit. The Grimkés, the Cordozos, the Prioleaus, the Mouzons, the Mischeaus, the De Reefs, the Mazycks, and the rest remind one of the list of original settlers.[23]

Speaking of the blood mixture of the races, South Carolina, especially Charleston and the lower counties, is noted for the composite progeny. In the coastal cities, along the waterline, the old French system of two families, one of either race, was quite prevalent, so much so that one-eighth Negro blood was as high as they deemed it safe to fix the definition of a white man. Congressman Tillman, a relative of the more famous Senator Tillman, said in the Constitutional Convention, that to raise the limit to the artificial exactions of one-thirty-second, would cause a number of counties to be bathed in blood.[24]

One of these days, the Society for the Study of Negro Life and History will undertake the study of the Free Negro in the several large cities of the South. It will prove to be an interesting and fascinating story when adequately and properly told. Charleston, New Orleans, Richmond, Savannah and the rest contain gold mines of rich and rare historical material.

Columbia next claims our attention. This is the capital of the state. Little need be said about the Negroes of this city until the days of reconstruction. In South Carolina and Louisiana, the Negroes actually held a majority of the legislatures. But the palmetto state had the advantage over its political rival in that it had a better basis of educated men to start with. Francis L. Cardoza had just finished his education in the universities of England and Scotland in time to corral the forces.[25] He sent for the New York *Tribune* and had it distributed among all of the Negro members of the Constitutional Convention, which kept them well posted as to the best methods to pursue. Educated Negroes, like Elliot, came down from Massachusetts to swell the intellectual forces.[26] Negroes filled all stations in the government, with the exception of governor, which was always accorded the white race. The Lieutenant Governor, Secretary of State, Treasurer, legislators and Congressmen were plentiful. As a boy, thirty miles away, my eyes and ears were just about beginning to be opened. I used to hear of the fabulous happenings going on in Columbia. I had relatives who went from Fairfield County as representatives and senators. They would tell me that Negroes often lit their cigars with five-dollar bills. Nowhere on earth did Negroes ever exercise so much political power as Columbia. Nor did they ever revel so extravagantly in the excrescences of power. Every Negro boy in the state was dreaming of a political career. Had I been ten years older I would have been in the thickest of the fray. But the bubble must soon break. Babylon must needs fall. South Carolina is the only state that admitted Negroes to the State University.[27] Of course, the whites left. Professor Richard T. Greener had the distinction of being the only Negro to be appointed professor in this famous institution.[28] I was with him in Columbia many years later when he could only stand at a distance and point out the room which he used to occupy. After the overthrow of reconstruction, when the whites regained control, all records of the Negro regime were destroyed as if there had been an inter regnum.

Many of the Negroes cast down from the seats of power cut a sorry figure. As many as could sought berths in the department service in Washington. When I was in Charleston last month I heard an eye witness tell of a former lieutenant governor becoming a street sweeper. Columbia dropped from the heights to the depths so far as the Negro was concerned. How did the mighty fall? But South Carolina has had the experience, and that is worth something. After the downfall in seventy-six, some of the old-liners held on to a lingering hope. General Robert Small, Thomas Miller and George W. Murray were elected to Congress from the blackest district.[29] But the rise of Tillman put an end to all of this. The Negro now has been driven from every vestige of political power. He makes no further effort, not even to function seriously in quadrennial election of Republican delegates.

The political experience gained in politics was quickly transferred to the several religious denominations and secret orders.

The Negro in South Carolina to-day is largely a farmer. The cotton manufacturing industry in the Piedmont section of the state is recruited mainly by white operatives. The only big chance now left the Negro in the state is on the farm, which he is prone to abandon for the allurements of the North.

The Negroes of my native state have had many ups and downs, but through it all they possess a courage and a determination to do worthwhile things. They possess a coherence and attachment for the old state that time and distance cannot destroy. After all, we love to be known as a South Carolinian. We have always had a large contingent of my fellow statesmen in Howard University. On an occasion some unworthy deed had been committed by a student, the South Carolina Club met to protect and defend the honor of its membership. The universal verdict was that "No South Carolinian could be guilty of such unbecoming conduct."

⋗ "The Disgrace of Democracy"

By KELLY MILLER
August 4, 1917.

Hon. Woodrow Wilson,
President of the United States,
The White House,
Washington, D.C.
Mr. President:

I am taking the liberty of intruding this letter upon you because I feel that the issues involved are as important as any questions now pressing upon your busy attention. The whole civilized world has been shocked at the recent occurrences in Memphis and East St. Louis.[30] These outbreaks call attention anew to the irritating race problem of which they are but eruptive symptoms which break forth ever and anon with Vesuvian violence. For fully a generation American statesmanship has striven to avoid, ignore or forget the perplexing race problem. But this persistent issue will not down at our bidding, and cannot be shunted from public attention by other questions however momentous or vital they may seem to be.

I know that I am taking unwarranted liberties with the ceremonial proprieties in writing such a letter to the President of the United States at the present time. It may seem to partake of the spirit of heckling after the manner of the suffragists.[31] Nothing is further from my purpose. No right-minded American would wish to add one featherweight to the burden that now so heavily taxes the mind and body of the President of the United States who labors under as heavy a load as human nature is capable of sustaining. Every citizen should strive to lighten rather than to aggravate that burden. It is, nevertheless, true that any suppressed and aggrieved class must run athwart the established code of procedure in order that their case may receive a just hearing. Ceremonial codes were enacted by those who are the beneficiaries of existing order which they wish to perpetuate and make unchangeable. They would estop all social and moral reform. The ardent suffragists find it necessary to ruthlessly violate the traditional and decorous modes of procedure in order to promote the reform which they have at heart. On one occasion you felt forced to terminate an interview with a committee of suffragists because they persisted in cross-examining the President of the United States.

There are 10,000,000 loyal citizens of African descent in the United States. They are rigorously excluded from a voice in the government by which they are controlled. They have no regularly constituted organ through which to present their case to the powers that be. They have no seat nor voice in the council of the nation. The late Doctor Booker T. Washington was the accepted spokesman and mediator of the race, but he has no successor. Under former administrations there was a small appointive official class of Negroes. Though derisively designated as the "Black Cabinet," they were on the inside of the circle of governmental control to which they had ready access in presenting the claims of the race.[32] But under the exaction of partisan exigencies even these have been excluded from official position under your administration. Several weeks ago a delegation of colored men from the State of Maryland sought an interview with you concerning the horrible crime of East St. Louis. You were good enough to write Senator France that you were too busy with other pressing issues to grant the request of an interview.[33] The failure of all other methods is my only excuse for resorting to an open letter as a means of reaching you and, through you, the nation at large, concerning the just grievances of 10,000,000 loyal American citizens.

The Negro feels that he is not regarded as a constituent part of American democracy. This is our fundamental grievance and lies at the basis of all the outrages inflicted upon this helpless race. It is the fundamental creed of democracy that no people are good enough to govern any other people without their consent and participation. The English are not good enough to govern the Irish. The Russians are not good enough to govern the Finns. The Germans are not good enough to govern the Belgians. The Belgians are not good enough to govern the people of the Congo. Men are not considered good enough to govern women. The white people of this country are not good enough to govern the Negro. As long as the black man is excluded from participation in the government of the nation, just so long will he be the victim of cruelty and outrage on the part of his white fellow citizens who assume lordship over him.

These periodic outbreaks of lawlessness are but the outgrowth of the disfavor and despite in which the race is held by public opinion. The evil is so widespread that the remedy lies in the hands of the national government.

Resolutions pending before both houses of Congress look toward investigation of the outrage at East St. Louis. I understand that you are sympathetically disposed toward this investigation by Federal authority. Such investigation is important only to the extent that it implies a tardy recognition of national responsibility for local lawlessness. There is no expectation that any additional comprehensive information will result. You may rest assured that there will be a half dozen similar outbreaks before this investigation is well under way. Indeed, since the East St. Louis atrocity there have already been lynchings in Georgia, Louisiana, Pennsylvania and Montana. Every intelligent American knows as much about the essential cause of this conflict as he will know after long and tedious investigation. The vital issues involved are apt to be obscured by technical wranglings over majority and minority reports. What the nation needs is not investigation of obvious fact, but determination and avowed declaration on the part of the President speaking for the people of the United States to put an end to lawlessness wherever it raises its hideous head. . . .

These outbreaks are not limited to the Southern States, although they occur there more frequently than elsewhere because of the relatively larger number of Negroes in the total population. There have been lynchings and burnings in Illinois, Kansas, Delaware, Ohio, Indiana, Colorado and other Northern States. The evil is indeed national in its range and scope, and the nation must provide the remedy. Striking indeed is the analogy between the spread of lawlessness today and the extension of the institution of slavery two generations ago. Like slavery, lawlessness cannot be localized. As the nation could not exist half slave and half free under Abraham Lincoln, so it cannot continue half law-abiding and half lawless under Woodrow Wilson. The evil tendency overcomes the good, just as the darker overlaps the brighter phase in the waning moon. If the Negro is allowed to be lynched in the South with impunity, he will soon be lynched in the North, so easy is the communicability of evil suggestion. The lynching of Negroes has become fashionable in some parts of the country. When a black man is accused of wrongdoing, "Lynch the Negro!" is the cry that springs spontaneously to the lips of man, woman and child. The fashion is spreading throughout the whole nation. If slavery could have been isolated and segregated in the South that institution might have existed even down to the present time. And so, if lynching could be localized and limited to the Southern States the nation as a whole would have less pretext for interfering. But this cannot be done. Senator Tombs of Georgia boasted that he would call the roll of his slaves under the shadow of the Bunker Hill monument, an ambition which, doubtless, might have been gratified had not the nation arisen in its moral might and blotted out the iniquitous institution altogether.[34] Unless the aroused conscience of the American people, efficiently asserting itself through Federal authority, shall stamp out the spirit of lawlessness, it is easy to prophesy that the Negro will yet be lynched not only in the shadow of the Bunker Hill monument, but on the campus of your beloved Princeton.[35] Already there have been burnings of human beings in the bleeding State of Old John Brown,[36] and in the city where lie the remains of Abraham Lincoln.[37] During the past thirty years nearly 3,000 Negroes have been lynched in various parts of the country. Scores of these have been burned at the stake. Even the bodies of women have been fed to the flames. Thousands of localities in the majority of the States of the Union have experienced these outrages. Our fair land of liberty is blotted over with these foul spots which cannot be washed out by all of the waters of the ocean. It is not easy to calculate the number of persons who have been involved in these lynchings, either as participants or as acquiescent lookers-on, all of whom were potential murderers. So general and widespread has become the practice that lynching may well be characterized as a national institution, to the eternal disgrace of American democracy.

Lynching cannot be confined to the Negro race. Hundreds of white men have been the victims of lawlessness and violence. While these words are flowing from my pen, news comes over the wire that a labor agitator has been lynched in the State of Montana.[38] Although the Negro is at present the chief victim of lawlessness, like any other evil disease, it cannot be limited by racial lines.

It is but hollow mockery of the Negro, when he is beaten and bruised and burned in all parts of the nation and flees to the national government for asylum, to be denied relief on the ground of doubtful jurisdiction. The black man asks for justice and is given a theory of government. He asks for protection and is confronted with a scheme of governmental checks and balances.

Mr. President, you are commander-in-chief of the Army and Navy. You express the voice of the American people in the great world conflict which involves practically the entire human race. You are the accepted spokesman of the world democracy. You have sounded forth the trumpet of democratization of the nations, which shall never call retreat. But, Mr. President, a chain is no stronger than its weakest link. A doctrine that breaks down at home is not fit to be propagated abroad. One is reminded of the pious slaveholder who became so deeply impressed with the plea for foreign missions that he sold one of his slaves to contribute liberally to the cause. Why democratize the nations of the earth if it leads them to delight in the burning of human beings after the manner of Springfield, Waco, Memphis, and East St. Louis while the nation looks helplessly on? You add nothing to the civilization of the world nor to the culture of the human spirit by the technical changes in forms of government. The old adage still remains true:

> "For forms of government let fools contest—
> What's best administered—is best."[39]

If democracy cannot control lawlessness, then democracy must be pronounced a failure. The nations of the world have a right to demand of us the workings of the institutions at home before they are promulgated abroad. The German press will, doubtless, gloat with ghoulish glee over American atrocities against the Negro. The outrages complained of against the Belgians become merciful performances by gruesome comparison.[40] Our frantic wail against the barbarity of Turk against Armenian, German upon Belgian, Russian upon Jew, are made of no effect. It cannot be said that these outbreaks are but the spontaneous ebullitions of popular feeling, without governmental sanction or approval. These outrages occur all over the nation. The nation must be responsible for what it permits. Sins of permission are as reprehensible as sins of commission. A few years ago a Turkish ambassador was handed his passports by you for calling attention to the inconsistency between our national practice and performance.[41] The nation was compelled, with a spirit of humiliation, to accept the reproach which he hurled into our teeth: "Thou hypocrite, first cast out the beam out of thine own eye; and then shalt thou see clearly to cast out the mote out of thy brother's eye."[42] Every high-minded American must be touched with a tinge of shame when he contemplates that his rallying cry for the liberation of humanity is made a delusion and a snare by these racial barbarities.

It is needless to attempt to place the blame on the helpless Negro. In the early stages of these outbreaks there was an attempt to fix an evil and lecherous reputation on the Negro race as lying at the basis of lynching and lawlessness. Statistics most clearly refute this contention. The great majority of the outbreaks cannot even allege rapeful assault in extenuation. It is undoubtedly true that there are imbruited and lawless members of the Negro race, as there are of the white race, capable of committing any outrageous and hideous offense. The Negro possesses the imperfections of his status. His virtues as well as his failures are simply human. It is a fatuous philosophy, however, that would resort to cruel and unusual punishment as a deterrent to crime. Lynching has never made one Negro virtuous nor planted the seed of right doing in the mind of a single American citizen. The Negro should be encouraged in all right directions to develop his best manly and human qualities. Where he deviates from the accepted standard he should be punished by due process of law. But as long as the Negro is held in general despite and suppressed below the level of human privilege, just so long will he produce a disproportionate number of imperfect individuals of evil propensity. To regulate the Negro to a status that encourages the baser instincts of humanity, and then denounce him because he does not stand forth as a model of human perfection, is of the same order of ironical cruelty as shown by the barbarous Teutons in Shakespeare, who cut off the hands and hacked out the tongue of the lovely Lavinia, and then upbraided her for not calling for perfumed water to wash her delicate hands.[43] The Negro is neither angelic nor diabolical, but merely human, and should be treated as such.

The vainglorious boast of Anglo-Saxon superiority will no longer avail to justify these outrages. The contact, adjustment and attrition of various races of mankind constitute a problem which is coterminous with the ends of the earth. The lighter and stronger races are coming into contact with the weaker and darker ones. The stronger breeds of men are relating themselves to the weaker members of the human family in all the ends of the earth. How does it happen that in the United States alone, of all civilized lands, these atrocious outrages are heaped upon the helpless Negro? The English nation has the largest colonial experience and success since the days of the Roman empire, and has come into relationship with the various weaker breeds of men in all parts of the world. But everywhere under English jurisdiction law and order prevail. In the West Indies, where Negroes outnumber the whites 20 to 1, rape and lynching have scarcely yet found a place in the local vocabulary. In Brazil, under a Latin dispensation, where a more complex racial situation exists than in the United States, racial peace and good-will prevail. Belgium furnishes the only parallel of civilized nations, in the atrocious treatment of a helpless people placed in their charge. But even the Belgians were forced to modify the rigors of their outrageous regime in the Congo, under the bombardment of moral sentiment of the more enlightened nations of the world.[44] America enjoys the evil distinction among all civilized nations of the earth of taking delight in murder and burning of human beings. Nowhere else do men, women and children dance with ghoulish glee and fight for ghastly souvenirs of human flesh and mock the dying groans of the helpless victim which sicken the air, while the flickering flames of the funereal pyre lighten the midnight sky with their dismal glare. . . .

The Negro's patriotism is vicarious and altruistic. It seems to be an anomaly of fate that the Negro, the man [who] of all men is held in despite, should stand out in conspicuous relief at every crisis of our national history. His blood offering is not for himself or for his race, but for his country. This blood flows like a stream through our national history, from Boston Commons to Carrizal.[45] Crispus Attucks was the first American to give his blood as an earnest of American independence. The Negro was with Washington in the dark days of Valley Forge, when the lamp of national liberty flickered almost to extinguishment. The black troops fought valiantly with Jackson behind the fleecy breastworks at New Orleans.[46] Two hundred thousand black boys in blue responded to the call of the immortal Lincoln for the preservation of the Union.[47] The Negro was the positive cause of the Civil War, and the negative cause of the united nation with which we face the world today.

The reckless daring of Negro troops on San Juan Hill marked the turning point in that struggle which drove the last vestige of Spanish power from the Western world.[48] It was but yesterday that we buried with honor at Arlington Cemetery the Negro soldiers who fell face forward while carrying the flag to the farthest point in the heart of Mexico, in quest of the bandit who dared place impious foot on American soil. In complete harmony with this marvelous patriotic record, it so happened that it was an American Negro who proved to be the first victim of ruthless submarine warfare, after you had distinctly announced to Germany that such outrage would be considered tantamount to war. In all of these ways has the Negro shown, purposely or unconsciously, his undeviating devotion to the glory and honor of the nation. Greater love hath no man than this, that he lay down his life for his country.

In the midst of the world war for the democratization of mankind the Negro will do his full share. I have personally always striven to urge the Negro to be patriotic and loyal in every emergency. At the Reserve Officers' Training Camp in Fort Des Moines there are over one hundred young colored men who have come under my instruction.[49] The deviltry of his fellow men cannot devise iniquities horrible enough to drive him from his patriotic devotion. The Negro, Mr. President, in this emergency, will stand by you and the nation. Will you and the nation stand by the Negro?

I believe, Mr. President, that to the victor belong the spoils, especially if these spoils be human liberty. After this war for the liberation of mankind has been won through the Negro's patriotic participation, he will repeat the lines of the old familiar hymn somewhat louder than ever:

> "Behold a stranger at the door,
> He gently knocks, has knocked before,
> Has waited long, is waiting still.
> You treat no other friend so ill."

As a student of public questions I have carefully watched your attitude on the race problem. You have preserved a lukewarm aloofness from the tangled issues of this problem. In searching your writings one finds little or no reference to this troubled phase of American life. It seems that you regard it as a regrettable social malady to be treated with cautious and calculated neglect. There is observable, however, a passive solicitude. You have kept the race problem in the back part of your mind. Your letter to Bishop Walters during your first campaign for the Presidency, expressing a generous concern for the welfare of the race, though of a general and passive character, caused many Negroes to give you their political support.[50] Under the stress and strain of other pressing issues and the partisan demands of your political supporters you have not yet translated this passive purpose into positive performance. There is, however, something of consolation in the fact that while during your entire career you have never done anything constructive for the Negro, you have never done anything destructive against him. Your constructive opportunity is now at hand. The time has come to make lawlessness a national issue, as a war measure if not from any higher consideration. As a patriotic and military necessity, I suggest that you ask the Congress of the United States to invest you with the power to prevent lynching and to quell lawlessness and violence in all parts of the country during the continuance of the war. Or at least you might quicken the conscience of the nation by a stirring message to Congress calling attention to this growing evil which is gnawing at the vitals of the nation. It is entirely probable that before the war is over you will have to resort to some such measure to control internal disturbances on other accounts. It is inconceivable that this nation should spend billions of dollars and sacrifice the lives of millions of its citizens without domestic uprising and revulsion. In such a time it becomes necessary for the President to exercise all but dictatorial power. . . .

Mr. President, Negroes all over this nation are aroused as they have never been before. It is not the wild hysterics of the hour, but a determined purpose that this country shall be made a safe place for American citizens to live and work and enjoy the pursuits of happiness. Ten thousand speechless men and women marched in silent array down Fifth Avenue in New York City as a spectral demonstration against the wrongs and cruelties heaped upon the race.[51] Negro women all over the nation have appointed a day of prayer in order that righteousness might be done to this people. The weaker sex of the weaker race are praying that God may use you as the instrument of His will to promote the cause of human freedom at home. . . .

Mr. President, ten million of your fellow citizens are looking to you and to the God whom you serve to grant them relief in this hour of their deepest distress. All moral reforms grow out of the people who suffer and stand in need of them. The Negro's helpless position may yet bring America to a realizing sense that righteousness exalteth a nation, but sin is a reproach to any people.

Yours truly,

KELLY MILLER.

NOTES

1. Miller, *Leopard's Spots,* 1.

2. Rodgers, "Kelly Miller," 290–91.

3. Miller's column was syndicated in newspapers such as the *New York Times,* the *Washington Post,* and the *Baltimore Sun,* among others.

4. Miller's titles include *The Everlasting Stain* (Washington, D.C.: Associated Publishers, 1924); *Kelly Miller's History of the World War for Human Rights* (Washington, D.C.: Austin Jenkins Company, 1919; repr., Charleston: Nabu Press, 2010); *Out of the House of Bondage* (New York: Neale Publishing Company, 1914; repr., New York: Arno Books, 1969); *Race Adjustment* (New York: Neale Publishing Company, 1908); and *A Review of Hoffman's Race Traits and Tendencies of the American Negro* (Washington, D.C.: American Negro Academy, 1897).

5. Miller, "Practical Value of Higher Education," 4–5.

6. Miller, *Race Adjustment Essays,* 12.

7. See Lutz and Ashton, *These 'Colored' United States.*

8. Holmes, "Phylon Profile IV," 121–25.

9. The Department of Military Censorship created a list of publications that were to be withdrawn from circulation on military bases during World War I; "The Disgrace of Democracy" was on the list. For more information, see Larson and Mock, "Lost Files," 5–29.

10. Jackson, *Ku Klux Klan in the City*, 45.

11. The historian Elliott Rudwick discusses the unreliable statistics available concerning this riot and notes that black sources such as the NAACP estimated that one hundred to two hundred black people were murdered. See Rudwick, *Race Riot*, 49–50.

12. Du Bois, "Returning Soldiers," 14. This reference was drawn to our attention by Jonathan Rosenberg, whose article gives a thorough and thoughtful evaluation of the context in which Miller's letter was written. See Rosenberg, "For Democracy, Not Hypocrisy," 592–625.

13. Known as "Old Hickory" for his leadership during the War of 1812, Andrew Jackson served as president of the United States from 1829 to 1837. John C. Calhoun served as vice president during Jackson's first term, a tumultuous period that included Jackson's approval of a tariff on European-made cotton goods. Southern farmers argued that this tariff and others like it benefited northern textile manufacturers to southerners' detriment. South Carolina, supported by Calhoun, declared that any state could "nullify," or declare void, any law that violated the U.S. Constitution, a theory that had been advocated at the end of the eighteenth century by Thomas Jefferson and others. South Carolina openly nullified the tariff, and in response Jackson proposed sending troops to South Carolina to force the collection of the tariff. Crisis was averted by Henry Clay, who suggested a compromise: the reduction of the tariff over time and passage of the Force Bill, which authorized the president to use force to ensure the enforcement of tariffs. South Carolina repealed its nullification of the tariff but symbolically issued a nullification of the Force Bill.

14. During the controversy regarding the status of slavery in Kansas, known as "Bleeding Kansas," tempers in Congress often ran high. In May 1856, Senator Charles Sumner of Massachusetts made a two-day speech that initially addressed the situation in Kansas but that turned to personal attacks against specific southern congressmen as it proceeded. One portion of the tirade was directed at Senator Andrew Butler of South Carolina and included a mocking reference to Butler's speech and his tendency to drool, side effects of a stroke that the elderly man had suffered. Two days later, Representative Preston Brooks of South Carolina, Butler's nephew, entered the Senate and beat Sumner unconscious with a cane in retaliation for the insult to his uncle's honor. A vote to expel Brooks from the House of Representatives failed because of overwhelming support among the other representatives from the South. The merchants of Charleston rewarded Brooks with a cane that was inscribed with "Hit him again!" He was censured and fined; he responded by resigning but was promptly re-elected.

15. Benjamin Ryan Tillman served as governor of South Carolina from 1890 to 1894 and as a U.S. senator from 1895 to 1918. He promoted the passage of Jim Crow laws and a new state constitution to circumvent the Fifteenth Amendment in South Carolina.

16. Coleman "Cole" Blease served as governor of South Carolina from 1911 to 1915 and as a U.S. senator from 1925 to 1931.

17. In 1837, John C. Calhoun gave a speech in the U.S. Senate that is one of the most famous defenses of slavery in nineteenth-century America. It is often known

as the "Positive Good" speech, as the primary argument is that not only is slavery not evil; it is in fact a positive good.

> Never before has the black race of Central Africa, from the dawn of history to the present day, attained a condition so civilized and so improved, not only physically, but morally and intellectually. It came among us in a low, degraded, and savage condition, and in the course of a few generations it has grown up under the fostering care of our institutions, reviled as they have been, to its present comparatively civilized condition. This, with the rapid increase of numbers, is conclusive proof of the general happiness of the race, in spite of all the exaggerated tales to the contrary. . . . I hold that in the present state of civilization, where two races of different origin, and distinguished by color, and other physical differences, as well as intellectual, are brought together, the relation now existing in the slaveholding States between the two, is, instead of an evil, a good—a positive good.

18. William Gilmore Simms (1806–1870) was a South Carolina writer who produced several novels set in the South, as well as history and geography books about South Carolina and South Carolinians. He edited several southern literary journals. An advocate for slavery, he wrote a novel in response to *Uncle Tom's Cabin*.

19. Abraham Lincoln to Albert G. Hodges, 4 April 1864, Manuscripts Division, Library of Congress; also Basler, *Collected Works of Abraham Lincoln*, 281. This quotation is taken from a letter from Lincoln to Albert G. Hodges, former U.S.senator from Kentucky. It is Lincoln's re-creation of a conversation about his views on slavery that took place among himself, Hodges, and two other men in 1864.

20. The Society for the Propagation of the Gospel in Foreign Parts was a missionary organization founded in London in 1701. Its work in North America included the conversion of Native Americans and slaves. Literacy was encouraged to enable converts to study the Bible. As a result, the Society often worked to open schools for slaves, including the school Miller discusses here. In 1743 the Society's Charleston-area representative, Alexander Garden, opened a school for black children. Garden purchased two young slaves, Harry and Andrew, to serve as its schoolmasters. The school operated for approximately twenty years and taught at least sixty pupils. For further information, see Monaghan, *Learning to Read.*

21. Denmark Vesey purchased his freedom after winning a lottery in 1799. He became a leader in the African Methodist Episcopal Church in Charleston. In 1822, he and other Church leaders began planning a slave revolt, the goals of which were to seize Charleston's arsenals, set fire to the city, and kill numerous government leaders and other white men. The revolt was planned for July, but several of the plot's leaders were arrested in June after some of the slaves who knew of the plot revealed it to their masters. Vesey was executed on July 2, and other leaders, at least thirty-five total, were executed later that month. A series of laws further restricting the movements of Charleston slaves was subsequently passed.

22. The Brown Fellowship Society, founded in 1790, was a benevolent society of free black and racially mixed men in Charleston. It was initially founded as a response to the denial of burial privileges in the official cemeteries of St. Philip's

Episcopal Church, which had many black members. The group purchased its own land for burials and served other social and political purposes for its members. As Miller notes, the group did not provide services to slaves. The organization's name was changed to the Century Fellowship in 1893. Many of its early records are now housed at the College of Charleston.

23. Miller notes many prominent families who were known to have produced mixed-race children. Henry Grimké and his mulatto slave Nancy Weston produced three children: Francis, Archibald, and John Grimké. Archibald Grimké and Francis Grimké are featured in the first unit of this collection.

24. George D. Tillman, brother of Benjamin "Ben" Tillman, served in the U.S. House of Representatives from 1883 to 1893. He also participated in the 1895 South Carolina Constitutional Convention, as did his brother Ben. During the debates over the wording of the 1895 Constitution, there was disagreement as to the definition of "Negro." Some representatives suggested that possession of any Negro blood made one a Negro, to which George Tillman protested. His grounds were that several respectable families with which he was acquainted, families that had sent soldiers to the Confederate Army, had some small amount of Negro blood. He further argued that there was not a representative at the Convention who possessed 100 percent pure Caucasian blood. For further information, see Tindall, "Question of Race," 277–303.

25. Francis L. Cardozo was the son of a white businessman and a free woman of color. Born in Charleston in 1836, he was educated in Europe. He served as South Carolina secretary of state from 1868 to 1872 and as South Carolina state treasurer from 1872 to 1876. He was tried and convicted of conspiracy in 1877 but was pardoned by the governor of South Carolina in 1879. Much of the evidence at his trial is considered to have been questionable and perhaps fabricated.

26. Robert Brown Elliott represented South Carolina in the U.S. House of Representatives from 1871 to 1874. He was also a leader at the 1868 South Carolina Constitutional Convention, the associate editor of a freedman's newspaper, and a member of the South Carolina House of Representatives.

27. From 1873 to 1877 the University of South Carolina admitted African American students. Many white students left the school, and several faculty members resigned. At the end of Reconstruction, this policy was ended, as South Carolina embraced the idea of segregated schools.

28. In 1870 Richard T. Greener became the first African American graduate of Harvard. In 1873, he accepted a position at the University of South Carolina, where he became the school's first African American faculty member. When the school was closed by the South Carolina legislature in 1877, he accepted a position as dean of the School of Law at Howard University.

29. Miller here is referring to "Robert Smalls." Robert Smalls served five terms in the U.S. House of Representatives: 1875–79, 1882–83, and 1884–87. He became a Civil War hero when he piloted the *Planter*, a small Confederate ship, out of the South and turned it over to the Union navy. Thomas Miller served in the U.S. House of Representatives from 1890 to 1891. George W. Murray was the only black member of the Fifty-Third and Fifty-Fourth Congresses. He served in the U.S. House of Representatives from 1893 to 1895 and from 1896 to 1897.

30. Miller likely refers here to the May 1917 lynching of Ell Person in Memphis, Tennessee, and the July 1917 race riot in East St. Louis.

31. Suffragists or suffragettes were women involved in the early twentieth-century struggle to gain more rights for women, particularly the right to vote. One of the tactics they used to draw the notice of politicians was "heckling," which often included yelling embarrassing, disparaging, or distracting comments at public gatherings. Wilson was often an object of heckling because of his failure to take a stand in support of women's right to vote.

32. The "Black Cabinet" is an informal term referring to a shifting group of influential African American figures who either held minor government or bureaucratic positions or were somehow considered influential experts on race affairs. The first identified group gathered during the somewhat sympathetic Taft administration (1909–13) but had little influence in shaping Taft's policies on antisegregation or antilynching legislation. Under the Wilson administration the Black Cabinet was dissolved because Wilson (a Democrat) dismissed almost all black office holders as soon as he became president.

33. Senator Joseph Irwin France was a Republican from Maryland who served from 1917 to 1923.

34. Robert Augustus Toombs served the state of Georgia in the U.S. House of Representatives from 1845 to 1853 and in the U.S. Senate from 1853 to 1861. In 1861 he resigned to become the first secretary of state for the Confederate States.

35. Wilson served as Princeton University's president from 1902 to 1910.

36. Miller may be referring to a highly publicized incident in which a black man named Fred Alexander was dragged from a jail and burned alive by a mob in Leavenworth, Kansas, in 1901.

37. Miller is likely referring to a 1908 race riot in Springfield, Illinois, the site of President Lincoln's tomb.

38. Frank Little, an executive board member of the Industrial Workers of the World, argued that industrial workers should refuse to fight in World War I. He was lynched in Montana in August 1917.

39. This passage is a quote from Alexander Pope's 1734 poem "An Essay on Man."

40. The Germans were alleged to have perpetrated many atrocities upon the Belgians during the first months of World War I.

41. In September 1914, the Turkish ambassador to the United States, A. Rustem Bey, requested a leave of absence from his official capacity. While his withdrawal was officially voluntary, the *New York Times* reported that Bey had been informed by the secretary of state that statements he had made regarding lynchings in the American South and the possible use of water torture in the Philippines had "ended his usefulness at this capital." "Turkish Diplomat to Leave Country."

42. Matthew 7:5.

43. William Shakespeare, *Titus Andronicus*.

44. In 1885, King Leopold II of Belgium announced the formation of the Congo Free State, with himself as its head. In 1908 Belgium officially annexed what was in essence the king's private colony after reports of killings and atrocities carried out on a massive scale by Leopold's agents sparked international protests.

45. The Battle of Carrizal was a violent skirmish with the Mexican army in Carrizal, Mexico, during which several "buffalo soldiers," African American troops from the Colored Tenth Cavalry, were taken prisoner in June 1916.

46. The Battle of New Orleans was a series of battles that occurred in December 1814 and January 1815 as part of the War of 1812. The American troops were commanded by Andrew Jackson, who later became president of the United States. The First and Second Battalions of Free Men of Color, which included more than six hundred men, played an important role in the battle, which was a decisive American victory.

47. According to the National Archives, roughly 179,000 African American soldiers served in the U.S. Army and approximately 19,000 served in the U.S. Navy during the Civil War. U.S. National Archives, "Teaching with Documents."

48. The Battle of (or at) San Juan Hill occurred in Cuba during the Spanish-American War in 1898. Of the approximately fifteen thousand American troops present, about two thousand were African American. Much of the heaviest fighting was carried out by the African American troops.

49. After persistent efforts by the Central Committee of Negro College Men, an organization led by Kelly Miller and other supporters from Howard University, the secretary of war authorized the establishment of a training camp in Iowa for African American officers in May 1917. In October, more than six hundred African American men graduated and received their commissions.

50. Bishop Alexander Walters of the African Methodist Episcopal Zion Church, a prominent civil rights leader, corresponded with Wilson during his first presidential campaign. W. E. B. Du Bois discussed the correspondence and reproduced one of the letters in a 1973 journal article. Du Bois and Wilson, "My Impressions," 453–59.

51. On July 28, 1917, a group of approximately eight thousand African Americans silently marched down Fifth Avenue in New York City carrying banners protesting general issues, such as segregation, as well as more specific incidents, such as individual lynchings and riots. For more information, see "Negroes in Protest March."

Mary Jane McLeod Bethune
(1875–1955)

೪◖ EDUCATOR, CLUB WOMAN, CIVIL SERVANT, ACTIVIST

The Negro wants to break out into the free realm of democratic citizenship. We can only have one of two responses. Either we must let him out wholly and completely in keeping with our ideals, or we must mimic Hitler and shove him back.

During World War II, Mary McLeod Bethune joined a cadre of civil rights and advocacy organizations that supported the "Double V" campaign, spearheaded by the African American newspaper the *Pittsburgh Courier,* to gain a dual victory over fascism abroad and racism at home. By 1944, Bethune had gained national recognition as an activist and educator who consulted with American presidents, collaborated with club women, networked with philanthropists, and educated African American youth. When the Howard University historian Rayford W. Logan asked her to submit an essay for his influential collection of essays by black intellectuals, *What the Negro Wants,* Bethune responded: "certain unalienable rights," a bold declaration of the nation's failure to ensure African American citizens' rights to "life, liberty, and the pursuit of happiness."

Mary Jane McLeod was born on her family's farm near Mayesville in Sumter County, South Carolina, to Samuel and Patsy McIntosh McLeod, former slaves. She was the fifteenth of seventeen children, eight of whom had labored as slaves. Her parents had saved money from their earnings to purchase the five-acre farm they called "The Homestead," distinguishing them from many African American southerners who languished in the sharecropping or renter systems. As she grew up, Mary Jane was profoundly influenced by the stories of courage and survival that she heard from her mother, Patsy, and her grandmother Sophie, both of whom had maintained a strong sense of family despite forced separations from their husbands and children during the antebellum period. Biblical stories of courageous women such as Esther, the Jewish orphan who became the queen of Persia and saved her people from annihilation, affirmed her belief in powerful women who wielded enormous influence as their people's intercessors and saviors.

Mary Jane gained basic literacy skills in Mayesville's segregated one-room schoolhouse, the Trinity Presbyterian Mission School, established by the Presbyterian Board of Missions. At her mother's insistence, she shared what she learned with neighborhood children who were unable to attend school in weekly Sunday gatherings. Her African American teacher Emma J. Wilson modeled how to be an effective instructor, administrator, and community leader as she garnered the support of parents, parishioners, county officials, and philanthropists to ensure the success of the Trinity School. A scholarship provided by Mary Crissman, a white Quaker educator from Denver, Colorado, enabled Mary Jane to continue her education at Scotia Seminary (now Barber-Scotia College) in Concord, North Carolina. There, she completed the Normal and Scientific Course in 1894. Scotia offered Mary Jane her first experience in an integrated setting and introduced her to benevolent white northern teacher-reformers who were committed to racial uplift. To fulfill her dream of entering mission service, Mary Jane enrolled in the Dwight Moody Institute for Home and Foreign Missions in Chicago, with the sponsorship of a second scholarship from Crissman, and was introduced to the Social Gospel Movement.[1] When she completed the program, in 1895, however, she discovered that there were no placements available for African American missionary teachers.

Undaunted in her desire to become an educator, Mary Jane returned to the South to teach African American children. In 1896 she moved back to Mayesville and worked with her former teacher at the mission school, which had been renamed the Mayesville Institute, before joining the staff at the Haines Normal and Industrial School, founded in Augusta, Georgia, by an African American educator and club woman, Lucy Craft Laney, in 1883. As Mary Jane gained additional insights on institution building and community activism from Laney, she began to envision the establishment of a school for African American girls. After a year at Haines, she transferred to the Kendall Institute in Sumter, South Carolina, where she met and married Albertus Bethune in 1898. A year later the couple relocated to Savannah and welcomed the birth of a son, Albert McLeod Bethune. The Bethune family then resettled in Palatka, Florida, where Mary McLeod Bethune operated a mission school for approximately five years.

Upon learning of a critical need for a school for the children of African American railroad workers in Daytona, Florida, Mary McLeod Bethune convinced her husband to move once again. In 1904 she opened the Daytona Educational and Industrial Institute for Negro Girls with five students in a four-room cottage that she rented for $11 per month. While her husband's varied business ventures languished, Mary McLeod Bethune's school thrived. Around 1908 Albertus Bethune returned to South Carolina, where he died of tuberculosis ten years later. Mary McLeod Bethune, however, remained in Florida and drew on her experiences with her former educators Wilson and Laney to gain the support of white philanthropists, notably James M. Gamble of Procter & Gamble and Thomas H. White of the White Sewing Machine Company. In 1923 she merged the Daytona Institute with the Cookman Institute, a school for African American boys in Jacksonville, Florida. By 1941, the coed high school had attained junior college status, become affiliated with the Methodist denomination, adopted a new name (Bethune-Cookman College), and gained approval from the Florida Board of Education to offer bachelor's degrees in the liberal arts and in education.

Mary McLeod Bethune's unique status as an African American female college president in early twentieth-century America catapulted her to the national stage as both a role model and a race woman. She affiliated herself with black club women and civil rights activists to extend her influence. Bethune served from 1917 to 1925 as president of the Florida Federation of Colored Women's Clubs,[2] an affiliate of the National Association of Colored Women (NACW), and was elected to a four-year term as national president of the NACW in 1924. By the mid-1930s, Bethune had streamlined and strengthened black club women's initiatives through the establishment of the National Council of Negro Women (NCNW), an association of independent black women's organizations that addressed national and global issues affecting women, families, and communities. Within three years, the NCNW convened the White House Conference on Governmental Cooperation in the Approach to the Problems of Negro Women and Children to support black women's participation in democracy. In 1936 Bethune was elected president of the Association for the Study of Negro Life and History, the influential black heritage society founded by the historian Carter G. Woodson. At the end of her four-year term, Bethune became vice president of the National Association for the Advancement of Colored People (NAACP).

Bethune also earned recognition and opportunities from U.S. government officials for her work as an educator and club woman. In 1925, during the Sixth Quinquennial Convention of the International Council of Women, she met President Calvin Coolidge at a White House reception. Four years later, President Herbert Hoover appointed her to the National Commission on Child Welfare and the Commission on Home Building and Home Ownership. In 1936 she accepted an appointment as a specialist in the National Youth Administration, which enabled her to ensure that New Deal grants supported a variety of education and employment initiatives for African Americans. She was also influential in establishing the Federal Council on Negro Affairs during the Roosevelt administration to press the administration for the inclusion of African Americans in federal positions and to keep the community's issues at the forefront of the national agenda.[3] During World War II, Bethune lobbied the Roosevelt administration for the enlistment of African American aviators, which led to the establishment of the flight training program at Tuskegee Institute. President Truman later appointed her to the Committee of Twelve for National Defense.

Bethune extended the scope of her influence by engaging with the public through her speeches and writings in delineating her positions on education, civil rights, politics, and women's rights. She presented lectures to a variety of organizations, including the World Assembly for Moral Re-Armament in Switzerland (1954)[4] and testified before the Senate Banking and Currency Committee on S. 1592 (1945), a bill that established federal housing regulations. She also corresponded with U.S. presidents, state legislators, and social service administrators; published letters to the editors of national periodicals such as the *New York Times;* and wrote essays and editorials for *Ebony,* the *Chicago Defender,* and the *Pittsburgh Courier.* In the essay presented here, "Certain Unalienable Rights" from Logan's anthology *What the Negro Wants* (Chapel Hill: University of North Carolina Press, 1996), Bethune equates the riots that broke out in black urban centers after the shooting of African American World War II veterans with the Boston Tea Party, staged by colonists to protest taxation without representation. In so doing, she validates both events as legitimate responses to persistent violations of the participants' "unalienable rights." Within the context of World War II, Bethune draws parallels between these struggles and the liberation efforts waged by various peoples throughout history to argue for the right of individuals to resist repression with violence, if necessary, to secure liberty. To mitigate the violence, however, Bethune recommends comprehensive directives for white and black Americans to follow in ensuring African Americans' enjoyment of the rights and privileges of citizenship. In keeping with her lifelong commitment to women's central role in racial advancement, Bethune ends the piece by offering African American women a three-point strategy for meeting the challenge of leading the civil rights struggle while their men are on the battlefield: draw on the legacy of their foremothers who survived slavery and the setbacks of the post-Reconstruction era, globalize their efforts through collaborations with women's movements in other nations, and exemplify Christian virtues in efforts to build a democratic society at home.

In 1942 Bethune resigned as president of Bethune-Cookman College, but she remained active in club work, politics, and civil rights for the next decade. Various organizations and institutions lauded her contributions to education reform and race relations. Bethune received eight honorary degrees in education and the humanities. The NAACP honored her with its Spingarn Medal in 1935 for the highest achievement by an African American during the previous year. Foreign governments also recognized her accomplishments. The Republic of Haiti invited her to visit in 1949 and awarded her the Order of Honor and Merit, its most prestigious award. Later that year, President Harry Truman joined other politicians and activists in celebrating her contributions to the NCNW. In 1952 she received the Order of the Star of Africa while visiting Liberia as the U.S. representative to the second inauguration of Liberian president William V. S. Tubman.

Mary McLeod Bethune died of a heart attack in May 1955 and is buried on the Bethune-Cookman College grounds.

⫷ "Certain Unalienable Rights"

It is a quiet night in December, 1773. A British merchant ship rides easily at anchor in Boston Harbor. Suddenly, some row boats move out from the shore. Dark stealthy figures in the boats appear to be Indians in buckskin jackets with feathers in their hair; but as they reach the ship, clamber aboard, climb down into the hold and carry out boxes of the cargo, the muffled voices speak English words. Their voices grow more excited and determined as they open the boxes and dump the King's tea into the ocean. The Boston Tea Party is in full swing. Resentment has reached flood tide. "Taxation without representation is tyranny!" The spark of the American Revolution has caught flame and the principle of the "consent of the governed" has been established by a gang disguised as Indians who take the law into their own hands. In this action a small and independent people struck out against restrictions and tyranny and oppression and gave initial expression to the ideal of a nation "that all men are created equal, that they are endowed by their Creator with certain unalienable rights."

It is a Sunday night in Harlem in the year of our Lord 1943. Along the quiet streets dimmed out against the possibility of an Axis air attack, colored Americans move to and fro or sit and talk and laugh. Suddenly electric rumor travels from mouth to ear: "A black soldier has been shot by a white policeman and has died in the arms of his mother." No one stops to ask how or why or if it be true. Crowds begin to gather. There is a rumbling of anger and resentment impelled by all the anger and all the resentment of all colored

Americans in all the black ghettos in all the cities in America—the resentment against the mistreatment of Negroes in uniform, against restriction and oppression and discrimination breaks loose. Crowds of young people in blind fury strike out against the only symbols of this oppression which are near at hand. Rocks hurtle, windows crash, stores are broken open. Merchants' goods are tumbled into the streets, destroyed or stolen. Police are openly challenged and attacked. There are killings and bodily injury. For hours a veritable reign of terror runs through the streets. All efforts at restraint are of no avail. Finally the blind rage blows itself out.[5]

Some are saying that a band of hoodlums have challenged law and order to burn to pillage and rob. Others look about them to remember riots in Detroit and Los Angeles and Beaumont.[6] They will look further and recall cities laid in ruins by a global war in which the forces of tyranny and oppression and race supremacy attempt to subdue and restrain all the freedom of the world. They are thinking deeply to realize that there is a ferment aloose among the oppressed little people everywhere, a "groping of the long inert masses." They will see depressed and repressed masses all over the world swelling to the breaking point against the walls of ghettos, against economic, social and political restrictions; they will find them breaking open the King's boxes and throwing the tea into the ocean and storming the Bastille stirred by the clarion call of the Four Freedoms. They are striking back against all that the Axis stands for. They are rising to achieve the ideals "that all men are created equal, that they are endowed by their Creator with certain unalienable Rights, that among these are Life, Liberty and the pursuit of Happiness." With the crash of the guns and the whir of the planes in their ears, led by the fighting voices of a Churchill and a Franklin Roosevelt, a Chiang Kai-shek[7] and a Stalin, they are realizing that "Governments are instituted among men" to achieve these aims and that these governments derive "their just power from the consent of the governed." They are a part of a people's war. The little people want "out." Just as the Colonists at the Boston Tea Party wanted "out" from under tyranny and oppression and taxation without representation, the Chinese want "out," the Indians want "out," and colored Americans want "out."

Throughout America today many people are alarmed and bewildered by the manifestation of this world ferment among the Negro masses. We say we are living in a period of "racial tension." They seem surprised that the Negro should be a part of this world movement. Really, all true Americans should not be surprised by this logical climax of American education. For several generations colored Americans have been brought up on the Boston Tea Party and the Declaration of Independence; on the principle of equality of opportunity, the possession of inalienable rights, the integrity and sanctity of the human personality. Along with other good Americans the Negro has been prepared to take his part in the fight against an enemy that threatens all these basic American principles. He is fighting now on land and sea and in the air to beat back these forces of oppression and tyranny and discrimination. Why, then, should we be surprised when at home as well as abroad he fights back against these same forces?

One who would really understand this racial tension which has broken out into actual conflict in riots as in Harlem, Detroit, and Los Angeles, must look to the roots and not be confused by the branches and the leaves. The tension rises out of the growing internal pressure of Negro masses to break through the wall of restriction which restrains them from full American citizenship. This mounting power is met by the unwillingness of white America to allow any approachable breach in this wall.

The hard core of internal pressure among the Negro masses in the United States today is undoubtedly their resentment over the mistreatment of colored men in the armed forces. The Negro faces restrictions in entering certain branches of the service, resistance to being assigned posts according to his ability; and above all there is the failure of the Army and his government to protect him in the uniform of his country from actual assault by civilians.

Letters from the men in Army camps have streamed into the homes of their parents and friends everywhere, telling of this mistreatment by officers, military police and civilians, of their difficulties in getting accommodations on trains and buses, of numerous incidents of long, tiresome journeys without meals and other concrete evidences of the failure of their government to protect and provide for its men, even when they are preparing to fight in defense of the principles of that government.

They need no agitation by newspaper accounts or the stimulation of so-called leaders. These things are the intimate experiences of the masses themselves. They know them and feel them intensely and resent them bitterly.

You must add to these deep-seated feelings a whole series of repercussions of the frustrated efforts of Negroes to find a place in war production: the absolute denial of employment in many cases, or employment far below the level of their skills, numerous restrictions in their efforts to get training, resistance of labor unions to the improving and utilization of their skills on the job. Pile on to these their inability to get adequate housing even for those employed in war work, and often, where houses are available, restrictions to segregated units in temporary war housing. At the same time they see around them unlimited opportunities offered to other groups to serve their country in the armed forces, to be employed at well-paying jobs, to get good housing financed by private concerns and FHA funds.[8]

Even those observers who have some understanding of the Negro's desire to break through all these restrictions will charge it to superficial causes, such as the agitation of the Negro press and leaders; or they counsel the Negro to "go slow." It is as though they admit that the patient is sick with fever and diagnosis reveals that he needs twelve grains of quinine, but they decide that because he is a Negro they had better give him only six. They admit that he is hungry and needs to be fed, but because he is a Negro they suggest that a half meal will suffice. This approach, of course, is a historical hang-over. It is a product of the half-hearted and timorous manner in which we have traditionally faced the Negro problem in America.

In order to maintain slavery, it was necessary to isolate black men from every possible manifestation of our culture. It was necessary to teach that they were inferior beings who could not profit from that culture. After the slave was freed, every effort has persisted to maintain "white supremacy" and wall the Negro in from every opportunity to challenge this concocted "supremacy." Many Americans said the Negro could not learn and they "proved" it by restricting his educational opportunities. When he surmounted these obstacles and achieved a measure of training, they said he did not know how to use it and proved it by restricting his employment opportunities. When it was necessary to employ him, they saw to it that he was confined to laborious and poorly-paid jobs. After they had made every effort to guarantee that his economic, social and cultural levels were low, they attributed his status to his race. Therefore, as he moved North and West after Reconstruction and during the Industrial Revolution, they saw to it that he was confined to living in veritable ghettos with covenants that were as hard and resistant as the walls of the ghettos of Warsaw.

They met every effort on his part to break through these barriers with stern resistance that would brook no challenge to our concept of white supremacy. Although they guaranteed him full citizenship under the Constitution and its Amendments, they saw to it that he was largely disfranchised and had little part in our hard won ideal of "the consent of the governed." In the midst of this anachronism, they increasingly educated his children in the American way of life—in its ideals of equality of all men before the law, and opportunities for the fullest possible development of the individual.

As this concept took hold among the Negro masses, it has evidenced itself through the years in a slow, growing, relentless pressure against every restriction which denied them their full citizenship. This pressure, intensified by those of other races who really believed in democracy, began to make a break through the walls here and there. It was given wide-spread impetus by the objectives of the New Deal with its emphasis on the rise of the forgotten man. With the coming of the Second World War, all the Negro's desires were given voice and support by the world leaders who fought back against Hitler and all he symbolizes. His efforts to break through have responded to Gandhi and Chiang Kai-shek, to Churchill and Franklin Roosevelt.

The radios and the press of the world have drummed into his ears the Four Freedoms, which would lead him to think that the world accepts as legitimate his claims as well as those of oppressed peoples all over the world. His drive for status has now swept past even most of his leaders, and has become imbedded in mass-consciousness which is pushing out of the way all the false prophets, be they white or black—or, be they at home or abroad.

The Negro wants to break out into the free realm of democratic citizenship. We can have only one of two responses. Either we must let him out wholly and completely in keeping with our ideals, or we must mimic Hitler and shove him back.

What, then, does the Negro want? His answer is very simple. He wants only what all other Americans want. He wants opportunity to make real what the Declaration of Independence and the Constitution and Bill of Rights say; what the four freedoms establish. While he knows these ideals are open to no man completely he wants only his equal chance to attain them. The Negro today wants specifically:

1. *Government leadership in building favorable public opinion.* Led by the President himself, the federal government should initiate a sound program carried out through appropriate federal agencies dedicated to indicate the importance of race in the war and post-war period. The cost of discrimination and segregation to a nation at war and the implications of American racial attitudes for our relationships with the other United Nations and their people should be delineated. Racial myths and superstitions should be exploded. The cooperation of the newspapers, the radio and the screen should be sought to replace caricature and slander with realistic interpretations of sound racial relationships.

2. *The victory of democracy over dictatorship.* Under democracy the Negro has the opportunity to work for an improvement in his status through the intelligent use of his vote, the creation of a more favorable public opinion, and the development of his native abilities. The ideals of democracy and Christianity work for equality. These ideals the dictatorships disavow. Experience has taught only too well the implications for him and all Americans of a Nazi victory.

3. *Democracy in the armed forces.* He wants a chance to serve his country in all branches of the armed forces to his full capacity. He sees clearly the fallacy of fostering discrimination and segregation in the very forces that are fighting against discrimination and segregation all over the world. He believes that the government should fully protect the persons and the rights of all who wear the uniform of its armed forces.

4. *The protection of his civil rights and an end to lynching.* He wants full protection of the rights guaranteed all Americans by the Constitution; equality before the law, the right to jury trial and service, the eradication

of lynching. Demanding these rights for himself, he will not be misled into any anti-foreign, Red-baiting, or anti-Semitic crusade to deny these rights to others. Appalled by the conditions prevailing in Washington, he joins in demanding the ballot for the District of Columbia and the protection of his rights now denied him within the shadow of the Capitol.

5. *The free ballot.* He wants the abolition of the poll tax[9] and of the "white primary";[10] he wants universal adult suffrage. He means to use it to vote out all the advocates of racism and vote in those whose records show that they actually practice democracy.

6. *Equal access to employment opportunities.* He wants the chance to work and advance in any job for which he has the training and capacity. To this end he wants equal access to training opportunities. In all public programs, federal, state and local, he wants policy-making and administrative posts as well as rank and file jobs without racial discrimination. He wants a fair share of jobs under Civil Service.

7. *Extension of federal programs in public housing, health, social security, education and relief under federal control.* Low income and local prejudice often deprive him of these basic social services. Private enterprise or local government units cannot or will not provide them. For efficiency and equity in administration of these programs, the Negro looks to the federal government until such time as he has gained the full and free use of the ballot in all states.

8. *Elimination of racial barriers in labor unions.* He demands the right of admission on equal terms to the unions having jurisdiction over the crafts or industries in which he is employed. He urges that job control on public works be denied to any union practicing discrimination.

9. *Realistic interracial co-operation.* He realizes the complete interdependence of underprivileged white people and Negroes, North and South—laborers and sharecroppers alike. He knows that they stay in the gutter together or rise to security together; that the hope of democracy lies in their co-operative effort to make their government responsive to their needs; that national unity demands their sharing together more fully in the benefits of freedom—not "one as the hand and separate as the fingers," but one as the clasped hands of friendly cooperation.[11]

Here, then, is a program for racial advancement and national unity. It adds up to the sum of the rights, privileges and responsibilities of full American citizenship. This is all that the Negro asks. He will not willingly accept less. As long as America offers less, she will be that much less a democracy. The whole way is the American way.

What can the Negro do himself to help get what he wants?

1. In the first place, he should accept his responsibility for a full part of the job of seeing to it that whites and Negroes alike understand the current

intensity of the Negro's fight for status as a part of a world people's movement. As individuals and as members of organizations, we must continue to use every channel open to affect public opinion, to get over to all Americans the real nature of this struggle. Those of us who accept some measure of responsibility for leadership, must realize that in such people's movements, the real leadership comes up out of the people themselves. All others who would give direction to such a movement must identify themselves with it, become a part of it, and interpret it to others. We must make plain to America that we have reached a critical stage in the assimilation of colored people.

We have large and growing numbers of young and older Negroes who have achieved by discipline and training a measure of culture which qualifies them for advanced status in our American life. To deny this opportunity creates on the one hand frustration with its attendant disintegration, and, on the other, deprives American civilization of the potential fruits of some thirteen millions of its sons and daughters.

Through our personal and group contacts with other racial groups, we must increasingly win their understanding and support. Only in this way can the swelling force among minority racial groups be channeled into creative progress rather than exploded into riots and conflicts, or dissipated in hoodlumism. While we seek on the one side to "educate" white America, we must continue relentlessly to make plain to ourselves and our associates the increased responsibility that goes with increased rights and privileges. Our fight for Fair Employment Practices legislation must go hand and hand with "Hold Your Job" campaigns;[12] our fight for anti-poll tax legislation must be supported equally by efforts of Negroes themselves to exercise fully and intelligently the right of franchise where they have it.

2. We must challenge, skillfully but resolutely, every sign of restriction or limitation on our full American citizenship. When I say challenge, I mean we must seek every opportunity to place the burden of responsibility upon him who denies it. If we simply accept and acquiesce in the face of discrimination, we accept the responsibility ourselves and allow those responsible to salve their conscience by believing that they have our acceptance and concurrence. We should, therefore, protest openly everything in the newspapers, on the radio, in the movies that smacks of discrimination or slander. We must take the seat that our ticket calls for and place upon the proprietor the responsibility of denying it to us.

We must challenge everywhere the principle and practice of enforced racial segregation. We must make it clear that where groups and individuals are striving for social and economic status, group isolation one from the other allows the rise of misunderstanding and suspicion, providing rich soil for the seeds of antagonism and conflict. Recently in the city of Detroit [during a racial upheaval], there was no rioting in the neighborhoods where whites and Negroes lived as neighbors, and there was no conflict in the plants where they worked side by side on the assembly-lines. Whenever one has the price or can fill the requirements for any privilege which is open to the entire public, that privilege must not be restricted on account of race.

Our appeal must be made to the attributes of which the Anglo-Saxon is so proud—his respect for law and justice, his love of fair-play and true sportsmanship.

3. We must understand that the great masses of our people are farmers and workers, and that their hopes for improvement in a large measure lie in association with organizations whose purpose is to improve their condition. This means membership in and support of labor and farmer unions. Within these organizations it means continuous efforts with our allies of all racial groups to remove all barriers which operate in the end to divide workers and defeat all of their purposes. The voice of organized labor has become one of the most powerful in the land and unless we have a part in that voice our people will not be heard.

4. We must take a full part in the political life of our community, state and nation. We must learn increasingly about political organization and techniques. We must prepare for and fight for places on the local, state, and national committees of our political parties. This is a representative government and the only way that our representatives can reflect our desires is for us to register and vote. In a large measure the whole of our national life is directed by the legislation and other activities of our governmental units. The only way to affect their action and to guarantee their democratic nature is to have a full hand in electing individuals who represent us. The national election of 1944[13] represents one of the most crucial in the life of this nation and of the world. The Congressional representatives that are elected to office will have a large hand in the type of peace treaty to be adopted and the entire nature of our post-war domestic economy. All of our organizations and individuals who supply leadership must fully acquaint our people with the requirements of registering and voting, see to it that they are cognizant of the issues involved and get out to register and vote.

Negro women and their organizations have a tremendous responsibility and opportunity to offer leadership and support to this struggle of the racial group to attain improved cultural status in America. We have always done a full part of this job. Now, with large numbers of our men in the armed forces and with considerable numbers of new people who have migrated into our communities to take their part in war production, we have a bigger job and a greater opportunity than ever. Our women know too well the disintegrating effect upon our family life of our low economic status. Discrimination and restriction have too often meant to us broken homes and the delinquency of our children. We have seen our dreams frustrated and our hopes broken. We have risen, however, out of our despair to help our men climb up the next rung of the ladder. We see now more than a glimmer of light on the horizon of a new hope. We feel behind us the surge of all women of China and India and of Africa who see the same light and look to us to march with them. We will reach out our hands to all women who struggle forward—white, black, brown, yellow—all. If we have the courage and tenacity of our forebears, who stood firmly like a rock against the lashings of slavery and the disruption of Reconstruction, we shall find a way to do for our day what they did for theirs. Above all we Negro women of all levels and classes must realize that this forward movement is a march of the masses and that all of us must go forward with it or be pushed aside by it. We will do our part. In order for us to have peace and justice and democracy for all, may I urge that we follow the example of the great humanitarian—Jesus Christ—in exemplifying in our lives both by word and action the fatherhood of God and the brotherhood of man?

NOTES

1. The Social Gospel Movement, founded by Washington Gladden in the late 1800s and initially known as Applied Christianity, grew out of Protestants' desire to Christianize the world by working among those in need rather than retreating from the world as advocates of reform and social justice. Settlement Movement leaders such as Jane Addams adopted this philosophy in the development of urban centers that addressed both the spiritual and the temporal needs of the poor and immigrants. Dorrien, *Social Ethics*, 60–61.

2. The Florida Federation of Colored Women's Clubs was the umbrella organization for more than 140 women's clubs that provided social services to their communities and were influential in civic affairs, particularly in matters that affected women such as suffrage rights.

3. Roosevelt's Federal Council on Negro Affairs was a small group of African Americans organized by Mary McLeod Bethune that advised President Roosevelt on policies concerning African Americans. This "Black Cabinet," as it was often designated, was largely responsible for shifting the African American vote to the Democratic Party.

4. Founded by Frank Buchman in 1938, the Moral Re-Armament (MRA) movement promoted international peace primarily through the hosting of large conferences. These conferences sought to end war by resolving tensions among warring nations.

5. On August 1, 1943, a white New York police officer shot and wounded Robert Bandy, an African American soldier, who objected to the officer's treatment of an African American woman who was being arresting for disturbing the peace. When word spread that Bandy had been killed, rioting and looting erupted in Harlem. Mayor Fiorello H. La Guardia mobilized 16,500 police and state guardsmen and 1,500 volunteers to quell the violence.

6. In the early 1940s a series of race riots broke out between the segregated black and white populations of cities across the nation. The exact causes of these riots were manifold, but they were sparked mainly by the increasing dissatisfaction of the African American population with its second-class status in American society and in the military during World War II.

7. Chiang Kai-shek (1887–1975) was a Chinese political leader who rose to power through military force in the 1930s and 1940s. His dictatorial nature and strong opposition to both communism and democracy made for a tenuous and complex relationship with the United States.

8. The Federal Housing Administration (FHA) was created through the National Housing Act of 1934 to promote affordable interest rates by insuring mortgage loans made by banks and lenders.

9. Payment of a poll tax was required by some states as a qualification for voting.

10. In the 1920s, white southerners introduced the white primary to disenfranchise African Americans by prohibiting their membership in the Democratic Party, which dominated elections in the South until the 1960s.

11. Likely an allusion to Booker T. Washington's 1895 Speech at the Atlanta Cotton Exposition.

12. In 1943, the National Council of Negro Women introduced the "Can You Hold Your Job" campaign to assist working-class African American women in cultivating traits that would enable them to exhibit respectability and maintain employment, namely being "clean, courteous, punctual, and affable." Shockley, *"We, Too, Are Americans,"* 61.

13. In November 1944, Franklin D. Roosevelt was elected to his fourth term as president; however, he died of a massive stroke about four months after his inauguration.

J. Max Barber,
Ill.

J. Max Barber
(1878–1949)

There is no peace in Atlanta.

The journalist Jesse Max Barber wrote those words not about the 1906 Atlanta race riot but about its aftermath in the hearts and minds of the city's black population. He saw what he called the "Atlanta Tragedy" as allowing a curtain to be lifted on "a veritable devil's caldron" of what can only be understood as social terrorism. Barber was run out of Atlanta by a cabal of white citizens for his public coverage of the riots, yet he was not hailed by the African American press or the power elites as a hero. Rather, by openly holding the white elites of Atlanta responsible for the riots, he ran afoul of enemies within the African American community, enemies who were to destroy his promising career as both journalist and race leader for the twentieth century. Barber rallied from the disappointments of a crushed career and was able to serve his causes in years to come, but the long silence imposed on him by the crush of the Tuskegee Machine ensured that his crusading work is little known today.[1]

At the turn of the twentieth century, however, Barber was a rising young voice of considerable influence. As an activist in black politics he became a close associate of W. E. B. Du Bois and worked with him as one of the founding members of the radical Niagara Movement in opposing the dominant policies of Booker T. Washington. Through his position as the managing editor and lead writer for the *Voice of the Negro* (January 1904–October 1907), one of the largest black periodicals in the country at the time and the first black-edited southern magazine, he helped fundamentally reframe and expand the possibilities for the expression of public thought and opinions about race at a time when there was considerable risk involved in such an undertaking.

J. Max Barber might also be classified as one of the most notable casualties of the ideological battles over black leadership waged by Washington against those who challenged his role as black spokesman for the nation. After the Atlanta race riots of 1906, the progressive, Atlanta-based *Voice of the Negro* could no longer function.[2] Booker T. Washington, who had become increasingly frustrated by Barber's radical stances, then used his long arm of influence to ensure that J. Max Barber would never again have such an influential platform from which to rail against white oppression, much less against Washingtonian conciliatory policies. In his later years, J. Max Barber supported himself as a dentist and remained sporadically active in politics. He served as president of both the Negro Professional Club of Philadelphia and the St. Marks Building and Loan Company and was elected the first black president of the Philadelphia chapter of the NAACP. He was never to resume his literary and journalistic career. This was a great loss to the profession for, as demonstrated by his compelling opinion pieces, Barber deployed his wit and incisive language with relentless passion and conviction to articulate the need of Americans, both black and white, to immediately embrace social change.

Barber, the child of ex-slave parents, was born in 1878 in Blackstock, South Carolina. He attended Friendship Normal and Industrial Institute at Rock Hill, Benedict College in Columbia, and Virginia Union University in Richmond, Virginia, graduating from Virginia Union in 1903.[3] He then moved to Atlanta and, upon the strength of having done editing work for the promotions department at Virginia Union, he was hired by the Illinois-based Hertel, Jenkins, and Company publishing house to help establish a new southern magazine, the *Voice of the Negro.* He was quickly promoted to managing editor and despite his youth managed to oversee its impressive growth and influence; by 1906 the magazine reportedly had a circulation of between twelve and fifteen thousand, a figure rivaled only by the circulation of the decidedly less radical *Colored American Magazine* (1900–1909). As the historian Walter Daniel describes it, for that period the *Voice of the Negro* was "the most prestigious black periodical in the nation."[4]

From early on, Booker T. Washington was concerned with the potential for the magazine to showcase troubling dissent from his own agenda of conciliatory and accommodationist policies for black America. Thus, although the magazine was independently funded, Emmett J. Scott, Booker T. Washington's secretary and confidant, agreed to serve as a part-time salaried associate editor who would help keep "an influence with this magazine that shall keep it working out way or at least not against us."[5] While Barber and his overseeing editor, William Bowen, officially stated that the *Voice of the Negro* was to be open to opinions from across the spectrum, Barber himself became increasingly sympathetic to Washington's critics and antagonistic toward Washington's protégé, Scott. With Bowen offering Barber much license and little oversight, the periodical quickly evolved as Barber's own. By July 1905, when Barber traveled to Canada for the meeting of twenty-nine black intellectuals and activists at which the Niagara Movement was formed as a counter to what they understood as the conciliatory racial policies of Washington, he irrevocably established himself as an enemy of Washington—a label that was to haunt and hound him for many decades. The *Voice of The Negro* thereafter became the unofficial mouthpiece for the short-lived but influential Niagara Movement.

Although Washington was an early contributor to the magazine before it swung irrevocably to the left, the *Voice of the Negro* also deserves note for highlighting new generations of black thinkers, including Kelly Miller, Mary Church Terrell, Archibald Grimké, William Pickens, and, of course, W. E. B. Du Bois, all of whom got important exposure in columns edited by Barber.[6] Barber's defiant and yet sober analysis of Atlanta's race riot represents the defining moment of his career; his account of what happened—the role of the press, the role of the white community—and even of his own actions remains one of the most compelling testimonies to the potent combination of calculated and random violence that marked one of the darkest moments in America's history.

In the first selection, we see Barber's celebration of a recently erected monument to Narciso G. Gonzales in Columbia, South Carolina, in 1905. The essay demonstrates how closely Barber followed South Carolina politics both black and white, even when working in Atlanta. It illustrates, too, his understanding of how the role of a free press was intrinsically connected to the future of the nation—an understanding that foreshadowed later turning points in his life.

The 1903 murder of Gonzales, a founder of the *State* newspaper in Columbia who came from a prominent Cuban American family that had married into the elite South Carolina planter class, attracted national attention not simply because of the victim's prominence or because his murder took place directly across the street from the State House in front of many witnesses. The murder also attracted national attention because the shooter was James Tillman, the nephew of "Pitchfork Ben" Tillman. Gonzales had long crusaded in the *State* against the career and political influence of both generations of Tillmans; his shooting thus resulted as much from simmering state political battles as from personal animosity.

When James Tillman was acquitted of murder on grounds of just cause and self-defense, the press outrage was especially huge. Many newspaper men across the nation understood the acquittal as tantamount to creating an open season on the press. It is thus not surprising that Barber, along with other journalists of the time, followed the case with special interest. The monument, however, put up only two years after Gonzales's death on a prominent site at the intersection of Senate and Sumter Streets close to the State House and, as rumor had it, intentionally placed where James Tillman would have to walk by it every day, heralded what Barber saw as a "triumph of righteousness in the Palmetto State." His account of the Gonzales monument in the *Voice of the Negro* offers insight into the less frenzied and impassioned voice of Barber and demonstrates how the tumultuous political scene in the Carolinas remained of particular significance to the national African American reading public.

In the second featured reading, Barber gives his version of what happened in the Atlanta riots in a powerful November 1906 article from the *Voice* (as the *Voice of the Negro* was renamed when Barber briefly relocated its editorial offices to Chicago in late 1906). Fanned by newspaper reports of alleged assaults of white women, presumably by black men, mobs of whites began rioting across Atlanta, destroying property, wounding unknown numbers of people, and killing perhaps twenty-four black people and two white people. What makes Barber's analysis of the Atlanta riot particularly compelling is his discussion of the role of the white press, which he argues deliberately manipulated its coverage in order to foment what he saw as essentially a war on his race.

Barber's essay was written, it must be noted, after he was run out of town for having wired a letter (signed "A Colored Citizen") to the *New York World* in which he accused John Temple Graves, the white editor of the *Atlanta Georgian,* of a "pageantry of high-sounding phrases" in which he sought "an excuse for a mob which was as lawless and godless as any savages that ever shocked civilization." Barber laid the blame for the riots on "sensationalist newspapers and unscrupulous politicians" and also reported that "emissaries" of Hoke Smith, the governor-elect of Georgia, had sent white men in blackface to knock down white women in order to justify further disenfranchisement and oppression of black citizens. A telegraph operator leaked Barber's name to investigators and the day after it was published representatives of the Board of Police Commissioners visited Barber and threatened him with arrest and sentencing to a chain gang if he didn't leave town immediately. Fearing arrest or worse, Barber fled—a decision that was used against him by Washington and others who later accused him of abandoning his Atlanta brethren in a fit of cowardice.[7] When Barber wrote his account of the riots immediately after arriving in Chicago in October 1906 (an account upheld in the main by historians of the event), he was freshly bitter and defensive in the face of these accusations of desertion. His somewhat frantic tone does not belie, however, some of the most vivid and influential reporting of one of the most horrifying race riots in the nation—news reporting that many scholars agree helped discredit Washington's accommodationist tactics and instead strengthened support for civil rights that would advance more aggressive approaches to achieving racial justice for the twentieth century.

?⊷ "The Monument to Gonzales"

The unveiling of a monument to N. G. Gonzales on December 12th at Columbia, S.C., is worthy of notice by the entire country.[8] It at once recalls the history and character of the man to whom this monument was reared. The character of a people may be judged by the monuments it builds to perpetuate the memory of its dead. One of the finest sources of ancient history is the monuments of the ancient people. Judged by the man South Carolina honored last month, there is still hope for the triumph of righteousness in the Palmetto State. Gonzales died at the hands of an assassin because he had courage enough to stand up for the truth. It will be recalled that Gonzales was shot by James Tilman [sic],[9] nephew of United States Senator Tilman,[10] in January 1903. Tilman had been a gubernatorial candidate in 1902. Mr. Gonzales, through his paper, The State,[11] had been largely instrumental in defeating Tilman and electing Heyward.[12] Although the Negro had been disfranchised in South Carolina eight years prior to this campaign, and in spite of the fact that Ben Tilman had argued that the disfranchisement of the Negro would settle the race problem, his nephew ran on an anti-Negro platform. The main plank in his platform was the one calling for a division of the school taxes between the races as they were paid in by the races. A fire-eater of the pronounced type, noted for his harsh, out-of-taste, uncharitable and uncouth language, he went up and down the State stirring up race antagonisms.[13] The spirit of justice stirred in the breast of Gonzales. It was then that his pen did work for which brave men must always give thanks. Hardly a day passed but that he did not expose some of Tilman's fallacies in the editorial columns of his paper. He appealed to the white people's sense of justice. He reminded them of their promise to treat the Negro justly if the North would keep hands off. He reminded them of their arguments during the campaign to disfranchise the Negro. It was then that the claim was made that to disfranchise the Negro would settle the race question in South Carolina. He made the argument that ignorance was dangerous, whether in the white man or in the black man. He said that it was the duty of the State to educate all of its citizens of whatever color. He showed by actual figures that if the taxes were divided as they were paid in, that the whites themselves would suffer. He brought up the question of the color of corporations that contributed through taxation to the general school fund and confounded the Tilmanites by showing that no color line could be drawn here. He showed the utter lack of fitness of Tilman for the governor's chair because of his gambling propensities and his general indecency. Gonzales' arguments prevailed even against the powerful influence of Senator Tilman. Some months later James Tilman met Gonzales on the streets of Columbia totally unarmed and peaceful. Tilman pulled out a revolver and shot him. Gonzales tottered back against a wall, and said: "Shoot again, you coward!" The coward walked off with a smoking revolver and left his victim to die. Tilman underwent a mock trial and was turned loose on the State, but South Carolina now honors Gonzales for the enemies he made. Gonzales was a man of lofty courage and patriotism. He knew no fear. He wrote with an unfettered pen and around his virile editorials there played the lambent lightnings of classical allusion. He was opposed to all kinds of lawlessness. As the orator of the unveiling occasion said, "there was no partnership between principle and policy; no alliance of conscience with cash." The policy of his paper was to espouse the cause of truth. He founded the cleanest and most fearless daily paper we have in the South, and in his death a potent voice for civic righteousness was hushed. South Carolina has done well to preserve the memory of this brave son on a tablet of stone.

?◄► "The Atlanta Tragedy"

The curtain rises on a veritable devil's caldron. An atmosphere overhead, usually resplendent with electric lights, blackened by a sheet of swirling dust and powder-smoke; beneath, the faint glitter of blue steel, the brandishing of dirks, the dull thud of wielded clubs, the whirr of stones, the crash of glass and the deafening report of guns; up from the very earth whence they have been struck down and trampled, the agonizing shrieks and wails of hapless men, women and children wounded and dying; the hoarse howl of contumely from the throat of this whirlwind of hoodlumism as an answering cry; the mad play of all the dreadful forces of primal savagery possible in an organized and well-directed mob;—who, having seen it, can never forget?[14] This is the true picture of Atlanta, Georgia, on the night of September 22, 1906.

This is the one night when the Negroes of Atlanta receive an outpouring of the black wine of the white man's wrath. All the white man's forces of evil are unleashed; and unbridled and unrestrained ruffianism hold a carnival.

The scene changes. At midnight pale faces in khaki garb with shouldered kragjorgensens tread Atlanta's highway.[15] Pandemonium subsides. Drunk with the blood of a score of the innocent, those who had flagitiously planned and executed this diabolism sneak home in the gray dawn of a Sabbath morning.[16] At sunrise haggard-faced black barbers, tailors, cobblers and shopkeepers crawl from under their ill-constructed barricades behind which they have crouched in darkness and fear all night long, peer cautiously into the streets, and then, passing through the broad avenues that shine with the glitter of bayonets and resound with the steady tramp and stern command of soldier and captain, they hurry home to painfully anxious wives and mothers. Atlanta is practically under martial law. On Sunday the church bells are significantly silent and the pulpits and pews are vacant. On the outskirts of the city groups of the snarling factory riff-raff prowl and prey. Neither colored women nor men dare venture beyond their thresholds lest they should be subject to the coarse vulgarity of unmannerly and insulting rowdies. There are many cases of violence. When the policemen are called these miniature mobs disperse like flies from a carcass when disturbed by an intruder. But they are hidden only behind houses and in allies and, like the carcass flies, return when the intruder is gone.

This running amuck of the mob is such an outrage upon the colored people that we have the feeble resentment of this infamy by a people who have heretofore accepted their blows with pathetic humility. The result is the wholesale arrest and disarming of colored people from college presidents down to hod-carriers—and the actual arming of white people. All the soldiery and police of the city at once become agents for Negro intimidation and white protection. Monday, Tuesday and Wednesday hardly anybody works. The industries of a great industrial center are paralyzed, business is at a standstill and more than a half-hundred thousand people hug their homes and porches for three dreadful days while deviltry broods and danger lurks.

Again the scene shifts. The captains depart. Behold! We have peace— No, not peace, but a wilderness called peace. Sixty or seventy colored people are in jail for killing one policeman while sixteen whites are in jail for the whole riot which resulted in the murdering and maiming of more than a hundred people. Five thousand of the city's most industrious citizens have gone to other towns and climes. Half of her best black population are preparing to leave daily. The newspapers which fomented the mob now treat us to a heavy dose of "editorial expurgations." There is a brief wave of pity for the bereaved, a tremor of indignation at rampant ruffianism, a weak spasm of patronizing virtue which results in scandalous leniency to mob leaders arrested red-handed, the flashing across the world of the lie that Negroes are brutes, the adroit and covert justification of the mob by Atlanta's leading publicists, and finally, the relapse of Atlanta back into her ancient ruts. Again we have a city that struts before the world as the liberal gateway of a great section but which is really the same old Atlanta steeped in the foul odours of ante-bellum traditions and held firmly in the remorseless clutch of a vile and reasonable race prejudice. . . .

Let me give to our readers the interpretation of the cause, the course and the aftermath of the Atlanta riots from the viewpoint of one who has lived in Atlanta for the last three years. Most likely this mob got its first psychological impulse from Tom Dixon's "Clansman."[17] The "Clansman," or the Ku Klux Klan, was a band of midnight marauders and murderers who held the whole Negro population of the South in terror during the seventies. Dixon has written and dramatized a story in glorification of this band of masked cowards. The "Clansman" came to Atlanta last winter. It was a very exquisite piece of deviltry. All the golden glory of two centuries were [sic] gathered before and behind the footlights. In the midst of a swirling carnival of color and a marvel of melody there passed a panorama of rape and plunder and murder as wicked and passion-stirring as ever searched the souls of a proud people. Behind the footlights the storm and stress period of reconstruction, with the nether side of society uppermost and with all the deftness of cunning deviltry, was portrayed.

The play stimulated and presaged the gathering of evil winds.

Dixon left; but the seed had been planted. Besides, there was in our midst a man who wanted to be our Governor and who was willing to stoop to any depths to capture the office. In former years Mr. Hoke Smith had been regarded as one of the broadest and most liberal white men in Atlanta.[18] A consistent member of the Presbyterian Church, a Sunday School teacher, a leading lawyer, an educator and a cabinet member—nobody esteemed him higher than the black people of Atlanta. Now that he wants to be Governor, he reverses all of his former ideas, repudiates his principles and turns demagogue. Mr. Smith went up and down the State railing against the "ignorant and purchasable Negro." In Russia he would have had a bomb placed under him; in Georgia he went to and fro calling not only for the disfranchisement of the Negro, but for the actual deportation from Georgia of those colored people who might complain against this constitutional knavery. It was not a short, snappy campaign like you have in the North; we had eighteen long months of his vituperation.

Dishonesty of government was all laid to the Negroes who have no part in law-making whatever. We did not have the slightest opportunity to fashion a legislature to our liking. Not one word was uttered that would tend to elevate an already vitiated sentiment to a place where a broad human sympathy would characterize the relations between the races. Nothing of patience with a weaker people, nothing of toleration, nothing of uplift, he uttered, not a word that smacked of the larger heroism. His mouth was a fountain of bitterness when he spoke of the Negro. And this is the case with most of our so-called Southern statesmen. They appeal not to reason, but passion. They advocate running the government according to the code of the highwayman. This is what they call reform. . . .

The man who deliberately fomented and precipitated the riot was the Editor of the *Atlanta News.*[19] . . . The day preceding the night of the riot *The News* flooded the neighborhood with "extras" with great glaring headlines, bigger than the headlines of the Hearst papers, telling of "Brutal Negro Assaults on White Women."[20] Such tactics would have excited a mob anywhere. It easily excited one in a hotbed of prejudice like Atlanta.

To show that the editor of the *News* had helped to plan and expected what happened Saturday night, it is but necessary to read his Sunday paper of September 23rd. Bear in mind too that this editorial matter was written either Saturday during the day or Saturday night while the mob yet held Atlanta in its mad grip. In the editorial columns of his paper on that broken Sabbath he says:

"Vicious blacks are surrounding the doom of their race.

"The wonder is that the white men do not begin in earnest a real warfare on the blacks.

"We prefer peace and order, but if it must be war, the white men are ready to face it.

"In the name of heaven, what else can white men do except to make war to the bitter end against the black devils who continue to attack defenseless white women?

"There is no use to deceive ourselves about the situation. A conflict, terrible in its consequences, is surely coming.

"The men of this community will stand it no longer. They will begin a warfare on the black race that will mean hell itself to every one of them. The blacks will be destroyed, annihilated and completely vanquished if they do not stop these crimes."

Later on he speaks of white men beginning "a real war-fare against the blacks" and of "preparations" that are being made for the conflict that "is coming."

And yet I had to leave Atlanta or be put on the chain gang because I sent a letter to the *New York World* accusing the *News* of fomenting the riot.

The average Southerner is incurably unreliable when discussing anything pertaining to the Negro. Graves, with an article on the riot in a Chicago magazine, and McElway, with one in a New York magazine, are cases in point.[21] Neither can the Negro nor the North afford to accept even a categorical promise from such men with any sense of security. They are leaders in the new oath-breaking reconstruction. They confound the noblest objects of citizenship with the ignoble motives of dastardly revenge. The only "Reign of Terror" there is in the South is the menace of the constitutionally lawless white man.

The white woman of the South is the best protected and best cared for woman in the world. Never before in the history of the world has woman been so adored as the Divine, the Incomprehensible, even though it be the "gaudy show of a spurious chivalry" which thus bows down to her. The black woman is the woman who is in real danger and is really left without protection in the South. Every time you see a yellow or mulatto child in the South, you may safely conclude that somewhere back in the past a black woman has been wronged by a white man. I say this in full knowledge of the fact that there are black criminals in abundance. But there is a wide difference between a race producing a percentage of criminals from its ranks and a race producing almost an entire progeny that is hostile to the fundamental laws of morality and of the land. Law can never reach or retain a high place in popular esteem when the makers of it are forever advocating disregard of existing law.

In justification for the way the citizens of Brownsville were treated McElway, in the *Outlook,* claims that the place had always been a source of disturbance.[22] The fact is instead of having always been a center of disturbance, this suburban village has a record for peace and sobriety unsurpassed, if equalled by any town of similar size and similarly situated in Georgia. It is practically a Negro college town and is without a saloon or a policeman.

Mr. McElway has recounted the history of rapes in and around Atlanta for the last year to show how the Atlanta whites were ultimately provoked to bloodshed. Some of his history is true and some of it is false. According to the newspapers and the courts a Negro named Walker did assault a white woman near Brookwood October 20, 1905. He was hanged forty-eight days later. At the time THE VOICE called attention to the fact that Walker's intellect was so dull and undeveloped that he could not think of two things at one time, such as crime and punishment. He could not spell the word "God," did not know the very first principle of Christianity and was so totally devoid of moral ideas as to be almost *unmoral* instead of *immoral.* When it was discovered that a committee of colored physicians were preparing to examine him to pronounce on his sanity on Monday, white physicians left church on Sunday to examine him and pronounced him sane. Thus it would have been a breach of courtesy and also of good judgment for colored physicians to have followed these white physicians with their examination. . . .

On August 20th two white girls were brutally assaulted on the outskirts of Atlanta. The white primary was only two days off. The police authorities and an armed posse with blood hounds were taken to the scene of the crime. A white man who was there and whose name I cannot mention—for he would be driven out of Atlanta—said that the dogs lost the trail at a white man's door. A second and third time these trained dogs did the same thing. They were called off and the chase was given up. This led this white man to conclude that in this case a white man had blacked his face and committed this deed either out of sheer lust or as an emissary of Hoke Smith to help inflame the voting whites against the blacks. Either case is reasonable. White politicians in the South will stoop to any dirt against the Negro to get into office. White men with blacked faces have been killed in South Carolina, Kentucky and Texas and one is now in jail in the District of Columbia for playing Negro while committing crime. There were any number of rumors of assaults the two days preceding Smith's election, all of which, save the cases mentioned above, upon investigation proved to be groundless. The newspapers reported the gathering of a great mob at Decatur on August the 20th to lynch a Negro,—which was an absolute fake. This information I also owe to a white man who quit his work and investigated. On August 24th a white woman was frightened from a spring by a passing Negro who never got near her and who in no way accosted her. But she was alone and the white newspapers had got the whole community unnerved so that white women were actually afraid to meet colored men alone. The Negro man thus met looked somewhat like a vagabond, and his very presence was called an attempt at assault.

But I forgot to mention the Carmichael case. That was July 31st. A young white woman said that she had been assaulted by a Negro in one of the suburbs of the city.[23] The woods were searched by an armed posse. All day men longed for blood, but no suspicious Negro could be found. Late in the afternoon one of the dogs belonging to the posse was found standing near a Negro cabin. In the hut were found four men and one woman. One of the men was marched to the home of the girl, identified and shot on the spot. He never confessed, was not dressed as described by the girl and was not given the semblance of a trial. But the mob demanded, like the Chattanooga juror, that the girl identify somebody. This time it was Frank Carmichael. Doctors afterwards said that the girl was not actually raped.

Of those cases the Saturday of the riot the *Georgian,* John Temple Graves' own paper, said in its issue of September 24th: "None was a real case of criminal assault," and yet when he wants to justify this mob before the outside world he counts the cases of Saturday with the "eleven assaults" and attempts within three weeks. As a matter of truth and record only one case of Saturday appeared to be an attempt at assault. Two were cases when Negro men knocked white women down in getting out of their way and the last was a case when a ninety year old woman, in closing her window blinds at bedtime, imagined she saw a Negro out in the yard. God knows the newspapers had been yellow enough to unnerve the woman![24]

Neither Graves nor McElway was fair enough to tell of the case of Mrs. Nancy Du Pree. Mrs. Du Pree is a grass widow.[25] She was found at the home where she worked with her throat badly cut, weltering in a pool of blood.

She barely whispered that a black brute had assaulted her. The usual armed posse with bloodhounds scoured the country looking for the brute. The dogs could not strike any trail. The woman did not die, but instead got well. A colored fortune teller, being sought, under the guise of an oracle, told the people that this woman had not been assaulted by a black man. Later the woman confessed to an attempt at suicide because of family unhappiness. What would have become of a Negro had he been found near that house by the armed posse. All know. Neither Graves nor McElway were fair enough to tell of the assault of an eight year old colored girl by a white brute last year in Atlanta. The white man was rescued from a mob of angry Negroes by the police and upon his own statement was given freedom. Neither Graves nor McElway told of the assault of white women by white men on the car line between Atlanta and the Chattahoochie River last year. No! No! They would select only those tidbits of testimony which would appear to make the Negro have a monopoly of rape.

As to the riot there is little necessity now for details. The newspapers themselves have told enough of the ghastly story to show the country where we are. I believe it was an organized mob, and these are my reasons. In several cases where colored men were working as assistants to white men, they were advised by these white men to go home early Saturday night. A white man who drives a laundry wagon told his Negro assistant that the white people intended to "clean up for the Nigger" after night. Then Charles Daniel, Editor of the *News,* had organized his so-called "Protective Association."[26] Add to this the fact that, instead of the utter repudiation of this godless mob, we have it openly stated that this anarchy has done good, that no soldiers could be had on the scene until the mob had done all the damage it cared and that for quite a while even the police did not interfere, and you will see why I believe the whole thing was planned.

The mob chased and killed all the colored people it could in the heart of town. Then it attacked the street cars, the cabs and even the Pullman cars in search of Negroes. Barber shops and restaurants were visited. Two barbers and a bootblack were killed and piled on each other. Everywhere in the heart of town there was a red tumultuous sea of blood. But the mob, who are always cowards at the core, never for once ventured into large Negro settlements. They knew better. Men who ought to know state that a half dozen or more whites were killed in the riot and it is a fact that almost as many whites as blacks had their wounds dressed at the Grady hospital. Those men who are scarred still live in Atlanta and could be found by the police if desired.

The Mayor ordered all saloons and hardware stores closed. The hardware stores were open all day Sunday, Monday, Tuesday and Wednesday. The whites bought all the arms they wanted. One store alone sold $17,000.00 worth of firearms and ammunition and not a dollar's worth of those goods was sold to Negroes. Instead Negroes on the streets were all searched. If found with guns, they were sent to jail. If the report of a gun was heard in a Negro settlement, it was an excuse for the police and militia disarming the whole settlement. That is the way the whites showed their superiority. The killing of an officer in Brownsville was unfortunate and to be deplored. If the man killed had been a mob member, the act would have called for approbation.

There are seven things I wish to emphasize in closing:

1. The Negro has no monopoly of rape. Many reported cases are fakes. Some are by white men disguised as Negroes. Some are cases of mutual consent. Only a small per cent are genuine.
2. This Atlanta riot cannot be charged entirely to hoodlums. If the mob were a pyramid, we would find hoodlums at the base but white politicians and newspaper editors at the apex. Tho launched by the rabble, the creative force of this mob was the upper class. And remember, too, that a doctor and a dentist were arrested in the mob as leaders.
3. Atlanta's leading publicists have not unqualifiedly condemned this mob. They all give the mob credit for making times better by making the Negro more humble. This was organized ruffianism and the object was to reform the Negro by humbling him.
4. The white man's wrath was not directed against the criminal Negro. Any colored man who attempted to beard that whirlwind went down. And in one case a colored woman was killed. "Humilate the progressive Negro" was the command to the mob.
5. Tho everybody admits that the authorities were criminally negligent on Saturday night, still black men have no ballot with which to rebuke them for their negligence. All the time our ebullient energy is displayed against Negro crime, but crime *per se* is seldom attacked. Law in the South is the weakest and most disrespected thing we have.
6. The South desires to go back to a period of semi-slavery for the Negro, and bound up with this aspiration is the desire to dictate the Negro policy of the nation.
7. There is no peace in Atlanta. The Negroes *may* be humbler and more polite, but they do not so impress me in their letters. They say that if they wrote what they felt, the paper upon which they wrote would shrivel into ashes. There is extensive and deep-seated dissatisfaction. There will be discontent as long as present conditions prevail.

If it is true that coming events always cast their shadows before them, what portent is it that creeps across the South land, lengthening daily like an evening shadow? And if right surely some day must triumph, what must be the fate of a fabric so toilsomely reared as our Southern kakistocracy?[27]

Atlanta represents the South. Let her remember the fate of the Harlot, Babylon, and desist from this species of political drunkenness and stupidity.[28]

NOTES

1. "Tuskegee Machine" refers to the influential network of Booker T. Washington's friends and allies. Many were or had been affiliated with Tuskegee University at some point, although many, both black and white, were simply supporters of his policies.

2. Barber managed to publish a few issues from Chicago, but the periodical didn't last for long.

3. Founded in 1891, Friendship Normal and Industrial Institute began by serving elementary and high school students but became a college in later decades, eventually closing in 1981. Benedict College and Virginia Union University are still operating today.

4. Daniel, *Black Journals,* 369. See Johnson and Johnson, "Away from Accommodation"; also Fultz, "'Morning Cometh.'"

5. Washington to Scott, 4 November 1903, *Washington Papers,* 328–29.

6. For an overview of the role of the *Voice of the Negro,* particularly in terms of how it showcased a new generation of talent, see Johnson, "Rise of the Negro Magazine," 13–14.

7. Harlan, "Washington and the *Voice,*" 58. Harlan speculates that either Washington or Scott wrote an unsigned letter to the editor of the *New York Age* that was published on October 1, 1906: "We will all be disappointed in Mr. Barber's bravery and sense of loyalty to the race if he deserts us in this trying hour. . . . If Mr. Barber, however, does leave us and go North, we very much hope that he will not follow the example of so many others, that is, after fleeing himself, spend his time in giving advice to the Negro from a long distance how he should conduct himself in the South."

8. Narciso Gener Gonzales (1859–1903) was a cofounder with his brother Ambrose E. Gonzales of the *State* newspaper in Columbia, South Carolina.

9. James H. Tillman (1869–1911), who served as South Carolina's lieutenant governor from 1901 to 1903, is known mostly for Gonzales's murder, which came to be known in South Carolina as the "Crime of the Century."

10. Benjamin "Pitchfork Ben" Tillman (1847–1918) served as South Carolina's governor from 1890 to 1894 and as a U.S. senator from 1895 until his death. He is known for helping found Clemson University and Winthrop College, passing legislation to disfranchise African American men in South Carolina, and encouraging violence against African Americans living in the South.

11. The *State,* South Carolina's most widely read newspaper, was first published on February 18, 1891.

12. Duncan Clinch Heyward (1864–1943) served as South Carolina's governor from 1903 to 1907.

13. Fire-eaters were an extremist, proslavery faction of politicians from the South who called for the secession of southern states and the formation of the Confederate States of America.

14. Contumely: insulting or deprecatory language.

15. Krag Jorgensen: a Norwegian-made automatic rifle that was used by the U.S. military in the late nineteenth and early twentieth centuries.

16. Flagitiously: to do something in a criminal or villainous manner.

17. *The Clansman: An Historical Romance of the Ku Klux Klan* was a novel written by Thomas Dixon Jr. in 1905. It played a significant role in reviving the KKK during the twentieth century and was adapted by D. W. Griffith into a film titled *The Birth of a Nation* (1915).

18. Michael Hoke Smith was the owner of the *Atlanta Evening Journal* until 1900, when he was appointed secretary of the interior by President Grover Cleveland. He served as governor of Georgia from 1907 to 1909.

19. Established in 1902, the *Atlanta News* was a daily newspaper edited by Charles Daniels. Fulton County made Daniels a special deputy sheriff for his fearmongering portrayal of African American men as rapists. See Shapiro, *White Violence and Black Response,* 97–98.

20. William Randolph Hearst was a wealthy newspaper owner in the late nineteenth and early twentieth centuries.

21. John Temple Graves was the first editor of the newspaper the *Atlanta Georgian* when it was established by Fred Seely in 1906. The influential southern writer and political activist Alexander J. McKelway served as editor of the *Presbyterian Standard,* a newspaper based in Charlotte, North Carolina.

22. In the early twentieth century, Brownsville was the predominantly African American southern section of Atlanta, Georgia. It is the home of two historically black colleges, Clark Atlanta University and Gammon Theological Seminary.

23. Annie Laurie Poole was the young girl who made this accusation against Frank Carmichael. See Burns, *Rage in the Gate City,* 22, 178.

24. "Yellow" refers to yellow journalism, defined as newspaper reporting that presents events on the basis of hearsay and sometimes even complete fabrications.

25. The term "grass widow" can refer to a divorced woman or to a mistress who has been abandoned by her lover.

26. The "Protective Association" was likely an informal armed patrol of white citizens.

27. "Kakistocracy" is the government of a society by its least capable citizens.

28. This refers to the Whore of Babylon in the book of Revelation, who seduces the kings of the earth. They become drunk on her "wine of immorality" and subsequently forfeit their authority on the earth. Rev 17:1–13 (NAS).

Jane Edna Harris Hunter
(1882–1971)

NURSE, SOCIAL ACTIVIST, ATTORNEY,
CLUB WOMAN, PHILANTHROPIST

*These words I had not heard before, for in the South Negro nurses were
favored by white people. . . ."I am not a nigger," was my reply, "and if
there are other nurses practicing in Cleveland, I have enough faith to
believe that I, too, can succeed."*

Hunter, Nickel and a Prayer, 71.

In 1905 Jane Edna Harris Hunter arrived in Cleveland, Ohio, during the
first wave of the Great Migration with her southern sensibilities regarding race relations intact, expecting little trouble in securing lucrative employment as a nurse at a city hospital or with affluent white doctors. Several
years earlier, after completing nursing training at the segregated Cannon
Street Hospital in Charleston, South Carolina, she had boldly approached
the city's most prominent white surgeon, Dr. Thomas Grange Simons, whose
clients included "Yankee" vacationers and "aristocratic" families like the
Wagners, owners of the Wagner Sleeping Car Company, and convinced him
to hire her.[1] About two years later, with Dr. Simons's encouragement, she
had enrolled in the advanced training program for nurses at Dixie Hospital,
affiliated with Hampton Institute, a historically black college in Hampton,
Virginia.[2] Completing the program bolstered her confidence and credentials.

The rejection of her job applications by white doctors in Cleveland introduced Hunter to the brutal realities of northern life for African American migrants, however. In her autobiography, *A Nickel and a Prayer* (1940), Hunter recalls that, after hearing her request for employment, one physician insisted that she "go back south—that white doctors did not employ 'nigger' nurses."[3]

Hunter ignored the doctor's advice and intensified her job search, eventually finding employment that inspired her to enlarge her vision for her lifework. She initially accepted work as a domestic servant to cover her living expenses. Her career prospects improved considerably when Dr. L. E. Sieglestein, the Cuyahoga county coroner, recommended her to the same type of clients she had served in Charleston: wealthy white families. Six years later, as she mourned the unexpected death of her mother and recalled her difficult transition into urban life, Hunter convinced several of her friends to save a nickel each week and to offer a prayer for the success of their Working Girls' Home Association, which they founded to provide affordable housing for African American working women. Within two years, Hunter changed the name of the organization to the Phillis Wheatley Association (PWA) to honor the first published African American woman poet and to distinguish it from a Cleveland settlement house, the Colored Working Girls' Christian Home. By 1925, the PWA had become a nationally recognized residential, employment, and recreation center, one of the largest and most successful social service agencies for black women and girls in early twentieth-century America.

Hunter's life began on Woodburn Farm, the former plantation where her ancestors had labored as slaves in Pendleton, South Carolina, a bustling village in the upstate region that lowcountry planters once favored for their summer homes. Her father, Edward Harris, the son of an enslaved African American woman and a white overseer, and her mother, Harriet Milliner Harris, the daughter of slaves, eked out a meager living as wage laborers to support Jane and her three siblings, Winston, Rebecca, and Rosa. Her father moved the family closer to Pendleton so that his children could attend the one-room Silver Spring School established by African American Baptists. After her father died, in 1892, Jane's mother placed the children in the homes of different friends and relatives, initiating a nomadic, often traumatic journey for Jane that included laboring as a domestic for an abusive family in Anderson, South Carolina; housekeeping for a licentious hotel proprietor on the Clemson College campus; and working in Woodburn's cotton fields as a field hand for Augustine T. Smythe, a former Confederate officer. Her fortunes changed dramatically after her mother reluctantly permitted her to complete the four-year program at Ferguson and Williams College in Abbeville, South Carolina.[4]

By 1900, Jane faced the daunting task of finding viable employment during the age of Jim Crow in South Carolina, when options for young, single black women were often limited to the domestic sphere, specifically working as a paid housekeeper or marrying and becoming a housewife. Seventeen-year-old Jane pursued both options, finding domestic work in Abbeville and a young lover in Pendleton, but her mother forced her into a loveless marriage to Edward Hunter, a wealthy man forty years her senior. Within sixteen months, Jane made the unusually bold decision to separate permanently from her father-figure husband. She relocated to Charleston, where she accepted employment as a live-in nurse for the children of Attorney Benjamin Rutledge Jr.[5] Her eagerness to explore new opportunities led Hunter to acquire nursing training in Charleston and at Hampton. She then took perhaps the most daring risk of her life: abruptly abandoning her plans to move to Florida in order to migrate north with Mr. and Mrs. William Coleman, family friends she was visiting in Richmond.

Hunter and the Colemans joined millions of African Americans who traveled from the South to the Northeast, Midwest, and West between 1905 and 1940 during the Great Migration, seeking better employment opportunities and safer living environments. Rather than take the traditional route to Philadelphia or New York that many African Americans preferred, however, they headed to Cleveland, a midwestern oil and steel town where an upwardly mobile but relatively tight-knit black middle class had brokered a fragile alliance with white Clevelanders that brought them a measure of comfort and a facade of progressiveness.[6] Prior to the Great Migration, Cleveland's African American population had totaled fewer than ten thousand people. After 1920 that number rose to more than thirty thousand, giving Cleveland the largest African American urban population in Ohio.[7] This sudden influx of thousands of African American southerners seeking affordable housing, wage-earning labor, and inexpensive entertainment precipitated a crisis after the city's major social service agencies, particularly the Young Women's Christian Association (YWCA), Young Men's Christian Association (YMCA), and Traveler's Aid, refused to assist the majority of black migrants.

In 1913 Hunter's PWA began meeting the varied needs of thousands of black women and girls who were migrating to Cleveland. She gradually expanded the Association's services to the larger community, providing support networks for young mothers, clubs such as the Girl Reserves, and activities as diverse as black history lectures and sophisticated fashion shows. The PWA also operated neighborhood centers and playgrounds in African American communities throughout Cleveland. By 1925, to meet the ever-expanding needs of black Clevelanders, Hunter initiated a $600,000 capital campaign, which received an enormous boost from oil magnate John D. Rockefeller Jr.'s $100,000 pledge, to fund the construction of a new eleven-story building for the PWA and to purchase property for a summer camp. That same year, she completed law school at Baldwin-Marshall College and passed the Ohio bar. She later received honorary degrees from several colleges, including Fisk University, and became increasingly active in the black women's club movement, particularly the National Association of Colored Women (NACW), the National Association of Colored People, and Republican Party politics.[8]

In *A Nickel and a Prayer,* Hunter adopts a personable style in recalling her formative years in the South in the first half of the text and then employs a more formal tone in detailing the establishment of the PWA and her outlook for African Americans in the second part of her narrative. She clearly perceives the book as both memoir and commentary, which causes her to shift between narrative styles. In the chapter presented here, titled "Starlight," Hunter recounts her triumphant confrontation with her nemesis, the local hustler Albert "Starlight" Boyd, whom she blames for introducing "commercialized vice" into Cleveland's black belt. This African American neighborhood was a bustling stretch of night clubs and smoking saloons. Starlight positioned himself as a formidable political foe by ingratiating himself with the African American community by providing inexpensive housing, entertainment, and services. Like many African American thinkers in this collection, Hunter overcomes challenges by drawing on the strong religious faith that she developed in South Carolina and boldly confronting her adversary. She evokes John Bunyan's *The Pilgrim's Progress* (1678) to characterize "commercialized vice" as Apollyon, a representative of Satan, and herself and Cleveland's black community as Christian, the protagonist. In so doing, she transforms the struggle into an allegorical battle between good and evil that Hunter and her supporters are destined, despite difficulties, to win.

Hunter's approach to social service work for black women and girls was also informed by her affiliation with the NACW. Cleveland's black club women had initially opposed the establishment of the PWA, a segregated facility that they viewed as a setback in race relations. As Cleveland and the nation slowly acknowledged Hunter's accomplishments in addressing the needs of black working women, however, black club women became some of her most loyal supporters. By 1930, the NACW had created a Phillis Wheatley Department, enabling Hunter to replicate the PWA's brand of earning respectability in ten affiliates throughout the nation, including an association in Greenville, South Carolina.

As Hunter gained more prominence as a social activist and club woman, she became increasingly popular on the African American activist lecture circuit, which offered new opportunities for her to implement racial uplift initiatives throughout the nation. The speech presented here, "An Opportunity for Club Women to Serve the Underprivileged Girl," highlights the recurring themes Hunter addressed in her speeches: democratic values, interracial cooperation, active faith, public service, and race pride and progress. Presented at the 1934 Central Association of Colored Women's regional meeting in Louisville, Kentucky, it reflects her reliance on religious beliefs and progressive ideologies to bridge the chasm between middle-class club women and working-class domestics. After acknowledging the enormous advances upwardly mobile club women like those in her audience had achieved during the post–World War I era, Hunter reproves them for neglecting members of their community who have been disproportionately affected by the Great Depression. Hunter then characterizes herself and her audience as self-appointed members of the "Talented Tenth," liberal arts–educated African Americans whom W. E. B. Du Bois had asserted should uplift the black working class. This characterization gives her the authority to chastise her club sisters for allowing their obsession with "regal entertainment and petty bickering for office" to undermine their commitment to their calling. She impels them to refocus their mission through the lens of Christian service, a lesson she had learned as matron of the cafeteria under Ella Williams's tutelage at Ferguson and Williams College. By positioning their efforts within a Christocentric perspective, Hunter reconfigures black club women as servants, thereby revealing an intimate connection between club work and domestic work. At the end of her speech, Hunter reinforces this alliance through her vision of a new model for club women, an interracial alliance comprising women from the secular and the sacred realms: the former slaves Sojourner Truth, Harriet Tubman, and Phillis Wheatley and the biblical figures Mary and Martha, revered women whose greatest legacy was service to their communities. Indeed, many African American thinkers from South Carolina advocated service to God, nation, and humanity to effect radical changes in early twentieth-century race relations.

After retiring from the PWA in 1948, Hunter founded the National Phillis Wheatley Foundation to provide college scholarships for African American women and remained active in club work and on the lecture circuit. In 1971, she died in Cleveland following a long illness and was buried in Lake View Cemetery. Hunter was eulogized as the "Godmother of America's Brown Daughters."[9]

❧ Excerpt from *A Nickel and a Prayer*

Chapter Eleven: "Starlight"

As a child on Woodburn Plantation I had often been thrown into teeth-chattering, blood-curdling panic by my terror of wildcats. Now, as a guardian of a social enterprise, I found myself facing a much more dreadful monster—commercialized vice. Like Apollyon[10] who bestrode the path of Christian, this creature, spawned by greed and ignorance, was hideous to behold. "Out of its belly came fire and smoke, and its mouth was as the mouth of a lion."[11] The service it imposed upon the wretched of my race was hard, "and its wages were death."[12] It tried to win us by fair promises; it wrestled with us, and had almost pressed to death. But when we fell, we rose. "And although we must continue to wage bitter warfare with it, we know that we shall be more than conquerors through Him that loved us."[13]

The story of American history, and, indeed, of all western history in the nineteenth century, is a record of unprecedented aggrandizement of urban populations. In Cleveland this mushroom growth, as regards its Negro population, achieved in the decade between 1910 and 1920 the phenomenal acceleration of three hundred per cent.[14] Drawn from rural regions and villages by the lure of better wages, the Negroes, like other underprivileged groups, offered a glaring mark for the rapacity of realtors and the dishonesty of politicians. Where once they had been scattered throughout the city, their very numbers now confined them to definite sections, and these "black belts"[15] quickly underwent a degeneration, civic and fiscal, of a type known to virtually all American cities.

Here was a golden opportunity for unscrupulous politicians; and greedily they seized upon it to serve their purposes, playing upon the ignorance of the Negro voter to entrench themselves in office, and then delivering the Negro over to every force of greed and vice which stalked around him. My second insight into this unholy alliance of organized vice and corrupt politics came to me in the course of my professional labors. Dr. A——,[16] from whom I took cases, maintained two practices—one in the downtown section, one for Negroes on the edge of the underworld. It was while attending one of his patients, the madame of a house of prostitution, that I acquired first-hand experience with a resort of this character, and learned the ties which linked its evils with municipal politics. There were two children in this evil den— one a child of two, my patient's daughter; the other her niece, a girl of fourteen who acted as a porter, admitting patrons and collecting the two dollars charged them for their visits.

It was from the latter, Willie Mae, that I learned the set-up and acquired my knowledge of "Starlight," the unsavory creature who thrived upon the tolls which he exacted from this place and hundreds like it. His name, Willie Mae told me, came from the fact that he always wore a large, flashing diamond beneath his black bow tie. He was the "Great Mogul" of organized vice. Suave, impressive, impervious to shame, and gifted with the art of leadership, he was a born political henchman; and many a young colored girl, misled by hopes of an easy, glamorous existence, became the victim of his false promises and found herself, too late, a hopeless prisoner of shame and degradation.

Chance brought me in immediate contact with his first victim, a beautiful mulatto girl named Osie,[17] whom he waylaid as she was on her way home from high school and won over with promises of marriage and a life of luxury. When her parents found her days later, she was living in a house of prostitution at Scovill Avenue and Fourteenth Street,[18] where gambling and liquor offered a good time to libertines of both races, and dissolute white men sought a thrill with loose Negro girls. Osie's task was to keep the patrons drinking; and when business boomed, to seek fresh recruits for the trade. Pending the addition of these recruits, the greed of her husband frequently compelled his helpless victims to entertain as many as forty men in a single night. The time came, however, when this helpless first wife, Osie, was divorced by "Starlight" and abandoned by all her associates. She went from bad to worse; the police, acting under "Starlight's" orders, had denied her even the right to practice her unsavory profession to which he had dragged her; and at length, broken in health, stricken with pneumonia, she crawled back to her mother's home to die there, mourned only by her own mother. I stood at her bedside when her eyes closed in death, and heard her unhappy mother cry, "Thanks be to God, now my trouble is over." Once more it was borne in upon me that only but for the grace of God this fate might easily enough have been mine, and I felt a renewed determination to help the homeless and imperiled daughters of my people.

"Starlight," meanwhile, waxed wealthier and more powerful each year. New houses of prostitution were opening frequently with procurers hunting Negro girls at our very doorsteps, and the issue had reached point where it was no longer possible to ignore it.

What to do? Very early in the history of our social work for girls, tours of dance halls, which I made with Mrs. Mary Rathburn Judd,[19] General Secretary to the Young Women's Christian Association, had opened my eyes to the evil influence which the commercial dance hall was exerting upon the morals of the Negroes. Even then it was apparent that the only answer lay in supplying similar recreation under wholesome influences; and though this step involved the risk of alienating those of our supporters to whom dancing under any auspices was abhorrent, I now determined that the Phillis Wheatley should inaugurate a recreational hall. We rented a barn in the rear of our home for ten dollars a month, put in a new floor, plastered the walls, and announced our first party. Guests came only on invitation; no admission was charged at the parties which were held twice a month. The new addition to the Phillis Wheatley Association proved a huge success. Not only did we use the hall for dances, but we had it fitted up as a gymnasium. A Sunday school in the neighborhood held a bazaar, and from the proceeds bought dumb bells, Indian clubs,[20] and other paraphernalia.

Preventive measures, however, were not enough. We determined to carry the warfare into the enemy's camp and do battle with the political corruption, "Starlight's" chief mainstay, which had made of our neighborhood a region of brawling vice, known throughout the city as the "Roaring Third."[21]

At the moment, the Democratic and Republican parties were engaged in one of their periodic battles over the local railway system; the Democrats declaring for reduced fare, the Republicans aligning themselves with the stockholders of the Street Railway Company[22] for "good service" at the existing fare. Eventually the issue came before the electorate, and fearing the outcome, the Republicans determined to clinch it by organizing the Negro vote in their favor. The task was not difficult. By tradition then the Negro vote was still overwhelmingly Republican,[23] and all that was needed was to ensure that this vote should be delivered in bloc. The respectable Negro vote, the vote largely of the church people, was won by appeals to racial pride. The other, a numerically stronger vote, was in the pocket of "Starlight," placed there by the far-flung ramifications of his evil influence. If you care to investigate this chapter of Cleveland politics, you will discover how completely "Starlight" justified the confidence that was reposed in him by his masters, the politicians, and how intimate can be the relations between a general and public economic issue like that of a street railway franchise and the more private, but basically not less, economic issue of the prevalence of organized vice.

The Republicans won in 1910, and a part of "Starlight's" share in the victory was the privilege of naming a councilman to be elected by that body from our district. Great was the pride of the Negroes in this person, Tim Flagman,[24] a popular young lawyer, who took his seat in the Councilmanic Chamber. Social leaders, especially those of us associated with the Phillis Wheatley, did not join in these plaudits, however, for well we knew what it foreboded; and when Tim was promptly slated for the all-important post of Chairman of the Fire and Police Committee, not the faintest doubt remained to us that evil days were upon us, and that henceforth vice would enjoy a free hand in the city. Our fears were not long in being realized. New dives and brothels opened all around us, all attempt at concealment was abandoned, the headway which the Negro had made toward the state of good citizenship at the time was tumbled gutterward, and faith in Negro leadership was turned to derision.

It was only this result, however, which could open the eyes of the gullible and misguided, and pave the way to a reaction. Now with evidence all around them of how shamefully they had been duped by "Starlight's" promises, the law-abiding citizens set to work to fight his baneful influence before and after municipal elections. Prominent in this movement were the members of St. John's AME Church, the Antioch Baptist Church, and other members of my group who had been "anti-Starlight" from the outset.

Our war cry was "Down with 'Starlight' and corruption," and we did not lack for campaign material; for scarcely a week went by that I was not summoned to police court to assume responsibility for some girl who had been arrested in a house of prostitution for which this monster was responsible. We had no campaign funds, but we did not lack enthusiasm. As the election drew near and our infectious zeal spread in every direction, our opponents began to feel a little worried. One ward-heeler[25] came to my office and asked what I was doing, what I wanted for my district—in short, where I was standing.

"Go back and tell your boys I'm not standing," I told him, "I'm on my knees."

"Hell, get up then," he blurted out rudely; "you've got the boys worried sick."

This was welcome news; and in the light of our enthusiasm, defeat now seemed impossible. Alas, for the simplicity of our illusions! Never once had it occurred to us that only the count determines an election, and that many a victory is won after the polls have closed. The returns were simply incredible! We were barely in the running. It was not until years later that I learned how we had been cheated out of a hard-earned victory.[26]

Politicians think their maneuvers irresistible. I was very much amused after this campaign by the various attempts which were made by "Starlight" and his crowd to tie the Phillis Wheatley to their chariot. "Starlight" went so far as to apply for membership in the Association; and when we respectfully returned the check he sent us for dues, he came back with an offer to furnish a living-room in the house. We informed him that we would not accept the offer, since his actions did not accord with the purposes and spirit of the Phillis Wheatley Association—a rebuff which he received with unruffled suavity.

His next move was covert and more successful. He sent to the Phillis Wheatley Home a light mulatto woman named Dora,[27] who was fairly well educated, had pleasant manners, and dressed like a Paris fashion plate. It was not generally known that Dora was a scout for the "Starlight-Tim" combination. As a free lancer, she sought to recruit new blood for their underworld practices, and became identified with numerous social, religious, and political groups. In this way she interested herself in the work of our Association. It happened that one of the girls living in the Phillis Wheatley was reported as keeping late hours, in violation of dormitory rules. Dora learned of this and came to me under the pretense of friendship for Inez, and requested that

I permit her to admonish the girl. Very soon it was discovered that Dora's real purpose was to entice Inez, because of her attractiveness, away from the institution and lure her into the "Starlight-Tim" dives, for this is where I subsequently found Inez. This experience was sufficient to put me on guard against future activities of this woman in the affairs of the Phillis Wheatley Association.

In fact it was necessary at all times to guard our girls from evil surroundings. I kept a vigilant ear at the switchboard[28] in my office to catch conversations of a doubtful character, and to intercept assignations. No effort we made to restrict tenancy to girls of good character could exclude the ignorant, the foolish, and the weak, for these had to be protected as well. In the company of a policeman whom I could trust, I would sometimes follow couples to places of assignation, rescue the girl, and assist in the arrest of her would-be seducer.

Two years passed, and once more we were facing an election. This time our candidate was Howard E. Murrell,[29] a successful business man with marked talents for organizing and directing a campaign. The contest proved much more bitter than the first one. Feeling on election day reached the pitch of violence. One of our workers, more daring than prudent, became engaged in controversy with one of "Starlight's" crowd, and had her coat torn from her shoulders. While I had always sought to avoid controversy, I could not stand by and allow one of my followers to be treated in this fashion, and I hurried to her succor.

My arch enemy saw me and stopped me forty paces from our door. "Might as well give up, 'Miss Janey,'" he announced suavely; "you're wasting time and energy. Go home and take it easy. Do now." The quiet insolence of the man made my blood boil. Everything decent and right which my parents had implanted in me and stood for, was affronted by his presence. I shook my finger in his face. "Some day I'll get you, you rascal."

The events of the next few hours, however, were to corroborate "Starlight's" boasting. Hour after hour, I sat in my office waiting for the belated returns from our district. Shortly before midnight, the issue still not known, I heard the crash of drums and the screeching of horns. It was "Starlight" and his forces, two thousand strong, sweeping down the street past the Phillis Wheatley, throwing their searchlights into our windows and shouting their derision. Out of defiance or a desire to show myself a good loser, I threw open the door on Central Avenue and stood there on the threshold. The unruly mob surged up the steps. One burly Negro rushed forward, his fist clenched to strike me. But someone in the crowd roared, "Don't you touch her," and he fell back. The mob rejoined the procession; and as they moved out on Central Avenue, I heard someone say, "Ain't Miss Hunter brave?" It was a pleasing tribute, doubly so in defeat; but the cold fact remained that we were in for two more years of "Starlight" and that our efforts had gone for nothing.

Then, abruptly, one month from the day I faced and denounced him, word of his death flashed through the district. He had contracted pneumonia; and, weakened by over-exertion and exposure during the election, had been unable to fight it. It seemed too good to be true. It was only when I stood watching the funeral procession that bore him to the church for burial that I felt sure that "Enemy No. 1" of Cleveland had at long last been vanquished. What a mockery it seemed—that procession, the masses of flowers, the stately music, the marching societies in gleaming regalia, the religious ceremony—all to honor a man who had destroyed virtue and spread ruin.

With the passing of "Starlight" in 1921, better days dawned for the Third District. Politicians had come to feel a certain respect for my influence, and the Phillis Wheatley Association continued to afford a safe refuge for the unprotected. From this time on I took no further active part in politics, except to keep our followers informed of the caliber of the men on the municipal and county tickets. Since direct campaigning seemed futile, the moral seemed to be that our best hope lay in our work of education and protection; and so we went on supplying recreation and beauty to the young, counsel and correction to the wayward, and a home to the homeless. Sweeping changes in social conditions we felt would have to await a more enlightened and responsible electorate.

But I am sorry to admit that the death of "Starlight" dealt no serious blow to open and protected prostitution. The evil was too deep-rooted for that; the foundations which he laid for an underworld of gambling, prostitution, and vice generally remained to menace unborn generations.

Dance halls have multiplied, and their unsavory atmosphere is a growing cause of concern to parents. Under a former city administration, measures were taken to supervise these places. A dance hall inspector was appointed, and the establishments that met certain standards were licensed for operation. This reform, however, has been largely nullified by political pressure exerted by unionized orchestras who dislike the peril to their livelihood presented by effective regulation and consequent reduction of attendance. Slot machines and the policy racket have also operated to set up lower dance hall standards. Few, indeed, are the commercialized amusements which have escaped exploitation and control by gangsters.

A survey made in 1939 of conditions in my neighborhood shows that the old evils still flourish in most places of amusement. The dice roll, strong liquor flows; lewd men and wretched women crowd about gambling tables in basements, often wagering as high as forty dollars, to emerge with a dime. They stagger out in the early morning, the men sometimes waiting to catch some innocent girl, as she rushes off to work or hurries home from a night job. Dives, run by Greeks and Italians in my district, flourish beside schools, and are frequented regularly by children of both the senior and junior high schools. At my instigation and with my assistance, a Negro policeman succeeded in having the license of one of these places revoked.

These are the ancient evils. But my last tour of inspection brought me in touch with something more anomalous; vice as a spectacle not for the ignorant or the unfortunate, but for patrons from society's leading families. It is located, this night club of which I am speaking, in the heart of a newly created Negro slum district, and its appointments are elaborate and costly. Here, to the tune of St. Louis voodoo blues,[30] half-naked Negro girls dance shameless dances with men in Spanish costumes, while daughters from highly respectable families, attended by escorts, clap their dainty, white hands and shout their approval. The whole atmosphere is one of unrestrained animality, the jungle faintly veneered with civilized trappings.

When one of the entertainers discovered my presence and announced in a loud voice that Miss Jane Hunter was present, the applause which greeted his announcement filled me with the deepest confusion. As unobtrusively as possible, I took my departure, saddened and disgusted.

Decent and self-respecting members of my race, I told myself, are not allowed to live in respectable white neighborhoods; yet a white aristocracy penetrates Negro slums to enjoy, patronize, and encourage the worst that my race has to offer. Interracial co-operation built the Phillis Wheatley Association and is carrying on its work; a co-operation of Negroes and whites for worthy purposes; which can gauge the spiritual contribution the Negro has made to American life, since his arrival in America. But in the meeting of blacks and whites in night clubs of the type I had encountered, there is to be found only cause for regret and head-hanging by both races. On the one side an exhibition of unbridled animality, on the other a blasé quest for novel sensations, a vicarious gratification of the dark and violent desires of man's nature, a voluntary return to the jungle.

And behind it all, the hideous god of greed; greedy landlords avowed to reap enhanced returns at the moral cost of the community; racketeers and gangsters frightening the honest but cowardly into the service of evil; and dishonest politicians using public office to undermine the decency and morality of society. Yet at the bottom, the responsibility rests with the citizens of our community. Given what is lacking, unselfishness, imagination, courage, they could easily enough rout the forces of vice which they have supinely allowed to flourish.

It was these virtues that made possible the building of Phillis Wheatley. Out of the prayers and nickels—the interested benevolence of a few Negro working women—has grown a movement which has erected buildings for the welfare of hundreds of homeless women, and radiated the influences of fellowship throughout an entire country. We have proved that white and black can co-operate unselfishly for the common social good.

?◆ "An Opportunity for Club Women to Serve the Underprivileged Girl"

I covet this opportunity to speak to the Central Association of Colored Women,[31] for I feel deeply that there is need to bring to the attention of club women everywhere the necessity for revamping our entire social program. The subject which I have chosen, namely, "An Opportunity for Club Women to Serve the Underprivileged Girl," itself suggests a challenge.

I fervently hope that what I say today shall not be interpreted as coming from a holier than thou attitude, but rather as a friendly admonition born of serious thinking and a definite desire to provoke action on the part of the women of our race to larger participation in the problems of racial self-preservation.

Today, on all sides, in the gradual emergence from a world-wide economic depression, our race is faced with problems, many and difficult. It has fallen our lot to bear the brunt of the siege of unemployment through which our country has undergone in the past six years. Notwithstanding the institution of the National Recovery program,[32] it is only here and there that its benefits have reached down to us, the greatest sufferers.

In the post-war inflation days when employment was easily obtained and labor was paid at fancy prices, we as a group in America were lulled to sleep by the oft repeated phrase "The American Negro has made more progress than any other race on earth during the short period of years since his emancipation." Throughout the United States the beautiful homes of our professional classes were pointed to with pride. The earning capacity of our laboring classes had increased to such a point that many of the luxuries of life previously unavailable had become the ordinary convenience of many households. It was the ambition of nearly every household to have their children become doctors, dentists, lawyers and teachers. Colleges of one kind or another to train the children of these ambitious families sprang up all over the country.

Such was the condition during the post-war inflation period. This condition of affairs was not only true of the Negro, but it was more emphatically true of the rest of our population. America itself was running in high gear and the Negro was merely seeking to keep step.

With the 1929 stock market crash the bottom dropped out of the American financial life, crushing beneath it the aspiring Negro. The devastating effect of the depression upon the Negro as a whole has somehow apparently escaped, or perhaps been ignored by many of us who claim the right to be the Talented Tenth.[33]

During the heyday of our post-war success, those of us who assumed the role of leadership had come to feel that the chief end of our activities lay in vying with each other for social position. We organized women's clubs, womens' societies and other organizations principally for the purpose of bringing ourselves favorably before the eyes of the general public. The programs of these various groups and organizations for the most part consisted in regal entertainment and petty bickering for office. So great a hold on us did these activities take that even now they form a major part of the program of our various national women's organizations. Today we are virtually fiddling while the Rome of our race's future security is burning.

Is it not time, may I ask of you, my fellow club women, for us to take stock of ourselves? Are there not great neglected opportunities demanding our attention?

In my opinion the moral and physical plight in which thousands of our young girls today find themselves affords opportunity for club women to engage in an unselfish service that will yield untold benefits not only to our generation but to those succeeding us.

Girls and women of our group have always suffered certain handicaps. In the earliest struggles of our adventure as participants in weaving the social fabric of our American life, living conditions were not as difficult nor was making a livelihood as complicated as we find them today.

A recent report of the women's Department of the Federal Labor Bureau[34] indicates that 85% of our women are engaged in personal service. To begin with this great army of wage earners stagger under terrific handicaps; first they are untrained; second, they come from overcrowded homes; third, they suffer from unsanitary living conditions, they have practically no academic background, they undergo a multitude of social barriers,—all of which makes them unprepared for the competition to be met in new and difficult surroundings.

Again we find our unattached girl seeking a livelihood as she finds her way into large cities thrown into the worst kind of environment, a sea of moral degeneracy. A situation which she finds herself unable to overcome in later years and there she is doomed by society to a rotten and discouraged future. We as club women in neglecting these girls, are overlooking the very fountain of our existence.

From the experiences of the depression, we have come to realize that the majority of those of us who have fitted ourselves for professional pursuits exist only when our working classes are employed. We learned too that this working class constitutes upward of 90% of the employable persons of our group. It seems to me that we should begin now to see the need of improving the condition of the mass of our people.

We must stop deceiving ourselves by frittering away our time and effort in the desire for social position. Let us as club women seize upon the opportunity to improve, encourage, and preserve this great host of underprivileged women. Let us commend and patronize those of us who engage in any commercial or industrial pursuit—let us look up to, instead of down on, those who have not enjoyed a more cultural existence. Let us teach, as did the Christ, the dignity of service.

I sincerely believe that the colored club women of America are in position to render an outstanding service, a service that will redound to the race and to the nation as a whole. That service lays in elevating the place of the working girl of America so that the job of performing household duties shall become as dignified as that of any other field of economic endeavor. There is no reason why this greatly desired result should not be accomplished.

The field for service is so large that one hesitates to confine oneself to one or two suggestions. It seems to me that the colored club women of America would do well to consider the projection of a program calculated to build up the home life in their several communities. Recently I had opportunity to serve as chairman of the sub-committee on home life working under the auspices of the National Conference on Fundamental Problems in the Education of the Negro.[35] In this study our committee reported that the average American family was composed of five persons, two adults and three children, and that the average income yearly varied from $1500 to $1800 per year. Comparing this to the home life status of the Negro group it reported that the average income of the Negro family ranged from $720.00 to $900.00 per year while the size of the Negro family generally reached the figure seven.

The Negro family of seven, our committee reported, finds the husband working at a small weekly wage and the wife out of necessity working as a servant or laundress at a very small wage. The children ranging from the ages of 12 to 2 are for the most part left alone at home while the parents are at work, or, if of school age are at school for part of the day and upon returning home are left alone until the parents return from their daily occupation. Little or no time, the committee reported, was available for the personal development of the members of the family group within the home itself. The whole matter of the development of the Negro child of the average Negro family is left to the public school system, the social welfare institutions and the church organizations. These organizations, however, fail in many essential matters to effectively fill the place which well developed home life activities are calculated to serve.

If the report of this committee is a correct evaluation of the present status of Negro home life then here lies a great opportunity for the club women of America to undertake to engage in activities which will assist in raising to a higher level the home life status of the Negro family. Certainly much can be done in this direction.

Another opportunity for service is clearly defined in a report coming from the office of Dr. Ambrose Caliver,[36] Senior Specialist in Negro Education, Department of Interior,[37]—in which we note close to a million Negro children of high school age are not in school. This fact alone offers to the club women fertile soil for active service. Here is an opportunity for service of a high order—indeed it is almost a duty. If we women in our varied communities would have our clubs interest themselves in the lives of the ambitious youths about us—seek out the promising ones and provide scholarships, where needed, we will be performing a work more compensating than any yet undertaken.

At present Negro leadership was never in greater need of strengthening than it is today. Unless the women of the race and especially club women direct their attention to this great army of neglected children and underprivileged girls, there is bound to be a draught in our leadership for the future.

In a word, I am commending to you a task of unselfish service—our day and our race are calling for Sojourner Truths,[38] for Harriet Tubmans,[39] for Phillis Wheatleys,[40] the Mary and Martha[41] type, for women imbued with a desire to render a real service of unselfishness—Can we supply this need? I think we can![42]

NOTES

1. In 1896, Alonzo C. McClellan, an African American physician, founded the Canon Street Hospital and Training School for Nurses in Charleston for the education of African American medical personnel. Drago, *Charleston's Avery Center*, 99. Thomas Grange Simons Jr. (1843–1927), a white physician and Confederate Army veteran, studied medicine and worked at the Charleston City Hospital before opening a private practice. Snowden and Cutler, *History of South Carolina*, 5:164–65. The Wagner Sleeping Car Company, founded in 1858 by a white businessman, Webster Wagner (1817–1882), was the second-largest sleeping car company in America. White, *American Railroad Passenger Car*, 655; Harter, *World Railways*, 250.

2. In 1870, the American Missionary Association founded Hampton Institute, which Union General Samuel Chapman Armstrong further developed to train African American teachers. In 1892, the school began offering nursing training in the Hampton Nurse Training School and Dixie Hospital. Peabody, *Education for Life*, 95–126 and Jones-Wilson, *Encyclopedia of African-American Education*, 336.

3. Hunter, *A Nickel and a Prayer*, 71.

4. Ferguson and Williams College was a boarding middle school founded in 1885 by two black Presbyterian missionaries, the Reverend Emory W. (?–1910) Williams and Mrs. Ella V. Chase Williams (1852 or 1854–?) to provide industrial training and religious, musical, and literary education for African American children.

Daniel and Brown, *Women Builders,* 168; Smith, *Notable Black American Women,* 2:14–16.

5. Rutledge's ancestors include Edward Rutledge, a signer of the Declaration of Independence and a former governor of South Carolina, and Edward's brother, John Rutledge, delegate to the First Continental Congress. Snowden and Cutler, *History of South Carolina,* 5:116.

6. Wilkerson, *Warmth of Other Suns,* 57.

7. For a discussion of Cleveland's dramatic growth, see Phillips, "'But It Is a Fine Place,'" 393–413.

8. The National Association of Colored Women was a national network of black women's clubs. It was founded in 1896 to nurture and affirm black womanhood and to advance the cause of the race.

9. "Phillis Wheatley Founder Dies," Cleveland Call and Post, 1A and 6A.

10. In John Bunyan's *The Pilgrim's Progress* (1678), Christian encounters the beast Apollyon, representative of Satan, immediately after he receives assurance of salvation. See Bunyan, *Pilgrim's Progress,* 65.

11. Hunter is referencing the description of Apollyon in *The Pilgrim's Progress:* "Now the monster was hideous to behold; he was clothed with scales like a fish (and they are his pride), he had wings like a dragon, feet like a bear, and out of his belly came fire and smoke, and his mouth was as the mouth of a lion." Ibid.

12. Hunter is citing Christian's response to Apollyon's assertion that sin lead to death: "I was born indeed in your dominion, but your service was hard and your wages such as a man could not live on, for 'the wages of sin is death' (Rom. vi. 23)." The biblical source is "For the wages of sin is death; but the gift of God is eternal life through Jesus Christ our Lord" (Rom. 6:23). Ibid., 66.

13. Christian wins his battle against Apollyon by wounding the monster: "Christian perceiving that, made at him again, saying, 'Nay, in all these things we are more than conquerors through him that loved us' (Rom. viii. 37). And with that Apollyon spread forth his dragon's wings, and sped him away, that Christian for a season saw him no more (Jam. iv. 7)." Hunter characterizes "commercialized vice" as "Apollyon" and herself and Cleveland's black community as "Christian" to posit their struggle as a crusade against evil that they will win. Ibid., 69.

14. In the second decade of the twentieth century, Cleveland's African American population grew 307.8 percent, increasing from 8,448 (1.5% of the total population) to 34,451 (4.3% of the total population). See U.S. Department, Bureau of the Census, *Negroes in the United States,* 393–413.

15. Hunter characterizes Cleveland's "black belt" as a crime-ridden area "north of Cedar Avenue and south of Quincy Avenue, between East 55th and 105th Streets" that is filled with clubs, smoking saloons, and restaurants. She urged Clevelanders to support legislative initiatives that would turn the neighborhood into a safe, prosperous community. "It's Our Problem: Voters in the Black Belt," *Open Door,* October 1938.

16. "Dr. A—" may be Dudley Peter Allen (1852–1915), who was associated with the Severances, Cleveland's homeopathic doctors, the Medical Library Association, and the Cleveland Museum of Art. See Ohio Medical Society, "Dudley P. Allen," 23–45.

17. Osie was Albert "Starlight" Boyd's first wife, Olive Azaler Boyd (1881–1920).

18. Albert "Starlight" Boyd owned and operated the house of prostitution that Hunter references. It included a barbershop, pool hall, and dance floor, and it functioned as the unofficial Republican Party headquarters of Cuyahoga's Eleventh Ward. See Jones, *Jane Edna Hunter,* 74–75; *Encyclopedia of Cleveland History* (hereafter *ECH*), "Boyd, Albert Duncan 'Starlight.'"

19. The white civic leader Mary Rathburn Judd served as the general secretary of the Cleveland YWCA and as a member of the Cooperative Board of the PWA. See Jones, *Jane Edna Hunter,* 62, 69.

20. Indian clubs were heavy wooden devices shaped like bowling pins; they were used in exercise routines. See Bornstein, *Manual of Instruction,* 7–11.

21. The "Roaring Third" was the predominately African American "red light district" under the jurisdiction of Cleveland's Third Police Precinct, which black leaders faulted for being more interested in arresting patrons than corrupt businessmen. Giffin, *African Americans and the Color Line,* 21–22.

22. Hunter is likely referring to the Cleveland Railway Company, which gained exclusive rights to the city's public railway franchise in the early 1900s. See *ECH,* "Cleveland Railway Co."

23. After the Civil War, many African Americans joined the Republican Party, the "Party of Lincoln," because of the Emancipation Proclamation and Republicans' support of Reconstruction legislation. By the 1940s, however, many switched to the Democratic Party, drawn by President Franklin D. Roosevelt's New Deal and the Democratic Party's aggressive recruitment initiatives. See Scroop, *Mr. Democrat,* 122.

24. Tim Flagman was actually the African American activist Thomas W. Fleming (1874–1948), an influential Republican Party operative who helped establish the *Cleveland Journal,* a weekly African American newspaper, and served on the Cleveland city council. Flagman supported the PWA because of his belief in all-black institutions. See Davis, *Black Americans in Cleveland,* 143–44; *ECH,* "Fleming, Thomas W"; Giffin, *African Americans and the Color Line;* Gerber, *Black Ohio and the Color Line,* 404–6.

25. A ward-heeler is an elected official who is as loyal to powerful politicians as a dog is to its master.

26. Hunter felt cheated after Cleveland adopted a "City Manager Plan" in 1921 that empowered councilmen elected from four districts to select the city's chief executive. See Maxey, "Cleveland Election," 83–86.

27. Dora is not yet identified.

28. Operators redirected calls that had been routed from a switchboard to telephone customers using distinct rings. After transmitting a call to a resident, the PWA telephone operator could stay on the line and listen in on the conversation.

29. In 1926, Howard E. Murrell (?–1926), a black businessman, became manager of the African American–owned Empire Savings and Loan Bank, founded in 1911 to serve Cleveland's black community. Murrell was a PWA trustee for twelve years. See Davis, *Black Americans in Cleveland,* 243–44; *ECH,* "Empire Savings and Loan"; *Open Door,* October 1923.

30. St. Louis voodoo blues posits musicians as conjurers who use dream imagery, charms, and curses to cast a spell over their listeners.

31. The Central Association of Colored Women was a consortium of black women's clubs located in Illinois, Indiana, Iowa, Kentucky, Michigan, Minnesota, Missouri, and Wisconsin. It was affiliated with the National Association of Colored Women. See Brown, *History of Central Association.*

32. The National Recovery program was a New Deal initiative by President Franklin D. Roosevelt that established the National Recovery Administration, which supervised the development and enforcement of labor, production, and marketing standards to stabilize businesses and ensure fair wages for American workers. See O'Sullivan and Keuchel, *American Economic History,* 178–79.

33. The Talented Tenth were the well-educated top 10 percent of the African American population that the African American activist W. E. B. Du Bois (1868–1963) believed would elevate the masses.

34. In 1918 the Women's Bureau was established as a war agency, Women in Industry Service, to address the need for female workers in war production as men were drafted for military service. In 1920 the agency's name was changed to the Women's Bureau, the white American social researcher and reformer Mary van Kleeck was appointed director, and the scope of its mission was redirected to the creation and implementation of public policy regarding fair wages, safe work environments, and employment opportunities for American working women. See Weber, *Women's Bureau.*

35. The 1934 National Conference on Fundamental Problems in the Education of the Negro was a New Deal initiative supported by First Lady Eleanor Roosevelt to address the inequities in public education opportunities for African American children.

36. The African American educator and civil servant Dr. Ambrose Caliver (1894–1962) worked as a high school teacher and principal and as director of vocational programs and dean at Fisk University before President Herbert Hoover appointed him to be Senior Specialist in the Education of Negroes for the U.S. Office of Education. President Franklin D. Roosevelt later selected him as a Specialist for Education Relief in the Federal Emergency Relief Administration. He was later named director of the Project for Literacy Education, adviser for the U.S. Displaced Persons Commission and the United Nations Special Commission on Non-Self Governing Territories, and president of the Adult Education Association. See Wilkins, "Section K: Ambrose Caliver," 212–13.

37. The Negro Education Specialist, a position first held by Dr. Caliver in the Department of the Interior, created and published public policy that addressed the educational needs of African Americans, including vocational, public and private school, collegiate, and gifted education.

38. Born into slavery and named Isabella Baumfree in Ulster County, New York, Sojourner Truth (1797–1883) gained her freedom after New York outlawed slavery, in 1828. Fifteen years later, believing she had received a call from God to preach, she renamed herself Sojourner Truth and traveled throughout the country, eventually

becoming one of the most influential antislavery and women's rights activists and orators of the nineteenth century.

39. Harriet Tubman (c. 1820–1913) was born into slavery in Dorchester County, Maryland, but escaped and eventually led more than one hundred enslaved African Americans to freedom in the North and in Canada, a feat that earned her the moniker Moses. Tubman also worked as a spy, cook, and nurse for the Union Army during the Civil War.

40. Phillis Wheatley (1753–1784), the first African American to publish a poetry collection, was born in West Africa. She was sold into slavery and transported to a Boston slave market where a white merchant, John Wheatley, purchased her as a lady's maid for his wife, Susannah Wheatley. The Wheatleys educated Phillis and helped arrange for the publication of her letters and poems. Phillis Wheatley gained her freedom after she returned from a trip to England to arrange for the publication of her poetry anthology.

41. Mary, known as a close friend of Jesus, was distinguished by her devotion to learning truths from the Savior. Her sister, Martha, is remembered as a fastidious host yet faithful follower whom Jesus gently scolded for being frustrated by Mary's preference for listening to His teachings rather than assisting with hospitality duties.

42. Hunter's speech was typed onto a series of index cards. The final card bears a handwritten note that reads as follows: "Irene, Please have Dr. Waring publish this speech given by Mrs. Jane Hunter at our Regional meeting in Louisville. Missed you much. Fondly, Ella." Ella, whose identity has not been determined, is likely referencing the African American educator and social activist Dr. Mary F. Waring (?–1958), the tenth president of the National Association of Colored Women.

Benjamin Elijah Mays
(1894–1984)

EDUCATOR, MINISTER, SCHOLAR, SOCIAL ACTIVIST

*Whatever you do, strive to do it so well that no man living and
no man dead, and no man yet to be born can do it any better.*

When he began his twenty-seven-year tenure as president of Morehouse College, a historically black institution of higher education for African American men in Atlanta, Georgia, Benjamin Elijah Mays initiated a tradition of preaching a sermon in chapel each Tuesday to inspire students to strive for excellence. Years after Dr. Clinton E. Warner graduated from Morehouse, he recalled a particular chapel talk from his and Mays's first year that still influenced his life. After chiding students for not valuing their education, Mays had offered these words of encouragement: "Whatever you do, strive to do it so well that no man living and no man dead, and no man yet to be born can do it any better."[1] Warner believes that Mays's aphorisms helped create the "Morehouse Mystique," a distinguishing characteristic of Morehouse Men that propelled thousands of graduates to distinguished careers in fields ranging from medicine to politics.

Mays's own thirst for education fueled his drive to overcome the limitations of Jim Crow laws imposed on African American South Carolinians by the South Carolina constitutional convention in 1895, the year after he was born. He was the eighth child of Louvenia Carter and Hezekiah Mays, former slaves who labored as farmers on land they rented near Ninety-Six,

South Carolina. During his formative years, Benjamin Mays attended the Brickhouse School for three to four months a year and helped his parents plant and harvest crops during the remaining months until he was about fifteen years old. At that time, his pastor, the Reverend James F. Marshall of the Old Mt. Zion Baptist Church, convinced his father to allow him to attend the Baptist Association School in McCormick for two years. Next, Mays enrolled in South Carolina State College's High School Department, despite his father's objections.[2] Hezekiah Mays viewed farming or preaching as his son's best career options, jobs he believed did not require formal education. Benjamin Mays forged ahead, buoyed by his mother's support, his church family's encouragement, and his own love of learning. At State College, he met African American faculty who had graduated from historically black institutions that specialized in preparing African Americans for teaching careers. In 1915 Mays graduated as valedictorian of his class. He continued his education at Virginia Union College, a historically black college in Richmond, Virginia.[3] One year later, he transferred to Bates College in Lewistown, Maine, with the encouragement and assistance of two Bates alumni who taught at Virginia and wrote letters of recommendation for him. Mays wanted to compete with whites at a New England college to dispel the myth of Negro inferiority. He financed his education by working as a Pullman porter during the summer and winning scholarships. Mays excelled academically and became president of the Debating Council and the Phil-Hellenic Club, a member of the Young Men's Christian Association (YMCA) Council, and graduated Phi Beta Kappa in 1920.[4]

Shortly after finishing college and beginning his career as an educator and pastor, Mays married Ellen Harvin. They settled in Atlanta, where he began working as a mathematics teacher and debate coach at Morehouse College in 1921. Within a year, he was ordained as a Baptist minister and appointed pastor of the Shiloh Baptist Church. Just as the young couple settled into their new life in Atlanta, however, tragedy marred their happiness. Ellen Harvin Mays died unexpectedly after a surgical procedure at a hospital in Atlanta. While mourning his wife's death, Mays redirected his energies to the pursuit of higher education. In 1925 he earned a master's degree from the University of Chicago's School of Religion, which introduced him to a "sociohistorical approach to religion" that enabled him to contextualize biblical and world events from political, sociological, and economic perspectives.[5] Upon graduation, he accepted a position as an English professor at his alma mater, South Carolina State College, where he married Sadie Gray, a social worker and a member of the faculty. The young couple began their forty-six-year marriage with a move to Tampa, Florida, for Mays's two-year stint at the Tampa Urban League and the Tampa Family Services Association. In 1928 the couple relocated to Atlanta, where Benjamin Mays worked as the national student secretary of the YMCA for two years. By 1930 he had initiated a two-year sociological study, sponsored by the Institute of Social and Religious Research in New York, of 609 urban and 185 rural African American churches in twelve cities.[6] His research on black churches led to the publication of his first book, *The Negro's Church*, coauthored with Joseph W. Nicholson, a pastor of the Colored Methodist Episcopal Church. The book presented a bleak assessment of African American churches in the early twentieth century as debt-ridden institutions managed mostly by pastors with poor academic credentials. Although Mays and Nicholson recommended radical changes in both the education of black pastors and the bent of African American theology, they acknowledged the critical role of black churches in sustaining hope, instilling pride, and nurturing identity in African Americans.

In 1932, Mays continued his exploration of the connection between Christianity and social activism through graduate studies and higher education administration. He initiated this new phase in his career by enrolling in the PhD program at the University of Chicago's Divinity School. After completing his studies, he became the dean of the School of Religion at Howard University in Washington, D.C., where he worked for six years. Under his leadership, enrollment increased, the faculty improved, the curriculum diversified, and the library expanded, achievements that garnered the highest commendation from the American Association of Theological Schools.

Professional success led to increased opportunities. In 1936 Mays was selected as one of twelve U.S. delegates to the World Conference of the YMCA in Mysore, India. While there, he met privately with Mahatma Gandhi to discuss nonviolent strategies for civil disobedience that would become a central component of the protest strategy of the 1960s civil rights movement. When he was appointed president of Morehouse College, in 1940, Mays transformed the fledging school into one of the nation's premier institutions of higher learning. Although the Great Depression and World War II had led to dramatic decreases in enrollment, Mays convinced the trustees to keep the college open. He implemented innovative recruitment initiatives, hired new faculty, strengthened the curriculum, and established a Phi Beta Kappa chapter. During his twenty-seven-year tenure at Morehouse, Mays devoted enormous energy to mentoring a cadre of civil rights leaders, notably his protegé Martin Luther King Jr., who described Mays as his "spiritual and intellectual father."[7] Mays later presented King with an honorary doctorate from Morehouse and delivered the eulogy at his funeral.

Mays extended the scope of his influence through affiliations with prominent educational, religious, and racial uplift organizations. When he retired from Morehouse, in 1969, he was elected to the Atlanta school board, where he became the first African American chairman and brokered the peaceful desegregation of the public schools. He also served in leadership positions with the NAACP, the Commission on Interracial Cooperation,[8] the Southern Regional Council,[9] the National Council of Churches,[10] and the United Negro College Fund.[11]

As a popular orator and prolific author, Mays disseminated discerning insights on religion and race relations that reached varied audiences ranging from the general public to academic scholars. His consummate skill as a public speaker earned him speaking engagements at colleges, universities, and churches throughout the nation. Mays published eight books, including *The Negro's God* and *A Gospel for the Social Awakening*, as well as a collection of sermons titled *Disturbed about Man*. He also contributed chapters to fifteen other books and wrote more than two thousand articles that were featured in leading periodicals such as *Crisis, The Journal of Negro Education, Saturday Review*, and the *Journal of Religious Thought*; in newspapers such as the *Pittsburgh Courier*, the *Atlanta Journal*, and the *Atlanta Constitution*; and in numerous pamphlets, including "The Christian and Race Relations." In the selection presented here, taken from his autobiography, *Born to Rebel*, Mays opens his narrative with a recollection of his earliest memory: his father's humiliation by a mob of rifle-carrying white men on horseback during the Phoenix Riot. He positions himself as a village griot–sociologist, interweaving his life narrative with stories from fellow black southerners who supplement and enrich his history of a resilient people who survived slavery and the setbacks of the post-Reconstruction era. A thread of race pride runs throughout the narrative, as Mays asserts, "We never felt sorry for ourselves because we were dark, and we accepted Africa as the home of our ancestors. Although I can appreciate the current emphasis on blackness, I am mighty glad I didn't have to wait seventy years for someone in the late 1960s is to teach me to appreciate what I am—black!" But his is pride tempered by the daily challenges of life in a racist society where negotiating the color lines was a matter of life and death for African Americans in the early twentieth century.

Throughout his career, Mays received national recognition for effective public service. In 1944 he was listed on the Schomburg Honor Roll of Race Relations. In 1974, he received an honorary doctorate from Lander University in Greenwood, South Carolina, the first of fifty-six he would be awarded over his lifetime. In 1980 the South Carolina state legislature authorized the installation of his portrait in the State House. In 1981, the intersection of Scotch Cross Road and U.S. Highway 178 near his birthplace was renamed "Mays Crossroads." In 1982 the NAACP awarded him the Spingarn Medal. In 1983 he was inducted into the South Carolina Hall of Fame.

Mays died on March 28, 1984. More than 2,500 people attended his funeral at Morehouse College. The U.S. Congress unanimously affirmed his selection as a recipient of the Presidential Medal of Freedom posthumously.

His childhood home has been preserved at the Benjamin E. Mays Historic Site in Greenwood, South Carolina.

⸾ Excerpt from *Born to Rebel: An Autobiography*

Chapter 1: *"In the Days of My Youth"*

I remember a crowd of white men who rode up on horseback with rifles on their shoulders. I was with my father when they rode up, and I remember starting to cry. They cursed my father, drew their guns and made him salute, made him take off his hat and bow down to them several times. Then they rode away. I was not yet five years old, but I have never forgotten them.

I know now that they were one of the mobs associated with the infamous Phoenix Riot which began in Greenwood County, South Carolina, on November 8, 1898, and spread terror throughout the countryside for many days thereafter.[12] My oldest sister, Susie, tells me, and newspaper reports of that period reveal, that several Negroes were lynched on the ninth and others on subsequent days.

That mob is my earliest memory.

Susie says I was born on August 1, 1895. The 1900 United States Census gives my birth date as August 1,1894, and this date I accept. My birthplace is ten miles from the town of Ninety Six, South Carolina, and fourteen miles from Greenwood, the county seat. The first post office l recall was named Rambo; later it was renamed "Epworth." Epworth is four miles from my birthplace, six miles from Ninety Six, and ten miles from Greenwood. The train ran through Ninety Six, which is seventy-five miles from Columbia. My birthplace is about midway between Greenwood and Saluda, not far from Edgefield.

Both my parents were born in slavery, my father, Hezekiah Mays, in 1856 and my mother, Louvenia Carter Mays, in 1862. My mother was too young to remember anything about slavery, but Father could, for he was nine years old when the Civil War came to an end in 1865.

I know virtually nothing about my ancestors. I have been told that my grandmother, Julia Mays, and her two children were sold as slaves by someone in Virginia to a buyer in South Carolina. Her daughter died early and her son was shot to death in the field by a white man. After coming to South Carolina, she married my grandfather, James Mays. Six children were born to them, four girls and two boys: Frances, Roenia, Janette, Polly, Hezekiah (my father), and Isaiah.

I never knew my grandfather, James Mays, but I remember my grandmother, Julia, quite distinctly. She lived to be ninety or more years old. As I remember her features, I think she might have had a strain of Indian or white blood. However, I do not recall ever hearing her or my parents make any reference to white ancestry. I never knew my maternal grandparents. My mother had three brothers and two sisters: Abner, Harper, John, Sarah, and Susie.

My mother and father were very dark-skinned, and the color of their children ranged from black to dark brown. Color was never a problem in my family, nor did we ever feel any discrimination based on color among Negroes in my community, whose colors ranged from black to white. To protect the "purity" of the white race, South Carolina had decreed that any person with one-eighth of Negro blood in his veins belonged to the Negro race.[13] So there were a good many mulattoes and white Negroes in my area. We never felt sorry for ourselves because we were dark, and we accepted Africa as the home of our ancestors. Although I can appreciate the current emphasis on blackness, I am mighty glad I didn't have to wait seventy years for someone in the late 1960s to teach me to appreciate what I am—black! Many times my mother, unlettered and untutored though she was, said to us children, "You are as good as anybody!" This assurance was helpful to me even though the white world did not accept my mother's philosophy!

My heroes were black. Every once in a while, some Negro came along selling pictures of, or pamphlets about, a few Negro leaders. Pictures of Frederick Douglass, Booker T. Washington, and Paul Laurence Dunbar hung on our walls.[14] In my high school days, Booker T. Washington meant more to me than George Washington; Frederick Douglass was more of a hero than William Lloyd Garrison; Dunbar inspired me more than Longfellow. I heard about Crispus Attucks and was thrilled. The Negro preachers and teachers in my county, I worshiped. I didn't know any of the white preachers and teachers. (I doubt that I would have worshiped them if I had!) The Negroes in the South Carolina Legislature during the Reconstruction and post-Reconstruction years were the men held up to us in high school history classes as being great men, and not the Negro-hating Benjamin Ryan Tillman and his kind, who strove so long and hard to deprive the black man of his vote.[15] I had identity.

My mother could neither read nor write. She enjoyed having me read to her, especially sections of the Bible. Until this day, I regret that I didn't teach my mother to read, write, and figure. Father could read printing fairly well but not script. I often wondered how my father—a slave for the first nine years of his life—had learned to read as well as he did. My sister Susie, ninety years old now, told me much about our parents when I visited her in the summer of 1967 as I was beginning this book. She remembers well two of my father's stories. He frequently told how the slave children on his master's plantation were fed. While the slaves were working in the fields, the master's wife would feed the slave children. She would pour milk into a trough and then call the slave children—my father among them. The children would rush to the trough, scoop up the milk in their hands and slurp it into their mouths. The other story is delightful. The slave master's son liked my father very much. Though it was unlawful to teach a slave to read, this white boy would take my father down in the woods to a secluded spot and there teach him to read.

I am the youngest of eight—three girls and five boys: Susie, Sarah, Mary, James, Isaiah, John, Hezekiah, and Benjamin—me. I never knew Isaiah, who died early. Hezekiah was the only one of my siblings to finish high school. The others went hardly beyond the fifth grade in our ungraded one-room school. The maximum school term of the Negro school was four months— November through February. The white school usually ran six months. Dis-crimination and farm work accounted for the shorter term for Negroes. Most of the cotton was picked in September and October; and early in March work on the farm began. It would never have occurred to the white people in charge of the schools that they should allow school to interfere with the work on the farms. I was nineteen years old before I was able to remain in school for the full term. . . .

In 1900, Greenwood County, in which I lived, had a population of 28,343, of which 18,906, or 66.7 percent, were Negroes. The fact that Negroes so far outnumbered the whites contributed to the whites' determination to exclude them from politics. The evil result of this determination was the infamous Phoenix Riot. Negroes in my county were heavily dependent upon the white people for land to till; the whites were equally dependent upon the Negroes to get their farms worked. In 1900, close to 20 percent of the Negro farmers in South Carolina owned their homes. However, in Greenwood County in 1910 only 112 Negroes owned their farms free of debt; ninety-five had farms but they were mortgaged; sixty-eight were part owners; 1,230 were cash ten-ants; 1,296 were share tenants; forty-three share-cash tenants; and eighty-nine were not specifically designated.[16] These figures add up to 2,933 farms run by Negroes. The free-of-debt owners, plus the owners with the mort-gages, and the part-owners totaled 275, or 9.4 percent who had some owner-ship in their farms. Roughly speaking, only one Negro farmer in ten owned his land, and only one in twenty-six owned a farm absolutely free of debt. Ninety percent of the Negro farmers in Greenwood County were renters, sharecroppers, and wage hands. Despite poverty, however, Negro life was very stable. As a rule, men did not desert their families. There were not many illegitimate children in my community. A girl who had an illegitimate child was usually looked down on as having brought disgrace to her family.

My father was a renter. As far back as I can remember, I think we owned our mules. Any man who owned his mules or horses, buggy, wagon, or other farm equipment occupied a little higher status than the one who worked for wages or was a sharecropper. The wage hand was one who worked by the month for ten, twelve, or fifteen dollars a month. The sharecropper, or the one who worked on "halves," had his house, mules, and other farm implements provided for him. The owner of the land received half of all the sharecropper made.

As I recall, Father usually rented forty acres of land for a two-mule farm, or sixty acres if we had three mules. The rent was two bales of cotton, weighing 500 pounds each, for every twenty acres rented. So the owner of the land got his two, four, or six bales out of the first cotton picked and ginned. Many Negroes rented as many as sixty acres of land, paying as rent six bales of cotton weighing 500 pounds each. From the first bales ginned, Father got only the money that came from selling the cottonseeds. I was elated when that time came, for my father always celebrated by buying a big wheel of sharp yellow cheese out of the first cottonseed money. I still enjoy the taste of cheese. I have eaten the finest varieties in many parts of the world, but nothing has ever tasted as good to me as the cheese my father used to bring home from the sale of cottonseeds.

Although I do not recall that we were ever hungry and unable to get food, we did have very little to go on. To make sixteen bales of cotton on a two-mule farm was considered excellent farming. After four bales were used to pay rent, we would have twelve bales left. The price of cotton fluctuated. If we received ten cents a pound, we would have somewhere between five and six hundred dollars, depending upon whether the bales of cotton weighed an average of 450, 475, or 500 pounds. When all of us children were at home we, with our father and mother, were ten. We lived in a four-room house, with no indoor plumbing—no toilet facilities, no running water. . . .

In later years, my wife was shocked when she first saw the Brickhouse School, for she had expected to see a real brick building. It was named the Brickhouse School after a large brick house nearby owned by a white man. It was a frame, one-room building with a wood stove in the center of the room, with boys seated on one side and girls on the other. The school ran for four months, from the first of November through February. When we moved from the Childs' place to the Mays' place, the round trip to school was increased from about six to approximately seven miles.

It was a happy day for me when I entered the Brickhouse School at the age of six. I discovered on that eventful day that I knew more than any of the other children who were entering school for the first time. Susie, my oldest sister, had taught me to say the alphabet, to count to a hundred, and to read a little. Since I was the only one in the beginners' class who could do these things, I was praised and highly complimented by the surprised teacher. As we put it, she "bragged on me." The next church Sunday, the second Sunday in November, my teacher sought my parents and told them, with other people standing around, "Bennie is smart." From that moment on, I was the star of that one-room school. The experience made a tremendous impression on me, so much so that I felt I had to live up to my teacher's expectations. I became Exhibit A when visitors came around and I was called upon to recite, which I was always eager and ready to do. I dearly loved the spelling class, where the best speller stood at the head of the class. If the boy or girl at the head of the class missed a word, the one who spelled the word correctly moved to the head of the class. I had been so impressed with myself that first day that I always strove thereafter to occupy the first place in class. I loved school so well that when the weather was bad and Mother kept me home I would weep. The student who was out of school a day had to go to the foot of the class, even though he had been standing at the head. When it did happen that I had to go to the foot for being absent, I took great delight in working my way up from the foot to the head.

I fell in love with my teacher, and I am sure I studied hard to please her as well as to learn. My first teacher was Ellen Waller, daughter of Tom Waller, the wealthy Negro farmer. Miss Waller was a high school graduate from Benedict College in Columbia, South Carolina. Very few Negroes went to college from my county.[17] I can think of only four, before my time, who went to college and received degrees. A fair number went to high school and were graduated. . . .

. . . As I sat as a boy in Sunday school, discussing the Sunday school lessons with the adults, asking questions and making comments, they encouraged me and gave me their blessings. Each Sunday in June, we had what was called "Children's Day." I do not remember exactly how old I was—possibly nine—when I participated, having committed to memory a portion of the Sermon on the Mount. After my recitation, the house went wild: old women waved their handkerchiefs, old men stamped their feet, and the people generally applauded long and loud. It was a terrific ovation, let alone a tremendous experience, for a nine-year-old boy. There were predictions that I would "go places" in life. The minister said I would preach; and from that moment on the Reverend Marshall manifested a special interest in me. All of this was part of the motivation that had started with my oldest sister's teaching me how to count and read and write, thereby winning for me the encouragement and praise given me by my first teacher, Ellen Waller. The people in the church did not contribute one dime to help me with my education. But they gave me something far more valuable. They gave me encouragement, the thing I most needed. They expressed such confidence in me that I always felt that I could never betray their trust, never let them down.

After the Phoenix Riot, never a year passed in my county that there were not several brutal incidents involving Negroes and whites. In the months following the Phoenix Riot, I had seen bloodhounds on our land with a mob looking for a Negro. I saw a Negro hiding in the swamps for fear of being caught and lynched. Negroes always got the worst of it. Guilt and innocence were meaningless words: the Negro was always blamed, always punished. Among themselves, Negroes talked much about these tragedies. They were impotent to do anything about them. They dared not even mention them to whites.

I was twelve years old when I read about the Atlanta Riot in the Greenwood *Index* and the Atlanta *Journal*, the two papers to which we subscribed.[18] As I recall, the papers played up the fact that the Atlanta Riot was the result of a series of attacks that Negro men were supposed to have made on white women. It was not until I was older that I realized that Hoke Smith, who campaigned for governor of Georgia on a white supremacy platform, and the four Atlanta newspapers which played up the accusations against the Negroes, not only struck the match but supplied the combustible material to ignite the flames that produced the Atlanta Riot.[19]

It was in this connection that I received a stern lecture from the man who was later to marry my sister Susie. He was an unlettered but highly intelligent man. Like Susie, he would have done well in anybody's college had he been given half a chance to go. He often walked miles to see my sister, and frequently if he left before dark he would invite me to walk a distance with him. During one of our walks, the Atlanta Riot was mentioned. I was old enough at the time to hear what my parents talked about in the home. I heard the gossip about things that happened in the community. My older brothers and sisters learned all the rumors of the county and talked freely about them at home and in the cotton fields. We knew that a beautiful, light-brown-skinned Negro woman was living in the house with a white man, and that Negro men knew enough to leave her alone. It was common knowledge that "Hamp," the mulatto Negro who lived in a house a white man built for him in his backyard and whom the white man kept there to work in his house and to drive his daughters around, was really the white man's son, born to a Negro woman, and therefore half brother to the white daughters. It was an accepted fact that "Polly," a beautiful Negro woman, was the paramour of "Lowden," a white man. Once Polly was caught in a buggy with a Negro man, and rumor had it that Lowden made her get out of the buggy and threatened to shoot the Negro man. This story was so deeply believed that fifty years later Negroes living in that community were still talking about Polly and Lowden, who both lingered ill and suffered for years before they died. Negroes say even now that God punished them for their sins. It no doubt was a comfort to believe that God would mete out the punishment that Negroes were powerless to inflict. Occasionally, too, a white baby turned up in a black home.

In the Atlanta Riot, which began on Saturday night, September 22, 1906, and extended through Tuesday, September 25, many Negroes were killed and many more wounded. One or two whites were killed and several wounded. The riot was allegedly caused by black men attacking white women. It was in this context that I asked my brother-in-law-to-be why it was that white men could do anything they wanted to Negro women but Negro men were lynched and killed if they did the same to white women or even if they were merely accused and innocent. My prospective brother-in-law stopped by the side of the road and gave me a stern lecture. He told me in positive language never to discuss that matter again. It was dangerous talk, and if I said such a thing in the presence of a white person it would not be good for me. . . .

I cannot close this chapter without words of commendation for my parents. My father was bitterly opposed to my efforts to get an education; and yet I owe much to my parents. I shall mention only two things:

My parents were industrious. There wasn't a lazy bone in their bodies. They didn't sit back and make the children do it. They did their part on the farm. In addition to cooking, seeing that our clothes were washed and ironed, and keeping the house clean, Mother hoed and picked cotton, and Father worked equally hard. I must have caught their spirit of work. To this day, I am impatient with lazy people. Father believed that a man should earn his living by the sweat of his brow, and that, to him, meant working on the farm in the blazing hot sun. And my parents were honest. I never heard them scheming how they might get something for nothing. I never suspected them of stealing anything from anybody. They taught their children honesty. I believe that not a single child in our family expected to get anything except through honest channels and by his own efforts. I am reminded of what John Hope, president of Morehouse College in Atlanta, once said.[20] He admitted that Morehouse was poor, but added, "We live in respectable poverty!" The Mays family was poor and lived on the ragged edge of poverty, but we lived in "respectable poverty."

The rugged honesty of my parents has stuck with me through all these years. I am intolerant of dishonesty, particularly intellectual dishonesty, wherein men ignore or distort the truth and plot to take advantage of others for their own indulgence. My parents did little or no ethical philosophizing, but they *lived* their ideals of industry and honesty. I am indebted to them for their living example, and I am grateful.

There were only a few books in the Mays' house and no magazines. We had the Bible, a dictionary, picture books about Booker T. Washington, Frederick Douglass, and Paul Laurence Dunbar, and Sunday school books. We read the Atlanta *Journal* and the Greenwood *Index*. And we had the school textbooks from which we learned to read, spell, and figure to a certain level. This was about it. Nobody in the family had gone beyond the fourth or fifth grade. I didn't seem to have much to go on. But I had learned industry and honesty from my parents. I had been inspired by my county teachers, encouraged by the Reverend Marshall, and motivated by the people in the church who made me believe that I could become something worthwhile in the world. These are the things that drove me on and, when they are summed up, I guess they amount to quite a lot.

Chapter 2: "Be Careful and Stay out of Trouble"

There wasn't much going for the Negro in the world in which I was born. The shades of darkness were falling fast upon and around him. The tides of the post-Reconstruction years were being turned deliberately and viciously against him. The ballot was being taken away. Segregation was being enacted into law. Lynching was widespread and vigorously defended. Injustice in the courts was taken for granted whenever a Negro was involved with a white man. Discrimination and inequity in education were accepted as morally right. Books and articles were being published, sermons preached, and anti-Negro speeches made, all saying in substance: *The Negro is a different breed. He is inferior to the white man. At any cost he must be kept down.*

The North and the South had reached an agreement about the Negro's role in the South and in the nation. It was to be a subordinate role, with the Southern white man free from Northern interference, whatever might be his treatment of Negroes. Poor whites, former slave masters, and the warring political factions among the whites shared one determination: the "inferior" Negro was not to be allowed to become a political threat to white supremacy. At every turn the black man was being dehumanized. In fact, the Negro was being enslaved again.

In this perilous world, if a black boy wanted to live a halfway normal life and die a natural death he had to learn early the art of how to get along with white folks.

The Negro's economic or educational status in no way modified the problem. It was always the Negro's responsibility to find ways and means to get along with white people; never need white people concern themselves with getting along with Negroes. Were a Negro slightly above the county poverty level, with a few dollars in the bank and the ability to read, write, and figure, it was all the more necessary for him to behave well and "walk humbly" among the white folks. Strange as it may seem to most Negroes and whites today, it was literally true, when I was a boy, that it behooved Negroes to be humble, meek, and subservient in the presence of white folks. It is even true in some backward sections of the South in 1970.

When my parents admonished their children, "Be careful and stay out of trouble," they had only one thing in mind: "Stay out of trouble with white people!" My parents were not more cautious or fearful than others; virtually all Negro parents tried in some way to protect their children from the ever-present menace of white violence. The meaning was unmistakably clear. It was dangerous to argue with a white person. No matter how false or stupid, his word was law and gospel. It was not to be disputed even in court. "Stay out of trouble" meant that if the white man cursed you, you were not to curse him back. Even if he struck you, it was not safe to strike back. The occasional few who did strike back either ran out of town under cover of night or sought the protection of some "boss" or other influential white man. No matter how they acted, it was not always possible for Negroes to "stay out of trouble"; the many who cringed and kowtowed to white people the most were in just as much danger as the few who did not. How could a Negro avoid trouble when his "place" was whatever any white man's whim dictated at any given time? Hundreds of innocent Negroes were insulted, cheated, beaten, even lynched for the sole reason that they had incurred the displeasure of some white man. The situation was the same in essence throughout the South, though the degree of brutality varied from one section to another. Inevitably, some Negroes decided to fight back and suffer the consequences. One in my area, in self-defense, killed two white men and tried to escape. He took refuge in an empty house. A mob burned the house down and shot the Negro to death as he ran out. . . .

It was customary in Greenwood County, and throughout the South, for Negroes to call white men and boys in their teens "Mister." The whites called Negroes, no matter what their age, "John," "Charlie," "boy," "Jane," "Sallie," "girl," "Uncle," "Aunt," and often "nigger." Among the 118 contemporaries interviewed, 107 (90 percent) said that they and members of their families always addressed white people formally, by titles such as "Sir," "Boss," "Cap," "Mrs," "Miss." So, as a technique of survival, most Negro parents in my community and elsewhere taught their children servility. Even here, however, there were a few exceptions. One Negro interviewed said that in her town Negroes and whites who grew up together called each other by their first names. She stated that it was not until she moved to Atlanta that she encountered the "Miss Ann" practice. "I was on my first nursing job in this exclusive Atlanta area," she said, "when I addressed a sixteen-year-old white girl as 'Nancy.' Her mother quickly informed me that I was to call her daughter 'Miss Nancy'!" There were other cases where Negroes and whites grew up and played together, but at a certain age the white boy or girl demanded that his Negro playmate call him or her "Mr." or "Miss."

I am not wise enough to say categorically what this system did to Negroes in Greenwood County. I can only speculate on the basis of what I saw and observed. It certainly "put the rabbit" in many Negroes. They were poor, inadequately trained, and dependent on the white man for work. Few dared to stand up to a white man. When one did, he got the worst of it. It was not unusual to hear that a certain Negro had been run out of town, or, fearing he would be, had left the county before "they" could get him. Most Negroes grinned, cringed, and kowtowed in the presence of white people. Those who could not take such subservience left for the city as soon as they could—with or without their father's permission. They went to Asheville, Columbia, and Washington, and some went North. As a Pullman porter, I met several hundred of these boys who had fled the South. I often heard them say, "I would rather be a lamppost on Lenox Avenue in Harlem than be the Governor of Mississippi!" There were others who, though they could not get away, never quite accepted in their minds the role they had to play. Some parents, thinking that they themselves were too old to adjust in a new place, permitted their sons and daughters to go away with their blessings.

Negroes lived under constant pressures and tensions all the time in my community. They knew they were not free. They knew that if attacked they dare not strike back—if they wanted to live. To be at ease, to be relaxed, to be free were luxuries unknown to Negroes in Greenwood County and in most sections of the South. Some Negroes grew bitter and hated white people—all white people. Ralph, a high school roommate of mine from Florida, was one of those who hated white people; and Ralph was not afraid. He was graduated from State College, from Lincoln University in Pennsylvania, and from Cornell. Though he did not return to Florida, he did teach in the South. I was always afraid that he would be killed. If he had been attacked, he would have fought. I believe to this day that Negroes in my county fought among themselves because they were taking out on other Negroes what they really wanted but feared to take out on whites. It was difficult, virtually impossible, to combine manhood and blackness under one skin in the days of my youth. To exercise manhood, as white men displayed it, was to invite disaster.

At revival time in August, people could go from one church to another for a whole month if they chose because there were churches within an eight- or ten-mile radius of our house that held preaching one Sunday each month, and August was "Big Meeting" month. For the church that held worship on the first Sunday in August, the Big Meeting, or Revival, was held the first week in August, and so on through the month. Many buggies and wagons were on the road. There were no paved roads; when it was dry the roads were very dusty, and when it rained they were very muddy. As a rule, Negroes did not pass white people on either a dusty or a muddy road. If a Negro did pass a white person, throwing dust on him, the Negro was supposed to apologize for passing. I have been with my father when he apologized for passing a white driver by saying, "Excuse me, Boss, I'm in a hurry." Did this mean that my father mentally accepted or emotionally approved this cringing be-havior? I doubt it. It was a technique of survival. But I have always wondered how long one can do a thing without eventually accepting it. I believe my father rebelled against the system as best he knew how. Dozens of times, I heard him tell, in gleeful tones and with a sparkle in his eyes, how when he was young he had whipped two white men. He knocked one of them down and, while that one was getting up, he knocked the other man down. Every time he told the story, he would laugh, and laugh, and laugh. It was his prize story.

I never had a white playmate; but seventy-two (63.7 percent) of those interviewed for my study said that they had had white playmates. The vast majority of them admitted that such shared play ceased in the pre-teen or early teen years, usually at twelve or thirteen. When play stopped, so did friendship.

My parents advised us further, especially my mother. They admonished my brothers and me to stay clear of white women. My mother told us that white women were dangerous and would surely get us into trouble. Whenever we met them on the road, or on the street in town, we were to "give them space and the time of day." If there were white women in the community whom we knew, we tipped our hats to them and passed on. Although Negroes were lynched for minor offenses as well as for major ones, real or trumped up, the white press tended to give the impression that Negroes were lynched only when white women were involved. . . .

While white men used physical force to protect white women or to avenge alleged attacks on white women by black men, Negro parents had to contrive other methods to protect their daughters, often without success. My parents did what they could to prevent exposure of my sisters to white men. My sisters were never allowed to work for white farmers unless one or more of their brothers worked along with them. When one of my sisters went to the store, one brother always went with her. As a rule, Father never permit-ted my sisters to cook for white families. Only my oldest sister, Susie, cooked out; and this was for the Childs family. We lived on their place, and Susie has told me that Dr. Childs was very kind to the family, particularly when all of us, except me, were ill with typhoid fever. I was two years old when the fever epidemic struck the family, and I never knew Dr. Childs. My brother Isaiah, whom I also never knew, was the only one of my family who died in the epidemic. Dr. Childs and God shared the credit for saving the other members of our family!

It is not my intention to give the impression that all white men made sexual overtures or advances to Negro women. Such an indictment would be far from the truth. But there was more than enough evidence to instill caution in Negro parents who cared about their daughters. Nor would I be so naïve as to imply that all Negro women were paragons of virtue at the turn of the century. Human nature and desires are essentially the same the world over. People are people regardless of race. But Negro parents knew during those difficult years that their daughters—irrespective of their feelings—had little or no chance to resist, let alone refuse, the sexual demands of any lecherous white man. *Any!* One of the persons interviewed for this study told of a Negro father who, hard up for money, hired out his daughter as a maid in a white man's home. Soon she complained of being pestered by one of the white males in the family. The father, accusing her of laziness, of trying to dodge work, insisted that she keep her job. Later on his daughter gave birth to a white baby. The Negroes in the community blamed the father. The following statement, written by one of the women interviewed, shows how little protection some Negro girls received: "I will never forget one Sunday evening in a little town in South Carolina. I was standing on a friend's porch. His sister asked their mother if she might go and buy some salt. She went into the woods and a white man followed her. Later she had a white baby."

The cautiousness of careful parents was understandable. In the thinking of all too many white people, Negroes "didn't count," so that if white men invaded the sexual privacy of Negro women, no moral code had been violated. Chastity was a virtue "for whites (white women, that is!) only" and had to be protected at whatever cost. It was rumored and believed by many Negroes in my county that white men sought to cohabit with Negro women in order to get experience in the sexual act before marriage to white women. Perhaps this self-righteous attitude of the white man in protecting the virtue of white women was an abortive atonement for the sins he committed against defenseless Negro women, with and without consent, during slavery and throughout the Reconstruction and post-Reconstruction eras....

As bad as things were in Greenwood County when I was a boy, I hear from others that they were worse in some other sections of the South, and even in certain other sections of South Carolina. We could walk on the sidewalks when we went to Greenwood, the county seat. But Negroes by and large were a subdued lot and they showed their abject condition by the way they moved around on the sidewalks and the servile way in which they behaved when they went into the stores to trade. Negroes were always careful never to brush up against a white person. Negroes in my county tried to stay out of trouble, with little success; and it was circulated that there were towns in South Carolina where Negroes coming to town on Saturdays walked in the streets and left the sidewalks to the whites. A white friend of mine, Mrs. Elizabeth Jonitis, who now lives in Maine and Florida, wrote me in June, 1968, that such was the case in Walterboro, South Carolina, in 1943, when she stopped off there; that Negroes meeting her would step off the sidewalk rather than share it with a white woman: and that this custom differed from that of Chestertown, Maryland, where she had once lived, where Negroes and whites by custom used different sides of the sidewalks.

I never felt completely at home in my native county. The experiences I had in my most impressionable years, hearing and seeing the mob, observing the way my people were treated, noting the way in which they responded to this treatment, never having developed any white friends in the county, and living all my early years in a rented house—all this left me with a feeling of alienation from the county of my birth. The chasm was so wide between black and white in my day that I never felt that any white person in Greenwood County or in South Carolina would be interested in anything I did.

It was surprising and delightful, therefore, when years later—1968—I visited the offices of the *Index-Journal* in Greenwood, South Carolina, to meet editor J. E. Chaffin and hear him express great satisfaction in my career. He gave me a copy of a most enlightened address on race which he had delivered at Erskine College.[21] He carried a good story about me in the *Index-Journal*. I was equally surprised, shocked, and delighted when I received the Man of the Year Award from the Greenville Chapter of the Society for the Advancement of Management that year. My rapport had been with Negroes—not whites.[22]

We always lived on the highway, a thoroughfare connecting Greenwood and Saluda and other small towns. When there was trouble, such as the Phoenix Riot, and when drunken men rode by at night cursing, using profane and obscene language, and sometimes shooting, it was not so good.

I trembled in my bed at night as white men passed by making the night hideous with their wild behavior. But there was also a pleasant side to living by the side of the road. Frequently people would stop for a few minutes to chat, en route to and from church and Greenwood. It was known that our spring water, about one-sixth of a mile away, was fresh and cool. Often we were sent to the spring to get fresh, cool water for a thirsty wayfarer. Some of these people who stopped to get water were white. In the country, we did not drink out of glasses. Dippers and gourds were used. And our white travelers drank out of our dippers and gourds. However, when we worked for white farmers by the day, if whites were working in the field with us, they maintained their "superior" status by drinking first.

The thing I remember best about our house by the side of the road was the handsome, big oak tree where we put up our swing. It was so close to the road that if we were swinging full blast it often proved frightening to the people on their way by. I loved that oak tree. For years, in passing by the place of my birth, I always looked for the oak and was glad to see it—still strong, stately, and handsome.

NOTES

1. Clinton E. Warner, an African American surgeon and civil rights activist, graduated from Morehouse College in 1958. He established the first African American surgical group in Atlanta, Georgia; served on the board of trustees for the Morehouse School of Medicine; and was honored as Physician of the Year in 1978 by the American Medical Association.

2. The 1895 South Carolina State Constitutional Convention authorized the establishment of the South Carolina State College as a public land-grant institution to provide agricultural and mechanical education for African American youth. The historically black college began operating in 1896.

3. Members of the American Baptist Home Mission Society founded Virginia Union College in 1865 to educate freedmen.

4. Formed at Bates College in Lewiston, Maine, the Phil-Hellenic Club was a Greek literary organization that sponsored various cultural events, particularly plays, on campus. Phi Beta Kappa, established at the College of William and Mary in 1776, was the first honor society to be identified by Greek lettering.

5. Dorrien, *Making of American Liberal Theology*, 417.

6. The Institute of Social and Religious Research, now known as the Religious Research Association, was founded in the early twentieth century with the aim of promoting the social application of religious research through interfaith collaboration among scholars and religious leaders.

7. King, "Statement Regarding the Retirement of Benjamin E. Mays," 1.

8. The Commission on Interracial Cooperation (CIC) was founded in 1919 in Atlanta, Georgia, and merged with the Southern Regional Council in 1944. It was formed largely in response to escalating racial tensions between white Americans and African Americans in the South. The CIC opposed racial violence and worked to educate whites about the negative influence of racism in their communities.

9. The sociologist Howard W. Odum established the Southern Regional Council to combat racism and promote civil rights for African Americans in the South.

10. The National Council of Churches was founded in 1850 to advocate ecumenical associations between American Christians.

11. Founded in 1944, the United Negro College Fund is an educational foundation that offers scholarships and grants to students attending private, historically black colleges and universities.

12. The Phoenix Riot occurred in 1898 after J. I. "Bose" Ethridge was shot and killed while attempting to remove a ballot box that a white Republican, Tom Tolbert, had placed in Phoenix, South Carolina, for African American supporters of his brother Robert Red Tolbert, who was running for Congress. Whites accused African Americans of the murder, while African Americans believed they were being disenfranchised. A race riot ensued, during which five African Americans were lynched and the Tolberts were driven from their homes.

13. According to the South Carolina Constitution of 1895 (Article 3, § 33), "The marriage of a white person with a negro, or mulatto, or person who shall have one-eighth or more negro blood, shall be unlawful and void."

14. Paul Laurence Dunbar (1876–1906), an African American poet, playwright, and novelist, gained national acclaim in the late nineteenth century.

15. African Americans were the majority delegation at the 1895 South Carolina constitutional convention and held major offices in the state legislature until the white Democratic revolution of 1876, which ousted Republican politicians. The segregationist Benjamin Ryan "Pitchfork Ben" Tillman, who was elected governor in 1890, orchestrated the enactment of Jim Crow laws in South Carolina during the 1895 constitutional convention.

16. Cash tenants paid a fixed sum to rent farmland and kept all of the profits from the crops. Share tenants used their own equipment and money to till the land in exchange for a share of the crops. Share-cash tenants paid a share of their crops and cash to rent farmland.

17. Founded in 1870 on a plantation near Columbia, South Carolina, Benedict College is a historically black liberal arts college established by northern Baptists. The original mission of the school was to educate recently emancipated African American slaves.

18. The Atlanta Race Riot of 1906 was a mass civil disturbance that began on September 22 and lasted approximately four days. Its principal cause was increased competition for jobs among both white and black persons, as well as a general dissatisfaction among African Americans with their lack of civil rights during the Reconstruction era.

19. Hoke Smith (1855–1931), an attorney and the publisher of the *Atlanta Journal,* was the governor of Georgia during the Atlanta Race Riot. Aligning himself with progressive Democrats, Smith supported the amendment of the state constitution with a grandfather clause that granted suffrage to citizens whose grandfathers were able to vote prior to 1866, effectively disenfranchising most African American voters.

20. Morehouse College is an outgrowth of the Augusta Institute in Augusta, Georgia, established in 1787 to educate ministers. In 1879, the institute moved to Atlanta and was renamed Atlanta Baptist Seminary and then Atlanta Baptist College in 1897. In the early twentieth century, John Hope, the first African American president of the seminary, expanded the curriculum to include liberal arts education, a direct challenge to Booker T. Washington's industrial education approach. In 1913 the seminary was renamed Morehouse College in honor of Henry L. Morehouse, the Northern Baptist Home Missionary Society's corresponding secretary.

21. In 1839 the Associated Reform Church founded Erskine College in Due West, South Carolina.

22. Founded in 1912 by supporters of Frederick Taylor, the "Father of Scientific Management," the Society for the Advancement of Management enables members to develop strong management skills in a variety of disciplines, including finance, marketing, research, and entrepreneurship.

Septima Poinsette Clark
(1898–1987)

➜ EDUCATOR, ACTIVIST, COMMUNITY ORGANIZER

Literacy means liberation.

　　Septima Clark, "Literacy and Liberation," 124.

S eptima Poinsette Clark creatively and effectively advocated literacy as an essential skill that would empower African Americans to organize and sustain the modern civil rights movement. By implementing grassroots projects that provided literacy skills and citizenship education to African American children and adults, and then training male and female community organizers to extend the work throughout the South, she wielded enormous influence over voter registration drives, nonviolent protests, and public education systems. Indeed, she was as comfortable speaking Gullah with students at her Citizenship Schools on Johns Island, South Carolina, as she was navigating contentious strategy sessions for civil rights initiatives with prominent activists like Martin Luther King Jr. and Ralph Abernathy for the Southern Christian Leadership Conference (SCLC). Her lasting influence is reflected in the prominent placement of her stately black and white photograph on the cover of Brian Laker's book *I Dream a World: Black Women Who Changed America*, an honor that moved *New York Times* reporter David Dunlap to characterize Clark as the "queen mother of the Civil Rights Movement."[1]

Charlestonian native Septima Earthaline Poinsette Clark was born on May 3, 1898. She was the second of eight children to Peter Porcher Poinsette, a caterer who had labored as a slave on Joel Roberts Poinsett's low country plantation, and free-born Victoria Warren Anderson Poinsette, a domestic who had spent her formative years in Haiti. After Septima completed the eighth grade, she continued her studies at the Avery Normal Institute at her mother's insistence and graduated in 1916 with a teacher's certificate.[2] Eighteen-year-old Septima's first job was in a one-room school for 132 African American students on Johns Island. She also developed literacy classes for adult learners. When she learned of the discrimination that black teachers experienced in pay inequity and inadequate facilities, she initiated a decades-long battle that eventually helped to change state laws regarding teacher compensation.[3] After teaching at the Johns Island School for three years, she returned to the Avery Institute for a one-year appointment as a sixth-grade teacher. Here she resumed her involvement in civil rights by developing a petitioning campaign that convinced the Charleston School Board to begin hiring African American teachers for the public schools in 1920.

Within a year of resettling in Charleston, she married Nerie Clark, a Navy cook whom she had met while serving on the welcoming committee for soldiers returning from World War I. The Clarks had one daughter who died within one month of her birth. While her husband was at sea, Septima Clark began pursuing a college degree. When Nerie Clark was discharged from the Navy, the couple moved to Ohio where their second child, Nerie Clark Jr., was born in 1925. Shortly after Nerie Jr.'s birth, his father Nerie Clark Sr. died of kidney disease. Septima Clark moved back to South Carolina and resumed her teaching job on Johns Island. After unsuccessfully attempting to find suitable living arrangements for herself and her son, she sent Nerie Jr. to live with his paternal grandparents in Hickory, North Carolina, and continued her education career.

Soon a teaching opportunity arose for Septima Clark in Columbia, South Carolina, that offered more pay and greater opportunities for involvement in social and political organizations, including the National Association for the Advancement of Colored People (NAACP). During her summer breaks, she took classes at Atlanta University with activist and sociologist W. E. B. Du Bois and at Columbia University in New York City. In 1935, she developed the South Carolina Adult Education Program for illiterate African American soldiers at Fort Jackson, teaching them practical skills such as counting, writing checks, and understanding bus routes. She resumed her undergraduate studies and graduated from Benedict College in 1942 and then earned a master's degree from Hampton Institute in 1946. While finishing her degrees, Septima Clark joined forces with NAACP attorney Thurgood Marshall, Booker T. Washington High School principal J. Andrew Simmons, and civil rights lawyer Harold R. Boulware to lobby for salary equity for South Carolina teachers based on education and experience, which federal district judge J. Waties Waring approved in 1945.

When Septima Clark returned to Charleston to teach and care for her ailing mother in 1947, she also became involved with several civic organizations, notably the Young Women's Christian Association, the Charleston Federation of Women's Clubs, and the NAACP. Her civic activism enabled her to establish a friendship with Judge Waring and his wife Elizabeth Waring, outspoken supporters of equality and integration. Septima Clark and Elizabeth Waring stoked the ire of segregationist-minded African American and white Charlestonians when Waring accepted Clark's invitation to tea in her home. But Clark faced even greater challenges after the U.S. Supreme Court ruled against segregated public schools in *Brown v. Board of Education* in 1954.[4] The South Carolina legislature and school administrators not only refused to comply, they also required teachers to list their civic affiliations and prohibited educators from holding memberships in civil rights organizations, particularly in the NAACP because of its pivotal role in the case. When Clark refused to relinquish her NAACP membership, she was fired from her job in the Charleston school system, including the retirement benefits she had earned during her fifty-eight-year teaching career. Thirty years later, she successfully petitioned the Charleston school board to have her benefits reinstated, but she did not receive all of her back pay until 1981.

After losing her job in Charleston, Clark affiliated herself with institutions that provided increasingly influential roles for her to shape the objectives of the civil rights movement and train thousands of activists who impacted every aspect of the struggle. She turned down several job offers with the South Carolina Council on Human Relations and the Voorhees Institute in Denmark, South Carolina, to become the director of workshops at the Highlander Folk School in Monteagle, Tennessee where she could continue her work with citizenship education. She had already facilitated programs and workshops there, including one attended by Rosa Parks prior to the Montgomery Bus Boycott. Highlander supported Clark's collaborations with Esau Jenkins and Bernice Robinson to develop Citizenship Schools on Johns Island that enabled residents to pass literacy tests required for voter registration. When the Highlander School lost its charter in 1961, its literary programs were transferred to the SCLC. Clark was appointed education and teaching director and continued establishing Citizenship Schools throughout the South for the SCLC's Voter Education Project. Over two million African Americans registered to vote during her tenure. In organizing the SCLC's Citizenship Schools, she worked closely with Martin Luther King Jr., who invited her to travel with him to Oslo, Norway, in 1964 when he received the Nobel Peace Prize, as well as with Ralph Albernathy and Hosea Williams.

The male-dominated black activist community proved to be a challenging work environment for African American women leaders, however. In the chapter from her memoir *Ready from Within: Septima Clark and the Civil Rights Movement* (Trenton, N.J.: Africa World Press, 1990) presented here, Clark provides a retrospective analysis of gender dynamics in civil rights organizations and African American southern families through the lens of feminism. She recalls encounters with civil rights luminaries such as Abernathy and King who viewed women more as "sex symbols" than equal partners and limited their roles in the movement. She notes the irony of sexist men advancing a movement that would eventually empower women. Clark traces the roots of sexism in the civil rights movement to the influence of overprotective African American mothers who shielded their sons from a racist environment that threatened black manhood, and who encouraged their daughters to be quiet to avoid trouble within and without the home. She locates her politicization to various encounters with white feminists who encouraged her to develop her own voice. Ultimately, Clark characterizes the voicelessness of women as a regional rather than cultural issue, born of traditions that favored men's authority over women's opinions. Nevertheless, she asserts that numerous African American women who discovered their voices by galvanizing their church groups and civic organizations were the secret to both the initiation and the success of the movement. The SCLC eventually acknowledged Clark's contributions to the struggle for human rights by awarding her its Drum Major for Justice award.

When she retired from the SCLC in 1970, Clark devoted more time to her family and remained active in Charleston's civic affairs. She carved out time to care for her two of her six grandchildren in her own home. In 1975, she was elected to the Charleston school board and served two terms, focusing her efforts on improving opportunities for African American students and teachers, and developing strong academic programs and citizenship training for African American children. Additionally, Clark remained active in women's organizations, supporting the parenting program in Alpha Kappa Alpha, her sorority, and advocating for women's rights and opportunities.

Her beliefs regarding a Christocentric, global commitment to citizenship initiatives are reflected in the second selection presented here, an essay published in the *Journal of Black Studies* titled "Citizenship and Gospel."[5] In the essay, Clark details different types of obstacles that people of African descent faced in their communities, the nation, and the world in exercising the "rights, privileges, and responsibilities of citizenship." These obstacles cropped up at the voting booth, on the historically black college campus, and in African nations like the Congo that attained independence from colonial rule. Drawing on her experiences in developing Citizenship Schools on Johns

Island, South Carolina, Clark replicated her efforts throughout the South by training members of varied communities to educate their neighbors and friends. Like nineteenth-century race woman Maria W. Stewart and other black female activist forerunners of the civil rights movement, Clark justifies the need for comprehensive race work by grounding the SCLC's efforts in the black jeremiad, specifically Isaiah's prophecy for a liberator of the oppressed that was fulfilled in Jesus' earthly ministry. For Clark, liberating the oppressed in America meant teaching African Americans how to read, write, and vote, as well as pressuring the Justice Department to eradicate laws and practices that disempowered them. While African Americans, members of the majority worldwide population of colored people, languished in a nation where the Supreme Court had recently declared the doctrine of "separate but equal" to be unconstitutional, America could not claim a place as world leader. Ultimately, biblical mandates rather than man-made laws would be the standard by which America was judged.

Clark earned local and national recognition for her activism. By 1982, she had received an honorary doctorate from the College of Charleston, the Order of the Palmetto from the state of South Carolina, the Race Relations Award from the National Education Association, and the Living Legacy Award from U.S. president Jimmy Carter. In 1987, her memoir *Ready From Within* won the American Book Award. Several schools have been named in her honor, including the Septima Clark Charter Public School in Washington, D.C., and the Septima P. Clark Corporate Academy in Charleston. Clark spent her final days in the Sea Island Health Care Center on Johns Island that had been founded by graduates of the Citizenship School she established early in her career. She died there in 1987.

❧ Excerpt from *Ready from Within: Septima Clark and the Civil Rights Movement*

"The Role of Women"

I was on the executive staff of SCLC [Southern Christian Leadership Conference],[6] but the men on it didn't listen to me too well. They liked to send me into many places, because I could always make a path in to get people to listen to what I have to say. But those men didn't have any faith in women, none whatsoever. They just thought that women were sex symbols and had no contribution to make. That's why Rev. Abernathy[7] would say continuously, "Why is Mrs. Clark on this staff?"

Dr. King would say, "Well, she has expanded our program. She has taken it into eleven deep south states." Rev. Abernathy'd come right back the next time and ask again.

I had a great feeling that Dr. King didn't think much of women either. He would laugh and say, "Ha, ha, ha. Mrs. Clark has expanded our program." That's all. But I think that he thought too much of me, because when I was in Europe with him, when he received the Nobel Peace Prize in 1964, the American Friends Service Committee[8] people wanted me to speak. In a sort of casual way he would say, "Anything I can't answer, ask Mrs. Clark." But he didn't mean it, because I never did get the chance to do any speaking to the American Friends Service Committee in London or to any of the other groups.

When I heard the men asking Dr. King to lead marches in various place, I'd say to them, "You're there. You going to ask the leader to come everywhere? Can't you do the leading in these places?"

I sent a letter to Dr. King asking him not to lead all the marches himself, but instead to develop leaders who could lead their own marches. Dr. King read that letter before the staff. It just tickled them; they just laughed. I had talked to the secretaries before about it, and when the letter was read they wouldn't say a word, not one of them. I had a feeling that they thought Dr. King would have to do the leading. If you think that another man should lead, then you are looking down on Dr. King. This was the way it was.

Here was somebody from Albany, from Waycross, Georgia, from Memphis, Tennessee, from Chicago, from Detroit—all wanting him to come and lead a march. I felt that it wasn't necessary. I thought that you develop leaders as you go along, and as you develop these people let them show forth their development by leading. That was my feeling, but that was too much for them. They didn't feel as if that should be.

I think that there is something among the Kings that makes them feel that they are the kings, and so you don't have a right to speak. You can work behind the scenes all you want. That's all right. But don't come forth and try to lead. That's not the kind of thing they want.

When I went into that little town out from Macon and presented those people certificates of appreciation, Dr. King's secretary was terribly worried because he was hurt by it. He thought that I presented them and didn't call his name. But I did call his name. I said, "In the name of Dr. King and the SCLC we are glad to have you as affiliates of SCLC. We want to work with you in this town to get people registered to vote. First, they have to learn to read and write." He didn't know that I had said that, and he was blaming his secretary for letting me have the appreciation certificates to present to them.

But in those days I didn't criticize Dr. King, other than asking him not to lead all the marches. I adored him. I supported him in every way I could because I greatly respected his courage, his service to others, and his nonviolence. The way I think about him now comes from my experience in the women's movement. But in those days, of course, in the black church men were always in charge. It was just the way things were.

Like other black ministers, Dr. King didn't think too much of the way women could contribute. But working in a movement he changed the lives of so many people that it was getting to the place where he would have to see that women are more than sex symbols. He always said that his wife should never leave home to do anything as long as they had small children. In 1965 I was in Pasadena, and Mrs. King was supposed to come out and give a concert because she was a great concert singer. She almost had to give up her career.[9] She hasn't gotten back to it, either, because the men didn't feel as if it was right.

I see this as one of the weaknesses of the civil rights movement, the way the men looked at women. I think I know how the men got that way. I think about my mother, who had a feeling that black boys in the South could be conspired upon. She wanted to keep her boys right under her nose; she never wanted them away from her. She would always say: "A girl will bring you one trouble, but a boy can bring so many others. He can be arrested for stealing. He can be arrested for looking at a white." She'd name all these things that I think caused black mothers to feel as if black boys have to be very docile. Because they resented that, the black boys grew up feeling that women should not have a say in anything. That's what I think.

When I was working over on Johns Island,[10] the women never could get up and give a suggestion. Esau Jenkins[11] wouldn't listen to them, not at all. I remember one woman said, "Don't pay attention to that silly Esau. He ain't goin' to listen to ya." And that was the truth.

When Dr. King visited at Esau's house, Dr. King said, "Do you mean to tell me that you built this house and furnished it and that your wife didn't have any part of it?"

And do you know what Mrs. Jenkins said? She said, "If Esau like it, I like it."

That was the way most women were reared. My mother wasn't reared like that, though. No, she was the boss of her house.

I found all over the South that whatever the man said had to be right. They had the whole say. The woman couldn't say a thing. Whatever the men said would be right, and the wives would have to accept it.

Out of these experiences I felt I wanted to be active in the women's liberation movement. Remember Virginia Durr,[12] that friend of Rosa Parks in Montgomery? She also proved to be an excellent friend to me.

Virginia was with the National Organization of Women.[13] When they had their first meeting in Washington, I think it must have been in 1958, she had me to come from Highlander[14] to talk about the women of the South who failed to speak up when they knew what they wanted, about white women who would see their husbands doing wrong but dared not tell them, about black women who wouldn't speak at all because the husband had the right to say whatever.

Virginia Durr got me a room at a swell hotel, and I'd never had such a thing before in my life—a room that was all treated up to look like a wonderful place to live. I had a bedroom, a restroom, and also a sort of a little parlor on the side, but I really didn't get to use it very much. I was too busy in meetings, where we talked about the things that were happening in Alabama, the kind of segregation that those people were living under.

I was able to get a whole lot of things done through those women, because later on I went back there to talk to them about the kinds of things that women had to face in voter registration. For example, in Louisiana a black woman even had to say that she was not the father of an illegitimate child. South Carolina had in its law that a person registering had to swear that "I'm not guilty of arson or of wife-beating."[15] One woman said, "How could I be a wife-beater, since I'm a woman?" Those were some of the things that came up in the liberation movement that I was able to talk to the women in Washington about.

I also went to Oak Ridge, Tennessee, to a meeting in May of '53 or '54.[16] There were numbers of women at Oak Ridge whose husbands had come to work in that big atomic research plant there. I found out that those women were different. They would speak out. They were concerned about black and white women from various parts of the South who would never speak out.

These southern women were worried about their children; they wanted their children to do what they had a feeling for, but it was not possible because the husband had the real power over the whole family. Nothing that the women said could go. It had to be what the man said. One woman said that she as the wife could see the husband doing whatever he wanted to do with the women who worked on his farm, and still she could say nothing about it. She had to let it go just as she saw it. She could not do one thing.

That was quite a meeting at Oak Ridge. The wives of the workers at the atomic plant told their feelings, how they felt. They didn't see how the men should have all the say. They didn't see why women couldn't talk about the discrepancies that they noted. Anyway, I worked along with them.

There were many things that I felt we needed to change, but there were some points that I had different ideas about. I saw women in Maine and in the mountains of North Carolina driving tractors, and to me that was a terrible thing. I just didn't think that women had strength enough to do that type of thing. But there they were.

I still have a feeling that women weren't made to do the heavy lifting, and I think I got that from my father. He didn't like for us to lift a tub of water, didn't like to see a white woman with a bag of groceries in her arms. He would always say, "Hand it here, Missy; it's too heavy for you." I still have that feeling that there are things too heavy for a woman. I think that her backbone is not made for that kind of lifting.

Once I read an article which said that women are made differently, that the bone that goes from the end of their back up to the brain doesn't have the same kind of tissue or strength that the men have. Women shouldn't drink, the article said, because the alcohol would ruin that same bone and would lead to the brain; that's why women get drunk quicker than men and act real silly. I never will forget that article. I still think that there is a difference, that women become alcoholics quicker than men.

Now I do serve wine for Thanksgiving dinner and for Christmas dinner. That's a custom. We used to make eggnog and have a big bowl in the middle of the table, and the neighbors would come in celebrating Christmas and the New Year. Instead of the eggnog now we serve the wine. But I still don't care for alcoholic drinks at all. They make you foolish, make you real foolish.

But even though I think women are physically weaker than men and get drunk faster, I am all for women's liberation. This country was built up from women keeping their mouths shut. It took fifty years for women, black and white, to learn to speak up. I had to learn myself, so I know what a struggle it was.

I used to feel that women couldn't speak up, because when district meetings were being held at my home on Henrietta Street in Charleston, I didn't feel as if I could tell them what I had in my mind. Not at all. I thought it was up to the men to do that talking. Of course, my father always said that a woman needs to be quiet and just be in the home. I grew up with the idea that women didn't have a word to say. But later on, I found out that women had a lot to say, and what they had to say was really worthwhile. I changed my mind about women being quiet when they had something to say. I felt that surely the talk that the women had would be worthwhile, as well as what the men had to say. So we started talking, and have been talking quite a bit since that time.

As I look back into the early twenties, I see women both white and black who never dared to give a thought in any home or meeting. They were silent at all times. They did the chores and failed even to speak out about any wrong. In the late fifties and sixties in the United States there was a tremendous upheaval for women. They gained success and recognition. Before that, it was difficult for any woman in the U.S. to be recognized for her intellectual ability. For black women, the problem was two-fold: being a woman and being black.

Until recently black women have just been ignored in history books. Now books are coming out that show the impact that black women have had on the shaping of America. One example is *Black Women of Valor* by Olive Burt that tells about four black women—Juliette Derricotte,[17] social worker; Maggie Mitchell Walker,[18] banker; Ida Wells Barnett,[19] journalist; and me—Septima Poinsette Clark, educator.

Many people think that the women's liberation movement came out of the civil rights movement, but the women's movement started quite a number of years before the civil rights movement. Virginia Durr asked me to come down and talk to the black women of the churches in Montgomery in 1955. I spoke at that church, and I was able to get a number of those women to come Highlander.

The women of Montgomery played a major role in organizing the bus boycott,[20] not just in carrying it out. Black women helped through their church groups, as well as through the Women's Political Council,[21] started at Alabama State College. The women believed that if they supported protest, then the men would go along. But the men couldn't be out front leading—they had more to lose.

In the spring of 1957, a few months after we won the bus boycott in Montgomery, women organized a march on Washington, D.C. It was called "The Prayer Pilgrimage."[22] That was six years before the big march of 200,000 people when Dr. King gave his "I Have a Dream" speech.[23] The march in '57 was the largest civil rights demonstration ever staged by black Americans up to that time, and Mrs. Coretta King did the speaking.

In stories about the civil rights movement you hear mostly about the black ministers. But if you talk to the women who were there, you'll hear another story. I think the civil rights movement would never have taken off if some women hadn't started to speak up. A lot more are just getting to the place now where they can speak out.

⸎ "Citizenship and Gospel"

Journal of Black Studies

The signs pointed to the left for white and to the right for colored. It seems everything in Georgia must be so labeled. Yet here in the Drivers License Bureau were two men, one white, one colored, standing together attempting to fill out the application for a license. The white man was doing the writing, but it was necessary for the Negro to spell each word for him. This was an odd combination indeed. The one with a basic skill, the other, no skill, but it was necessary for the Negro to spell each word for him. This was an odd combination indeed. The one with a basic skill the other, no skill, but a phenomenal memory and obvious intelligence.

This scene might be duplicated in many cities across the South. There are 8.5 million functional illiterates in the United States. Many of these are southern Negroes. This fact is tragic, because there are often persons with a great deal of natural intelligence who have ben deprived of the basic opportunity of public school education. Often in the course of travels through small towns and underprivileged communities, one is astonished to find "Ph.D. minds" who have had opportunity for only a few years of formal training.

Until 1954, there was little attempt to provide adequate education for Negro citizens. The school year was broken up by the cotton crop, the tobacco crop, and any other crop which needed harvest or care. Thanks to the Supreme Court, Negro Education came to the attention of the nation as a whole and the South in particular. Many of the ills of Negro education are being corrected. In the future, Negro children may hope for an adequate education. But what of those who received their training prior to 1954?[24] These were bleak years of so-called separate but equal facilities which always managed to be separated, that left the Negro child in a one-room school with a small blackboard, a bucket, a dipper, and the battered textbooks that were passed down from the white school children after they were too ragged for their use. In spite of the inequity, this system was proven detrimental to the masses of both races.

Television and travel have brought to every American home the promise of democracy. Now everyone knows the advantage we advertise as the fruits of a free society. Adult American Negroes do not want to remain in their underprivileged state. Our society is now presented with the challenge of nurturing these citizens into the mainstream of American life as full-fledged participants.

The Southern Christian Leadership Conference has accepted the challenge to lead the masses of Negro citizens into full participation in a desegregated society. Under the vision and leadership of its president, Dr. Martin Luther King Jr., a South-wide program in citizenship education has been launched. This Citizenship Education Program is designed to train local community leaders to conduct Citizenship Schools.

The Citizenship School helps persons to overcome the handicaps which have been inflicted upon them in a segregated society. First the school attempts to provide basic literacy skills. It is amazing how fast the adult students can acquire these skills when they are motivated by the goal of first class citizenship.

In every corner of the globe, there is now heard the cry for freedom. Our Christian Mission stations at home and abroad have done a great deal to plant concepts of freedom, justice, and equality in the hearts of men.[25] Now the march is on to actualize these concepts. At times it scares us, as in the Congo where untrained masses are turned loose with little preparation for running a government, but we realize that this is a part of a dream which is both Christian and American in its inspiration—our fear should be transformed into concern.[26]

The Gospel Challenge

The first words of Jesus' public ministry were quoted from the prophet Isaiah:

The Spirit of the Lord is upon me, because he hath anointed me to preach the gospel to the poor; he hath sent me to heal the brokenhearted, to preach deliverance to the captives, and recovering the sight to the blind, so set at liberty them that are oppressed [Luke 4:18].

Throughout the New Testament, the concern for the poor and underprivileged is expressed as one of the fruits of grace. Where there is obedience to the gospel, there will be concern for the less fortunate. "The *least* of these my brethren *are* no less *brothers* in Christ than one's social counterparts."

Long experience in Christian missions has taught us that this love and concern for others must be made concrete. Our missionaries could not be content preaching the gospel to hungry folk. They had to also teach them new agricultural methods and help them to provide food for themselves and their families. They provide clinics and hospitals to improve the health of the people, and established schools for the education of these new converts.

In recent years we have realized that still another step is necessary. To feed or educate or heal an individual with no thought for the type of community life, or system of government which has contributed to the deprived state of the individual, is too shortsighted indeed. If we really are to contribute to the "deliverance of the captives" it is necessary to do something to redeem the system which keeps them in captivity.

Even in America, there are social injustices which occur as our government is caught up in an ever-changing set of domestic and world pressures. The one great pressure created by the millions of black men who were brought to this country as slaves and who now make up one-tenth of our total population.

Full Citizenship

The Negro came to this country in the lowest possible social state—as slaves. Two hundred years later the conscience of our nation was kindled to go to war in an attempt to abolish the slave status. In the one hundred years since slavery the Negro has struggled to overcome the attempts to transform that once legal slavery into more subtle forms of educational, economic, and political slavery. This is the genesis of the present fight for full citizenship.

Certainly a great deal has been accomplished in the last hundred years. We read magazine articles on "Our Negro Aristocracy," books on "The Black Bourgeoisie," all of which indicate that there has been great progress over the years.[27] But Christians can never be content with token progress by a fortunate few. They must continually remain sensitive to the will of God for the redemption of "the saints of rank and file," the people of the land around whom Jesus centered his earthly ministry.

The Citizenship Education Program is attempting to provide an opportunity for these people to help themselves and their neighbors. By training one or two persons from each community we are able to help them to teach their neighbors about the American way of life and the way in which the ballot is used to create and continue the rule of liberty and justice for all (even dark-skinned persons in Mississippi).

To date, over five hundred local community leaders have received one week of training at Dorchester Center, McIntosh, Georgia. These persons have come from all southern states: Louisiana, Mississippi, Alabama, Georgia, South Carolina, Arkansas, Virginia, Tennessee, and Florida. They represent local community leadership from over one hundred towns and rural areas. At Dorchester Center, these persons live together and spend almost fourteen hours daily learning to face community problems, understand basic facts about local government, and how to teach their neighbors to read and write.

The literacy test is the newest means of keeping the Negro citizen from being a full citizen. In many states these tests are far beyond the normal demands of literacy. In Alabama, Negro professors with Ph.D. degrees were consistently turned down at the registration office. Finally after an investigation by the Justice Department, they were given the right to vote. These situations are numerous across the South. Often the tests are just made so difficult that it requires a special school to prepare persons to vote. In many ways this is good, however, because it forces us to give our new registrants some preparation for voting. This system becomes unjust because it is not applied to all.

A young white minister in the Episcopal Church reported to me that as he came to his first parish and attempted to register, he was met by a three-page questionnaire. He informed the registrar that he was sorry but he did not know these answers, but that he would study and return to take the test. The registrar replied, "Oh that's alright Reverend, you don't have to worry about that. Those are just to keep the niggars from voting."

Young and Old

There is no age limit on our requirements for teachers. We have had teachers from seventeen to seventy. In Georgia where it is permissible for eighteen year olds to vote, we have trained many high school graduates and college students to work in the program. Our major requirements are that the persons be able to read well aloud, and that they write legibly on a blackboard. It has been our experience that these persons, without a great deal of formal training, can be taught to teach a few basic things, and that often they make better teachers than persons with a great deal of academic background. Their approach is a "folk" approach to learning rather than a classical one. Their vocabularies are similar, and there is usually an existing relationship upon which we build.

In our January 1961 workshop, we had nineteen college students who had been expelled from Albany State College in Georgia for having participated in the recent protest over violations of the rights of Negroes to use interstate bus facilities on a desegregated basis.[28] These youths were suspended for a quarter, but wanted to work during their suspension to help their community.

Since receiving the training courses, they started classes for adults in the community and conducted a voter registration drive. In 1962 and 1963 Mississippi has sent more than one hundred in. They are conducting schools and voter registration campaigns.

Where Do We Go from Here?

Our immediate objective is to help Negro citizens to assume the rights, privileges, and responsibilities of first-class Americans, but there are some significant by-products. The Southern Christian Leadership Conference makes the claim on its stationery, "Redeeming the Soul of America." At first glance this seems like a rather arrogant claim, but on further consideration, one can see the problem of racial inequality as the glaring moral dilemma of American life. The ability of the United States to cope with racial difference within her borders is the key to her role as a leader of a world that is made up largely of colored peoples. Our day of judgment may well be decided by the way we treat the least of these, our brothers, within our midst.

NOTES

1. Dunlap, "Parting Glance."
2. Originally known as the Saxton School, Avery Normal Institute was founded by the American Missionary Society in 1865 to provide normal, or teacher, training for African American children in Charleston, South Carolina. Drago, *Charleston's Avery Center*, 57–58.
3. By the beginning of the 1915–16 academic year, South Carolina had invested more than $5 million in schools for white children but only $600,000 in educational institutions for African Americans, most of which were constructed of logs and located in churches or lodge halls. The state spent approximately $17.02 in educating each white student and $1.09 for each African American student. Black teachers received half as much pay or less than their white counterparts and were often required to teach more than twice the number of students. *Forty-Eighth Annual Report*, 140, 146.

4. In 1954, the U.S. Supreme Court ruled that state laws mandating segregated public schools were unconstitutional in *Brown v. Board of Education of Topeka*, 347 U.S. 483. The class action suit contained five cases, including *Briggs v. Elliot* 342 U.S. 350 (1952), a South Carolina lawsuit based in Clarendon County that demanded equal transportation and education for African American students in state schools.

5. Although the article was published in 1980, Clark's references to events such as the civil war in Congo and training of the students who were expelled from Albany State College suggest that she likely wrote the article in the early 1960s.

6. The Southern Christian Leadership Conference (SCLC) is an African American civil rights organization founded in 1957 by Dr. Martin Luther King Jr. and several other black ministers.

7. The African American civil rights activist the Reverend Ralph David Abernathy (1926–1990) assumed the leadership of the SCLC after Dr. King was assassinated.

8. The American Friends Service Committee (AFSC) is a religious organization devoted to promoting peace and social justice in the United States and abroad. The AFSC was founded in 1917 to aid civilian victims of the First World War.

9. Coretta Scott King (1927–2006) studied concert singing at the New England Conservatory of Music in Boston, Massachusetts. Although she relinquished her pursuit of a singing career after her fourth child was born, she continued to organize Freedom Concerts during the civil rights movement.

10. Johns Island is a Sea Island near Charleston, South Carolina, where Clark was a schoolteacher in an impoverished rural school district.

11. Esau Jenkins (1910–1972) was an African American civil rights leader and founder, with Septima Clark, of the Citizenship schools in Charleston County.

12. Virginia Durr (1903–1999), a white civil rights activist, was married to Clifford Durr, the attorney who represented Rosa Parks when she challenged the constitutionality of the Jim Crow laws that required the segregation of public bus passengers.

13. The National Organization of Women was founded in 1966 by participants in the Third National Conference of the Commission on the Status of Women and is currently the largest active women's rights organization in the United States.

14. Founded in 1933 in Grundy County, Tennessee, by Myles Horton and Don West, the Highlander Folk School (now known as the Highlander Research and Education Center) gradually shifted its focus from nurturing the labor movement to supporting the civil rights movement, particularly in developing citizenship schools, offering cultural workshops for the creation of freedom songs, and spearheading desegregation initiatives through interracial alliances.

15. See Oath Required of Applicant, Code of Laws of South Carolina § 23–68 (1952).

16. Oak Ridge, Tennessee, was a rural area that the federal government chose as the site for the development of the Manhattan Project and the construction of the world's first atomic bomb.

17. The African American civil rights activist and educator Juliette Derricotte (1897–1931) was the first female trustee at Talladega College and a member of the general committee of the World Student Christian Federation. She was refused admittance to a whites-only hospital following a car accident, and her subsequent death provoked an outcry from the African American community.

18. Maggie Mitchell Walker (1864–1934), an African American businesswoman and educator, was the first woman to charter a bank in the United States.

19. The African American journalist and social activist Ida Wells-Barnett (1862–1931) published her investigative report about lynchings in the southern United States in *A Red Record* (1895).

20. The African American activist Jo Ann Robinson and the Women's Political Council originally proposed the Montgomery bus boycott and circulated a pamphlet throughout the African American community of Montgomery to garner support.

21. The Women's Political Council, founded in 1946 in Montgomery, was a social activist organization that contributed to the civil rights movement.

22. The Prayer Pilgrimage for Freedom, endorsed by the NAACP and the SCLC, was a peaceful protest demonstration, staged in front of the Lincoln Memorial on May 17, 1957, that provided Dr. King his first opportunity to address a national audience.

23. The March on Washington for Jobs and Freedom, the largest political rally of the civil rights movement, was the venue for Dr. King's influential "I Have a Dream" speech and precipitated the passage of the Civil Rights Act of 1964 and the Voting Rights Act of 1965.

24. Here Clark is referencing the US Supreme Court decision *Brown v. Board of Education* that mandated the desegregation of public schools in 1954.

25. Christian Mission stations were built on land allocated by local leaders in foreign countries, particularly Africa, where resident missionaries could establish themselves within communities to provide education and medical care, as well as assistance with negotiating disputes with colonial powers.

26. After the Congo won independence from Belgium in 1960, the young nation was continually plagued with problems stemming from the legacy of colonialism, initiated when Congolese soldiers in the army mutinied shortly after the first elections, which led to the Congo Civil War, 1960–1964.

27. Clark is referencing Bill Davidson, "Our Negro Aristocracy," *The Saturday Evening Post*, January 13, 1962, and Frank Frazier, *The Black Bourgeoisie* (New York: Simon and Schuster, 1957).

28. In 1903, Joseph Winthrop Holley, the son of former slaves, founded the Albany Bible and Training Institute for African American students after learning of the desperate condition of the Albany's African American community in W. E. B. Du Bois' *The Souls of Black Folk*. After attaining four-year status in 1943, its name was changed to Albany State College (now Albany State University). During the civil rights movement, Albany State students organized the Albany Movement, which attracted the support of Martin Luther King Jr. The student protest in 1961

was sparked by the expulsion of two students who were arrested after refusing to leave the waiting room at a local bus station where they had purchased tickets for a trip home over the Thanksgiving holidays. Albany State's president, concerned about being forced out of office over the incident, expelled the students, which sparked protests both on campus and in the community.

The Civil Rights Legacy

PART III

Marian Wright Edelman
(b. 1939)

🐍 ACTIVIST, EDUCATOR

"I take responsibility."

How do we make a world that is stronger and safer? We make it by protecting each child we see before us and every child that we do not see, especially children born into poverty. Or that seems to be the answer Marian Wright Edelman would give. She is a woman who has married struggles for civil rights with an international crusade for child advocacy and in doing so has become one of the most influential social activists in the world, winning numerous awards, including the MacArthur Prize Fellowship, the Albert Schweitzer Humanitarian Award, and the nation's highest civilian award, the Presidential Medal of Freedom. Her writing has ranged from best-selling inspirational and autobiographical works to scholarly sociological and legal studies, and her lectures take her around the world.

The trajectory of Edelman's intellectual and political life was launched by her early engagement with the civil rights movement. While her attention has, in recent decades, turned to the struggle to improve the quality of children's lives around the world, her early upbringing in South Carolina evidently gave her much of the courage and conviction she needed to see how these causes were deeply and inextricably aligned. As she wrote, "I have always felt blessed to be born who I was, where I was, when I was, and with the parents I had. As a Black girl child growing up in a small segregated town, I could never take anything for granted and never for a moment lacked a purpose worth fighting, living, and dying for, or an opportunity to make a difference if I wanted to."[1]

Edelman was one of five children born to a Baptist preacher, Arthur Jerome Wright, and his wife, Maggie Leola (Bowen) Wright, in Bennettsville, South Carolina. The deep social connections and care that surrounded Edelman in her poor but loving community modeled for her the possibilities for what a larger community of care might be. When her father, for example, realized that there were no lunch counters or playgrounds open to black children, he opened a canteen and a playground behind his church. Realizing that there weren't adequate facilities for caring for the elderly in their community, Edelman's family established the Wright House for the Aged. Her much beloved father passed away when Edelman was fourteen, yet her mother went on to take in nearly a dozen foster children. Seeing firsthand not merely the suffering that segregation, ignorance, and poverty caused but also the ways in which individual action could collectively make a difference, Edelman grew increasingly committed to a career in service.

She began that career at Spelman College in Atlanta, where she grew as a scholar and as an engaged citizen under the mentorship of Benjamin Mays, who was then teaching at Morehouse, and her professor Howard Zinn. Thanks to a nomination by Zinn, she was awarded a Merrill Scholarship to travel and study in Europe. She went on to win a Lisle Fellowship, which sent her for further study in the Soviet Union. Although she cherished her experiences abroad both in Europe and in the Soviet Union, she returned to the States even more intent on dedicating her life to overthrowing the strictures of the segregated South, having seen what life was like in non–segregated societies.

Increasingly committed to alleviating social injustice, Edelman decided to attend Yale Law School in order to serve the civil rights movement. She was particularly determined to work in Mississippi at the epicenter of racial turmoil and hatred of that era. Her mentor, Zinn, arranged for his friend and fellow antiwar activist the Reverend William Sloane Coffin to house her with his family in New Haven during her law school years, when there were very few appropriate housing options for a young black female student. Coffin, too, became a lifetime mentor and helped shape Edelman's future career in civil rights activism.

As a young graduate of Yale Law School, she moved back south to head up the NAACP's Legal Defense and Education Fund's office in Jackson, Mississippi. There, she became the first African American woman admitted to the Mississippi state bar. During her years in Mississippi, she also met Peter Edelman, a legislative assistant to Robert F. Kennedy. In 1968 they were married in Virginia at a wedding officiated by Reverend Coffin and former Supreme

Court Justice Arthur Goldberg. It was the first interracial marriage in Virginia since the Supreme Court had thrown out that state's antimiscegenation statute.[2]

While working closely with Medgar Evers, Robert Kennedy, and other luminaries of the civil rights era, Edelman became counsel to the Poor People's Campaign, organized by Martin Luther King and the Southern Christian Leadership Conference. King's assassination notwithstanding, she stood with the movement and its continuing campaign to end the Vietnam War and to construct what was essentially an economic bill of rights for the nation's poor. To that end, she lobbied Congress for expanded child and family nutrition programs and an expanded Head Start program on behalf of a group she founded called the Washington Research Project.

She established the Children's Defense Fund (CDF) in 1973 to continue Dr. Martin Luther King's call for justice and to "ensure a level playing field for all children."[3] To that end, the CDF lobbies for poor and minority children as well as for children with disabilities and children suffering from abuse. Since its founding, the CDF has functioned not only as a lobbying group for political legislation on behalf of children and children's issues but also as a research center to develop policies and recommendations to help children.

In the reading featured here, the final chapter from her best-seller, *The Measure of Our Success: A Letter to My Children and Yours* (Boston: Beacon Press, 1992), Edelman models how personal uplift is meaningless without specific civic uplift for others left behind. Indeed, she takes the lessons of her South Carolina upbringing to the state house. As one critic in the *Harvard Education Review* writes, "She—like no one since Thurgood Marshall—has found ways to straddle the difficult line between opposing government policies and working with the government to enact systematic change."[4]

Like many child advocates, she refers to specific incidents and cases. Edelman raises the famous case of Baby Jessica McClure, for example, who became an object of national media fixation in 1987 when she had to be rescued from a Texas well. But unlike others who might invoke the incident merely to illustrate how much we, as a nation, care for children, Edelman also notes that Jessica was in an unregulated family day care center that placed her in "a danger she should not have come close to in the first place." Edelman remarks on the horror of Lisa Steinberg, another child who captured national attention in 1987 after being abused and murdered by her would-be father. As Edelman frames it, though, Lisa's tragedy was in part the tragedy of being failed by a civic system that neither ensured that her adoption was legal nor detected her horrific abuse. And then, most starkly, Edelman presents, in contrast, the story of eight-month-old Shamal Jackson, who died from a combination of "poverty and homelessness" and who was neglected first by the state and then by a nation that failed to even notice.

Edelman follows these anecdotes with a list of statistics that renders them all the more poignant and painful. She cites, for example, predictions that 9,208 children age nineteen and younger would commit suicide and 3.6 million infants would be born into poverty between 1993 and 1997. In each case, though, she has built up such authorial credibility that one can sense her commitment not merely to drawing our emotional engagement with each human tragedy behind those numbers. Rather, she is committed to forcing readers to confront the necessarily uncomfortable and difficult civic decisions that must be made in order to stop the torrent of individual horrors from becoming collective statistics. She asks her readers for pledges of specific action—not simply to promise to be kinder or more fair. She asks them to vote. She asks them to spend time visiting hospital neonatal intensive care nurseries and rocking AIDS babies who need love.

Edelman ends her selection with a version of "A Prayer for Children," a poem by Ina Hughes.[5] The poem's refrain consists of variations on the words "We pray for children who . . ." Edelman, however, exhorts the reader to add to each instance of "we pray" the following promise: "I take responsibility for. . . ." This charge brazenly redirects any false satisfaction the poem might offer and sums up the savvy, persuasive, and deeply invested rhetoric that has defined Edelman's role in the public discourse for the past fifty years.

ॐ Excerpt from *The Measure of Our Success:*
A Letter to My Children and Yours

If the Child is Safe: A Struggle for America's Conscience and Future

> *If the child is safe everyone is safe.*
>
> G. Campbell Morgan, "The Children's Playground in the
> City of God," Westminster Pulpit (circa 1908)

> *There is no finer investment for any country than*
> *putting milk into babies.*
>
> Winston Churchill

The most important work to help our children is done quietly—in our homes and neighborhoods, our parishes and community organizations. No government can love a child and no policy can substitute for a family's care, but clearly families can be helped or hurt in their irreplaceable roles. Government can either support or undermine families as they cope with the moral, social, and economic stresses of caring for children.

There has been an unfortunate, unnecessary, and unreal polarization in discussions of how best to help families. Some emphasize the primary role of moral values and personal responsibility, the sacrifices to be made and the personal behaviors to be avoided, but often ignore or de-emphasize the broader forces which hurt families, e.g., the impact of economics, discrimination, and anti-family policies. Others emphasize the social and economic forces that undermine families and the responsibility of government to meet human needs, but they often neglect the importance of basic values and personal responsibility.

The undeniable fact is that our children's future is shaped both by the values of their parents and the policies of our nation.

> *Putting Children and Families First: A Challenge for our Church, Nation, and World, National Conference of Catholic Bishops—Pastoral Letter, November 1991*

The 1990s' struggle is for America's conscience and future—a future that is being determined right now in the bodies and minds and spirits of *every* American child—white, African American, Latino, Asian American, Native American, rich, middle class, and poor. Many of the battles for this future will not be as dramatic as Gettysburg or Vietnam or Desert Storm, but they will shape our place in the twenty-first century no less.[6]

Ironically, as Communism is collapsing all around the world, the American Dream is collapsing all around America for millions of children, youths, and families in all racial and income groups. American is pitted against American as economic uncertainty and downturn increase our fears, our business failures, our poverty rates, our racial divisions, and the dangers of political demagoguery.

Family and community values and supports are disintegrating among all races and income groups, reflecting the spiritual as well as economic poverty of our nation. All our children are growing up today in an ethically polluted nation where instant sex without responsibility, instant gratification without effort, instant solutions without sacrifice, getting rather than giving, and hoarding rather than sharing are the too-frequent signals of our mass media, business, and political life.

All our children are threatened by pesticides and toxic wastes and chemicals polluting the air, water, and earth. No parent can shut out completely the pollution of our airwaves and popular culture, which glorify excessive violence, profligate consumption, easy sex and greed, and depict deadly alcohol and tobacco products as fun, glamorous, and macho.

All our children are affected by the absence of enough heroines and heroes in public and daily life, as the standard for success for too many

Americans has become personal greed rather than common good, and as it has become enough to just get by rather than do one's best.

All our children are affected by escalating violence fueled by unbridled trafficking in guns and in the drugs that are pervasive in suburb, rural area, and inner city alike.

Young families of all races, on whom we count to raise healthy children for America's future, are in extraordinary trouble. They have suffered since the early 1970s a frightening cycle of plummeting earnings, a near doubling of birth rates among unmarried women, increasing numbers of single-parent families, falling income—the median income of young families with children fell by 26 percent between 1973 and 1989—and skyrocketing poverty rates. Forty percent of all children in families with a household head under thirty are poor. While many middle-class youths and young families see the future as a choice between a house and a child, many undereducated, jobless, poor youths and young adults trapped in inner-city war zones see the future as a choice between prison or death at the hands of gangs and drug dealers.

More and more Americans feel their children are being left behind. But poor children suffer most, and their numbers are growing—841,000 in 1990 alone. They are the small, faceless victims who have no one to speak and fight for them. We were mesmerized by the 1987 death of Lisa Steinberg, a child whose adoption was never completed or abuse detected by our overburdened, inadequate child welfare system.[7] We cheered when Jessica McClure was rescued from an open well shaft in the yard of an unregulated family day care center run by a relative, a danger she should not have come close to in the first place.[8] But when eight-month-old Shamal Jackson died in New York City from low birth-weight, poor nutrition, and viral infection— from poverty and homelessness—we didn't hear much about him.[9] During his short life, he slept in shelters with strangers, in hospitals, in welfare hotels, in the welfare office, and in the subways he and his mother rode late at night when there was no place else to go. In the richest nation on earth, he never slept in an apartment or house. Nor have we heard about two-pound "Jason" fighting for his life at Children's Hospital in Washington, D.C., or about thousands of other babies in similar neonatal intensive care wards all over America. At birth—three months before he was due—Jason weighed just over one pound. He lives because tubes connect his lungs and every available vein to the many machines that are needed to feed him and keep him warm and enable him to take his next breath. He has a heart problem and has already suffered seizures because of damage to his nervous system caused by bleeding into his head—damage that, if he lives, will probably be permanent.

What exactly led to Jason's premature birth will never be known. We do know, however, that unless a mother receives early and ongoing prenatal care, conditions that lead to prematurity cannot be detected or treated. A third of our mothers do not receive the care they need because our health care system, unlike that of every other major industrialized nation, does not provide universal basic coverage for mothers and children.

Remember these children behind the statistics. All over America, they are the small human tragedies who will determine the quality and safety and economic security of America's future as much as your and my children will. The decision you and I and our leaders must make is whether we are going to invest in every American child or continue to produce thousands of school dropouts, teen parents, welfare recipients, criminals—many of whom are alienated from a society that turns a deaf ear to the basic human needs and longings of every child.

If recent trends continue, by the end of the century poverty will overtake one in every four children, and the share of children living with single parents will also rise. One in every five births and more than one in three black births in the year 2000 will be to a mother who did not receive cost-effective early prenatal care. One of every five twenty-year-old women will be a mother, and more than four out of five of those young mothers will not be married. And the social security system that all of us count on to support us in our old age will depend on the contributions of fewer children—children we are failing today.

If we do not act immediately to protect America's children and change the misguided national choices that leave too many of them unhealthy, unhoused, ill-fed, and undereducated, during the next four years

1,080,000	American babies will be born at low birth-weight, multiplying their risk of death or disability,
143,619	babies will die before their first birthday,
4,400,000	babies will be born to unmarried women,
2,000,000	babies will be born to teen mothers,
15,856	children 19 or younger will die by firearms,
2,784	children younger than 5 will die by homicide,
9,208	children 19 or younger will commit suicide,
1,620,000	young people ages 16 to 24 will fail to complete high school,
3,780,000	young people will finish high school but not enroll in college,
599,076	children younger than 18 will be arrested for alcohol-related offenses, 359,600 for drug offenses, and 338,292 for violent crimes,
7,911,532	public school students will be suspended, and
3,600,000	infants will be born into poverty.

It is a spiritually impoverished nation that permits infants and children to be the poorest Americans. Over 13 million children in our rich land go without the basic amenities of life—more than the total population of Illinois,

Pennsylvania, or Florida. If every citizen in the state of Florida became poor, the president would declare a national disaster. Yet he and Congress have yet to recognize child and family poverty and financial insecurity as the national disaster it is and to attack it with a fraction of the zeal and shared commitment we now apply to digging out after a devastating hurricane or earthquake or fire. We moved more than 1.7 million elderly persons out of poverty in the three years following the 1972 revisions to the Social Security Act that indexed senior citizens' benefits to inflation. Surely we can provide families with children equitable treatment.

It is a morally lost nation that is unable and unwilling to disarm our children and those who kill our children in their school buses, strollers, yards, and schools, in movie theaters, and in McDonald's. Death stalks America's playgrounds and streets without a declaration of war—or even a sustained declaration of concern by our president, Congress, governors, state and local elected officials, and citizen.

Every day, 135,000 children bring a gun to school. In 1987, 415,000 violent crimes occurred in and around schools. Some inner-city children are exposed to violence so routinely that they exhibit post-traumatic stress symptoms similar to those that plague many Vietnam combat veterans. Still, our country is unwilling to take semiautomatic machine guns out of the hands of its citizens. Where are the moral guerrillas and protesters crying out that life at home is as precious as life abroad? Isn't it time for a critical mass of Americans to join our law enforcement agencies and force our political leaders to halt the proliferation of guns? Every day twenty-three teens and young adults are killed by firearms in America.

In response to a distant tyrant,[10] we sent hundreds of thousands of American mothers and fathers, sons and daughters, husbands and wives, sisters and brothers to the Persian Gulf. According to Secretary of State James Baker, the Gulf War was fought to protect our "life style" and standard of living and the rights of the Kuwaiti people.[11] No deficit or recession was allowed to stand in the way. How, then, can we reconcile our failure to engage equally the enemies of poverty and violence and family disintegration within our own nation? When are we going to mobilize and send troops to fight for the "life style" of the 100,000 American children who are homeless each night, to fight for the standard of living of thousands of young families whose earning capacity is eroding and who are struggling to buy homes, pay off college loans, and find and afford child care? Where are the leaders coming to the rescue of millions of poor working- and middle-class families fighting to hold together their fragile households on declining wages and jobs? Why are they not acting to help the one in six families with children headed by a working single mother—29 percent of whom are poor? Isn't it time to tell our leaders to bail out our young families with the same zeal as they bailed out failed thrift and banking institutions to the tune of an estimated $115 billion by 1992?

What do we *really* value as Americans when the president's 1992 budget proposed only $100 million to increase Head Start for *one year* and no addition for child care for working families,[12] but $500 million *each day* for Desert Storm, $90 million *each day* to bail out profligate savings and loan institutions,[13] and hundreds of millions more to give capital gains tax breaks to the rich? Between 1979 and 1989, the average income (adjusted for inflation) of the bottom fifth of families dropped by 6 percent while that of the top fifth surged upward by 17 percent. The poorest fifth of American families with children lost 21 percent of their income.

Why were we able to put hundreds of thousands of troops and support personnel in Saudi Arabia within a few months to fight Saddam Hussein when we are unable to mobilize hundreds of teachers or doctors and nurses and social workers for desperately underserved inner cities and rural areas to fight the tyranny of poverty and ignorance and child neglect and abuse?

Isn't it time for the president and Congress and all of us to redefine our national security and invest as much time and leadership and energy to solving our problems at home as we do to our problems abroad?

It is an ethically confused nation that has allowed truth-telling and moral example to become devalued commodities. Too many of us hold to the philosophy that "government is not the solution to our problems, government is the problem." If government is seen as an illegitimate enterprise, if the public purposes of one's job are not considered a high calling, and if government has no purpose other than its own destruction, the restraints against unethical behavior in both the public and private sectors quickly erode. As a result, for every Michael Deaver and for every Elliot Abrams,[14] from the public sector, there is an Ivan Boesky or a Reverend Jim Bakker in the private sector.[15] If the only principle our society adheres to is economist Adam Smith's "Invisible Hand,"[16] it leaves little or no room for the human hand, or the hand of God, whom the prophet Micah said enjoined us "to be fair and just and merciful." There is a hollowness at the core of a society if its members share no common purpose, no mutual goals, no joint vision—nothing to believe in except self-aggrandizement.

Isn't it time for us to hold our political leaders to their professed beliefs and promises about getting children ready for school and providing them health care and education?

It is a dangerously short-sighted nation that fantasizes absolute self-sufficiency as the only correct way of life. Throughout our history, we have given government help to our people and then have forgotten that fact when it came time to celebrate our people's achievements. Two hundred years ago, Congress granted federal lands to the states to help maintain public schools.

In 1862, President Lincoln signed the Morrill Land-Grant Act, granting land for colleges. The first food voucher and energy assistance programs came, not during the New Deal or the War on Poverty,[17] but at the end of the Civil War, when Congress and President Lincoln created the Freedman's Bureau.[18] Federal help for vaccinations, vocational education, and maternal health began, not with Kennedy, Johnson, and Carter, but under Madison, Wilson, and Harding, respectively.[19]

Our parents, grandparents, and great-grandparents benefited from this government help just as we all do today. Only the most blind of economists could doubt that American prosperity, like Japan's, is built on the synergistic relations between government and private initiative. But it is some of the most blind economists, political scientists, and "moral philosophers" who have the ear of many of our leaders or are themselves political leaders. Too many of them suffer from the peculiarly American amnesia or hypocrisy that wants us to think that poor and middle-class families must fend entirely for themselves; that makes us forget how government helps us all, regardless of class; and that makes us believe that the government is simply wasting its billions supporting a wholly dependent, self-perpetuating class of poor people, while doing nothing but taxing the rest of us.

Chrysler and Lee Iacocca didn't do it alone.[20] Defense contractors don't do it alone. Welfare queens can't hold a candle to corporate kings in raiding the public purse. Most wealthy and middle-class families don't do it alone. Yet some begrudge the same security for low-and moderate-income families with children who must grow up healthy, educated, and productive to support our aging population.

The president and Congress and public must take the time and have the courage to make specific choices and not wield an indiscriminate budget ax or hide behind uniform but unjust freezes of current inequalities. They must also take time to distinguish between programs that work (like immunization, preventive health care, and Head Start) and programs that don't (like the B-2 stealth bomber).[21] They must apply the same standards of accountability for programs benefiting the rich and poor and middle class alike. They must hold the Pentagon to the same standards of efficiency as social programs. And isn't it time for the president and Congress to invest more in preventing rather than trying to mop up problems after the fact? Isn't it time to reassess national investment priorities in light of changing national and world needs? Does it make sense for our federal government to spend each hour this fiscal year $33.7 million on national defense, $23.6 million on the national debt, $8.7 million on the savings and loan bailout, $2.9 million on education, and $1.8 million on children's health?

Making hard choices and investing in our own people may help restore the confidence of citizens in government. The overarching task of leadership today in every segment of American society is to give our youths, and all Americans, a sense that we can be engaged in enterprises that lend meaning to life, that we can regain control over our families and our national destiny, and that we can make a positive difference individually and collectively in building a decent, safe nation and world.

America cannot afford to waste resources by failing to prevent and curb the national human deficit, which cripples our children's welfare today and costs billions in later remedial and custodial dollars. Every dollar we invest in preventive health care for mothers and children saves more than $3 later. Every dollar put into quality preschool education like Head Start saves $4.75 later. It costs more than twice as much to place a child in foster care as to provide family preservation services. The question is not whether we can afford to invest in every child; it is whether we can afford not to. At a time when future demographic trends guarantee a shortage of young adults who will be workers, soldiers, leaders, and parents, America cannot afford to waste a single child. With unprecedented economic competition from abroad and changing patterns of production at home that demand higher basic educational skills, America cannot wait another minute to do whatever is needed to ensure that today's and tomorrow's workers are well prepared rather than useless and alienated—whatever their color.

We cannot go back and change the last decade's birth rates. But we can prevent and reduce the damages to our children and families and ensure every child a healthy start, a head start, and a fair start right now. In the waning years of the twentieth century, doing what is right for children and doing what is necessary to save our national economic skin have converged.

When the new century dawns with new global economic and military challenges, America will be ready to compete economically and lead morally only if we

1. stop cheating and neglecting our children for selfish, short-sighted, personal, and political gain;
2. stop clinging to our racial past and recognize that America's ideals, future, and fate are as inextricably intertwined with the fate of its poor and nonwhite children as with its privileged and white ones;
3. love our children more than we fear each other and our perceived or real external enemies;
4. acquire the discipline to invest preventively and systematically in all of our children *now* in order to reap a better trained work force and more stable future *tomorrow;*
5. curb the desires of the overprivileged so that the survival needs of the less privileged may be met, and spend less on weapons of death and more on lifelines of constructive development for our citizens;

6. set clear, national, state, city, community, and personal goals for child survival and development, and invest whatever leadership, commitment, time, money, and sustained effort are needed to achieve them;

7. struggle to begin to live our lives in less selfish and more purposeful ways, redefining success by national and individual character and service rather than by national consumption and the superficial barriers of race and class.

The mounting crisis of our children and families is a rebuke to everything America professes to be. While the cost of repairing our crumbling national foundation will be expensive in more ways than one, the cost of not repairing it, or of patching cosmetically, may be fatal.

The place to begin is with ourselves. Care. As you read about or meet some of the children and families in this country who need your help, put yourself in their places as fellow Americans. Imagine you or your spouse being pregnant, and not being able to get enough to eat or see a doctor or know that you have a hospital for delivery. Imagine your child hungry or injured, and you cannot pay for food or find health care. Imagine losing your job and having no income, having your unemployment compensation run out, not being able to pay your note or rent, having no place to sleep with your children, having nothing. Imagine having to stand in a soup line at a church or Salvation Army station after you've worked all your life, or having to sleep in a shelter with strangers and get up and out early each morning, find some place to go with your children, and not know if you can sleep there again that night. If you take the time to imagine this, perhaps you can also take the time to do for them what you would want a fellow citizen to do for you. Volunteer in a homeless shelter or soup kitchen or an afterschool tutoring or mentoring program. Vote. Help to organize your community to speak out for the children who need you. Visit a hospital neonatal intensive care nursery or AIDS and boarder baby ward and spend time rocking and caring for an individual child. Adopt as a pen pal a lonely child who never gets a letter from anyone. Give a youth a summer job. Teach your child tolerance and empathy by your example.

Essential individual service and private charity are not substitutes for public justice, or enough alone to right what's wrong in America. Collective mobilization and political action are also necessary to move our nation forward in the quest for fairness and opportunity for every American.

So pledge to take responsibility not only for your child but for all children or at least for one child who may not be your own. Finally, as you read the prayer below by Ina J. Hughs, include with every "we pray" the promise "I take responsibility for":

We pray for children
who sneak popsicles before supper,
who erase holes in math workbooks,
who can never find their shoes.
And we pray for those
who stare at photographers from behind barbed wire,
who can't bound down the street in a new pair of sneakers,
who never "counted potatoes,"
who are born in places we wouldn't be-caught dead,
who never go to the circus,
who live in an X-rated world.
We pray for children
who bring us sticky kisses and fistfuls of dandelions,
who hug us in a hurry and forget their lunch money.
And we pray for those
who never get dessert,
who have no safe blanket to drag behind them,
who watch their parents watch them die,
who can't find any bread to steal,
who don't have any rooms to clean up,
whose pictures aren't on anybody's dresser,
whose monsters are real.
We pray for children
who spend all their allowance before Tuesday,
who throw tantrums in the grocery store and pick at their food,
who like ghost stories,
who shove dirty clothes under the bed, and never rinse out the tub,
who get visits from the tooth fairy,
who don't like to be kissed in front of the carpool,
who squirm in church or temple and scream in the phone,
whose tears we sometimes laugh at and
whose smiles can make us cry.
And we pray for those
whose nightmares come in the daytime,
who will eat anything,
who have never seen a dentist,
who aren't spoiled by anybody,
who go to bed hungry and cry themselves to sleep,
who live and move, but have no being.
We pray for children who want to be carried
and for those who must,

for those we never give up on and for those
who don't get a second chance.
For those we smother . . . and for those who will grab
the hand of anybody kind enough to offer it."[22]

Please offer your hands to them so that no child is left behind because we did not act.

NOTES

1. Edelman, *Lanterns*, xiii.

2. In the *Loving v. Virginia*, 388 U.S. 1 (1967) decision the U.S. Supreme Court overturned *Pace v. Alabama*, 106 U.S. 583 (1883), and declared Virginia's Racial Integrity Act of 1924 unconstitutional. This landmark civil rights case ended all race-based legal restrictions on marriage in the United States. See also Wallenstein, "Interracial Marriage."

3. Children's Defense Fund, "About Us."

4. Reardon, review of *Measure of Our Success*, 111.

5. Hughs, "Prayer for Children," xiv–xv.

6. Desert Storm is also known as the Persian Gulf War.

7. Lisa Steinberg was illegally adopted by Joel Steinberg, a defense attorney who was convicted of manslaughter in 1987 for hitting Lisa on the head and then failing to seek immediate medical attention for the child, who died in a hospital three days later at the age of six.

8. Jessica McClure became famous in 1987 when she was rescued from a well in Midland, Texas, after being trapped for fifty-eight hours.

9. Basler, "Blind and Deaf Infant's Short Life." The child of a homeless family, Shamal Jackson died in May of 1985.

10. Saddam Hussein served as the fifth president of Iraq from 1979 to 2003, when he was overthrown during a U.S.-led invasion that came to be known as Operation Iraqi Freedom.

11. The Persian Gulf War was the U.N.-sanctioned military response to Iraq's invasion of Kuwait in 1990. The United States led coalition troops from thirty-four nations against Iraqi armed forces from August 1990 to February 1991.

12. Founded in 1965, Head Start is a federally sponsored program that provides educational services for three- to five-year-old children in low-income families.

13. A savings and loan institution is a financial organization that accepts money through savings deposits and lends money to borrowers in the form of mortgages, car loans, or personal loans. Thanks to the lifting of much regulatory legislation as well as the laying off of Federal Home Loan Bank Board regulatory staff members, these institutions have faced little oversight. Speculative real estate and commercial investments increasingly caused these institutions to fail throughout the 1980s. By 1989 more than half of the nation's savings and loans banks had failed, as had the federal fund that was supposed to have insured them. Estimates suggest that

by 1999, the crisis cost taxpayers and industry $153 billion, with taxpayers footing the bill for $124 billion of that total. See Curry and Shibut, "Cost of the Savings and Loan Crisis."

14. Michael Deaver served as President Ronald Reagan's White House deputy chief of staff from 1981 to 1985. Deaver was convicted of perjury in 1987 for the congressional testimony he submitted concerning his lobbying activities. Elliot Abrams served in various foreign policy positions for presidents Ronald Reagan and George W. Bush. In 1982 Abrams spoke out against reports of civilians being massacred by the government in El Salvador. It was later discovered that Salvadoran forces had executed up to five thousand civilians.

15. Ivan Boesky was an American stock trader who was convicted of insider trading in the late 1980s. James Bakker was a prominent televangelist and host of a popular 1980s television show, *The PTL Club* (the "Praise the Lord" Club). Caught up in financial and sex scandals, he resigned from his ministry in 1987.

16. The economist Adam Smith's concept of the "invisible hand" refers to the idea that competitive economic production by individuals propels society toward mutually desirable ends.

17. The New Deal is the term given to President Franklin Roosevelt's overall economic recovery plan, implemented from 1933 to 1936, in response to the Great Depression. The War on Poverty is the colloquial name for legislation that was introduced in 1964 by President Lyndon B. Johnson in response to the 19 percent poverty rate in the United States.

18. Established by President Lincoln in 1865, the Freedmen's Bureau was created to aid freed slaves by providing them with essentials such as food and housing.

19. The men to whom Edelman is referring served as president of the United States: John F. Kennedy (1961–63), Lyndon B. Johnson (1963–69), James E. Carter (1977–81), James Madison (1809–17), Woodrow Wilson (1913–21), and Warren G. Harding (1921–23).

20. Lee Iacocca was the president and CEO of the auto manufacturer Chrysler from 1978 to 1992. In 1979, Iacocca secured a loan from the federal government that saved the company from bankruptcy.

21. The B-2 bomber is a military aircraft equipped with stealth technology. Its production sparked controversy in the 1990s because of its price tag of $737 million per plane.

22. A version of this poem appears in Ina Hughs's book *A Prayer for Children* (New York: William Morrow, 1995).

James E. Clyburn
(b. 1940)

✒ CIVIL RIGHTS ACTIVIST, CONGRESSMAN, DEMOCRATIC LEADER

We can be no more or no less than what our experiences allow us to be.

James Enos "Jim" Clyburn is not only the most influential African American congressman of the early twenty-first century, but he is the proud heir of an activist intellectual legacy—his great-great uncle was George Washington Murray, the son of slaves who nonetheless became the only black member of the Fifty-Third and Fifty-Fourth Congresses (from 1893 to 1897). Clyburn's career followed a similarly unlikely ascent. Clyburn was born in Sumter, South Carolina, in 1940, to parents of modest means; his father, Enos, was a minister and his mother, Almeta, a beautician.

Raised to engage, Clyburn became president of the local youth chapter of the NAACP when he was only twelve years old. He entered South Carolina State College to study history and rose to become the leader of the college chapter of the Student Nonviolent Coordinating Committee.[1] As leader he participated in and helped organize several demonstrations and sits-ins protesting segregation. Arrested repeatedly, he actually met his future wife, Emily England, a sit-in participant, in jail; they married in 1961. One of the most significant actions he helped organize was a 1961 march on the state capitol that led to the landmark *Edwards v. South Carolina* case, in which the state was found to have violated the petitioners' right to free speech and assembly by forcing the peaceful protest to disperse.[2] This decision helped pave the way for activist and protest rights during the coming decade and struck a significant blow against the segregationist and conservative powers seeking to silence dissent in South Carolina.

As Clyburn takes pain to note in interviews and public statements, his role in the civil rights movement was in part circumstantial. Because his parents were not public-sector employees, he could become involved without fearing they would face retaliation for his actions. But this sort of humility has also been mirrored by a fierce pride and confidence. It was confidence that enabled him to use early exposure to what political work could accomplish in conjunction with grassroots activism that led him to a complicated career trajectory. As he once said: "We can be no more or no less than what our experiences allow us to be"[3] Hence, he increasingly combined personal and political work to agitate for justice.

Clyburn worked with the South Carolina State Employment Security Commission from 1965 to 1966 and as director of the Charleston County Neighborhood Youth Corps and New Careers Projects from 1966 to 1968. His increasing experience and understanding of community engagement and the needs of South Carolinians led him to a position as executive director of the South Carolina State Commission for Farm Workers from 1968 to 1971.

Clyburn increasingly came to see himself as effecting change as a politician. Although he lost a race for the House in 1970 (and also lost bids for South Carolina secretary of state in 1978 and 1986), he honed his skills by studying at the University of South Carolina Law School from 1972 to 1974 and working as a staff member for Governor John C. West from 1971 to 1974. Clyburn was the first African American adviser to a South Carolina governor since Reconstruction.[4] Four years later, shortly after the Orangeburg Massacre had brought South Carolina race relations to the forefront of state and national policy issues, Governor West appointed Clyburn human affairs commissioner.[5] Clyburn held this position under four governors, both Democratic and Republican, until 1992, when he was elected to the newly created and largely African American Sixth Congressional District. As chair of the Democratic Congressional Campaign Committee, Clyburn helped raise money to elect thirty more Democrats to the House and when, in 2006, the Democrats came to hold the majority position in the 110th Congress, Clyburn became the party whip, a title he held until the Republican majority win in 2010. He was named assistant Democratic leader in 2011, making him the third most highly ranked Democrat in the House of Representatives.

One incident that illustrates the kind of leader Clyburn wanted to be took place when he first took on the title "party whip." When he was invited to participate in the ceremonial tradition of receiving an actual leather horsewhip from the outgoing officeholder, in this case the white GOP party whip at the time, Roy Blunt, he sought to reshape the ceremony. Clyburn was uncomfortable with the symbolism, no matter how good the intentions, of an actual horsewhip being handed off to a black man from a white man. For Clyburn, evidently the legacy of American slavery suggested too many troubling interpretations for such a public act. He thus arranged instead to receive a whip handed to him by William Gray, a Democrat from Pennsylvania, who, in 1989, had been the first black majority whip.[6] This kind of attentive care to the evolving nature of government and to new possibilities for defining cross-cultural relationships in the era after a two-term black president has been elected, is indicative of Clyburn's current career in public service.

While he doesn't specifically reference this event in our first featured selection, his public statement "Whom Much Has Been Given," his choice to redefine the ceremonial whip tradition informs his declaration of mission. He notes instead his pride in being the first *South Carolinian* to hold the position of majority whip, not merely the second African American to hold such a position. Indeed, he discusses concerns that being too nice a "southern gentleman" could impede his success at "herding cats" whether he was black or white. He will be, as he says "a different kind of whip."

Yet being a different kind of political leader didn't mean that Clyburn was willing to allow false poses of honor to get in the way of acknowledging suffering and promoting action. One of the most telling aspects of Clyburn's 2009 "Proper Response to Ty'Sheoma's Letter," which we feature in this collection, isn't his acknowledgment of the horrific school conditions within the Sixth Congressional District. Rather, it is his emphasis on the role of Congress and congressionally directed spending that merits note inasmuch as it demonstrates his faith in the role of a representative government. He honors the sentimental and rhetorical power of a child's voice yet he harnesses it to concrete political action. Clyburn invokes this eighth grader's letter to argue that there should be a special or at least a more immediate and nuanced relationship between the federal government and congressional representatives in order to ensure that congressionally directed spending will be allocated for the good of constituents. Coming from a man who has seen firsthand how the federal government has served as one of the only bulwarks against state-sponsored racism, his rails against legislative earmarks and the ways in which congressional representatives are powerless to help their own constituents have a deeper contextual resonance. Clyburn's response was written with a personal and historical sensitivity to the consequences of centralized power in a state known for racial inequality. While Ty'Sheoma's story (which is more fully explored in our Afterword) continues and the school she wrote of has since been replaced with a new building, Clyburn continues in his position in the U.S. Congress to work toward responsible and equitable governance.

‚◗ "Whom Much Has Been Given, Much Is Required"

This has been a remarkable year for South Carolina and me. When the 110th Congress was sworn in last January,[7] John Spratt became Chair of the House Budget Committee[8] and I became the House Majority Whip, the third ranking leadership position in the U.S. House of Representatives. We were both elected to our positions by unanimous votes of the House Democratic Caucus, and in my case, it is the first time a South Carolinian has ever risen to this level of leadership in the United States House. And it is only the second time an African American has ever done so. The importance of this achievement does not escape me.

I am often asked, what does being the Whip mean? I believe defining the title gives insight into the job. The term "Whip" originated in the British Parliament, the body after which our government was patterned. They took the term from the sport of fox hunting. Foxhunters rode horses following hounds that pursued and flushed out the foxes. Because the hounds would sometimes get distracted and lose focus, members of the hunt were assigned to ride alongside the hounds responsible for keeping the foxhounds focused on their mission. They carried whips and were called "whipper ins."

Essentially, I am responsible for counting the votes and helping my colleagues keep focused on our mission. My team—this is definitely a job that no one can do alone—maintains constant communication with the members, counts votes, addresses members' concerns and works to persuade our colleagues on both sides of the aisle to support our legislative agenda.

A Different Kind of Whip

Since assuming this position, it has been often noted that my approach is much different than some of my high profile predecessors. It has even been written that I may be too nice a Southern gentleman to do the job effectively. Everyone seems to remember Tom DeLay whose service as House Majority Whip earned him the nickname "Hammer" for his strong-armed style that seemed to have worked well for him.[9] But I have always maintained that we can be no more and no less than what our experiences allow us to be, and my experiences make it hard for me to believe that people would rather be coerced and threatened than to be counseled and consulted.

My approach stems from important lessons I learned in the home in which I was raised, the schools in which I was taught, and the social and political environments in which I developed. From my father I learned that, "the first sign of a good education is good manners," and from one of my mentors, Governor John West I learned that, "you catch more flies with honey than with vinegar."[10] From my wife I learned that, "when you win, brag gently, when you lose, weep softly," and from my mother I learned that no matter how many times you fail, "never give up." And as hard as it sometimes is, I never give up on any of my colleagues.

When I became the Majority Whip last January, I had spent seven of my 14 years in Congress holding leadership positions to which I was elected by my colleagues. I had served as President of my Freshman Class (1994), Chair of the Congressional Black Caucus (1999–2001), Vice Chair of the House Democratic Caucus (2003–06), and Chair of the House Democratic Caucus (2006).

The House Democratic Caucus is very reflective of the diversity of our nation. We are seven distinct caucuses. All of them are well organized with highly competent elected leadership. We have the Asian-Pacific Islanders Caucus, the "Blue Dog" Democrats Caucus, the Progressive Caucus, the New Democrats Coalition, and the Women's Working Group.[11] Also, our 21-member Congressional Hispanic Caucus has several ethnic backgrounds, and our 42-member Congressional Black Caucus has varied backgrounds and experiences. If one can imagine herding cats, one can get a good feel for what it may like being the House Democratic Whip. To whip successfully, one must honor and respect this make-up. It requires a different kind of whip.

I believe, however, that my background and experiences prepared me well for this job. My years as a teacher in the Charleston County Public Schools, Director of the Neighborhood Youth Corps, Executive Director of the South Carolina Commission for Farm Workers, Assistant to Governor John West and South Carolina Human Affairs Commissioner,[12] have provided me a solid foundation, a good set of skills and a faith-based value system.

While I technically represent only one sixth of South Carolina's citizens, many of my legislative initiatives have benefited communities outside my district. The Gullah/Geechee Cultural Heritage Corridor follows Highway 17 along the entire South Carolina coast.[13] This has been my most popular initiative, yet only small portions of the Corridor are in the Sixth Congressional District. But tourism—and heritage tourism specifically—are extraordinarily important to our state's economy. This is also the reason I authored legislation to create the South Carolina National Heritage Corridor.[14] Much of that corridor is outside of my district, but I continue to secure $1 million in federal funding each year to continue generating an estimated $80 million annually for our state's economy.

I was humbled by the invitation to address a joint session of the South Carolina General Assembly in April. While I recognized it as an historic moment, I did not dwell upon that. Instead, I discussed initiatives I believe will benefit all South Carolinians. I called for major investments to put South Carolina in the forefront of developing alternative energy sources. In addition to addressing America's addiction to foreign oil, it will also boost our rural economies by creating markets for cellulosic crops that can replace our withering cotton and tobacco fields.[15]

I also used that speech to encourage more lottery funds for need-based scholarships. Too many of our young graduates are being unduly and unfairly burdened by the cost of obtaining a higher education. According to a recent *Greenville News* editorial, Clemson and University of South Carolina students graduate with an average of $18,000 in student loans. Incurring this crushing debt deters many from pursuing a higher education, and often sends our most promising graduates out of state where they can find higher salaries in order to repay their loans.

Finally, I urged lawmakers to seek a balance between our state's environment and our citizens' economic needs. Both are important and can coexist if we control our emotions, give just due to scientific research, and put proper regulations and safeguards in place at all levels of government.

My parents had great dreams for my siblings and me. I doubt, however, that they ever dreamed that one of their sons would one day occupy an opulent office in the U.S. Capitol with a breathtaking view down the National Mall. It is a far cry from our earlier days growing up in Kershaw and Lee counties and on Walker Avenue and Bartlette Streets in Sumter.

My ears often ring with the biblical admonition "to whom much is given, much is required." I am deeply humbled by the opportunities I have been given, and not a day goes by that I don't seek ways to use my position to give back. It is my strongest desire that South Carolina will be the ultimate beneficiary of this extraordinary and unprecedented gift.

?⬥ "Proper Response to Ty'Sheoma's Letter"

When I picked up Sunday's edition of my hometown newspaper, *The State,* I was greeted with a headline that read, "Ex-senator vents on state's schools, politics." Former U.S. Sen. Fritz Hollings, who retired four years ago, was lamenting that decades after he helped move the first 3-cent state sales tax through the South Carolina Legislature, "here we've got little Ty'Sheoma in Dillon, 50 years later, still begging for a decent school."[16] Hollings expressed embarrassment over her letter seeking "federal help to rebuild aging J.V. Martin Junior High she attends because South Carolina has dallied so long in upgrading its education system."

All South Carolinians should be embarrassed by the conditions that precipitated Ty'Sheoma Bethea's cries, but I, for one, was not embarrassed by her letter. To the contrary, I was buoyed by her bold initiative, and I was extremely pleased by the response of President Barack Obama and first lady Michelle Obama at the joint address before Congress last week.

Dillon County is bisected by Interstate 95, which runs for 200 miles through South Carolina, and has been dubbed "the corridor of shame."[17] Two-thirds of that corridor lies in the 6th Congressional District that I proudly represent. The J.V. Martin school is not an anomaly. Unfortunately, the conditions at J.V. Martin are all too common along that corridor.

I, and many members of Congress, hear cries for help like Ty'Sheoma's every time we visit our districts. Most of us have tried to respond as best we can, personally and politically. We hold town meetings, workshops and seminars to impart information and improve communities. We sponsor internships, fellowships and scholarships to provide individual assistance through various public and private entities. But to really improve conditions, our responses need to be at least as bold as Ty'Sheoma's initiative.

I think it is instructive that although Obama visited her school during his presidential campaign, Ty'Sheoma addressed her letter "Dear Congress of the United States." It's her congressman who visits her school, attends her family reunion and participates in local parades. She has been taught by school officials and counseled by family and friends to write her congressman to address her concerns, and we are constitutionally and dutybound to respond. I do not believe that a canned referral to an administrative agency run by a faceless bureaucrat is an effective, or even proper, response.

If I could, I would have dedicated some of the American Recovery and Reinvestment Act[18] to replacing schools and upgrading communities along the corridor of shame. I would have done so under the new "transparency and accountability" rules instituted by Democrats in the last Congress, just as I did to further develop the Lake Marion Regional Water Agency at the 98-mile marker on the I-95 corridor.[19] It was an earmark for which I was criticized, but because of it, a $600 million investment was recently announced that will create an initial 3,000 jobs in an area that has suffered double-digit unemployment for as long as I can remember.[20]

Unfortunately, Ty'Sheoma and her classmates are at the mercy of a governor whose political ideology makes him reluctant to provide the help they need. He has been allocated millions, but the American Recovery and Reinvestment Act effectively replaces congressional earmarks with gubernatorial earmarks. So Gov. Mark Sanford is free to do whatever he pleases for whoever pleases him.[21]

Because of Ty'Sheoma's actions, and national attention, J.V. Martin may get some much-needed attention, but what about other schools along the I-95 corridor: Bamberg-Ehrhardt,[22] which needs to replace a 60-year-old roof, or Lafayette Academy in New Orleans? Who will be Ty'Sheoma for these schools? Their teachers, students and parents send representatives to Congress expecting them to address their needs and concerns as they pursue their dreams and aspirations.

I trust Obama to make the right investments in education, access to health care, energy independence and American ingenuity to lead the country on the path toward recovery. But I believe that lawmakers who were elected by the people they live among, and who see firsthand the day-to-day challenges their neighbors face, should play a role in directing some of those federal investments.

In the past decade, earmarks quadrupled and the word "earmark" became a bad word because of a few bad actors. But we have dramatically reformed the process, reducing earmarks to less than 1 percent of discretionary spending and instituting openness, transparency and accountability so we can discourage, expose and properly punish the bad guys. Those with a political agenda will demonize congressionally directed spending, but to me, it's an appropriate answer to Ty'Sheoma's letter and a proper response to schools such as J. V. Martin and communities along the corridor of shame.

NOTES

1. Known as South Carolina State College since 1954, the institution officially changed its name to South Carolina State University in 1992.

2. The Supreme Court decision in *Edwards et al. v. South Carolina,* 372 U.S. 229 (1963), was handed down in February 1963. The basis of the case was the 1961 arrest and conviction of nearly two hundred peaceful demonstrators, mostly African American students, in Columbia, South Carolina, for breach of the peace, despite the fact that there was neither violence nor threat of violence by the demonstrators or by those watching the demonstration. The U.S. Supreme Court, in overturning the decision of the South Carolina Supreme Court, determined that the treatment of the demonstrators violated their rights under the First and Fourteenth Amendments to the U.S. Constitution; South Carolina had specifically violated their rights of free speech, freedom of assembly, and freedom to petition for redress of grievances. In the majority opinion, the court noted, "The Fourteenth Amendment does not permit a State to make criminal the peaceful expression of unpopular views."

3. Clyburn, "Creation of the Student Nonviolent Coordinating Committee."

4. For more information on West and his impact on desegregation in South Carolina, see Saxon, "John C. West."

5. On the night of February 8, 1968, nine highway patrol officers fired into a crowd of protesters at South Carolina State College in Orangeburg, South Carolina. This action came in the wake of a protest against the segregation of Orangeburg's only bowling alley that had taken place two days earlier. At least thirty people were wounded in the shootings. Two South Carolina State students and a local high school student died. The incident, which became known as the Orangeburg Massacre, occurred more than two years before the Kent State shootings in Ohio that resulted in the deaths of four students in May 1970.

6. William Herbert Gray III served in the U.S. House of Representatives from 1979 to 1991. He resigned his seat in 1991 to become president of the United Negro College Fund, a position he held until 2004.

7. The 110th Congress of the United States was sworn in on January 4, 2007. Its term ended at noon on January 4, 2009.

8. John Spratt served in Congress as a representative from South Carolina from 1982 to 2010.

9. Tom DeLay served as a representative from Texas in the U.S. House of Representatives from 1985 to 2006. He served as House majority leader from 2002 to 2005, when he resigned from the position. In 2011, he was sentenced to three years in prison for his involvement in a scheme to illegally funnel corporate money to political candidates from Texas.

10. John C. West served as the governor of South Carolina from 1971 to 1975 and as the U.S. ambassador to Saudi Arabia from 1977 to 1981.

11. Founded in 1994, the Congressional Asian Pacific American Caucus (CAPAC) is composed of members of Congress of Asian and Pacific Islander descent as well as members of Congress who have a strong dedication to promoting the well-being of the Asian American and Pacific Islander community. Formed in 1995, the Blue Dog Coalition is composed of fiscally conservative Democrats in Congress. As of the 112th Congress, there were twenty-five members of the Blue Dog Coalition. Established in 1991, the Congressional Progressive Caucus was formed to promote a more just and humane society and to reflect the diversity of America; it is the largest caucus within the House Democratic Caucus. The New Democratic Coalition, often known as the NDC or "New Dems," was founded in 1997. The group seeks to promote a "common sense" policy agenda. The Democratic Women's Working Group was founded in 2010 to promote equality and opportunity for women.

12. Clyburn taught social studies at C. A. Brown High School in Charleston. He joined the staff of Governor John C. West in 1971. In 1974, Governor West appointed him South Carolina's human affairs commissioner. He held this position until 1992, when he stepped down to run for Congress.

13. The Gullah/Geechee Cultural Heritage Corridor was designated by Congress in 2006. It stretches from Wilmington, North Carolina, to Jacksonville, Florida, and was created to recognize the culture and traditions brought to the area by the West and Central Africans who came to the southern United States as slaves.

14. The South Carolina National Heritage Corridor was designated a National Heritage Area by Congress in 1996. It stretches 240 miles and crosses seventeen counties. Locations of special cultural, environmental, and historical significance are identified along its length.

15. Cellulosic bioenergy crops are crops that can be converted to biofuels.

16. Frederick "Fritz" Hollings (b. 1922) served as a Democratic senator from South Carolina from 1966 to 2005.

17. In 1993 thirty-six South Carolina school districts filed a case against the state of South Carolina alleging violations of state and federal funding laws and violations of the South Carolina and U.S. Constitutions in reference to the funding of

rural South Carolina schools. The resulting Supreme Court decision is known as *Abbeville County School District, et al. v. State of South Carolina, et al.* The evidence presented at the trial is documented in a film titled "Corridor of Shame: The Neglect of South Carolina's Rural Schools."

18. Congress passed the American Recovery and Reinvestment Act (ARRA) on February 17, 2009. It increased federal funds for education and health care and provided tax cuts to create jobs, save existing jobs, and spur economic growth. It included stringent reporting requirements in order to foster high levels of accountability.

19. On March 29, 2006, Congress passed the Legislative Transparency and Accountability Act of 2006. It required that members of Congress who propose an earmark be identified, that the positive points of an earmark be identified, and that provisions be made for removal of earmarks. The Earmark Transparency Act of 2010 passed and created a clear public government website with a searchable database of congressional earmarks. The Lake Marion Regional Water System is a multimunicipality system that uses treated water from Lake Marion. It is owned and operated by Santee Cooper and governed by the Lake Marion Water Agency.

20. An "earmark" is a legislative provision that directs that funds be spent on a specific project. Legislators frequently attempt to allocate earmark money to organizations and projects in their home states.

21. Marshall Clement "Mark" Sanford Jr. (b. 1960) was South Carolina's 115th governor, serving from 2003 to 2011.

22. Bamberg-Ehrhardt High School is located in Bamberg, South Carolina. It is part of Bamberg School District 1, which includes schools built as early as 1937. In March 2010, Bamberg County voters approved a referendum allowing the district to borrow $29 million from the federal government to replace the high school's roof and to make other improvements.

Jesse Jackson
(b. 1941)

❧ CIVIL RIGHTS ACTIVIST, BAPTIST MINISTER, POLITICIAN

They wonder, "Why does Jesse run?" because they see me running
for the White House. They don't see the house I'm running from.

During his historic 1988 Democratic Convention speech, Jesse Louis Jackson used these words to remind listeners that although he had garnered international attention through an unprecedented second run for the White House, he had been born in obscurity in Greenville, South Carolina, to an unwed mother. Family and friends ostracized his mother, Helen Burns, because of her pregnancy, which resulted from an affair with her married next-door neighbor, compelling the young woman they once admired for her beautiful singing voice to consider an abortion. After consulting with her pastor, however, she decided to keep her baby. She named her son Jesse Louis Burns, after his paternal grandfather, Jesse Louis Robinson. A few years after her son's birth, Helen Burn married Charles Henry Jackson, who adopted Jesse when he was about fifteen years old. Jesse's parents tried to protect him from the stigma associated with the circumstances of his birth, but they could not shield him from the taunts of neighbors and classmates. Jesse Jackson later insisted that he was not traumatized by the revelation of his parentage; he reveled in the fact that he had two fathers who loved him.

Jackson grew up in an impoverished African American neighborhood lined with an assortment of wood frame and brick homes that lacked running water and included outhouses in the backyards. Despite his dire socioeconomic status, he excelled academically and athletically. After graduating tenth in his high school class, he enrolled in the University of Illinois-Chicago (UIC) on a football scholarship. Disillusioned by the racism and discrimination he encountered in the Midwest, Jackson transferred to the historically black North Carolina Agricultural and Technical College (AT&T) in Greensboro, North Carolina, where he became student body president, played quarterback, and joined the Congress on Racial Equality (CORE). As a member of CORE, Jackson organized numerous sit-ins and marches to protest segregation. His bold leadership style brought him to the attention of national civil rights organizations. Jackson quickly attained high-profile, influential positions, including president of the North Carolina Intercollegiate Council on Human Rights and CORE field director. During this period he was married, in 1962, to Jacqueline Lavinia Brown, with whom he eventually had five children: Santita, Jesse Jr., Jonathan Luther, Yusef Du Bois, and Jacqueline Lavinia.[1] He graduated from AT&T in 1964 with a degree in sociology. After receiving a Rockefeller grant, Jackson enrolled in the Chicago Theological Seminary and became a volunteer for the Coordinating Committee of Community Organizations.

In 1965 Jackson's life took a dramatic turn when he organized a group of students to participate in demonstrations with Martin Luther King Jr. and the Southern Christian Leadership Conference (SCLC) in Selma, Alabama. Before returning to Chicago, Jackson secured a staff position in the SCLC to help extend civil rights initiatives into the North through the Chicago Campaign. He soon left the seminary to become involved full-time in the civil rights movement, starting as coordinator and then becoming national director of Operation Breadbasket, the SCLC's economic development and empowerment program.[2]

Jackson became known nationally overnight when, in 1968, he was present at the Lorraine Hotel as Martin Luther King Jr. was assassinated. While other SCLC members rushed to the hospital with King, Jackson remained at the hotel and took media questions that day and the next with King's blood still on his shirt. While versions of what precisely occurred on that evening vary, Jackson's readiness to take on, whether by intention or by default, King's mission and mantle became apparent, and he quickly became a powerful voice for the new generation of civil rights leaders. Indeed, although it was actually Ralph Abernathy who replaced King as the leader of the SCLC, many came to view Jackson as King's successor in the broader sense of leading the nation in its quest for civil rights. As Jackson and Abernathy sought to fulfill King's dream, they repeatedly disagreed about the direction of the movement, however, and parted ways in 1971. Jackson soon founded Operation PUSH (People United to Save Humanity), which widened the scope of his civil rights, social activism, and political change initiatives to an international scale.

Jackson's involvement with international issues made headlines when, in 1983, he flew to Damascus with a group of other ministers to successfully negotiate with Syrian president Hafez al-Assad for the release of an American aerial navigator, Navy Lieutenant Robert Goodman Jr. The fame he received from this success helped launch his 1984 presidential campaign, supported by a "Rainbow Coalition" platform that promoted equality for all Americans. While he did not win the Democratic nomination, he outperformed most expectations by ultimately obtaining approximately 18 percent of the popular vote and 465.5 delegates. He also founded the National Rainbow Coalition, a multiracial political organization, to empower the poor, minorities, and the working class. Jackson continued to lobby for civil rights at home and international justice abroad by assisting with negotiations that eventually freed hostages held in Cuba in 1984, in Iraq in 1991, and in Serbia in 1999. Since the 1970s he has repeatedly traveled overseas to bring media attention to international issues such as apartheid in South Africa, the crisis of the Palestinian people, and setbacks in the Northern Ireland peace process. In 1997 President Bill Clinton and Secretary of State Madeleine Albright appointed him to represent U.S. interests as a special envoy to Africa.

In the 1986 *Harper's* magazine interview that we feature here, Jackson pushes back in his discussions with Charles Murray, the conservative social theorist, with comradely recognition of shared interests yet retaining his own resolute focus on how America should respond to the crisis of poverty. Jackson consistently reminds Murray and their audience that America's reaction to social crisis cannot be constructed out of fear or self-righteousness. When Jackson first replies to Murray's framing of the question "What does the government owe the poor?," Jackson not only rebuts the assumptions about the ineffective nature of historical government intervention but does so in a manner that demonstrates his oratorical training and artful debate style. He gently posits Murray as a proponent of simplistic truths, and with graceful repetition and structural shaping he builds his case that we cannot condemn all inconvenient social intervention while ignoring the parallel government work that has benefited so many. Jackson states:

> We cannot be blindly anti-government. The government has made significant interventions in many, many areas for the common good. Without public schools, most Americans would not be educated.

Without land-grant colleges, the United States would not have the number one agricultural system in the world. Without federal transit programs, we would not have an interstate highway system. Without subsidized hospitals, most Americans could not afford decent medical care. And the government has played a significant role in providing a base for many American industries. The defense industries, for example, may be considered private, part of the market, but many of them are almost wholly supported by government contracts.

Jackson's and Murray's sparring seems jovial throughout, but their differences lie deep, and therein we can see the same characteristics of Jackson that have allowed him to negotiate with some of the world's most ferociously unyielding governments and individuals.

In another passage, Jackson and Murray exchange a quip that, while humorous, nonetheless illustrates the deep cynicism that underscores Murray's worldview and how it contrasts with the essential faith Jackson seems to have in people. Murray, displaying an assumption that was soon to fuel the epically controversial arguments about IQ and race later to be published in Murray's study, *The Bell Curve*,[3] questions whether Jackson's social solutions would benefit the less intelligent (a genetic trait, he assumes) and, even more important, the less industrious (a trait he implies is possibly genetic but certainly cultural).

> MURRAY: Now, what about the youngster who is offered an opportunity but who is below average in intelligence? I mean, half the country is below average in intelligence, and in industriousness.
> JACKSON: Does that apply all the way through the government?

Jackson's clever retort efficiently points out the class and race assumptions that fuel Murray's comments in a simultaneously sharp and jovial manner (for surely everyone can agree there are stupid people in government, he seems to imply). But his reply also demonstrates the courage to resist going down the path of false syllogisms and misleading warrants. Jackson wrestles the conversation away from Murray and claims the terms of the interview as his own. The optimism that Jackson demonstrates is not surprising, for it comes from a man who had run a failed attempt at the presidency in 1984 but, unbowed, was to run again in 1988.

The standing he acquired in the early 1980s both as a patriot and as a player on the international stage helped Jackson do even better in his 1988 presidential bid. This time around he received about 29 percent of the votes in local primary elections and came in second to Massachusetts governor Michael Dukakis, who went on to win the Democratic Party nomination but lost the presidential election in a landslide. Jackson's historic accomplishment as the first African American candidate to come so close to achieving a major party nomination was almost overshadowed, however, by his stirring Democratic Convention speech, featured here. It was and has since been hailed as one of the most remarkable moments in American oratory. From the outset of the speech, Jackson advances a philosophy of inclusiveness that urges Americans to acknowledge and celebrate diversity. He refashions America's founding motto, "Out of many, one," into a series of mantras that stress commonalities—common good, common ground, common sense, and common threads. Those threads are best represented in what is perhaps the most familiar image in the speech: his grandmother's quilt. Indeed, Jackson's speech functions like a quilt, a patchwork of deftly woven rhetorical strategies that reflects the rhythmic cadences of a Baptist preacher's sermon and the fiery oratory of a seasoned politician's stump speech. He provides a new vision for inclusiveness and equality that emerges when an African American South Carolinian born in poverty dramatically shifts the political landscape during his remarkable second run for the White House.

In 1990 Jackson won his first public office when the Washington, D.C., city council elected him a "shadow senator" whose duties were primarily to lobby for genuine senatorial representation for the District of Columbia. He returned to Chicago yet again in 1996 and merged Operation PUSH with the Rainbow Coalition to form the Rainbow PUSH Coalition, which creates economic and political opportunities for minority populations and advocates for peace and justice internationally. His work has ranged from spearheading voter registration drives to negotiating agreements with mortgage companies to aid homeowners. In 2001 it was revealed that he had fathered a daughter, Ashley, with a staffer, Karin Stanford, in 1999. The scandal caused him to slow down his activism for a period, but it has not stopped his career of engagement.

Through the years, Jackson has received recognition for his public service. In 1989 he received the NAACP's Spingarn Medal for his achievements as a religious leader, civil rights activist, and politician. In 2000 President Clinton honored him by presenting him with the Presidential Medal of Freedom. In 2009 British prime minister Gordon Brown acknowledged his work with the Global Diversity and Inclusion Award. Numerous organizations throughout the nation and around the world have recognized his contributions to civil rights, social justice, and political empowerment. Jackson has been awarded forty honorary degrees, and he was inducted into the Cambridge Union Society in England in 2010. He has also been invited to lecture at major universities throughout the United States, including Princeton, Harvard, Morehouse, Stanford, Yale, and Columbia.

✐❧ "What Does the Government Owe the Poor?"

CHARLES MURRAY *is a senior research fellow at the Manhattan Institute for Policy Research. He is the author of* Losing Ground: American Social Policy, 1950–1980, *which criticizes the effects of social programs on the poor. He was formerly chief scientist at the American Institutes for Research, where he evaluated government programs involving urban education, welfare services, child nutrition, day care, adolescent pregnancy, juvenile delinquency, and criminal justice.*

JESSE JACKSON *is president of the National Rainbow Coalition and co-pastor of the Fellowship Missionary Baptist Church in Chicago. From 1967 to 1971 he served as national director of the Southern Christian Leadership Conference's Operation Breadbasket. In 1971 he founded Operation PUSH, which promotes excellence in inner-city public schools and negotiates with major corporations to increase the amount of business they do with minority-owned companies. Jackson sought the Democratic presidential nomination in 1984.*

CHARLES MURRAY: How can government help the poor? The problem is that, so far, we haven't been very good at it. During the late 1960s and early 1970s, we began a major effort to bring people out of poverty, to educate the uneducated, to employ the unemployable. We have to confront the fact that the effort to help the poor did not have the desired effect. In terms of education, crime, family stability, the lives of poor people have gotten worse since the 1960s, and we have to explain why.

During those years we, in effect, changed the rules of the game for poor people. Essentially we said in a variety of ways: "It's not your fault. If you are not learning in school, it is because the educational system is biased; if you are committing crimes, it is because the environment is poor; if you have a baby that you can't care for, it's because your own upbringing was bad." Having absolved everybody of responsibility, we then said: "You can get along without holding a job. You can get along if you have a baby but have no husband and no income. You can survive without participating in society the way your parents had to." And lots of young people took the bait. So the question remains: What, if anything, does the government owe the poor?

JESSE JACKSON: I'm as unimpressed with boundless liberalism as I am with heartless conservatism. Creative thinking has to take place. But to begin to think creatively, we have to be realistic: about the role of government, for example.

We cannot be blindly anti-government. The government has made significant interventions in many, many areas for the common good. Without public schools, most Americans would not be educated. Without land-grant colleges, the United States would not have the number one agricultural system in the world. Without federal transit programs, we would not have an interstate highway system. Without subsidized hospitals, most Americans could not afford decent medical care. And the government has played a significant role in providing a base for many American industries. The defense industries, for example, may be considered private, part of the market, but many of them are almost wholly supported by government contracts.

Now, we consider spending the public's money toward these ends to be in our national interest. When we saw the devastation in Europe after World War II, we devised the Marshall Plan—a comprehensive, long-term program.[4] Had the Marshall Plan been a five-year investment program—as the War on Poverty essentially was—Europe would have collapsed. But we determined that the redevelopment of Europe was in our national interest. That's an instance where a vigorous government investment made something positive happen.

But when we shift from the notion of subsidy as something that serves our national interest, to that of welfare, the attitudes suddenly shift from positive to negative. In this country there is a negative predisposition toward the poor. We must learn to see the *development* of people who are poor as in our national interest, as cost-efficient, as an investment that can bring an enormous return to every American. The government definitely has a big role to play.

MURRAY: I agree it has a role. There are some things government *can* do, and one of them is to ensure that a whole range of opportunities is available to everyone. For example, in my ideal world, whether a child lived in the inner city or in the suburbs, everything from preschool to graduate school would be available to him—free. In this ideal world, if someone really looked for a job and just couldn't find one, perhaps because of a downturn in the economy, some minimal unemployment insurance would be in place to help him.

Opportunity should be assured, but attempts at achieving equal outcome abandoned. What would happen if you took away all other government-supported welfare, if the system were dismantled? Well, believe it or not, a lot of good things would begin to happen.

JACKSON: The notion of "opportunity" is more complicated than it sounds. For example, some people are poor *because* of government. When a nation is 51 percent female yet can't get an equal rights amendment passed; when many women still cannot borrow money with the same freedom men can, cannot pursue their ideas and aspirations in the marketplace because they are not equally protected—that amounts to government interference, too, but on the side of the status quo. Many blacks and Hispanics cannot borrow money from banks, on subjective grounds—because some bank official doesn't like their color, or because whole neighborhoods are red-lined so that money will not be loaned to anyone living there. Government must be committed to the vigorous enforcement of equal protection under the law and other basic principles; without that enforcement, it is not a government handout that's the issue as much as it is the government's shoving people into a hole and not *letting* them out. When Legal Aid is cut and the poor no longer have access to the courts, that's an example of government playing a role in perpetuating poverty.[5]

MURRAY: If you try to rent an inexpensive apartment in my hometown of Newton, Iowa, even if you're white, you may very well not be able to rent that apartment, on "subjective grounds." I mean, you come to the door, and because of the way you act or the way you look or whatever the landlord says to himself: "My apartment's going to get trashed." These subjective grounds often have a basis in fact. And its real tough for people renting out apartments—and maybe even for banks—to operate in ways that enable them to make money if they aren't permitted to make these kinds of subjective judgments.

JACKSON: Dr. Murray, the farmer wearing his bib overalls who walks up to that apartment door and is rejected for the way he looks is not a victim of racial prejudgment. That man could put on a suit and get the apartment. Blacks can't change color. The idea is that bankers choose not to make loans to blacks *institutionally.*

Now, I'm not just throwing around a charge here. John H. Johnson, the president of Johnson Publishing Company, which publishes *Ebony,* is perhaps the most established black businessman in the country. Yet several banks turned down his loan application to build in downtown Chicago. Maybe the most established black businessman in the country was turned down for a loan simply because of the institutional racism of banks. And so we need laws enforced, we need the government to protect people who are black or Hispanic or Asian or Indian or female, from the bankers' ability to do that.

A lot of people, to this day, are simply locked out. Until 1967, there had never been more than a couple of black car dealerships, because the automobile industry's policy was not to allow a black to invest in a car dealership or to learn to run one in any neighborhood, black or white. So blacks now have fewer than 240 dealerships out of the 22,050 in this country. Blacks always had the ability, but they were locked out by race, even if they had the money. Operation PUSH confronted Ford as late as July 1982, when there were fewer than 40 black automobile dealerships out of 5,600.[6] Ford finally agreed to grant thirty new black dealerships in one year, which they had previously claimed was impossible. Well, those thirty dealerships are still operating, employing an average of more than fifty people each, and those jobs represent the alternative to welfare and despair.

MURRAY: If you say that in 1960 blacks as a people were locked out, well, I have no problem with that. But that is no longer accurate. Let's talk about black youth unemployment. Are you saying that America's black youth are marching resolutely from door to door, interviewing for jobs, and that they are getting turned down because they're black? If so, then a jobs program ought to do wonders. CETA ought to have done wonders.[7] But it didn't.

JACKSON: The private economy, by being so closed for so long, has pushed many people into the public economy. There's just no reason why, in a population of 30 million blacks, there are only two black beverage-bottling franchises. You can't explain it by lack of ambition or an unwillingness to take risks, because for the past twenty years blacks have been the top salesmen in that industry. A lot of people got locked into poverty because of the government's failure to enforce equal protection under the law. Until the Civil Rights Act of 1964 and Lyndon Johnson's executive order of 1965, beverage companies could get lucrative government contracts to operate on U.S. military bases around the world, even though they locked out a significant body of Americans.

MURRAY: I'm not in a position to argue with you about wholesalers and franchises. But I don't think we can assume that if blacks gain more access to entrepreneurial business positions—which I'm all in favor of—it will have a fundamental effect on poverty and the underclass.

JACKSON: If there is an artificial ceiling limiting the growth of the so-called talented 10 percent—I use the term advisedly—then it compounds the problem of the disinherited 90 percent.[8] If where we live, our money won't "spend" because of redlining, which becomes a de facto law; if where we live, our money cannot buy a car franchise or a beer franchise or a soft-drink franchise—which are some of the great American ways out of poverty—then blacks are effectively locked out of the private economy.[9] And so, just as the political grandfather clause locked blacks out of the political system, economic grandfather clauses have effectively locked blacks out of the economic system. Blacks today can take over a town politically, because its population is mostly black. But the economic territory—the entrepreneurial opportunities, beyond mom-and-pop businesses, which allow a people to develop a leadership class in the private economy, which in turn begins to lift others as it hires them and trains them—is still closed. Blacks who worked as salesmen and saleswomen for the first generation of black entrepreneurs now have franchises of their own, because they have access to the franchise head. But that has not happened historically.

MURRAY: Why is it that the Koreans and Vietnamese and all sorts of other people who come here with very few resources do well, including West

Indian blacks? They come here, start businesses, and manage to earn a median income which rivals or surpasses that of whites. I'm not trying to say racism doesn't exist. I'm saying it doesn't explain nearly as much as it ought to.

JACKSON: Do not underestimate the impact of 250 years of legal slavery followed by a hundred years of legal segregation. The damage it did to the minds of the oppressor and the oppressed must not be played down. When I grew up in South Carolina, I could caddy but I couldn't play golf. That's why I can't play golf now; I could have been arrested for hitting a golf ball at the Greenville Country Club. I could shag balls, but couldn't play tennis.[10] I could shine shoes, but I couldn't sit on the stand and couldn't own a stand at the train station. I could wait tables, but I couldn't sit at them; and I could not borrow money to build a competing establishment.

The other groups you mentioned have not known that level of degradation. The Cubans came to Miami as beneficiaries of a cold war between this country and Cuba; we used money and subsidies to induce them to come here, and those who came were in large measure from a class that had some history of business acumen. Many of the Vietnamese were beneficiaries of the same kind of cold war policy.

Now, shagging balls and not playing tennis, caddying and not playing golf, not voting and seeing others vote—all of this had the cumulative effect of lowering people's ambitions and limiting their horizons. Let me give an example. I saw a story in *USA Today* last summer headlined "More Blacks Graduating from High School, Fewer Going to College." A young lady from Chicago was quoted in the story, and I decided to meet with her and her mother. It turned out she had a B+ average, was a member of the National Honor Society—the whole business. I said to the girl, "Do you want to go to college?" She said she did. I said, "Well, have you taken the SAT tests?" She said she hadn't. "Why not?" "Well, the counselor told me that since I couldn't afford to go to college, that stuff was a waste of time." In other words, she was being programmed for failure, taught to be mediocre, programmed downward.

Once I discovered what was happening, I went on the radio and asked any high school student—black, white, brown—who had every college qualification except money to come to Operation PUSH. Seven hundred fifty young people came with their parents; we have placed 250 of them in colleges, including that young lady. But if that young lady hadn't gone to college, she would have been written off three or four years later: people would have said the family was subsidized, dependent; she didn't go to college; now she's pregnant; and the whole cycle begins again. She was programmed into lower ambition, programmed away from college. Yet many schools, especially the better ones like Harvard and Columbia, provide scholarship money. But so many students don't know this; it's a well-kept secret. Those who have, know; the circle remains essentially closed.

MURRAY: Getting that information out would serve as an *incentive*. I know how I'd spend money on educational programs. I'd put up a bunch of posters saying that anybody who gets such-and-such a score on the SATs will get a free ride through college. I'm willing to bet that I'd get more results from my program than the government would get by trying directly to improve the schools.

JACKSON: There's a role for that kind of motivation. There's also a role for increasing opportunity. Often it's not lack of ability or ambition that locks people out, but lack of information.

MURRAY: I'm worried, because I'm starting to agree with you too much!

JACKSON: Just give me time, you'll be all right. . . .

The present welfare system should be replaced with a human development system. As presently constructed, the welfare system has built-in snares: there's no earn-incentive, no learn-incentive to get out. Assume you are locked into this box: a girl with a tenth-grade education and a baby. If she's making, say, $200 a month on welfare, why not provide some positive incentives? If she went back to school and got her junior college degree, she should get $240, $250. Why? Because that's making her employable, moving her closer to the market, where she can earn her own money. She can go back to junior college and study computer science, or learn cosmetology or business. The way it is now in most states, if she went out and found a job and made $200, they would take away $200 from welfare. So why earn the $200? Maybe if she earns $200 she should keep at least $100. The point is that incentives to earn and learn must be built into the system. As it is now, if the young man who fathered the child doesn't have a job but comes back to live with the mother, she loses her check. So there's an incentive to keep the father away. And one of the few ways she can get any extra money is by engaging in an activity that may get her an extra child.

Now this young girl—white, black, Hispanic, Asian, Indian—is the victim of a system that is not oriented toward human development. We must take away the punishment and threats and disincentives and move toward a sense of optimism and increasing options.

MURRAY: One part of me endorses what you're saying in principle. But when I think of all the practical difficulties I get depressed. Most of all, it is extremely difficult to make much progress with youngsters who already have certain behavior patterns. If we go to a poor part of New York City, white or black, and pick a hundred kids who really have problems—drugs, illegitimate kids, the rest of it—and I say: "Here's a blank check; hire the best people, use the latest technologies, do whatever you can." At the end of three or four or even five years, if you start with seventeen- or eighteen-year-olds, *maybe* you will be able to point to ten or fifteen out of that hundred who show any major signs of getting somewhere.

Human beings aren't plastic. We don't know how to deal with certain kinds of problems after a certain age. The only route we have is prevention. So if you're hearing me say we're going to have to write off a generation, you can certainly back me into that corner.

JACKSON: Dr. Murray, I have seen these same kids, who you say can't do anything, volunteer for the Army, and in six to eight months they are building bridges, assuming responsibility. Why? Because it's an effective program that teaches, inspires, and sets clear goals.

So many young people step into sex and have babies because of ignorance, lack of discipline, and the like. If there was sex education before the fact, as well as the teaching of moral values, then there'd be less debate about abortion after the fact. Today, there is this whole group of people who *love* the fetus; they march across America to save a fetus and march right back to cut off aid for a baby.

Aid to women for prenatal care has a lot of value. The Head Start program saved and salvaged a whole generation.[11] The drive to wipe out malnutrition by Senators McGovern and Hollings in the food stamp program annually worked; it brought about balanced diets where there had been none.[12] We should drop programs that aren't working, not those that are.

MURRAY: It is beginning to percolate into the consciousness of policymakers that we just don't know how to affect large numbers of people who are leading blighted lives. The only way we can deal with this is by prevention.

JACKSON: I agree that there are ways to change this situation without just paying another top-heavy layer of overseers and administrators who'd be sending paperwork back to Albany. I would take 500 young people and say, "How many of you would like this neighborhood to be cleaner?" Most hands would go up. "How many of you would like to have windows in your buildings in the wintertime?" Hands would go up. "How many of you would like to make $12 to $20 an hour?" Many hands. "Then here's what you must do if you want to make $12 to $20 an hour. We'll teach you how to be a mason. You can lay bricks and not throw them. You can learn how to be a glazier, how to be a plasterer. And at the end of this time we'll get you certified in a trade union. You will then have the skill to build where you live; if the floor's buckling in your gymnasium, you can fix it."

And so these young men and women would be empowered and enfranchised: they would much rather make $20 an hour than be on welfare. Just to do things *for* them while keeping them economically disenfranchised is no systemic change at all. And, Dr. Murray, people who can lay bricks and carpet and cut glass have no intention of going back on welfare.

MURRAY: I should point out that in my ideal world, by God, any black youngster who wants to can become a glazier, any poor youngster can earn a trade. And, Reverend Jackson, in my ideal world I would also clone *you,* because I've heard you speak to these kids.

JACKSON: But why do you think black kids everywhere are playing basketball so well? I submit to you that they're playing basketball and football and baseball so well and in such great numbers because there is a clear and obvious reward; there's a carrot. Do this and you'll be in the paper, on the radio, on television. And you'll get a college scholarship. And if you're real good, you'll get a professional contract. So these same kinds that you say are unreachable and unteachable will gravitate to a carrot if they can see it. There must be a way out. And right now we must come up with ways out.

MURRAY: Yes, education and training opportunity—the carrots—are absolutely central. But once you have those, you have to have a support system, and this is where we've got a real problem. For example, let's say a youngster graduates from high school without many skills. He gets into a good job-training program, one that will really teach him a skill if he buckles down. But the youngster has never learned good work habits, so he flunks out of the training program. For that youngster to come out of high school ready to take advantage of a training program, there must be changes in the school he came from.

Now, what about the youngster who is offered an opportunity but who is below average in intelligence? I mean, half the country is below average in intelligence, and in industriousness.

JACKSON: Does that apply all the way through the government?

MURRAY: Let's just say this youngster is no great shakes, not much of anything. How is this youngster going to have a life that lets him look back when he's sixty and say, "Well, I did O.K., given what I had. At least I always supported myself and raised my kids and so on." The only way that eighteen-year-old kid is ever going to get to that position is by taking jobs that aren't much fun and don't pay much money. In order to reach the point where he feels good about supporting himself and his family, he's got to survive those years of eighteen, nineteen, twenty, when kids want to do things which make a whole lot of sense when you're that age but turn out to have been real stupid by the time you're thirty. Here is where, after you've provided the opportunities, which I am for in abundance, you've still got to worry.

JACKSON: But Dr. Murray, democracy must first guarantee opportunity. It doesn't guarantee success. Now, why do you think these ghetto and barrio youngsters are doing so well in athletics?

MURRAY: Because they see people just like them, who came out of those same streets, making a whole lot of money doing it.

JACKSON: So successful role models are a great motivator.

MURRAY: They make a huge difference. Now, how do we get the Jesse Jacksons of the world to be more visible role models?

JACKSON: Well, I've been working on that for a few years. But the point is that where the rules are clear, even though the work is hard, the locked-out tend to achieve. Ain't no low-class and high-class touchdowns. But there are no black baseball managers and no black professional football coaches. Why? Because in those areas where the decisions are made behind closed doors and where the rules are not so clear, those who are locked out don't do well.

That is basically true in the private economy: the more subjective the rules, the less the penetration. When people go behind closed doors to, say, determine who the dean of the medical school will be, eight people who are doctors, all of them graduated from the same school, tend to come up with someone from the same lineage. Why are there so many blacks in government [employment]? Because if you do well on the test you can get in, and the rules of seniority are established.

MURRAY: In 1983, the New York City Police Department gave a sergeant's exam, and 10.6 percent of the white candidates passed but only 1.6 percent of the blacks. So it was decided that even though the rules were clear, some blacks who had failed the test would be promoted in order to fill a quota. Now, either you assume that the test measured nothing relevant to being a sergeant and that skill is randomly distributed, so it didn't make any difference that a whole bunch of blacks were arbitrarily promoted despite the fact that they didn't pass the test, or you assume that the test did in fact measure abilities that are important to advancement. If that's true, a few years down the road very few of the black sergeants will become lieutenants. This ensures, in an almost diabolically clever way, that no matter how able blacks become, they will continue to be segmented, and whites will always be looking at black co-workers who aren't quite as good at their jobs as the whites are. You build in an appearance of inferiority where none need exist.

Now, your son went to St. Albans and my daughters go to National Cathedral. These are among the finest schools in Washington. Your son, when he applies for a job, doesn't need or want any special consideration. The fact that he's black is irrelevant.

JACKSON: You're making dangerous comparisons here, Doctor, which tend to inflame weak minds. My son is not a good example because, like his father, his achievements are above average. The fact is that all of America, in some sense, must be educated about its past and must face the corrective surgery that is needed.

When there's moral leadership from the White House and from the academy, people tend to adjust. When Lyndon Johnson said—with the moral authority of a converted Texan—that to make a great society we must make adjustments, people took the Voting Rights Act and affirmative action and said, "Let's go."

There are a lot of positive examples around the country where integrated schools have worked, where busing has worked, where affirmative action has worked, when that spirit of moral leadership was present. The same school where the National Guard had to take two blacks to school in 1961—the University of Georgia—is where Herschel Walker won the Heisman Trophy. Later he was able to marry a white woman without protest in rural Georgia. Why? Because people had been taught that it was all right.

MURRAY: You've got the cart before the horse. By the mid-1960s, white folks finally, after far too long, had had their consciousnesses raised. They said to themselves, "We've done wrong. We have violated a principle that's one of the taproots of America; we haven't given people a fair shot just because their skin's a different color." A chord was struck that triggered a strong desire not only to stop doing the bad things but also to help people make up for lost ground.

That additional response was, from the very beginning, sort of pushing it. The principle that had actually been violated was that of the fair shot; but the black civil rights movement isn't feeding off that important nutrient anymore. It's gone beyond that. Today, when white folks aren't making public pronouncements, I hear far too many of them saying things which are pretty damned racist. I see a convergence of the old racism, which is still out there, with a new racism, from people who are saying, "Well, gee, it's been twenty years now. You'd think they'd be catching up by now."

JACKSON: They're getting strong signals from the highest pulpit in the nation. When the White House and the Justice Department close their doors to the Afro-American leadership; when the Congressional Black Caucus cannot meet with the President of the United States, when the government closes its doors to the NAACP,[13] the SCLC,[14] the Urban League,[15] Operation PUSH; when the White House will not meet with the Conference of Black Mayors; when those who work in the vineyards daily will not even engage in the dialogue you and I have engaged in today—that's reprehensible behavior. It sends out signals that hurt people. When leadership is present, people behave differently.

MURRAY: In addition to spending a lot of time talking to white people in general, I also spend a lot of time talking to conservatives. And I happen to know that their passion for a colorblind society is not just rhetoric.

Jackson: Are you a consultant for an optometrist? Because the only people who would benefit from people going colorblind would be optometrists.

Nobody wants to be that way, man. We don't *need* to be colorblind; we need to affirm the beauty of colors and the diversity of people. I do not have to see you as some color other than what you are to affirm your person.

MURRAY: I mean that the ideal of giving everybody a fair shot—of not saying to anyone, "Because you're black I'm going to refuse to give you a chance"—is something which a lot of conservatives feel more passionately about than a lot of your putative friends do.

JACKSON: But if two people are in a one-mile race and one starts off with a half-mile head start and one starts off at point zero—O.K., now let's take the chains off, every man for himself—well, such a race is not just. We are starting out behind. I mean, of the top 600 television executives, fewer than fifteen are black.

MURRAY: I had a talk with somebody from one of the networks a few weeks ago, as a matter of fact. He said to me: "Well, we figured we ought to have a black producer, so we went out and hired the best one we could find. But he really isn't very good, so we do most of his work for him. Now, insofar as people aren't allowed to be TV producers because they're black, that's bad. But insofar as white people go around saying, "We had to get our black TV producer, so we brought in someone who can't make it on his own," they are not doing blacks a service.

JACKSON: Man, for most of my life, I have seen black people train white people to be their boss. Incompetent whites have stood on the shoulders of blacks for a long time. Do you know how impressed I am when a white rock singer who is selling millions of records explains how he got his inspiration from a black artist, who can't even afford to come to the white man's concert? A few months ago *Time* said in an article that Gary Hart was the only Democrat who has run a coast-to-coast campaign.[16] I was on the cover of *Time* twice during the 1984 campaign. But Hart's the only one. Isn't that a strange phenomenon? It's like Ralph Ellison's invisible man: they look at you but they don't see you.[17]

By and large, the black people the White House sees are those one or two exceptions who did something great. They take a Hispanic kid or a black person and try to impose that model on the nation. I could take the position, "Well, if I can make it from a poor community in South Carolina, explain to me how a white person can be in poverty," and it would be absurd. But I could argue it and get lots of applause.

MURRAY: I'm willing to grant that we shouldn't make so much of the exception if you grant me that just because folks may be against certain kinds of programs, it doesn't mean that they're mean-spirited, or don't care about problems.

JACKSON: If we can avoid the demagogy and turn debate into dialogue and stereotypes into creative thinking, we can begin to develop ideas. I mean, I agree that this welfare system hurts people fundamentally. Many of the things that come from this Administration, like the enterprise zone idea, have a lot of validity. If an enterprise zone creates a green line, instead of a red line, where if you live in that area you get certain incentives—that idea has merit. It may mean that a young man or a young woman teaching school will want to move to a district because of a tax incentive, or perhaps a doctor or a lawyer will want to move his office there. You establish an incentive for people to locate there, through the tax system or otherwise, you begin to shift capital and the people who live there have first option on the new jobs. But the Administration has never really discussed this idea with those who would have to communicate with the masses about it. So that idea has merit. Together we could make sense of such an idea. I'm anxious to open up the door of social policy, and I'm impressed with this opportunity today.

✒ 1988 Democratic National Convention Address

Tonight, we pause and give praise and honor to God for being good enough to allow us to be at this place at this time.[18] When I look out at this convention, I see the face of America: Red, Yellow, Brown, Black and White. We're all precious in God's sight—the real rainbow coalition.[19]

All of us—All of us who are here think that we are seated. But we're really standing on someone's shoulders. Ladies and gentlemen, Mrs. Rosa Parks—the mother of the civil rights movement.[20]

[Mrs. Rosa Parks is brought to the podium.]

I want to express my deep love and appreciation for the support my family has given me over these past months. They have endured pain, anxiety, threat, and fear. But they have been strengthened and made secure by our faith in God, in America, and in you. Your love has protected us and made us strong. To my wife Jackie, the foundation of our family; to our five children whom you met tonight; to my mother, Mrs. Helen Jackson, who is present tonight; and to our grandmother, Mrs. Matilda Burns; to my brother Chuck and his family; to my mother-in-law, Mrs. Gertrude Brown, who just last month at age sixty-one graduated from Hampton Institute—a marvelous achievement.[21]

I offer my appreciation to Mayor Andrew Young who has provided such gracious hospitality to all of us this week.[22]

And a special salute to President Jimmy Carter.[23] President Carter restored honor to the White House after Watergate. He gave many of us a special opportunity to grow. For his kind words, for his unwavering commitment to peace in the world, and for the voters that came from his family, every member of his family, led by Billy and Amy, I offer my special thanks to the Carter family.

My right and my privilege to stand here before you has been won, won in my lifetime, by the blood and the sweat of the innocent.

Twenty-four years ago, the late Fannie Lou Hamer and Aaron Henry—who sits here tonight from Mississippi—were locked out onto the streets in Atlantic City; the head of the Mississippi Freedom Democratic Party.[24]

But tonight, a Black and White delegation from Mississippi is headed by Ed Cole, a Black man from Mississippi; twenty-four years later.[25]

Many were lost in the struggle for the right to vote: Jimmy Lee Jackson, a young student, gave his life; Viola Liuzzo, a White mother from Detroit, called "nigger lover," and brains blown out at point blank range; [Michael] Schwerner, [Andrew] Goodman and [James] Chaney—two Jews and a Black —found in a common grave, bodies riddled with bullets in Mississippi; the four darling little girls in a church in Birmingham, Alabama. They died that we might have a right to live.[26]

Dr. Martin Luther King Jr. lies only a few miles from us tonight.[27] Tonight he must feel good as he looks down upon us. We sit here together, a rainbow, a coalition—the sons and daughters of slavemasters and the sons and daughters of slaves, sitting together around a common table, to decide the direction of our party and our country. His heart would be full tonight.

As a testament to the struggles of those who have gone before; as a legacy for those who will come after; as a tribute to the endurance, the patience, the courage of our forefathers and mothers; as an assurance that their prayers are being answered, that their work has not been in vain, and, that hope is eternal, tomorrow night my name will go into nomination for the Presidency of the United States of America.

We meet tonight at the crossroads, a point of decision. Shall we expand, be inclusive, find unity and power; or suffer division and impotence?

We've come to Atlanta, the cradle of the Old South, the crucible of the New South. Tonight, there is a sense of celebration, because we are moved, fundamentally moved from racial battlegrounds by law, to economic common ground. Tomorrow we'll challenge to move to higher ground.

Common ground. Think of Jerusalem, the intersection where many trails met. A small village that became the birthplace for three great religions—Judaism, Christianity, and Islam. Why was this village so blessed? Because it provided a crossroads where different people met, different cultures, different civilizations could meet and find common ground. When people come together, flowers always flourish—the air is rich with the aroma of a new spring.

Take New York, the dynamic metropolis. What makes New York so special? It's the invitation at the Statue of Liberty, "Give me your tired, your poor, your huddled masses who yearn to breathe free." Not restricted to English only. Many people, many cultures, many languages with one thing in common: They yearn to breathe free. Common ground.

Tonight in Atlanta, for the first time in this century, we convene in the South; a state where Governors once stood in school house doors; where Julian Bond was denied a seat in the State Legislature because of his conscientious objection to the Vietnam War; a city that, through its five Black Universities, has graduated more black students than any city in the world.[28] Atlanta, now a modern intersection of the New South.

Common ground. That's the challenge of our party tonight—left wing, right wing.

Progress will not come through boundless liberalism nor static conservatism, but at the critical mass of mutual survival—not at boundless liberalism nor static conservatism, but at the critical mass of mutual survival. It takes two wings to fly. Whether you're a hawk or a dove, you're just a bird living in the same environment, in the same world.

The Bible teaches that when lions and lambs lie down together, none will be afraid, and there will be peace in the valley. It sounds impossible. Lions eat lambs. Lambs sensibly flee from lions. Yet even lions and lambs find common ground. Why? Because neither lions nor lambs want the forest to catch on fire. Neither lions nor lambs want acid rain to fall. Neither lions nor lambs can survive nuclear war. If lions and lambs can find common ground, surely we can as well—as civilized people.

The only time that we win is when we come together. In 1960, John Kennedy, the late John Kennedy, beat Richard Nixon by only 112,000 votes—less than one vote per precinct. He won by the margin of our hope. He brought us together. He reached out. He had the courage to defy his advisors and inquire about Dr. King's jailing in Albany, Georgia. We won by the margin of our hope, inspired by courageous leadership. In 1964, Lyndon Johnson brought both wings together—the thesis, the antithesis, and the creative synthesis—and together we won.[29] In 1976, Jimmy Carter unified us again, and we won. When we do not come together, we never win. In 1968, the division and despair in July led to our defeat in November. In 1980, rancor in the spring and the summer led to Reagan in the fall.[30] When we divide, we cannot win. We must find common ground as the basis for survival and development and change and growth.

Today when we debated, differed, deliberated, agreed to agree, agreed to disagree, when we had the good judgment to argue a case and then not self-destruct, George Bush was just a little further away from the White House and a little closer to private life.

Tonight, I salute Governor Michael Dukakis. He has run—He has run a well-managed and a dignified campaign. No matter how tired or how tried, he always resisted the temptation to stoop to demagoguery.

I've watched a good mind fast at work, with steel nerves, guiding his campaign out of the crowded field without appeal to the worst in us. I've watched his perspective grow as his environment has expanded. I've seen his toughness and tenacity close up. I know his commitment to public service. Mike Dukakis' parents were a doctor and a teacher; my parents a maid, a beautician, and a janitor. There's a great gap between Brookline, Massachusetts and Haney Street in the Fieldcrest Village housing projects in Greenville, South Carolina.

He studied law; I studied theology. There are differences of religion, region, and race; differences in experiences and perspectives. But the genius of America is that out of the many we become one.

Providence has enabled our paths to intersect. His foreparents came to America on immigrant ships; my foreparents came to America on slave ships. But whatever the original ships, we're in the same boat tonight.

Our ships could pass in the night—if we have a false sense of independence—or they could collide and crash. We would lose our passengers. We can seek a high reality and a greater good. Apart, we can drift on the broken pieces of Reaganomics, satisfy our baser instincts, and exploit the fears of our people.[31] At our highest, we can call upon noble instincts and navigate this vessel to safety. The greater good is the common good.

As Jesus said, "Not My will, but Thine be done." It was his way of saying there's a higher good beyond personal comfort or position.[32]

The good of our Nation is at stake. It's commitment to working men and women, to the poor and the vulnerable, to the many in the world.

With so many guided missiles, and so much misguided leadership, the stakes are exceedingly high. Our choice? Full participation in a democratic government, or more abandonment and neglect. And so this night, we choose not a false sense of independence, not our capacity to survive and endure. Tonight we choose interdependency, and our capacity to act and unite for the greater good.

Common good is finding commitment to new priorities to expansion and inclusion. A commitment to expanded participation in the Democratic Party at every level. A commitment to a shared national campaign strategy and involvement at every level.

A commitment to new priorities that insure that hope will be kept alive. A common ground commitment to a legislative agenda for empowerment, for the John Conyers bill—universal, on-site, same-day registration everywhere.[33] A commitment to D.C. statehood and empowerment—D.C. deserves statehood. A commitment to economic set-asides, commitment to the

Dellums bill for comprehensive sanctions against South Africa.[34] A shared commitment to a common direction.

Common ground.

Easier said than done. Where do you find common ground? At the point of challenge. This campaign has shown that politics need not be marketed by politicians, packaged by pollsters and pundits. Politics can be a moral arena where people come together to find common ground.

We find common ground at the plant gate that closes on workers without notice. We find common ground at the farm auction, where a good farmer loses his or her land to bad loans or diminishing markets. Common ground at the school yard where teachers cannot get adequate pay, and students cannot get a scholarship, and can't make a loan. Common ground at the hospital admitting room, where somebody tonight is dying because they cannot afford to go upstairs to a bed that's empty waiting for someone with insurance to get sick. We are a better nation than that. We must do better.

Common ground. What is leadership if not present help in a time of crisis? And so I met you at the point of challenge. In Jay, Maine, where paper workers were striking for fair wages; in Greenville, Iowa, where family farmers struggle for a fair price; in Cleveland, Ohio, where working women seek comparable worth; in McFarland, California, where the children of Hispanic farm workers may be dying from poisoned land, dying in clusters with cancer; in an AIDS hospice in Houston, Texas, where the sick support one another, too often rejected by their own parents and friends.

Common ground. America is not a blanket woven from one thread, one color, one cloth. When I was a child growing up in Greenville, South Carolina and grandmamma could not afford a blanket, she didn't complain and we did not freeze. Instead she took pieces of old cloth—patches, wool, silk, gabardine, crockersack—only patches, barely good enough to wipe off your shoes with. But they didn't stay that way very long. With sturdy hands and a strong cord, she sewed them together into a quilt, a thing of beauty and power and culture. Now, Democrats, we must build such a quilt.

Farmers, you seek fair prices and you are right—but you cannot stand alone. Your patch is not big enough.

Workers, you fight for fair wages, you are right—but your patch labor is not big enough.

Women, you seek comparable worth and pay equity, you are right—but your patch is not big enough.

Women, mothers, who seek Head Start, and day care and prenatal care on the front side of life, relevant jail care and welfare on the back side of life, you are right—but your patch is not big enough.

Students, you seek scholarships, you are right—but your patch is not big enough.

Blacks and Hispanics, when we fight for civil rights, we are right—but our patch is not big enough.

Gays and lesbians, when you fight against discrimination and a cure for AIDS, you are right—but your patch is not big enough.

Conservatives and progressives, when you fight for what you believe, right wing, left wing, hawk, dove, you are right from your point of view, but your point of view is not enough.

But don't despair. Be as wise as my grandmamma. Pull the patches and the pieces together, bound by a common thread. When we form a great quilt of unity and common ground, we'll have the power to bring about health care and housing and jobs and education and hope to our Nation.

We, the people, can win.

We stand at the end of a long dark night of reaction. We stand tonight united in the commitment to a new direction. For almost eight years we've been led by those who view social good coming from private interest, who view public life as a means to increase private wealth. They have been prepared to sacrifice the common good of the many to satisfy the private interests and the wealth of a few.

We believe in a government that's a tool of our democracy in service to the public, not an instrument of the aristocracy in search of private wealth. We believe in government with the consent of the governed, "of, for and by the people." We must now emerge into a new day with a new direction.

Reaganomics: Based on the belief that the rich had too much money [*sic*]—too little money and the poor had too much. That's classic Reaganomics. They believe that the poor had too much money and the rich had too little money,—so they engaged in reverse Robin Hood—took from the poor, gave to the rich, paid for by the middle class. We cannot stand four more years of Reaganomics in any version, in any disguise.

How do I document that case? Seven years later, the richest 1 percent of our society pays 20 percent less in taxes. The poorest 10 percent pay 20 percent more: Reaganomics.

Reagan gave the rich and the powerful a multibillion-dollar party. Now the party is over. He expects the people to pay for the damage. I take this principal position, convention, let us not raise taxes on the poor and the middle-class, but those who had the party, the rich and the powerful, must pay for the party.

I just want to take common sense to high places. We're spending one hundred and fifty billion dollars a year defending Europe and Japan 43 years after the war is over. We have more troops in Europe tonight than we had seven years ago. Yet the threat of war is ever more remote.

Germany and Japan are now creditor nations; that means they've got a surplus. We are a debtor nation—means we are in debt. Let them share more of the burden of their own defense. Use some of that money to build decent housing. Use some of that money to educate our children. Use some of that money for long-term health care. Use some of that money to wipe out these slums and put America back to work!

I just want to take common sense to high places. If we can bail out Europe and Japan; if we can bail out Continental Bank and Chrysler—and Mr. Iacocca, make [*sic*] 8,000 dollars an hour—we can bail out the family farmer.[35]

I just want to make common sense. It does not make sense to close down six hundred and fifty thousand family farms in this country while importing food from abroad subsidized by the U.S. Government. Let's make sense.

It does not make sense to be escorting all our tankers up and down the Persian Gulf paying $2.50 for every one dollar worth of oil we bring out, while oil wells are capped in Texas, Oklahoma, and Louisiana. I just want to make sense.

Leadership must meet the moral challenge of its day. What's the moral challenge of our day? We have public accommodations. We have the right to vote. We have open housing. What's the fundamental challenge of our day? It is to end economic violence. Plant closings without notice—economic violence. Even the greedy do not profit long from greed—economic violence.

Most poor people are not lazy. They are not black. They are not brown. They are mostly White and female and young. But whether White, Black or Brown, a hungry baby's belly turned inside out is the same color—color it pain; color it hurt; color it agony.

Most poor people are not on welfare. Some of them are illiterate and can't read the want-ad sections. And when they can, they can't find a job that matches the address. They work hard everyday.

I know. I live amongst them. I'm one of them. I know they work. I'm a witness. They catch the early bus. They work every day.

They raise other people's children. They work everyday.

They clean the streets. They work everyday. They drive dangerous cabs. They work everyday. They change the beds you slept in in these hotels last night and can't get a union contract. They work everyday.

No, no, they are not lazy! Someone must defend them because it's right, and they cannot speak for themselves. They work in hospitals. I know they do. They wipe the bodies of those who are sick with fever and pain. They empty their bedpans. They clean out their commodes. No job is beneath them, and yet when they get sick they cannot lie in the bed they made up every day. America, that is not right. We are a better Nation than that. We are a better Nation than that.

We need a real war on drugs. You can't "just say no." It's deeper than that. You can't just get a palm reader or an astrologer. It's more profound than that.[36]

We are spending a hundred and fifty billion dollars on drugs a year. We've gone from ignoring it to focusing on the children. Children cannot buy a hundred and fifty billion dollars worth of drugs a year; a few high-profile athletes—athletes are not laundering a hundred and fifty billion dollars a year—bankers are.

I met the children in Watts, who, unfortunately, in their despair, their grapes of hope have become raisins of despair, and they're turning on each other and they're self-destructing.[37] But I stayed with them all night long. I wanted to hear their case.

They said, "Jesse Jackson, as you challenge us to say no to drugs, you're right; and to not sell them, you're right; and not use these guns, you're right." (And by the way, the promise of CETA [Comprehensive Employment and Training Act]; they displaced CETA—they did not replace CETA.)[38]

"We have neither jobs nor houses nor services nor training—no way out. Some of us take drugs as anesthesia for our pain. Some take drugs as a way of pleasure, good short-term pleasure and long-term pain. Some sell drugs to make money. It's wrong, we know, but you need to know that we know. We can go and buy the drugs by the boxes at the port. If we can buy the drugs at the port, don't you believe the Federal government can stop it if they want to?"

They say, "We don't have Saturday night specials anymore."[39] They say, "We buy AS–47s and Uzi's, the latest make of weapons. We buy them across the counter along these boulevards."[40]

You cannot fight a war on drugs unless and until you're going to challenge the bankers and the gun sellers and those who grow them. Don't just focus on the children; let's stop drugs at the level of supply and demand. We must end the scourge on the American Culture.

Leadership. What difference will we make? Leadership. Cannot just go along to get along. We must do more than change Presidents. We must change direction.

Leadership must face the moral challenge of our day. The nuclear war build-up is irrational. Strong leadership cannot desire to look tough and let that stand in the way of the pursuit of peace. Leadership must reverse the arms race. At least we should pledge no first use. Why? Because first use begets first retaliation. And that's mutual annihilation. That's not a rational way out.

No use at all. Let's think it out and not fight it our because it's an un-winnable fight. Why hold a card that you can never drop? Let's give peace a chance.

Leadership. We now have this marvelous opportunity to have a break-through with the Soviets. Last year 200,000 Americans visited the Soviet Union. There's a chance for joint ventures into space—not Star Wars and war arms escalation but a space defense initiative.[41] Let's build in the space together and demilitarize the heavens. There's a way out.

America, let us expand. When Mr. Reagan and Mr. Gorbachev met there was a big meeting.[42] They represented together one-eighth of the human race. Seven-eighths of the human race was locked out of that room. Most people in the world tonight—half are Asian, one-half of them are Chinese. There are 22 nations in the Middle East. There's Europe; 40 million Latin Americans next door to us; the Caribbean; Africa—a half-billion people.

Most people in the world today are Yellow or Brown or Black, non-Christian, poor, female, young and don't speak English in the real world.

This generation must offer leadership to the real world. We're losing ground in Latin America, Middle East, South Africa because we're not focusing on the real world. That's the real world. We must use basic principles—support international law. We stand the most to gain from it. Support human rights—we believe in that. Support self-determination—we're built on that. Support economic development—you know it's right. Be consistent and gain our moral authority in the world. I challenge you tonight, my friends, let's be bigger and better as a Nation and as a Party.

We have basic challenges—freedom in South Africa. We've already agreed as Democrats to declare South Africa to be a terrorist state. But don't just stop there. Get South Africa out of Angola; free Namibia; support the front line states. We must have a new humane human rights consistent policy in Africa.

I'm often asked, "Jesse, why do you take on these tough issues? They're not very political. We can't win that way."

If an issue is morally right, it will eventually be political. It may be political and never be right. Fannie Lou Hamer didn't have the most votes in Atlantic City, but her principles have outlasted every delegate who voted to lock her out. Rosa Parks did not have the most votes, but she was morally right. Dr. King didn't have the most votes about the Vietnam War, but he was morally right. If we are principled first, our politics will fall in place.

"Jesse, why do you take these big bold initiatives?" A poem by an unknown author went something like this: "We mastered the air, we conquered the sea, annihilated distance and prolonged life, but we're not wise enough to live on this earth without war and without hate."

As for Jesse Jackson: "I'm tired of sailing my little boat, far inside the harbor bar. I want to go out where the big ships float, out on the deep where the great ones are. And should my frail craft prove too slight for waves that sweep those billows o'er, I'd rather go down in the stirring fight than drowse to death at the sheltered shore."

We've got to go out, my friends, where the big boats are.

And then for our children. Young America, hold your head high now. We can win. We must not lose you to drugs and violence, premature pregnancy, suicide, cynicism, pessimism and despair. We can win. Wherever you are tonight, I challenge you to hope and to dream. Don't submerge your dreams. Exercise above all else, even on drugs, dream of the day you are drug free. Even in the gutter, dream of the day that you will be up on your feet again.

You must never stop dreaming. Face reality, yes, but don't stop with the way things are. Dream of things as they ought to be. Dream. Face pain, but love, hope, faith and dreams will help you rise above the pain. Use hope and imagination as weapons of survival and progress, but you keep on dreaming, young America. Dream of peace. Peace is rational and reasonable. War is irrationable [*sic*] in this age, and unwinnable.

Dream of teachers who teach for life and not for a living. Dream of doctors who are concerned more about public health than private wealth. Dream of lawyers more concerned about justice than a judgeship. Dream of preachers who are concerned more about prophecy than profiteering. Dream on the high road with sound values.

And then America, as we go forth to September, October, November and then beyond, America must never surrender to a high moral challenge.

Do not surrender to drugs. The best drug policy is a "no first use." Don't surrender with needles and cynicism. Let's have "no first use" on the one hand, or clinics on the other. Never surrender, young America. Go forward.

America must never surrender to malnutrition. We can feed the hungry and clothe the naked. We must never surrender. We must go forward.

We must never surrender to illiteracy. Invest in our children. Never surrender; and go forward. We must never surrender to inequality. Women cannot compromise ERA or comparable worth. Women are making 60 cents on the dollar to what a man makes.[43] Women cannot buy meat cheaper. Women cannot buy bread cheaper. Women cannot buy milk cheaper. Women deserve to get paid for the work that you do. It's right! And it's fair.

Don't surrender, my friends. Those who have AIDS tonight, you deserve our compassion. Even with AIDS you must not surrender.

In your wheelchairs. I see you sitting here tonight in those wheelchairs. I've stayed with you. I've reached out to you across our Nation. And don't you give up. I know it's tough sometimes. People look down on you. It took you a little more effort to get here tonight. And no one should look down on you, but sometimes mean people do. The only justification we have for looking down on someone is that we're going to stop and pick them up.

But even in your wheelchairs, don't you give up. We cannot forget 50 years ago when our backs were against the wall, Roosevelt was in a wheelchair. I would rather have Roosevelt in a wheelchair than Reagan and Bush on a horse. Don't you surrender and don't you give up. Don't surrender and don't give up!

Why I cannot challenge you this way? "Jesse Jackson, you don't understand my situation. You be on television. You don't understand. I see you with the big people. You don't understand my situation."

I understand. You see me on TV, but you don't know the me that makes me, me. They wonder, "Why does Jesse run?" because they see me running for the White House. They don't see the house I'm running from.

I have a story. I wasn't always on television. Writers were not always outside my door. When I was born late one afternoon, October 8th, in Greenville, South Carolina, no writers asked my mother her name. Nobody chose to write down our address. My mama was not supposed to make it, and I was not supposed to make it. You see, I was born of a teen-age mother, who was born of a teen-age mother.

I understand. I know abandonment, and people being mean to you, and saying you're nothing and nobody and can never be anything.

I understand. Jesse Jackson is my third name. I'm adopted. When I had no name, my grandmother gave me her name. My name was Jesse Burns 'til I was 12. So I wouldn't have a blank space, she gave me a name to hold me over. I understand when nobody knows your name. I understand when you have no name.

I understand. I wasn't born in the hospital. Mama didn't have insurance. I was born in the bed at [the] house. I really do understand. Born in a three-room house, bathroom in the backyard, slop jar by the bed, no hot and cold running water. I understand. Wallpaper used for decoration? No. For a windbreaker. I understand. I'm a working person's person. That's why I understand you whether you're Black or White. I understand work. I was not born with a silver spoon in my mouth. I had a shovel programmed for my hand.

My mother, a working woman. So many of the days she went to work early, with runs in her stockings. She knew better, but she wore runs in her stockings so that my brother and I could have matching socks and not be laughed at school. I understand.

At 3 o'clock on Thanksgiving Day, we couldn't eat turkey because momma was preparing somebody else's turkey at 3 o'clock. We had to play football to entertain ourselves. And then around 6 o'clock she would get off the Alta Vista bus and we would bring up the leftovers and eat our turkey—leftovers, the carcass, the cranberries—around 8 o'clock at night. I really do understand.

Every one of these funny labels they put on you, those of you who are watching this broadcast tonight in the projects, on the corners, I understand. Call you outcast, low down, you can't make it, you're nothing, you're from nobody, subclass, underclass; when you see Jesse Jackson, when my name goes in nomination, your name goes in nomination.

I was born in the slum, but the slum was not born in me. And it wasn't born in you, and you can make it.

Wherever you are tonight, you can make it. Hold your head high; stick your chest out. You can make it. It gets dark sometimes, but the morning comes. Don't you surrender!

Suffering breeds character, character breeds faith. In the end faith will not disappoint.

You must not surrender! You may or may not get there but just know that you're qualified! And you hold on, and hold out! We must never surrender!! America will get better and better.

Keep hope alive. Keep hope alive! Keep hope alive! On tomorrow night and beyond, keep hope alive!

I love you very much. I love you very much.

NOTES

1. His son, Jesse Jackson Jr., has followed in his father's footsteps, representing a Chicago district in Congress from 1995 to 2012.

2. In 1968 Jackson was ordained as a Baptist minister. In 2000 the Chicago Theological Seminary awarded him a master of divinity degree based on his years of experience as a minister and activist.

3. Richard J. Herrnstein and Charles Murray, *The Bell Curve: Intelligence and Class Structure in American Life* (New York: Free Press, 1994).

4. The Marshall Plan was an American aid program designed to help European countries rebuild their economies and prevent the spread of Soviet communism after the Second World War.

5. Legal aid is a federal provision designed to assist persons unable to afford legal representation and offer them access to the court system. The central purpose of legal aid is to uphold equality before the law, the right to counsel, and the right to a fair trial.

6. Operation PUSH (People United to Save Humanity) is a nonprofit organization Jesse Jackson founded in 1971 to pursue social justice, civil rights, and political activism. The organization has since merged with the National Rainbow Coalition (also founded by Jackson, in 1984) to form Rainbow/PUSH.

7. Comprehensive Employment Training Act (CETA): a federal law enacted in 1973 that created programs to train low-income workers and provide them with public service jobs.

8. Jackson seems to be alluding to the notion of the "Talented Tenth," an idea first popularized by W. E. B. Du Bois in 1903 in a collection of essays by leading African American intellectuals called *The Negro Problem*.

9. "Redlining" is a discriminatory practice of denying loans or mortgages to borrowers in particular, often minority or poor areas. This unethical practice assumes

high default rates in general, rather than assessing individual credit worthiness in particular.

10. Shagging balls: gathering up golf or tennis balls for other players.

11. The Head Start program is a division of the U.S. Department of Health and Human Services and is responsible for providing comprehensive education, health, nutrition, and parent involvement services to low-income children and their families.

12. The Food Stamp Program, officially known as the Supplemental Nutrition Assistance Program (SNAP), provides federal assistance to impoverished families in the United States.

13. The National Association for the Advancement of Colored People (NAACP) was originally formed in 1909.

14. The Southern Christian Leadership Conference (SCLC) is an American civil rights organization usually associated with Dr. Martin Luther King, who served as the organization's first president.

15. Founded in 1910, the National Urban League (NUL) is an American civil rights organization based in New York City.

16. Gary Hart served as a Democratic senator from Colorado from 1975 to 1987 and ran for U.S. president in 1984 and 1988.

17. *Invisible Man,* a novel by Ralph Ellison, won the National Book Award in 1953. It features an unnamed protagonist who believes he is both literally and figuratively invisible because he is black.

18. This speech, delivered July 19, 1988, at the Omni Coliseum in Atlanta, Georgia, was Jackson's last public address before losing the Democratic presidential nomination to Michael Dukakis.

19. The Rainbow Coalition was a nonprofit political advocacy organization founded after Jackson's unsuccessful 1984 presidential campaign. The name "Rainbow Coalition" was the title of Jackson's keynote address at the 1984 Democratic National Convention, in which he called for a variety of ethnic minority groups, small farmers, and LGBT persons to unite for social and political advancement.

20. Rosa Parks (1913–2005) was a civil rights activist who became famous for refusing to give up her seat on a public bus in Montgomery, Alabama, to make room for a white passenger.

21. The Hampton Institute, accredited as Hampton University in 1984, is a historically black university in Hampton, Virginia. It was founded by the American Missionary Association in 1868 to provide education for recently emancipated slaves.

22. Andrew Jackson Young (b. 1932) is a pastor, politician, and activist who has served as the mayor of Atlanta, Georgia, from 1981 to 1989, as a congressman from Georgia's Fifth District from 1973 to 1977, and as the U.S. ambassador to the United Nations from 1977 to 1979.

23. James Earl "Jimmy" Carter (b. 1924) served as president of the United States from 1977 to 1981.

24. Fannie Lou Hamer (1917–1977) was an activist and civil rights leader who helped organize the Mississippi Freedom Summer for the Student Nonviolent Coordinating Committee. Aaron Henry (1922–1997) was also an activist and civil

rights leader ; he cofounded the Mississippi Freedom Democratic Party and was head of the Mississippi branch of the NAACP.

25. Ed Cole was elected chairperson of the Mississippi Democratic Party in 1988 and was the nation's first black state party chairperson.

26. Jimmie Lee Jackson (1938–1965) was a protestor in the civil rights movement who was shot and killed by an Alabama state trooper. His death became the primary catalyst for the Selma-to-Montgomery march that took place several days later. Viola Liuzzo (1925–1965) was a housewife and civil rights activist from Michigan who was murdered by members of the Ku Klux Klan for participating in the Selma-to-Montgomery march. Michael Schwerner, Andrew Goodman, and James Chaney were three men working for the Congress of Racial Equality (CORE) in Philadelphia, Mississippi; they were killed by the Ku Klux Klan for their civil rights work.

27. King (1929–1968) is interred at the Martin Luther King Jr. Center for Nonviolent Social Change in Atlanta, Georgia, at the corner of Auburn Avenue and Jackson Street.

28. Julian Bond (b. 1940) is a civil rights activist who helped found the Student Nonviolent Coordinating Committee while attending Morehouse College during the early 1960s. He is likely referring to Morehouse College, Spelman College, Morris Brown College, Clark College and Atlanta University (which merged in 1988 to become Clark–Atlanta University). He might also have been referring to Morehouse Medical School and / or the Interdenominational Theological Seminary, both of which are also historically black institutions in Atlanta. The Atlanta University Center Consortium currently consists of four historically black colleges: Clark Atlanta University, Spelman College, Morehouse College, and the Morehouse School of Medicine.

29. Lyndon B. Johnson (1908–1973) served as vice president of the United States from 1961 to 1963 and became president after the assassination of President John F. Kennedy in 1963. Johnson won reelection in 1964 and served until 1969.

30. Ronald Reagan (1911–2004) served as president of the United States from 1981 to 1989.

31. "Reaganomics" is a pejorative term that refers to the economic policies promoted by the White House during Ronald Reagan's presidency.

32. Luke 22:42.

33. Election-day voter registration allows eligible voters to register to vote on election day at the polling location.

34. The Comprehensive Anti-Apartheid Act of 1986 was introduced by U.S. congressman Ron Dellums. It called for trade restrictions against South Africa and immediate divestment by U.S. corporations.

35. The U.S. government loaned money to the Chrysler Corporation in 1980 and to the Continental Illinois National Bank and Trust Company in 1984 to help them avoid bankruptcy. Lee Iacocca (b. 1924) is an American business executive who served as president and CEO of the Chrysler Corporation from 1978 to 1992.

36. "Just say no" was a slogan coined by First Lady Nancy Reagan during the Reagan presidency to promote the "War on Drugs" during the 1980s.

37. Watts is a neighborhood in Los Angeles, California, known for its history of poverty and civil unrest.

38. The Comprehensive Employment and Training Act of 1973 (CETA) was enacted to train persons with low incomes and the long-term unemployed and to provide them with jobs in the public service.

39. "Saturday night special" is a slang term used in North America to refer to small, cheap handguns.

40. An AK-47 is a gas-powered assault rifle developed by the Soviet military. It has become the most commonly smuggled firearm that is eventually sold to governments, rebel organizations, civilians, and criminals. An Uzi is a powerful, hand-held submachine gun that was first developed in Israel in the late 1940s.

41. Jackson is referring to the Strategic Defense Initiative (SDI), proposed by Reagan in the 1980s. SDI is often referred to pejoratively as "Star Wars."

42. Mikhail Gorbachev (b. 1931) served as general secretary of the Communist Party of the Soviet Union from 1985 to 1991.

43. The American Equal Rights Association (AERA) was a political activist organization formed in 1866 by African American and women's rights activists with the aim of joining the causes of gender and racial equality.

PART IV

The Media Generation

Randall L. Kennedy
(b. 1954)

❧ ATTORNEY, PROFESSOR, COMMENTATOR

One of the things [critics] find disconcerting is that I ask questions.
I actually question the premise of my own thinking and push my own
conclusions hard. I thought that was what intellectuals were supposed
to do.

    Donegan, "Battle of the N-Word."

Randall L. Kennedy is indisputably one of the most thought-provoking intellectuals to emerge from South Carolina in the twentieth century. He unabashedly investigates contentious issues that other thinkers and scholars broach cautiously or avoid. Kennedy has examined the propriety of the racial epithet "nigger," the persistence of the social pariah the "sellout," and the presence of the color line in post–civil rights movement America. Kennedy's willingness to speak candidly about controversial topics regarding race has garnered him both acclaim and criticism. Some laud his rigorous approach to meticulously researching inflammatory subjects while others disdain his stances that challenge long-held beliefs and traditions within the African American community and the nation. Kennedy has distinguished himself as an intellectual by posing probing questions to the public and policymakers, as well as to himself.

Kennedy spent his early years in Columbia, South Carolina, the second of three children born to Henry and Rachel Kennedy. Pivotal events from his formative years influenced his perspectives on critical issues within the African American community; these included his grandmother's use of the term "nigger," his father's encounters with racist police officers, and his mother's aural passing by affecting an accent many have associated with white women, while conducting business over the phone. In the 1960s Kennedy's family moved to Washington, D.C., where he completed high school at St. Albans School. He then earned his undergraduate degree at Princeton University. In 1979, as a Rhodes Scholar at Oxford University's Balliol College, Kennedy studied history before being awarded an Earl Warren Legal Training Scholarship to Yale Law School, from which he graduated in 1982. He worked as a law clerk for the U.S. Court of Appeals judge J. Skelly Wright and later for U.S. Supreme Court justice Thurgood Marshall, whom his father had watched argue cases for the NAACP in South Carolina. By 1983 Kennedy had passed the bar in the District of Columbia and gained admission to argue before the U.S. Supreme Court. A year later he became an assistant professor of law at Harvard University, where he is currently the Michael R. Klein Professor of Law. In 1985 Kennedy married Yvedt Matory, a cancer researcher, surgeon, and entrepreneur. They have three children, Rachel, Thaddeus, and Henry. Matory died of cancer in 2005.

Kennedy develops his intellectual queries out of the complex intersections of race, law, and life in America. He first drew national attention through his inquiry into the efficacy of affirmative action, including the question of whether "racism is partially responsible for the growing opposition" to this contentious legal remedy for racial discrimination.[1] He earned further acclaim as a Robert F. Kennedy Book Award recipient for *Race, Crime, and the Law* (New York: Pantheon Books, 1997). In *Interracial Intimacies: Sex, Marriage, Identity and Adoption* (New York: Pantheon Books, 2003) Kennedy continued to pose probing questions regarding the history and continued existence of "state-supported racial separatism."[2] He argued for permeable boundaries in racial categories that facilitate both the acceptance and the rejection of racial markers. He examined another taboo subject in *Sellout: The Politics of Racial Betrayal* (New York: Pantheon Books, 2008), shifting readers' attention away from simplistic aphorisms regarding race traitors and toward a more complex characterization of individuals that requires critics to question character and motive rather than superficially evaluate actions. Kennedy courted more controversy when he challenged popular notions of a postracial American in *The Persistence of the Color Line: Racial Politics and the Obama Presidency* (New York: Pantheon Books, 2011). He maintains that Barack Obama's campaign, presidency, and reelection affirm the persistence of a color line in the twenty-first century that requires Obama to deftly walk a narrow line between being black enough but not too black so that he is acceptable to both white and black Americans.

The book that has provoked the most impassioned debates, however, is *Nigger: The Strange Career of a Troublesome Word* (New York: Vantage Books, 2002). The contradictions in the word that Kennedy describes as a "paradigmatic slur" compelled him to examine the etymology, cultural currency, and legal ramifications of the term.[3] In the excerpts presented here, Kennedy begins by recalling how "nigger" was used as a term of both endearment and derision within his family and his community in South Carolina and Washington, D.C. He then poses a series of penetrating questions regarding the definition, usage, and legalities of "nigger" in America culture. Kennedy continues his inquiry with etymology, suggesting that the historical development of the meaning of this term is critical to understanding its continued polarizing effect in American society. Kennedy provides readers with a dazzling array of texts in which "nigger" appears, including nursery rhymes, comedy routines, legal cases, rap music, political speech, and recollections of notable Americans ranging from Charles Sumner to Michael Jordan. In so doing, he reiterates the troublesome nature of the word, which can be viewed as a racial epithet, a punch line, a compliment, or an expression of solidarity—depending upon the individuals and circumstances associated with its usage. Indeed, contextualization is a critical element in Kennedy's argument for the careful use of "nigger." He decries "eradicationists" who advocate banning the term from entertainment, particularly rap and comedy. According to Kennedy, "There is nothing necessarily wrong with a white person saying 'nigger,' just as there is nothing necessarily wrong with a black person saying it. What matters is the context in which the word is spoken—the speaker's aims, effects, alternatives."[4] This stance emerged as a point of contention among Kennedy's critics, who accused him of sheltering racists from criticism by affirming white and black entertainers' right to use the term "nigger." Kennedy conceded that while his position risks emboldening bigots to continue using the term, it offers a greater measure of protection for free speech, which requires a willingness to ask questions of the speaker and oneself in making distinctions between abusive and appropriate usages of the term "nigger."

As a prolific writer and influential commentator, Kennedy specializes in civil rights and liberties, civil rights legislation, and the Supreme Court. He is a member of the American Law Institute, the American Academy of Arts and Sciences, the American Philosophical Association, and the editorial boards of *The Nation, Dissent,* and *The American Prospect.* He has contributed chapters to a variety of books that investigate law, politics, and culture; publishes frequently in law journals, newspapers, and periodicals; writes a blog for the *Huffington Post* website and commentary for the *Atlantic Monthly;* and often weighs in on matters of race as a media commentator. Kennedy received an honorary degree from Haverford College and has served as a Princeton University trustee.

૨✊ Excerpt from *Nigger: The Strange Career of a Troublesome Word*

Introduction to the Vintage Edition

Nigger has accompanied me throughout my life. As a child growing up in Columbia, South Carolina, and Washington, D.C., in the '50s and '60s I assumed that *nigger* (along with various other racial slurs including *cracker* or *peckerwood*) would be in the minds, if not on the lips, of participants in any altercation pitting whites against blacks. I do not remember the first time that a white person called me "nigger," but I do remember the first time that responding to it gave rise to a discussion between me and my parents. The episode occurred in the early 1960s. After battling a white boy for what seemed like hours on a D.C. playground (at the Takoma Elementary School), I walked home and at dinner calmly related the events of the day. I asked my parents for advice on how best to react to a white person who called me "nigger." They gave me contradictory advice. My father said that I had standing permission from him to "go to war." He warned me against rushing into a fight if I was badly outnumbered. Otherwise, though, he urged me to respond with fists, or if necessary, with bottles, sticks, or bricks. My mother, on the other hand, recommended that I pay no heed to racial taunts, avoid bullies, and let bigots stew in their own poisonous prejudices. She insisted that while "sticks and stones may break your bones, words need never harm you."

Yet it was a word—this word *nigger*—that lay at the core of a recollection that revealed to me the pain my mother continues to feel on account of wounds inflicted upon her by racists during the era of Jim Crow segregation. Several years ago I asked her to tell me about her earliest memory of the color line. She began laughingly, telling me about how, in Columbia, she had often accompanied her mother to white folks' homes to pick up and return laundry. Although they typically traveled on public buses, my mother had failed to notice that her mother, Big Mama, always took her to the back of the bus where Negroes were segregated. One day, Big Mama asked my mother to run an errand that required her to catch a bus on which they had often ridden together. This errand marked the first time that my mother rode the bus on her own. She stood at the correct stop, got on the right bus, and deposited the appropriate fare. Being a bit scared, however, she sat down immediately behind the bus driver. After about a block, the driver pulled the bus over to the curb, cut the engine, and suddenly wheeled around and began to scream at my mother who was all of about eight or nine years old—"Nigger, you know better than to sit there! Get to the back where you belong!"

At this point in the storytelling, my mother was no longer laughing. A tear dropped onto her cheek, as she recalled running away from the bus overcome by fright.

I have been called "nigger" to my face on a couple of occasions by people who sought to convey their racial hatred or contempt for all blacks including me. In the spring of 1978, a motorist in Oxford, England, slowed down, rolled down the window of his car, and made a gesture indicating that he needed assistance. When I reached the side of his auto, he screamed "Nigger go home!" and sped off. Seven years later, on my first day in residence as a member of the faculty at Harvard Law School, a cabbie called me "nigger" (as well as "coon," and "jigaboo") on the basis of no apparent provocation other than my race.

I have also encountered *nigger* in dealings with acquaintances. Explaining why there were no blacks on a swimming team to which he belonged, a white elementary school classmate innocently allowed me access to familial information that I am sure his parents would have preferred for him to have kept private. My classmate told me that he had heard his parents and their friends say that they needed some "relief from niggers."

Years later, at a junior tennis tournament, I found myself sharing a hotel room with a white youngster from Mobile, Alabama. Late one evening, right as we were about to shut off the lights and go to sleep, this guy decided to tell me a final joke, one in which a reference to a "nigger" constituted the punch line. As soon as that line escaped his lips, his eyes bulged while the rest of his face froze. He knew immediately that he had made himself vulnerable to a judgment that he deeply feared. Why had he done so? I suspect that he had become so comfortable with me that he ceased, at least temporarily, to see me in terms of race. Or perhaps he had merely granted me the status of an honorary white. Either way, the reference to "nigger" seems to have suddenly made him aware anew of my blackness and thus the need to treat me differently than other acquaintances. I said nothing during the awkward silence that enveloped the room as his voice trailed away from the failed joke.

He apologized.

I do not recall whether or not I actually felt offended, but I do remember that from that moment on, the ease that had marked our budding friendship vanished.

For many people, saying or hearing *nigger* is easier in monoracial as opposed to multiracial settings. That has often been my experience. In my final year at my wonderful high school, St. Albans School for Boys, a black friend jokingly referred to me as a nigger in the presence of one of our white classmates. If he and I had been alone, I might have overlooked his comment or even laughed. But given the presence of the white classmate, I concluded immediately that a show of forceful disapproval was imperative. My concern was twofold and had to do in part with my position as student body president. I did not want the white classmate—and, through him, other white classmates—to get the impression that *nigger* was less injurious and more acceptable than what they had probably been taught at home. Aware of the ignorance of many of my white classmates regarding things racial, I regarded it as my duty to impress upon them the conventional wisdom which declared that *nigger* is an ugly, evil, irredeemable word. For reasons I will discuss below, my real beliefs regarding the N-word were more complicated but I thought that it would be impossible to relate those nuances to my white classmates. So I decided simply to condemn "nigger" wholesale. In addition, I believed that I had to come down as hard on my black classmate as I would have come down on a white classmate or else be subject to charges of hypocrisy, or even prejudice. So I sternly told my black classmate to refrain from referring to me by "that word" and that if he failed to restrain himself I would give him demerits that would force him to attend a disciplinary session at the school on a Saturday morning.

I think that my black classmate knew what I was thinking. But he was in no mood to go along. He laughed in my face, pointed at me, and with a raised voice cackled "nigger-nigger-nigger-nigger-nigger-nigger!" I immediately gave him a couple of hours of demerits and joined him on Saturday to make sure that he was present for his punishment.

Because of the way that *nigger* was used in my household I learned at an early age that it could be said in many ways, put to many uses, and mean many things. Big Mama peppered her speech with references to "niggers" by which she meant discreditable Negroes, a group that, in her view, constituted a large sector of the African American population. If Big Mama saw blacks misbehaving she would often roll her eyes, purse her lips, and then declare in a mournful tone, "Nigguhs!" According to Big Mama, "niggers can't get along, not even in church" and "are always late, even to their own funerals." She swore that she would never allow a "nigger doctor" to care for her and repeatedly warned that "if you see a bunch of niggers coming, turn around and go the other way."

Big Mama had clearly internalized antiblack prejudice. She truly believed that white people's water was wetter than black people's water, that as a rule, whites were nicer, better looking, and more capable than blacks. There was no affection or irony in her use of *nigger*. She deployed it exclusively for purposes of denigration. But life, of course, is complicated. This same Big Mama was a pillar of her all-black community in Columbia and a stalwart supporter of her children, grandchildren, and great-grandchildren— black folk who loved, indeed, idolized her. We recognized with sadness her antiblack prejudice but thoroughly rejected it as a consequence of competing influences, particularly the black college students who so magnificently spearheaded the southern struggle for emancipation from Jim Crow pigmentocracy.

As I attained maturity in the '60s and '70s, relatives and friends used *nigger* but in ways that differed substantially from Big Mama's usage. Some deployed it as a signal that they understood that blacks remained mere "niggers" in the eyes of many whites. For them, referring to blacks as niggers was a way of holding up a clarifying mirror to society and reminding all within earshot of what they saw as an unchanging reality of American life—"ofays on top, niggers on the bottom." Others used the term with a large twist of irony to speak admiringly of someone, as in "James Brown is a sho nuff nigger," meaning that the great entertainer was wholly willing to be himself without apology. If Big Mama said that a person had acted like a nigger, it could only mean that, in her view, someone had behaved badly. By contrast, when my cousins and their friends said that someone had acted like a nigger it might mean that that person had reacted to racist challenge with laudable militancy. Big Mama warned us about "bad niggers" by which she meant Negroes who were in trouble with the law. But among my cousins, as among many blacks, being a certain sort of "bad nigger"—the sort that bravely confronted the laws of white supremacy—was glamorous and admirable. Big Mama warned her charges against "acting like niggers." But a popular saying among the youngsters was "Never give up your right to act like a nigger," by which they meant that Negroes should be unafraid to speak up loudly and act out militantly on behalf of their interests.

There was often a generational difference in evidence in competing uses of the N-word with the younger people experimenting with nonderogatory versions. On the other hand, while some of my younger relatives are adamantly opposed to any use of *nigger,* believing it to be only and unalterably a debasing slur, some of my older relatives anticipated by many years the transformation of *nigger* (or "nigga") that is now widely attributed to the hip-hop culture. Long before the rapper Ice-T insisted upon being called a nigger, my father declared that he was proud to be a "stone nigger"—by which he meant a black man without pretensions who was unafraid to enjoy himself openly and loudly despite the objections of condescending whites or insecure blacks.

How could the man who gave me permission to "go to war" against racial insult turn around and proudly refer to himself as a nigger? My father could do so because he intuited what Justice Oliver Wendell Holmes once observed—that "a word is not a crystal, transparent and unchanged," but is instead "the skin of a living thought [that] may vary greatly in color and content according to the circumstances and time in which it is used."

I relate some of my own direct experiences with the N-word in response to questions I have received since the publication of *Nigger*. . . . Many people have asked whether or under what circumstances I have personally had to grapple with the word. For some questioners, my book is more authentic and acceptable insofar as I have been called a nigger and have otherwise been forced to encounter it in my own life. I make no such claim on my own behalf. I do not believe that my experiences entitle me to any more deference than that which is due on the strength of my writing alone. Experience is only an opportunity; what matters is what one makes of it. The extent to which my writing is appreciated or deferred to should be determined solely on the basis of *its* character. The best evidence of that is found on the page.

Chapter 1: "The Protean N-Word"

How should *nigger* be defined? Is it a part of the American cultural inheritance that warrants preservation? Why does *nigger* generate such powerful reactions? Is it a more hurtful racial epithet than insults such as *kike, wop, wetback, mick, chink,* and *gook*? Am I wrongfully offending the sensibilities of readers right now by spelling out *nigger* instead of using a euphemism such as *N-word*? Should blacks be able to use *nigger* in ways forbidden to others? Should the law view *nigger* as a provocation that reduces the culpability of a person who responds to it violently? Under what circumstances, if any, should a person be ousted from his or her job for saying "nigger"? What methods are useful for depriving *nigger* of destructiveness? In the pages that follow, I will pursue these and related questions. I will put a tracer on *nigger,* report on its use, and assess the controversies to which it gives rise. I have invested energy in this endeavor because *nigger* is a key word in the lexicon of race relations and thus an important term in American politics. To be ignorant of its meanings and effects is to make oneself vulnerable to all manner of perils, including the loss of a job, a reputation, a friend, even one's life.

Let's turn first to etymology. *Nigger* is derived from the Latin word for the color black, *niger.* According to the *Random House Historical Dictionary of American Slang,* it did not originate as a slur but took on a derogatory connotation over time. *Nigger* and other words related to it have been spelled in a variety of ways, including niggah, nigguh, niggur, and niggar. When John Rolfe recorded in his journal the first shipment of Africans to Virginia in 1619, he listed them as "negars." A 1689 inventory of an estate in Brooklyn, New York, made mention of an enslaved "niggor" boy. The seminal lexicographer Noah Webster referred to Negroes as "negers." (Currently some people insist upon distinguishing *nigger*—which they see as exclusively an insult—from *nigga,* which they view as a term capable of signaling friendly salutation.) In the 1700s *niger* appeared in what the dictionary describes as "dignified argumentation" such as Samuel Sewall's denunciation of slavery, *The Selling of Joseph*.[5] No one knows precisely when or how *niger* turned derisively into *nigger* and attained a pejorative meaning. We do know, however, that by the end of the first third of the nineteenth century, *nigger* had already become a familiar and influential insult.

In *A Treatise on the Intellectual Character and Civil and Political Condition of the Colored People of the United States: and the Prejudice Exercised Towards Them* (1837), Hosea Easton wrote that nigger "is an opprobrious term, employed to impose contempt upon [blacks] as an inferior race. . . . The term in itself would be perfectly harmless were it used only to distinguish one class of society from another; but it is not used with that intent. . . . It flows from the fountain of purpose to injure."[6] Easton averred that often the earliest instruction white adults gave to white children prominently featured the word nigger. Adults reprimanded them for being "worse than niggers," for being "ignorant as niggers," for having "no more credit than niggers"; they disciplined them by telling them that unless they behaved they would be carried off by "the old nigger" or made to sit with "niggers" or consigned to the "nigger seat," which was, of course, a place of shame.

Nigger has seeped into practically every aspect of American culture, from literature to political debates, from cartoons to song. Throughout the 1800s and for much of the 1900s as well, writers of popular music generated countless lyrics that lampooned blacks, in songs such as "Philadelphia Riots; or, I Guess It Wasn't de Niggas Dis Time," "De Nigga Gal's Dream," "Who's Dat Nigga Dar A-Peepin?" . . .

Throughout American history, *nigger* has cropped up in children's rhymes, perhaps the best known of which is

> Eeny-meeny-miney-mo!
> Catch a nigger by the toe!
> If he hollers, let him go!
> Eeny-meeny-miney-mo!

Today, on the Internet, whole sites are devoted to nigger jokes. At KKKomedy Central—Micetrap's Nigger Joke Center, for instance, the "Nigger Ghetto Gazette" contains numerous jokes such as the following:

> *Q.* What do you call a nigger boy riding a bike?
> *A.* Thief! . . .

Nigger has been a familiar part of the vocabularies of whites high and low. It has often been the calling card of so-called white trash—poor, disreputable, uneducated Euro-Americans. Partly to distance themselves from this ilk, some whites of higher standing have aggressively forsworn the use of *nigger*. Such was the case, for example, with senators Strom Thurmond and Richard

Russell, both white supremacists who never used the N-word. For many whites in positions of authority, however, referring to blacks as niggers was once a safe indulgence. Reacting to news that Booker T. Washington had dined at the White House, Senator Benjamin Tillman of South Carolina predicted, "The action of President Roosevelt in entertaining that nigger will necessitate our killing a thousand niggers in the South before they will learn their place again." During his (ultimately successful) reelection campaign of 1912, the governor of South Carolina, Coleman Livingston Blease, declared with reference to his opponent, Ira Jones, the chief justice of the state supreme court, "You people who want social equality [with the Negro] vote for Jones. You men who have nigger children vote for Jones. You who have a nigger wife in your backyard vote for Jones."

During an early debate in the United States House of Representatives over a proposed federal antilynching bill, black people sitting in the galleries cheered when a representative from Wisconsin rebuked a colleague from Mississippi for blaming lynching on Negro criminality. In response, according to James Weldon Johnson of the National Association for the Advancement of Colored People (NAACP), white southern politicians shouted from the floor of the House, "Sit down, niggers." In 1938, when the majority leader of the United States Senate, Alben Barkley, placed antilynching legislation on the agenda, Senator James Byrnes of South Carolina (who would later become a supreme court justice and secretary of state) faulted the black NAACP official Walter White. Barkley, Byrnes declared, "can't do anything without talking to that nigger first."

A complete list of prominent whites who have referred at some point or other to blacks demeaningly as niggers would be lengthy indeed. It would include such otherwise disparate figures as Richard Nixon and Flannery O'Connor.

Given whites' use of *nigger,* it should come as no surprise that for many blacks the N-word has constituted a major and menacing presence that has sometimes shifted the course of their lives. Former slaves featured it in their memoirs about bondage. Recalling her lecherous master's refusal to permit her to marry a free man of color, Harriet Jacobs related the following colloquy:

"So you want to be married do you?" he said, "and to a free nigger."

"Yes, sir."

"Well, I'll soon convince you whether I am your master, or the nigger fellow you honor so highly. If you *must* have a husband, you may take up with one of my slaves."

Nigger figures noticeably, too, in Frederick Douglass's autobiography. Re-creating the scene in which his master objected to his being taught to read and write, the great abolitionist imagined that the man might have said,

"If you give a nigger an inch he will take an ell. A nigger should know nothing but to obey his master. . . . Learning would *spoil* the best nigger in the world."

In the years since the Civil War, no one has more searingly dramatized *nigger*-as-insult than Richard Wright. Anyone who wants to learn in a brief compass what lies behind African American anger and anguish when *nigger* is deployed as a slur by whites should read Wright's *The Ethics of Living Jim Crow.* In this memoir about his life in the South during the teens and twenties of the twentieth century, Wright attacked the Jim Crow regime by showing its ugly manifestations in day-to-day racial interactions. Wright's first job took him to a small optical company in Jackson, Mississippi, where things went smoothly in the beginning. Then Wright made the mistake of asking the seventeen-year-old white youth with whom he worked to tell him more about the business. The youth viewed this sign of curiosity and ambition as an unpardonable affront. Wright narrated the confrontation that followed:

"What yuh tryin' t' do, nigger, git smart?" he asked.

"Naw; I ain' tryin' t' git smart," I said.

"Well, don't, if yuh know what's good for yuh! . . . Nigger, you think you're *white,* don't you?"

"No sir!"

"This is *white* man's work around here, and you better watch yourself."

From then on, the white youth so terrorized Wright that he ended up quitting. . . .

Among the ubiquitous stories featuring *nigger* that appear in literature by and about black Americans, several others also stand out. . . .

Malcolm X remembered that during his childhood, after his family fell apart following the murder of his father, the whites who served as his guardians openly referred to blacks as niggers. And then there was his encounter with a white teacher who, in recommending a career in carpentry rather than the law, urged young Malcolm to be "realistic about being a nigger."

When Jackie Robinson reported to the Brooklyn Dodgers' top minor-league team, the manager earnestly asked the team's owner whether he really thought that niggers were human beings. Robinson, of course, would have to contend with *nigger* throughout his fabled career. During a game played on April 22, 1947, he recalled hearing hatred pour forth from the dugout of the Philadelphia Phillies "as if it had been synchronized by some master conductor":

"Hey, nigger, why don't you go back to the cotton field where you belong?"

"They're waiting for you in the jungles, black boy!"

"We don't want you here, nigger." . . .

In the early 1960s, at the height of his celebrity as a comedian, Dick Gregory ventured south to join other activists in protesting blacks' exclusion from the voting booth. In his autobiography, he recounted an altercation he had with a policeman in Greenwood, Mississippi, who, without just provocation, shoved him and ordered,

"Move on, Nigger."

"Thanks a million."

"Thanks for what?"

"Up north police don't escort me across the street against the red light."

"I said, move on, nigger."

"I don't know my way, I'm new in this town."

The cop yanked on my arm and turned his head. "Send someone over to show this nigger where to go," he hollered. . . .

I pulled one of my arms free and pointed at the crowd.

"Ask that white woman over there to come here and show me where to go."

The cop's face got red, and there was spittle at the corner of his mouth. All he could say was: "Nigger, dirty nigger. . . ."

I looked at him. "Your momma's a nigger. Probably got more Negro blood in her than I could ever hope to have in me."

He dropped my other arm then, and backed away, and his hand was on his gun. I thought he was going to explode. But nothing happened. I was sopping wet and too excited to be scared. . . .

Michael Jordan was suspended from school for hitting a white girl who called him "nigger" during a fight over a seat on a school bus in Wilmington, North Carolina.

Tiger Woods was tied up in kindergarten by older schoolmates who called him "nigger."

Recalling the difficulties she faced in raising her black son in a household with her white female lover, the poet Audre Lorde noted that "for years in the name-calling at school, boys shouted at [her son] not—'your mother's a lesbian'—but rather—'your mother's a nigger.'"

The musician Branford Marsalis has said he cannot remember a time when he was *not* being called "nigger." "If you grew up in the South," he observed, whites "called you nigger from the time you were born." . . .

In 1973, at the very moment he stood poised to break Babe Ruth's record for career home runs, the baseball superstar Hank Aaron encountered *nigger*-as-insult on a massive scale, largely in the form of hateful letters:

Dear Nigger,

Everybody loved Babe Ruth. You will be the most hated man in this country if you break his career home run record. . . .

An offshoot of *nigger* is *nigger lover*, a label affixed to nonblacks who become friendly with African Americans or openly side with them in racial controversies. In the Civil War era, Republicans' antislavery politics won them the appellation "black Republicans" or "nigger lovers." To discredit Abraham Lincoln, his racist Democratic party opponents wrote a "Black Republican Prayer" that ended with the "benediction"

> May the blessings of Emancipation extend throughout our unhappy land, and the illustrious, sweet-scented Sambo nestle in the bosom of every Abolition woman . . . and the distinction of color be forever consigned to oblivion [so] that we may live in bands of fraternal love, union and equality with the Almighty Nigger, henceforth, now and forever. Amen.

One of Senator Charles Sumner's white constituents in Massachusetts suggested sneeringly that his exertions in favor of abolition amounted only to "riding the 'nigger' hobby." Another dissatisfied constituent maintained that the senator suffered from "a deep-seated nigger cancer," that he could "speak of nothing but the 'sublime nigger,'" and that his speeches offered nothing but "the nigger at the beginning, nigger in the middle, and nigger at the end."

A century later, during the civil rights revolution, whites who joined black civil rights protesters were frequently referred to as nigger lovers. When white and black "freedom riders" rode together on a bus in violation of (unlawful) local Jim Crow custom, a bigoted white driver took delight in delivering them to a furious crowd of racists in Anniston, Alabama. Cheerfully anticipating the beatings to come, the driver yelled to the mob, "Well, boys, here they are. I brought you some niggers and nigger lovers." Speaking to a rally in Baltimore, Maryland, a spokesman for the National States Rights Party declared confidently that most "nigger lovers are sick in the mind" and "should be bound, hung, and killed."[7]

The term *nigger lover* continues to be heard amid the background noise that accompanies racial conflict. Whites who refrain from discriminating against blacks, whites who become intimate with blacks, whites who confront antiblack practices, whites who work on the electoral campaigns of black candidates, whites who nominate blacks for membership in clubs, whites who protect blacks in the course of their official duties, and whites who merely socialize with blacks are all subject to being derided as "nigger lovers."

Over the years, *nigger* has become the best known of the American language's many racial insults, evolving into the paradigmatic slur. It is the epithet that generates epithets. That is why Arabs are called "sand niggers," Irish "the niggers of Europe," and Palestinians "the niggers of the Middle

East"; why black bowling balls have been called "nigger eggs," games of craps "nigger golf," watermelons "nigger hams," rolls of one-dollar bills "nigger rolls," bad luck "nigger luck," gossip "nigger news," and heavy boots "nigger stompers."

Observers have made strong claims on behalf of the special status of *nigger* as a racial insult. The journalist Farai Chideya describes it as "the all-American trump card, the nuclear bomb of racial epithets." The writer Andrew Hacker has asserted that among slurs of any sort, *nigger* "stands alone [in] its power to tear at one's insides." Judge Stephen Reinhardt deems *nigger* "the most noxious racial epithet in the contemporary American lexicon." And prosecutor Christopher Darden famously branded *nigger* the "filthiest, dirtiest, nastiest word in the English language."

The claim that *nigger* is the superlative racial epithet—the *most* hurtful, the *most* fearsome, the *most* dangerous, the *most* noxious—necessarily involves comparing oppressions and prioritizing victim status. Some scoff at this enterprise. Objecting to a columnist's assertion that being called a honky was not in the same league as being called a nigger, one reader responded, "We should be in the business of ending racism, not measuring on a politically correct thermometer the degree to which one is more victimized than another." Declining to enter into a discussion comparing the Holocaust with American slavery, a distinguished historian quipped that he refused to become an accountant of atrocity. His demurral is understandable: sometimes the process of comparison degenerates into divisive competitions among minority groups that insist upon jealously defending their victim status. Because the Jewish Holocaust is the best known and most widely vilified atrocity in modern times, many use it as an analogical yardstick for the purpose of highlighting their own tragedies. Hence Iris Chang dubbed the Japanese army's Rape of Nanking during World War II "the forgotten holocaust," Larry Kramer titled his reportage on the early days of the AIDS crisis *Reports from the Holocaust,* and Toni Morrison dedicated her novel *Beloved* to the "sixty million and more"—a figure undoubtedly calculated to play off the familiar six million, the number of Jews generally thought to have perished at the hands of the Nazis. At the same time, some who are intent upon propounding the uniqueness of the Holocaust aggressively reject analogies to it, as if comparing it to other atrocities could only belittle the Nazis' heinous crime.

We could, of course, avoid making comparisons. Instead of saying that the Holocaust was the *worst* atrocity of the twentieth century, we could say simply that the Holocaust was terrible. Instead of saying that *nigger* has been the *most* socially destructive racial epithet in the American language, we could say merely that, when used derogatorily, *nigger* is a socially destructive epithet. Although such a strategy may have certain diplomatic merits, it deprives audiences of assistance in making qualitative judgments. After all, there is a difference between the massacre that kills fifty and the one that kills five hundred—or five thousand or fifty thousand. By the same token, the stigmatizing power of different racial insults can vary. . . .

It is impossible to declare with confidence that when hurled as an insult, *nigger* necessarily inflicts more distress than other racial epithets. Individuals beset by thugs may well feel equally terrified whether those thugs are screaming "Kill the honky" or "Kill the nigger." In the aggregate, though, *nigger* is and has long been the most socially consequential racial insult. Consider, for example, the striking disparity of incidence that distinguishes *nigger* from other racial epithets appearing in reported court opinions. In reported federal and state cases in the LEXIS-NEXIS data base (as of July 2001), *kike* appears in eighty-four cases, *wetback* in fifty, *gook* in ninety, and *honky* in 286. These cases reveal cruelty, terror, brutality, and heartache. Still, the frequency of these slurs is overwhelmed by that of *nigger,* which appears in 4,219 reported decisions.

Reported court opinions are hardly a perfect mirror of social life in America; they are merely an opaque reflection that poses real difficulties of interpretation. The social meaning of litigation is ambiguous. It may represent an attempt to remedy real injury, or it may mark cynical exploitation of increased intolerance for racism. The very act of bringing a lawsuit may express a sense of empowerment, but declining to bring one may do so as well, signaling that a person or group has means other than cumbersome litigation by which to settle scores or vindicate rights. That there is more litigation in which *nigger* appears could mean that usage of the term is more prevalent than usage of analogous epithets; that its usage is associated with more dramatic injuries; that targets of *nigger* are more aggrieved or more willing and able to sue; or that authorities—police, prosecutors, judges, or juries—are more receptive to this species of complaint. I do not know which of these hypotheses best explains the salience of *nigger* in the jurisprudence of racial epithets. What cannot plausibly be doubted, however, is the fact of *nigger*'s baleful preeminence.

Nigger first appears in the reports of the United States Supreme Court in a decision announced in 1871. The case, *Blyew v. United States,* dealt with the prosecution for murder of two white men who, for racial reasons, had hacked to death several members of a black family. According to a witness, one of the codefendants had declared that "there would soon be another war about the niggers" and that when it came, he "intended to go to killing niggers."

In the years since, federal and state courts have heard hundreds of cases in which the word *nigger* figured in episodes of racially motivated violence, threats, and arson. Particularly memorable among these was the successful prosecution of Robert Montgomery for violation of federal criminal statutes. In 1988, in Indianapolis, state authorities established a residential treatment center for convicted child molesters in an all-white neighborhood. From the center's opening until mid-1991—a period during which all of the residents of the center were white—neighbors voiced no objections. In June 1991, however, authorities converted the center into a shelter for approximately forty homeless veterans, twenty-five of whom were black. Soon thereafter trouble erupted as a group of whites, including Montgomery, loudly proclaimed their opposition to the encroachment of "niggers" and burned a cross and vandalized a car to express their feelings. An all-white cadre of child molesters was evidently acceptable, but the presence of blacks made a racially integrated group of homeless *veterans* intolerable!

If *nigger* represented only an insulting slur and was associated only with racial animus, this book would not exist, for the term would be insufficiently interesting to warrant extended study. *Nigger* is fascinating precisely because it has been put to a variety of uses and can radiate a wide array of meanings. Unsurprisingly, blacks have often used *nigger* to different purposes than racist whites. To lampoon slavery, blacks created the story of the slave caught eating one of his master's pigs. "Yes, suh, Massa," the slave quipped, "you got less pig now, but you sho' got more nigger." To poke fun at the grisly phenomenon of lynching, African Americans told of the black man who, upon seeing a white woman pass by, said, "Lawd, will I ever?" A white man responded, "No, nigger, never." The black man replied, "Where there's life, there's hope." And the white man declared, "Where there's a nigger, there's a rope." To dramatize the tragic reality of Jim Crow subjugation, African Americans recounted the tale of the Negro who got off a bus down south. Seeing a white policeman, he politely asked for the time. The policeman hit him twice with a club and said, "Two o'clock, nigger. Why?" "No reason, Cap'n," the black man answered. "I's just glad it ain't twelve." And to satirize "legal" disenfranchisement, African Americans told the joke about the black man who attempted to register to vote. After the man answered a battery of questions that were far more difficult than any posed to whites, an official confronted him with a headline in a Chinese paper and demanded a translation. "Yeah, I know what it means," the black man said. "It means that niggers don't vote in Mississippi again this year."

In the 1960s and 1970s, protest became more direct and more assertive. Drafted to fight a "white man's war" in Vietnam, Muhammad Ali refused to be inducted into the U.S. Army, explaining, "No Vietcong ever called me 'nigger.'" Emphasizing the depth of white racism all across the United States, activists joked, "What is a Negro with a Ph.D.?" Their response? "Dr. Nigger."

In his famous "Letter from a Birmingham Jail," Martin Luther King Jr. continued to agitate, listing in wrenching detail the indignities that prompted his impatience with tardy reform. He cited having to sleep in automobiles because of racial exclusion from motels, having to explain to his children why they could not go to amusement parks open to the white public, and being "harried by day and haunted by night by the fact that you are a Negro, living constantly at tip-toe stance never quite knowing what to expect next." Among King's litany of abuses was the humiliating way in which whites routinely addressed blacks: "Your wife and mother," he observed, "are never given the respected title 'Mrs.,'" and under the etiquette of Jim Crow, "your first name becomes 'nigger' and your middle name becomes 'boy' (however old you are) and your last name becomes 'John.'"

For some observers, the only legitimate use of *nigger* is as a rhetorical boomerang against racists. There are others, however, who approvingly note a wide range of additional usages. According to Professor Clarence Major, when *nigger* is "used by black people among themselves, [it] is a racial term with undertones of warmth and good will—reflecting . . . a tragicomic sensibility that is aware of black history." The writer Claude Brown once admiringly described *nigger* as "perhaps the most soulful word in the world," and journalist Jarvis DeBerry calls it "beautiful in its multiplicity of functions." "I am not aware," DeBerry writes, "of any other word capable of expressing so many contradictory emotions." Traditionally an insult, *nigger* can also be a compliment, as in "He played like a nigger." Historically a signal of hostility, it can also be a salutation announcing affection, as in "This is my main nigger." A term of belittlement, *nigger* can also be a term of respect, as in "James Brown is a straight-up nigger." A word that can bring forth bitter tears in certain circumstances, *nigger* can prompt joyful laughter in others. . . .

Nigger has long been featured in black folk humor. There is the story, for example, of the young boy inspired by a minister's sermon on loving all of God's creatures. Finding a frozen rattlesnake, he nicely put the animal under his shirt to warm it up. "Nigger, I'm gonna bite the hell out of you!" the snake announced upon its revival. "Mr. Snake," the boy asked, "you mean to say you gonna bite me after I followed the preacher's teaching and took you to my bosom?" "Hell yeah, nigger," the snake replied. "You knew I was a snake, didn't you?"

Before the 1970s, however, *nigger* seldom figured in the routines of professional comedians. It was especially rare in the acts of those who performed for racially mixed audiences. Asserting that unmentionable slurs derived much of their seductive power from their taboo status, the iconoclastic white comedian Lenny Bruce recommended a strategy of subversion through overuse. In a 1963 routine, Bruce suggested with characteristic verve that "if President Kennedy got on television and said, 'Tonight I'd like to introduce the niggers in my cabinet,' and he yelled 'Niggerniggernigger-niggerniggerniggernigger' at every nigger he saw. . . till *nigger* didn't mean anything anymore, till *nigger* lost its meaning . . . you'd never hear any four-year-old nigger cry when he came home from school."

But Bruce was unusual, and in terms of the N-word, he failed to inspire emulation. While the hip comedians of the 1950s and 1960s—Dick Gregory, Nipsey Russell, Mort Sahl, Godfrey Cambridge, Moms Mabley, Redd Foxx—told sexually risqué or politically barbed jokes, *nigger* for the most part remained off-limits.

All that changed with the emergence of Richard Pryor. Through live performances and a string of albums, he brought *nigger* to center stage in stand-up comedy, displaying with consummate artistry its multiple meanings.

Pryor's single best performance may be heard on the aptly titled *That Nigger's Crazy,* winner of the 1974 Grammy Award for best comedy recording. The album explores Pryor's professional fears ("Hope I'm funny . . . because I know niggers ready to kick ass"), blacks' alleged ability to avoid certain sorts of danger ("Niggers never get burned up in buildings. . . . White folks just panic, run to the door, fall all over each other. . . . Niggers get outside, *then* argue"), black parenting styles ("My father was one of them eleven-o'clock niggers"), comparative sociology ("White folks fuck quiet; niggers make noise"), racial anthropology ("White folks . . . don't know how to play the dozens"), and social commentary ("Nothin' can scare a nigger after four hundred years of this shit"). . . .

Mel Watkins has rightly maintained that what made Richard Pryor a pathbreaking figure was that he "introduce[d] and popularize[d]) that unique, previously concealed or rejected part of African-American humor that thrived in the lowest, most unassimilated portion of the black community." He broke free, at least for a while, of all those—whites and blacks alike—who, sometimes for different reasons, shared an aversion to too much realism. He seemed radically unconcerned with deferring to any social conventions, particularly those that accepted black comedians as clowns but rejected them as satirists. Nothing more vividly symbolized his defiant, risk-taking spirit than his unprecedented playfulness regarding the explosive N-word in performances before racially mixed audiences.

In the years since the release of *That Nigger's Crazy,* the N-word has become a staple in the routine of many black comedians. Among these, the one who most jarringly deploys it is Chris Rock, whose signature skit begins with the declaration "I love black people, but I hate niggers." . . .

According to Rock, "niggers always want credit for some shit they're *supposed* to do. They'll say something like 'I took care of my kids.'" . . .

Rock asserts that "the worst thing about niggers is that they love to *not know.*" That's because, he says, "niggers don't read. Books are like Kryptonite to a nigger."

Aware that some may condemn his routine as latter-day minstrelsy, racial betrayal, or a false pandering to antiblack prejudice, Rock exclaims near the end of his performance,

> I know what all you black [listeners] think.
> "Man, why you got to say that? . . . It isn't us, it's the *media*. The media has distorted our image to make us look bad. Why must you come down on us like that, brother? It's not us, it's the media."
> Please cut the shit. When I go to the money machine at night, I'm not looking over my shoulder for the media.
> I'm looking for niggers.
> Ted Koppel never took anything from me. Niggers have. Do you think I've got three guns in my house because the media's outside my door trying to bust in?

Rap is another genre of entertainment suffused with instances of *nigger*. A cursory survey just of titles yields Dr. Dre's "The Day the Niggas Took Over," A Tribe Called Quest's "Sucka Nigga," Jay-Z's "Real Nigger," the Geto Boys' "Trigga Happy Nigga," DMX's "My Niggas," and Cypress Hill's "Killa Hill Nigga." . . .

One of the seminal influences in gangsta rap called itself N.W.A., short for "Niggaz Wit Attitude." One of this group's most popular albums was *Efil-4zaggin* which, read backward, is "Niggaz 4 Life." Tupac Shakur proclaimed that to him, *nigga* stood for "Never Ignorant, Gets Goals Accomplished."

Some people—I call them eradicationists—seek to drive *nigger* out of rap, comedy, and all other categories of entertainment even when (perhaps *especially* when) blacks themselves are the ones using the N-word. They see this usage as bestowing legitimacy on *nigger* and misleading those whites who have little direct interaction with African Americans. Eradicationists also maintain that blacks' use of *nigger* is symptomatic of racial self-hatred or the internalization of white racism, thus the rhetorical equivalent of black-on-black crime.

There is something to both of these points. The use of *nigger* by black rappers and comedians has given the term a new currency and enhanced cachet such that many young whites yearn to use the term like the blacks whom they see as heroes or trendsetters. It is undoubtedly true, moreover, that in some cases, blacks' use of *nigger* is indicative of an antiblack, self-hating prejudice. I myself first became aware of the term as a child in an all-black setting—my family household in Columbia, South Carolina—in which older relatives routinely attributed to negritude traits they disparaged, including tardiness, dishonesty, rudeness, impoverishment, cowardice, and stupidity. Such racial disparagement *of* blacks *by* blacks was by no means idiosyncratic. It is a widespread feature of African American culture that has given rise to a distinctive corpus of racial abasement typified by admonishments, epigraphs, and doggerel such as:

Stop acting like a nigger.

I don't want nothing black but a Cadillac.

Niggers and flies. Flies and niggers. The more I see niggers, the more I like flies. . . .

This tendency toward racial self-abnegation has been much diminished since the civil rights revolution. But it still retains a grip on the psyches of many black Americans and is searingly evident in a phrase well known in black circles: "Niggers ain't shit."

Self-hatred, however, is an implausible explanation for why many assertive, politically progressive African Americans continue to say "nigger" openly and frequently in conversations with one another. These are African Americans who, in their own minds at least, use *nigger* not in subjection to racial subordination but in defiance of it. Some deploy a long tradition, especially evident in black nationalist rhetoric, of using abusive criticism to spur action that is intended to erase any factual predicate for the condemnation voiced. An example is writing by the Last Poets, a group established in 1968 that merged poetry, music, and politics in forms that anticipated certain types of rap. A famous item in the Last Poets' repertoire was "Niggers are Scared of Revolution," in which they charged that

> Niggers are scared of revolution but niggers shouldn't be scared of revolution because revolution is nothing but change, and all niggers do is change. Niggers come in from work and change into pimping clothes to hit the streets to make some quick change. Niggers change their hair from black to red to blond and hope like hell their looks will change. Niggers kill other niggers just because one didn't receive the correct change. . . .

Describing their intentions, Umar Bin Hassan writes that the poem constituted a "call to arms" because "niggers are human beings lost in somebody else's system of values and morals."

Many blacks also do with *nigger* what other members of marginalized groups have done with slurs aimed at shaming them. They have thrown the slur right back in their oppressors' faces. They have added a positive meaning to *nigger,* just as women, gays, lesbians, poor whites, and children born out of wedlock have defiantly appropriated and revalued such words as *bitch, cunt, queer, dyke, redneck, cracker,* and *bastard.*

Yet another source of allegiance to *nigger* is a pessimistic view of the African American predicament. Many blacks who use *nigger* before racially mixed audiences disdain dressing up their colloquial language. They do not even attempt to put their best foot forward for the purpose of impressing whites or eroding stereotypes because they see such missions as a lost cause. They like to use *nigger* because it is a shorthand way of reminding themselves and everyone else precisely where they perceive themselves as standing in American society—the message being, "Always remember you's a nigger." As Bruce A. Jacobs observes, "To proclaim oneself a nigger is to declare to the disapproving mainstream, 'You can't fire me. I quit.' Hence the perennial popularity of the word. Among poor black youth who . . . carry a burning resentment of white society. To growl that one is a nigga is a seductive gesture . . . that can feel bitterly empowering."

Two additional considerations also warrant notice here, both of them having to do with the power of words to simultaneously create and divide communities. Some blacks use *nigger* to set themselves off from Negroes who refuse to use it. To proclaim oneself a nigger is to identify oneself as real, authentic, uncut, unassimilated, and unassimilable—the opposite, in short, of a Negro, someone whose rejection of *nigger* is seen as part of an effort to blend into the white mainstream. Sprinkling one's language with *niggers* is thus a way to "keep it real."

Roping off cultural turf is another aim of some blacks who continue to use *nigger* in spite of its stigmatized status. Certain forms of black cultural expression have become commercially valuable, and black cultural entrepreneurs fear that these forms will be exploited by white performers who will adopt them and, tapping white-skin privilege, obtain compensation far outstripping that paid to black performers. This is, of course, a realistic fear in light of the long history of white entertainers' becoming rich and famous by marketing in whiteface cultural innovations authored by their underappreciated black counterparts. A counterstrategy is to seed black cultural expression with gestures that are widely viewed as being off-limits to whites. Saying "nigger" is one such gesture. Even whites who immerse themselves in black hip-hop culture typically refrain from openly and unabashedly saying "nigger" like their black heroes or colleagues, for fear that it might be perceived as a sign of disrespect rather than one of solidarity.

Some nonwhite entertainers have used *nigger* in their acts. John Lennon and Yoko Ono, for example, entitled a song "Woman Is the Nigger of the World," and Patti Smith wrote "Rock 'n' Roll Nigger." But Lennon, Ono, and Smith performed in overwhelmingly white milieus. Rap, by contrast, is dominated by blacks. A few white rappers have achieved commercial success and won the respect of black artists and audiences. I am thinking here especially of the white rapper Eminem, a superstar in the hip-hop culture. Eminem has assumed many of the distinctive mannerisms of his black rap colleagues, making himself into a "brother" in many ways—in his music, his diction, his gait, his clothes, his associations. He refuses to say, however, any version of a word that his black hip-hop colleagues employ constantly as a matter of course; the nonchalance with which he tosses around epithets such as *bitch and faggot* does not extend to *nigger.* "That word," he insists, "'is not even in my vocabulary."

Eminem is certainly following a prudent course, for many people, white and black alike, disapprove of a white person saying "nigger" under virtually any circumstance. "When we call each other 'nigger' it means no harm," Ice Cube remarks. "But if a white person uses it, it's something different, it's a racist word." Professor Michael Eric Dyson likewise asserts that whites must know and stay in their racial place when it comes to saying "nigger." He writes that "most white folk attracted to black culture know better than to cross a line drawn in the sand of racial history. *Nigger* has never been cool when spit from white lips."

The race line that Dyson applauds, however, is a specious divide. There is nothing necessarily wrong with a white person saying "nigger," just as there is nothing necessarily wrong with a black person saying it. What should matter is the context in which the word is spoken—the speaker's aims, effects, alternatives. To condemn whites who use the N-word without regard to context is simply to make a fetish of *nigger.* Harriet Beecher Stowe (*Uncle Tom's Cabin*), Mark Twain (*Huckleberry Finn*), William Dean Howells (*An Imperative Duty*), Edward Sheldon (*The Nigger*), Eugene O'Neill (*All God's Chillun*), Lillian Smith (*Strange Fruit*), Sinclair Lewis (*Kingsblood Royal*), Joyce Carol Oates (*Them*), E. L. Doctorow (*Ragtime*), John Grisham (*A Time to Kill*), and numerous other white writers have unveiled *nigger*-as-insult in order to dramatize and condemn racism's baleful presence.

In 1967, President Lyndon Baines Johnson decided to appoint an African American to the Supreme Court for the first time in American history. First on Johnson's list of candidates was Thurgood Marshall—"Mr. Civil Rights," the hero of *Brown v. Board of Education* and, of course, the man he ended up putting on the Court. But before he announced his selection, Johnson asked an assistant to identify some other possible candidates. The aide mentioned A. Leon Higginbotham, whom Johnson had appointed to the federal trial bench. Reportedly, the president dismissed the suggestion with the comment "The only two people who have ever heard of Judge Higginbotham are you and his momma. When I appoint a nigger to the [Supreme Court], I want everyone to know he's a nigger." Was the use of *nigger* in this context a venting of racial prejudice? Maybe. Johnson had been raised in a thoroughly racist environment, had supported racist policies for a long period, and, as we have seen, casually used *nigger* as part of his private vocabulary before he became president. On this particular occasion, however, it seems likely that he was merely seeking to highlight the racial exclusion against which he was acting, parodying the old regime even as he sought to reform it. If this is an accurate assessment of the situation, I see nothing wrong with what Johnson said, and I applaud what he did.

Can a relationship between a black person and a white one be such that the white person should properly feel authorized, at least within the confines of that relationship, to use the N-word? For me the answer is yes. Carl Van Vechten, for instance, wrote of "niggers" in correspondence with his friend Langston Hughes, and Hughes did not object (though he did once write that *nigger* was a red flag for all Negroes). *Should* Hughes have objected? No. Van Vechten, a key supporter of the Harlem Renaissance, had shown time and again that he abhorred racial prejudice, would do what he could to improve the fortunes of African Americans, and treasured his black friends. It was against this backdrop of achieved trust that Hughes (and other black writers) rightly permitted Van Vechten to use *nigger* as so many African Americans have used it—as an ironic, shorthand spoof on the absurdity of American race relations.

As we have seen, *nigger* can mean many different things, depending upon, among other variables, intonation, the location of the interaction, and the relationship between the speaker and those to whom he is speaking. Generally a reference to people of color, particularly blacks, *nigger* can refer to people of any hue. Senator Robert C. Byrd (D-West Virginia) got into trouble for saying publicly that he "had seen a lot of white niggers in [his] time." But more and more the word is being applied ecumenically. Sociologist John Hartigan reports that poor whites in Detroit often refer to their white neighbors as *niggers*. Typically they mean the word as an insult. But they do not necessarily mean for it to be a *racial* insult. Responding to an inquiry about a white-on-white deployment of *nigger,* one of the participants in Hartigan's study remarked: "He's a nigger, man, and you know what I mean by that. He's an asshole, and it doesn't matter whether a person's black or white, orange or plaid, he can still be a nigger if he runs his mouth like that asshole." Another white Detroiter observed by Hartigan echoed this sentiment. "You don't have to be black to be a nigger," he declared. "Niggers come in all colors." (Interestingly, he added "we are all colored. . . . There's about a hundred shades of white.") . . .

More vividly than most words, then, *nigger* illustrates Justice Oliver Wendell Holmes's observation that "a word is not a crystal, transparent and unchanged." A word is instead "the skin of a living thought [that] may vary greatly in color and content according to the circumstances and the time in which it is used."

NOTES

1. Kennedy, "Persuasion and Distrust," 1137.

2. Kennedy, *Interracial Intimacies*, 35.

3. Kennedy, *Nigger*, 22.

4. Ibid., 41.

5. Published in 1700, Samuel Sewall's essay *The Selling of Joseph* is considered a seminal antislavery treatise and possibly the first of its kind to be published in America. Sewall is also infamous for his relationship to the Salem witch trials, over which he presided as a judge. He later publicly apologized for his role in the proceedings.

6. In his *Treatise*, the free black writer, minister, and abolitionist Hosea Easton (1798–?) deplored the degradation of black men and women through slavery and racial prejudice.

7. A white-supremacist political organization formed in 1958 by J. B. Stoner, the National States Rights Party favored states' rights and segregation and advocated the deportation of African Americans to Africa.

Eugene Robinson
(b. 1955)

⅏ JOURNALIST, COMMENTATOR

*. . . seeing Obama in the White House obliterates any logic behind
self-imposed limits on imagination and ambition.*

Judges for the 2009 Pulitzer Prize praised Robinson's "eloquent columns on the 2008 presidential campaign that focus on the election of
the first African-American president, showcasing graceful writing and
grasp of the larger historic picture." The commentary award, given to him for
his work in the *Washington Post,* was a signal achievement for Robinson but
only one of many career accolades.

Robinson was born in 1955 in Orangeburg, South Carolina, a town he
understands as the quintessential small college town yet more emphatically
describes as a town rumored to house "more black PhDs per capita than
any other city or town in the nation."[1] His mother worked as head librarian
at Claflin University, where his father, who held a law degree, also taught
for a time. Consequently, Robinson describes the Claflin and South Carolina
State University (then South Carolina State College) campuses in Orangeburg as being as familiar to him as his "own backyard."[2] This familiarity not
only shaped his middle-class and intellectual upbringing but also informed
much of his later journalism and commentary, most particularly his analyses
of the black middle class in both South Carolina and the United States—a

perspective that has taken on new clout and timeliness with the prominence of an African American president.

Robinson's reflections on his youth in Orangeburg make it clear that while class differences within the black community were certainly powerful and occasionally tense, the overwhelming attribute that defined the people in the community was simply that they were black, and "to be black was to live under assault."[3] Indeed, Robinson speculates that "Racial apartheid, imposed and enforced by others, ironically had fostered great social cohesion among African Americans, binding together social and economic classes that otherwise might have drifted apart."[4]

Robinson chose to attend his father's alma mater, the University of Michigan, where he became focused on writing after winning an essay contest with an analysis of the 1968 Orangeburg Massacre.[5] He switched his major to journalism, started to write for the *Michigan Daily,* and rose in its ranks to become the first black coeditor-in-chief of the university paper. After graduating, he moved out west, where he found work as a junior reporter covering the Patty Hearst trial for the *San Francisco Chronicle* in 1976. He went on to cover city politics in San Francisco until 1980, when he was recruited to the *Washington Post* by Bob Woodward, who was working as the *Post*'s metro editor at the time.

In his early days at the *Washington Post* he covered the tumultuous career of Marion Barry, the African American mayor of Washington, D.C. As Robinson later pointed out, this meant that even as a relatively new reporter there, he wrote articles that frequently appeared on the front page.[6] His long relationship with the *Washington Post* evolved from position to position as he worked as assistant city editor, city editor, South America correspondent, London bureau chief, foreign editor, and assistant managing editor. In the fall of 1987 Robinson took a year off to conduct research as a Nieman Fellow at the Nieman Foundation for Journalism at Harvard University, where he studied Latin American history and politics. With this newly acquired expertise, he was soon thereafter appointed the South American correspondent for the *Post.* He has written opinion columns for the paper since 2005, and in addition to his regular print work he appears several times a week on various television news shows, especially those on MSNBC.

In his January 20, 2009, *Washington Post* column presented here, "This Consequential Presidency," Robinson observes that, despite the spectacular significance of Obama's race for all Americans, it is ironic that, "in the end, race is likely to be secondary in defining Obama's place in history." Robinson instead sees the enormous challenges of a collapsing economy, multiple international violent conflicts, and a deteriorating natural environment as the tests that ultimately will measure Obama's consequentiality. Nonetheless, with his hallmark concern for race framing his analysis, Robinson sees race as only one part of the "mental furniture" that will need rearranging in the American psyche ahead.

In addition to the thousands of newspaper columns and articles he has published, Robinson has authored several books. *Coal to Cream: A Black Man's Journey beyond Color to an Affirmation of Race* (New York: Free Press, 1999) was informed by his work in South and Central America from 1988 to 1992. Another book, *Last Dance in Havana: The Final Days of Fidel and the Start of the New Cuban Revolution* (New York: Free Press, 2004) examined the role of musicians in Cuba's changing culture. In his most recent book, *Disintegration: The Splintering of Black America* (New York: Doubleday, 2010), which we excerpt here, Robinson argues that the monolithic nature of black culture as imagined by mainstream white-identified society is a myth that not only has always been inaccurate but has become ever more so. Instead he delineates four distinct black Americas—a Mainstream middle-class majority, an Abandoned minority, a Transcendent elite, and an Emergent collective of both mixed-race Americans and foreign-born black immigrants. Robinson sees these categories as reshaping the models we use to analyze the working of class and culture and, most of all, race in America. His reading of how a homecoming game at South Carolina State University exemplifies a middle-class black America that is wholly invisible to the media demonstrates his larger point about a national issue about how difficult it is for middle-class people of color to be recognized in the culture wars of our day. It also, however, illustrates how the culture of black middle-class South Carolinians is simultaneously insular and national—old paradigms of class and racial caste are redefined for a scene distinctly local but proudly American.

?● "This Consequential Presidency"

Washington Post, January 20, 2009

Barack Obama staged his arrival in Washington to evoke Abraham Lincoln's, but the historical echo is faint. Lincoln's famous train ride to his 1861 inauguration traversed a landscape of bitterness and strife. He had to speed through Baltimore "like a thief in the night" for fear of riots and possible assassination. Obama, by contrast, was met by tens of thousands of Baltimoreans who braved subfreezing temperatures to cheer the new president. As Obama made his way to the capital, he crossed a landscape of hope.

Rarely has a new presidency been greeted with such a consensus of goodwill—and rarely has a new president so needed it.

The importance of Obama's mind-blowing historical breakthrough can hardly be overstated. Slavery vexed the Founding Fathers; if not for Lincoln's iron determination, it would have ripped the nation apart. For nearly a century after African Americans were freed from bondage, American society still relegated us to a corner reserved for second-class citizens. Having a black man as president does not magically eliminate racial disparities in income or wealth; it does not fix inner-city schools, repair crumbling neighborhoods or heal dysfunctional families. Psychologically, though, it changes everything.

Our mental furniture is being rearranged. The advent of Obama's presidency brings the African American experience to center stage but does so in a way that allows society to congratulate itself on having come so far. The implications for black Americans are even more profound, because seeing Obama in the White House obliterates any logic behind self-imposed limits on imagination and ambition.

These are huge impacts—making it ironic that, in the end, race is likely to be secondary in defining Obama's place in history.

Since Obama's election, I've heard more than one friend joke sardonically that the nation has said: Sure, a black man can run the country; go right ahead and take your turn—now that the economy is in the tubes, the financial system is a wreck, we're mired in two wars, global warming is parboiling the planet, the government has been forced to spend a trillion dollars or more just to stave off utter ruin, and there's precious little money left to finance desperately needed reforms in health care, education, energy, infrastructure. . . .

Expectations that Obama will be able to solve this daunting array of problems are strikingly high. A new *Post* poll finds that 61 percent of Americans have a "good amount" or "great deal" of confidence that Obama will make the right decisions for the country. A remarkable 72 percent are "fairly" or "very" confident that Obama's economic program—whatever it ultimately turns out to be—will improve the economy.

An Associated Press poll reports that 65 percent of Americans believe Obama will be an "above average" president, including 28 percent who expect him to be "outstanding." Almost two-thirds of Americans, the AP finds, believe their own financial situation will improve early in the Obama administration.

The conventional wisdom is that Obama risks losing public support through disillusionment as people discover that he can't wave a magic wand and make everything better. But the conventional wisdom has been wrong about Obama so many times over the past year that I use it more as a guide to what's *not* likely to happen.

The truth is that no one knows whether Barack Obama will be a good president, much less a great president. All that anyone, including Obama, can be sure of is that his will be a consequential presidency. That is an important piece of knowledge. It took the Sept. 11, 2001, attacks to broaden the scope and ambition of George W. Bush's presidency, for better or worse.

Obama takes office knowing beyond all doubt that he has no choice but to swing for the fences.

Two years ago, as Obama was launching his campaign—over the objections of the Democratic Party establishment, which was still listening to the conventional wisdom —I interviewed him in his Senate office. I was struck by his confidence and his conviction that this was his time, and especially by how unflappable he appeared to be. I saw him last week, after a campaign that had the rest of us on the edge of our seats for months and months, and he seemed temperamentally unchanged.

Our new president is a man who knows exactly who he is. The nation, filled with hope, is about to find out.

✃ Excerpts from *Disintegration: The Splintering of Black America*

"The Mainstream: A Double Life"

If O'Reilly or anyone else wanted to meet the black Mainstream in a setting where outsiders rarely venture, I'd suggest going to homecoming weekend on a historically black college campus.[7] The last time a visit to see my family happened to coincide with South Carolina State University's homecoming, I went to the game. When someone asked me about it later, I was able to report that the contest had been a squeaker, with the home team winning after several lead changes and momentum shifts. But for the life of me I couldn't recall who the opponent was. And I hadn't been drinking.

A friend of mine who lives in Washington—an SCSU graduate who retired not long ago after running a successful engineering consulting firm for many years—drives down to homecoming every year without fail, and never sets foot inside the stadium. He never even bothers to buy a ticket. If you were to conduct a survey asking what the point of SCSU's homecoming is, watching football would score pretty low. Watching halftime would score higher. The normal pattern is reversed: The stands actually *fill* when the second quarter ends, only to thin out again when the third quarter begins. Nobody wants to miss the spectacle.

The year I went, there was a controversy about the other team's cheerleaders, who were not just scantily and suggestively clad but whose routine included a lot of bumping, grinding, pelvis-thrusting, and booty-bouncing. "They look like a bunch of hoochie mamas," was the consensus of the women sitting in my row; the men wisely kept their opinions to themselves. SCSU's cheerleaders were only marginally more demure, however, and their performance only slightly less sexual. The advent of dance-troupe cheerleading squads that look as if they've escaped from a hip-hop music video is a hotly debated innovation in black-college football, but everybody's doing it.

Halftime's main event was the traditional battle of the marching bands. The visitors, who were from Norfolk State University in Virginia—I looked it up—performed first, and they were good. Surprisingly good. No one ever goes to a football game between historically black colleges expecting to hear a bad marching band, but Norfolk State momentarily stunned the crowd. SCSU has one of the nation's elite bands. The Marching 101 are expected to blow the competition away, not barely win the musical showdown. But that's what happened: a narrow victory, owing to more sophisticated choreography, tighter formations, and richer sound.

After halftime, people started drifting away to where the real action was. Sprawled across an area large enough to accommodate several football fields that cool, rainy Saturday afternoon was a soggy but high-spirited encampment. There were huge, Winnebago-style RVs, most with awnings that unfurled from the sides or the rear to provide shelter. There were pickup trucks with trailers on which were mounted barbecue grills large enough to cook a whole pig. There were hundreds and hundreds of cars, of course—SUVs, mostly, but also luxury cars, politically correct hybrids, the occasional vintage Mustang or Corvette. Everywhere there were party tents, some emblazoned with Greek letters signifying a fraternity or sorority. Vendors had set up tables to sell T-shirts, hats, and various tchotchkes. This was 2008, just a few weeks before the presidential election, and merchandise with the SCSU logo was running a poor second to anything labeled Obama.

Oh, and the people: thousands of men and women who belong to the black Mainstream, an unseen majority.

The invisibility of the black middle class is by now a standard trope of modern media criticism, but the phenomenon persists. Black dysfunction has always been newsworthy. Black achievement gets reported because those stories make everyone feel better, score points with black readers or viewers, and partly compensate for all the coverage of black dysfunction. Black normalcy is no more surprising, shocking, or heartwarming than any other color of normalcy, so it's really no surprise that it doesn't make the front page. But Mainstream black Americans seldom make the inside pages, either—the feature stories, for example, that are about neighborhood disputes over speed bumps, as opposed to neighborhood disputes about drug gangs.

There are black college professors who spend their professional lives studying international relations, but they aren't the experts that newspaper reporters and television producers keep on speed dial to offer wisdom about the latest crisis in Honduras or East Timor. There are black scuba clubs that jet off to explore the coast of Belize or the Great Barrier Reef, but their members aren't featured in stories about the impact of climate change on sensitive coral populations. There are African American motorcycle clubs that occasionally get written about, but only in a look-at-this, man-bites-dog sort of way; the president of Atlanta's biggest organized group of black Harley-Davidson riders would be quoted in a story whose point was how interesting it is that such a club exists but almost surely wouldn't be called for comment about a new mandatory helmet law.

In part, this is because society finds it so difficult to see the black experience as universal. For that matter, society has a hard time seeing anything other than what is considered the majority experience as universal. It caused not a ripple when Supreme Court justice Samuel Alito, in his Senate confirmation hearings, spoke of how his heritage as a descendant of Italian immigrants had a positive impact on the way he approached cases as an appellate judge.[8] "Old country" roots, family passage through Ellis Island, hard-won assimilation, a sense of ethnic solidarity—that story, specific to only a minority of citizens, is seen as a quintessentially American narrative. But Justice Sonia Sotomayor, in her confirmation hearings, was scolded, excoriated, and accused of un-American bias over a years-old speech in which she mused about how her heritage as a "wise Latina" might make her a better judge. The Nuyorican narrative is one that the nation seems to have more trouble accepting as legitimately American, for some reason.[9] Imagine the uproar that would have ensued if Barack Obama, during the campaign, had claimed that his African American heritage would make him a better president. Remember the uproar that *did* ensue when videotapes surfaced of the Reverend Jeremiah Wright, in flowing robes and full rhetorical flight, presenting an Afrocentric narrative of the country he had served honorably as a U.S. Marine.[10]

This societal chauvinism is absurd, frustrating, at times even infuriating. I've appeared dozens of times on television with the conservative commentator Pat Buchanan and managed to keep my cool, but the one time I lost it— my eyes got round and crazy, friends say, and apparently I looked as if I were about to smack him—was when he adamantly, even aggressively refused to acknowledge my point that Sotomayor's personal history was every bit as American as his own. He's an intelligent man who reads books and knows history, but he could not bring himself to admit that a Puerto Rican girl's childhood in the Bronx was just as red, white, and blue as an Irish American boy's childhood in Washington. What made me berserk was that Buchanan wasn't just taking an extreme position for the sake of debate. He genuinely didn't get it.

The notion that there's something privileged and somehow sacred about the many variations of the Euro-Caucasian experience in America is destined to fade away. By 2045 or perhaps earlier, depending on which projection you believe, there will be no racial or ethnic majority in the United States.

We will be a huge and varied collection of minorities. This is already the case in our most populous states, California and Texas, and soon may be true in New York as well. White is right as a fundamental assumption, with or without racist intent, cannot possibly be long for this nation—or for this world, if you consider reasonable projections about the rise of China, India, Brazil, and other fast-developing nations that are not European or Anglo-American. But chauvinism is only one reason why the black middle-class experience is so seldom recognized as universal.

The other is the "two worlds" reality—the fact that we tend to keep so much of the black Mainstream experience to ourselves.

At the SCSU homecoming, a man who was selling Obama paraphernalia recognized me from my television appearances and called me over. He offered to give me a T-shirt, my choice of color. "I might give you two if you're a Q," he said.

"I didn't pledge," I told him, "but my father's an Alpha."

"Well, then, I don't know about this whole thing," he said playfully. "I always liked what you had to say when you were up there with Chris Matthews and Keith Olbermann, but I might have to do a reevaluation."

Translation: By asking about my being a Q, he was inquiring whether I was a member of the African American fraternity Omega Psi Phi. The Greek letter omega looks a bit like a capital Q that someone neglected to close at the bottom. Members often have the letter branded on one shoulder—literally burned into the skin with a branding iron, leaving a raised omega-shaped scar. Omega Psi Phi is one of the two most prominent black fraternities; the other is Alpha Phi Alpha, to which my late father belonged. Wherever you find a critical mass of college-educated black men, and I mean *wherever,* you'll find some Qs and some Alphas—and they'll be engaged in friendly, trash-talking rivalry. If your father was a Q, and you decide to pledge, then you naturally become a Q as well. The fraternity system is stronger on historically black campuses, but it's alive and well at white-majority schools as well. Alpha Phi Alpha was founded in 1906 at Cornell, and my father pledged while he was at the University of Michigan. If I hadn't arrived in Ann Arbor in 1970—a moment when the whole Greek thing seemed hopelessly out of touch with the social, cultural, and political revolution that was taking place—I'd surely have become an Alpha, too.

Similarly, sororities are an important lifelong affiliation for many college-educated black women. My mother is a member of Delta Sigma Theta, and naturally my sister, Ellen, when she arrived at Spelman College and decided to pledge, became a Delta, too. The trash-talking between Delta Sigma Theta and Alpha Kappa Alpha—which, truth be told, is the oldest black sorority, predating the Deltas by three years—is more demure than what you hear among the guys, but the rivalry is there just the same. Deltas have a thing about the color red. Whenever you're at an event with a lot of middle-class black women and you notice a statistically significant overabundance of red dresses, you're almost surely among a bunch of Deltas.

Aretha Franklin and Nikki Giovanni are Deltas. Dionne Warwick belongs to another sorority, Zeta Phi Beta. Toni Morrison is an Alpha Kappa Alpha, as was Marian Anderson. Martin Luther King Jr. and W. E. B. Du Bois were Alphas. Bill Cosby, Vernon Jordan, and Michael Jordan are Qs, as were Langston Hughes and Roy Wilkins. These are lifelong affiliations, and while some men and women take them more seriously than others, few who have pledged a black fraternity or sorority take the commitment lightly. When African Americans speak of someone as "my fraternity brother" or "my sorority sister," a connection and even an obligation are implied.

There is nothing secretive or sinister, nothing skull-and-bones-ish about any of these organizations.[11] They were established, beginning about a hundred years ago, to provide mutual support and encouragement among blacks who knew that when they graduated from college they would be taking their hard-won learning into a cruel, openly racist world. Obviously the world today is a different place. But the black fraternities and sororities have endured—and they have remained black.

There's one more African American fraternity I should mention. It isn't a campus affiliation but instead can only be joined—invitation only—by grown men: Sigma Pi Phi, known colloquially as the Boule, from an archaic Greek word meaning "representative assembly." The Boule (pronounced boo-lay) is for high-achieving black professionals, and its reach is nationwide. Once in Sacramento, which few would think of as a magnet for African Americans, my wife, Avis, and I were invited as guests to a Boule Sunday-afternoon get-together. The venue was the expansive, Spanish-colonial style home of a prominent young developer who was serving a term as head of the local Boule chapter. Present were college professors, former campus radicals, doctors, lawyers, financiers, and the like, along with their equally accomplished spouses. The only items on the agenda were food and fellowship. There was talk about the recession and its impact on the California real estate market. There was a certain amount of networking, I suppose, although these were men and women who had known one another long enough to have already made all the possible connections. The real point of the gathering was to gather—to laugh, commiserate, solve the problems of the world, debate the prospects of the Sacramento Kings, and agree on tee times for the coming week. There was something warm and almost womb-like about the afternoon—easy comfort in a house full of total strangers. There was so much we knew about one another's lives without even having to ask.

Everyone present was black. This slice of Mainstream black life—like so much of the cake—is for us. Not for anybody else.

*   *   *

Also, it may not be for long.

The us-against-the-world solidarity of Mainstream black culture is dissipating. On balance, it's hard to argue that this is a bad thing. In fact, it's hard to argue that it's not tremendously encouraging, given our nation's history with race. If there's no longer a bunker mentality, that must mean that those once in the bunker no longer feel themselves under attack. What's happening is assimilation, which is an odd term to use about a group whose first members landed before the *Mayflower*. It seems wrong to speak of assimilating into a society we literally helped build, counterintuitive to think of learning a culture to which we so lavishly contributed. But that's where the black Mainstream is headed—not this generation, perhaps, but surely the next.

My generation, like those that came before, was forged in an all-black context amid a hostile society. I went to all-black schools until integration, at which point I became a member of an embattled black clique. In higher education, the nation was reaching a tipping point: Before, most African Americans had attended historically black colleges and universities, but I graduated high school at a moment when white-majority institutions were actively seeking to attract black students. Today, only about 20 percent of black college students are attending historically black colleges and universities—a complete reversal within just a few decades.

My wife and I grew up in black neighborhoods; one result of integration is that our sons did not. Most of the friends they had while growing up were white. But times had changed, and what we once thought of as "proprietary" black culture had spread beyond any narrow racial context. Black became not just acceptable but cool. Both of my sons have had white friends who spoke Ebonics much more fluently than they did.[12] Likewise, young African Americans are acculturated and can easily converse in today's dialects of Valleyspeak.[13] In black-majority Mainstream community like Prince George's or DeKalb,[14] it is not impossible for white kids to be cool and popular. And it is likely that black students, even if they grow up in mostly black or all-black neighborhoods, will eventually find themselves on white-majority college campuses. The lifelong friends they meet in the dorms will be white, Asian, Latino—the law of averages says they're unlikely to be black. When these Mainstream kids go out with their friends to hear music, it will be in integrated venues—not an all-black nightclub like the Bohemian Caverns of old.[15] My generation had many of these world-expanding college experiences, too. But we had lived through the civil rights movement, the assassination of Dr. King, the riots, the emergence of the Black

Panthers.[16] . . . We had the kind of race consciousness that comes from experience, not a history book.

All of which is a long way of saying that race doesn't matter to our children's generation in the same way it does to ours. It matters less. Change is good. But even welcome, long-awaited changes aren't easy.

For example, teenage angst and rebellion are innovations that Mainstream black America has found hard to accept. When there was a single black America, one of its cultural characteristics was respect for elders. It's not that teenagers or young adults always obeyed their parents—far from it—or that they didn't argue. But most of the insubordination was surreptitious. You did not sass your parents to their faces, no matter how unreasonable the command or how unjust the punishment you were being forced to endure. Once out of the house, of course, you did what you pleased. But you didn't provoke a confrontation. And if a direct confrontation did take place, you knew that even if you were absolutely right on the merits, you were still in the wrong for having forced the issue instead of finding some other way of making your point. You also did not sulk, mope, or whine like the sulky, mopey, whiny white teenagers you saw on television. From what we could tell, it seemed as if black juvenile delinquents were more respectful to their parents than white honor students were to theirs.

Now, Mainstream parents are often confronted with the kind of sassing, sulking, whining, and moping that their own parents never would have tolerated. Perhaps this is an inevitable step in the assimilation process, analogous to young Indian Americans who refuse to go along with arranged marriages, or young Korean Americans who balk at joining the family business. It is a less profound form of rebellion than those other examples. But it frustrates parents and sometimes strains family bonds in a way that many African Americans find alien and distressing.

Another adjustment for Mainstream parents is that the girlfriends and boyfriends their children bring home from high school or college may not be African American. This sets up a conflict between two strongly held Mainstream values—on one side an absolute belief in Dr. King's dream that all be judged solely by the content of their character, on the other a fierce determination that African American history and culture be not only revered but also perpetuated.

Mainstream black America, then, seems in many ways a paradoxical place. We demanded and won the right to live wherever we want, but many of us decide to live together in clumps. We complain, with justification, that the nation seems not to know or acknowledge that middle-class black Americans even exist, but we conduct much of middle-class black American life out of the larger society's field of vision. We marched, studied, and worked our way to the point where we are assimilating, but we have reservations about assimilation if it means giving up our separate identity.

For the Mainstream, race shouldn't matter. But it does.

NOTES

1. Robinson, *Disintegration,* 39.

2. Ibid. Claflin University is a historically black private college founded in 1869, and South Carolina State University is a historically black land-grant institution founded in 1890.

3. Ibid., 41.

4. Ibid., 43.

5. On February 8, 1968, an unarmed group of demonstrators gathered at a local bowling alley in Orangeburg, South Carolina, to protest the owner's segregationist policies. When the mob became agitated, nine South Carolina highway patrol officers fired into the crowd, killing three men and injuring twenty-eight more.

6. Berman, "After They Walk."

7. Bill O'Reilly is a political commentator for the conservative Fox News channel. He is also the author of more than ten books that offer a conservative commentary on American politics and society.

8. Following the retirement of Justice Sandra Day O'Connor, Alito was nominated to the Supreme Court by President George W. Bush in 2005. He is the second Italian American to be elected to the Supreme Court.

9. Originating in the 1970s, "Nuyorican" combines "New York" and "Puerto Rican." It refers to people of Puerto Rican descent who were either born in or immigrated to the New York City area. This term can be used to designate either a person, a group of people, or aspects of a culture.

10. The Reverend Wright is best known for being Barak Obama's former pastor and for the controversial and stylized nature of his sermons. During Obama's presidential campaign, ABC News broadcast clips from several of Wright's sermons in which he is often featured in African-inspired robes deploring the oppressive policies of "white America."

11. Skull and Bones is a secret society of college students founded at Yale University in the late nineteenth century. This society has long been featured in conspiracy theories and myths of popular culture.

12. A term that emerged in the 1990s, "Ebonics" refers to colloquial African American English.

13. "Valleyspeak" refers to the slang, vernacular, and speech patterns of young girls from the San Fernando Valley in California. It was popularized by teen movies and television in the 1990s.

14. Prince George's, Maryland, and DeKalb, Georgia, are counties whose populations are predominantly African American.

15. Established in 1926, this Washington, D.C., nightclub showcased some of the most prominent African American jazz artists of the twentieth century, including Duke Ellington, John Coltrane, and Charles Mingus.

16. Active from 1966 to 1982, the Black Panthers were a black nationalist organization characterized by a militant, socialistic, and revolutionary rhetoric.

Armstrong Williams
(b. 1959)

ᴣ◗ COMMENTATOR

Yes, I voted for Barack Obama.

One of the most controversial conservative voices in America, Armstrong Williams has seen a tumultuous career in media and politics mired in scandals and triumphs. A Christian pundit who champions what he describes as morality, the virtues of capitalism, the sanctity of life, and the sacredness of parenting, he calls for a "revitalization of American society, politics and culture by updating the values of our Founding Fathers and bringing them full force into the twenty-first century."[1] Williams has long straddled a complicated identity as both an insider and an outsider in the world of mainstream journalism and has demonstrated a remarkable professional resiliency that has kept him in the public eye for decades.

Raised with nine siblings on a two-hundred-acre tobacco and swine farm in Marion, South Carolina, Armstrong Williams is a proud third-generation Republican who graduated from South Carolina State University in 1981, having served for two years as student body president. A protégé of South Carolina senator Strom Thurmond, he was—perhaps improbably—given his first glimpse of national politics when he was granted an internship in the famous former segregationist's office. Williams quickly established himself as one of the most notable young black conservatives working in Washington, D.C. He moved among several government positions, working as a legislative aide for South Carolina Republican congressman Carroll Campbell (who later served as governor of South Carolina from 1987 to 1995) and also for South Carolina Republican congressman Floyd Spence in 1981. A critical opportunity came when, at age twenty-one, he was appointed by President Ronald Reagan as a legislative assistant in the U.S. Department of Agriculture (USDA). It was during this time that he first met his mentor, Clarence Thomas, who was working as an attorney for an agricultural firm. While Williams was at the USDA, he was repeatedly frustrated by the assumption that he would be especially interested in "black issues," and yet when Thomas was appointed chairman of the Equal Employment Opportunity Commission (EEOC), Williams went to work for him as his personal assistant from 1983 to 1987.[2]

In a canny move that was to prove either ironic or helpful in the challenges to come, Williams was appointed a vice president of a public relations firm, B & C Associates. He later founded a partnership, with Stedman Graham (educator, entrepreneur, and perhaps best known as the consort of Oprah Winfrey), called the Graham Williams Group (an organization whose name has remained the same but in which Graham no longer has any financial stake).[3]

Williams's involvement with media escalated after 1991, when Clarence Thomas, a nominee for the U.S. Supreme Court, faced accusations of having sexually harassed Anita Hill, a subordinate, during his time at the EEOC. Fervently defending Thomas, Williams used his growing media platform on talk radio—particularly the Washington, D.C., station WOL—to rally black Americans to support Thomas's nomination. His local radio show, *The Right Side with Armstrong Williams,* was syndicated in 1995 and distributed to increasingly large media markets across the nation. From 2002 to 2005 Williams hosted *On Point with Armstrong Williams,* a cable television news program. His first book, an account of a dialogue with an anonymous street hustler, titled *Beyond Blame: How We Can Succeed by Breaking the Dependency Barrier* (New York: Free Press, 1995), helped propel his reputation as a man with a vast resource of advice and a compelling command of oratory and rhetoric.

His rising career came to a sudden halt, however, when he became the central figure in a Bush administration scandal. In 2005, *USA Today* reported that Williams had accepted $240,000 from a PR firm that was contracted by the U.S. Department of Education to promote the No Child Left Behind Act (NCLB). While Williams acknowledged later that he had taken the money and that doing so had been an instance of "poor judgment" from which he had learned, he argued that it never altered his feeling that the Act was in the best interests of America's children:[4] "I had long endorsed school vouchers as an instrument of empowerment for children—mostly of color—languishing in underfunded public schools. I had been promoting the ideas of NCLB in my writings and speeches before the program even existed."[5]

Nonetheless, in the wake of what many media watchdogs described as an egregious violation of both the government's legal obligation to refrain from propagandizing and the media's ethical duty to avoid the appearance that its opinions could be purchased, Williams's contract with Tribune Media Services (which had syndicated his work) was terminated. As the president of the National Society of Newspaper Columnists, Suzette Standring commented on the Department of Education's subsequent report on the event in 2005: "The report comes across as a chagrined 'oopsie!' It describes Armstrong's hiring to shill for No Child Left Behind policies as 'poor judgment.' We maintain 'ethical lapse.' They say 'mistake,' we say 'abuse.' In our dictionary, the Department of Education's 'public relations minority outreach' is better defined under 'covert propaganda.' You say potahto, I say 'payola.'"[6]

These brutal assessments were hard to recover from. When the Government Accountability Office released a report of its own later in 2005 concluding that because there had not been any public disclosure of the government's role in this PR effort, the Department of Education's payments to Williams had been illegal, Williams's career was shattered.

Williams reflects upon these events in the featured excerpt from his latest book, *Reawakening Virtues: Restoring What Makes America Great* (Sarasota, Fla.: New Chapter, 2011). He writes: "I was forced to take a sabbatical—a long, compulsory Sabbath." Williams is evidently done with his sabbatical now, however, and into the full swing of a workweek with an expanding list of newspaper columns and blog posts. Since 2008 he has hosted a number of radio shows and been regularly featured on the speakers' circuit for conservative media programs. He has appeared on Fox News as a commentator as well as occasionally on NPR, MSNBC, and CNN. As of 2011, despite some skepticism from his critics, he became a regular columnist for the *Washington Times* and a frequent contributor to *The Hill*, an influential newspaper and website that covers Congress.[7]

With the publication of *Reawakening Virtues*, Williams may be on the ascendancy again. His reflections on race politics in America and the Obama presidency now receive a wide audience and perhaps demonstrate that it took the election of a black president to allow a discredited foe the platform not only to opine against the new status quo but to re-create himself.

ཉ❧ Excerpt from Reawakening Virtues: Restoring What Makes America Great

"The Virtue of the Sabbath"

Growing up in the Williams household in South Carolina in the 1960s, all of us worked cropping tobacco, slopping hogs, tending to the cattle, picking the garden, baling hay, caring for the chickens or cultivating the land with the tractor. We worked every day from dawn to as long as there was sunlight, Monday through Saturday. There was always still more to be done at sundown; you couldn't ever get ahead. While other people had two days off on the weekend, we only had Sunday, our celebration of the Sabbath. On Sunday morning, instead of rising at 5:00 A.M., we didn't have to be out of bed until 7:00 A.M., and boy, those two hours were a big deal! It was only expected of us to have breakfast as a family, and attend Sunday school and church. When church finally let out around 1:00 P.M. or 2:30 P.M., depending on which service we attended, we had the whole afternoon to ourselves to play or watch sports, sleep and relax! Let me tell you, did we ever need that time to rest. Monday was always the worst day of the week, perhaps because we knew it would be six more days until we had another Sunday. The Sabbath was something I really looked forward to, because even when in church, I fell asleep half the time—that's how tired I was.

In life, we are generally more effective when we set aside time to recharge. Retirement is one type of rest in the celebration of accomplishments, but the Sabbath is a day-long period each week when we are meant to renew ourselves. In so doing, we become more effective at work as we have something positive to anticipate each week, and can enter each work week refreshed. According to Jesus, the Sabbath was made for man.

Still, daily, people from all walks of life often say they are just too busy and wish they could find more time to relax and revitalize. The pressures of work and family, the ringing of cell phones, the piles of e-mails; they can sap our energy and dampen our spirits. Unless, of course, amidst all of this work we can find the means to renew ourselves, and to rejoice in the beauty of the world, the caring of our friends and the precious moments that we have.

You may think it odd for me to start a book about reawakening virtues with a chapter on resting, especially in difficult times, when having all hands on deck to right the ship is critical. Well, I believe that especially in such times, rather than charging into the fray, it is crucial to take a step back to understand why we got in this mess in the first place in order to come up with a coherent plan to move forward. Sometimes, just taking time out to reconnect with our inner self, our sense of purpose and our spiritual truths may be the most sensible and productive thing we can do in the short run. We would do well to make the Sabbath a regular part of our lives and honor it more often.

My Own Wake-up Call

I'd like to share a deeply personal experience that reacquainted me with the importance and power of the Sabbath—a story that starts with one of the lowest points of my entire life, but ends in one of its greatest awakenings.

The last several years have been very challenging for me. My career as a political commentator and public media figure was effectively destroyed in 2005 after it was disclosed that I had accepted money from the Bush administration to help promote the No Child Left Behind Act (NCLB), and that I had used my nationally syndicated TV show to advertise the cause.[8] At that time, I honestly didn't give much thought to helping the administration spread its message on education reform. I had long endorsed school vouchers as an instrument of empowerment for children—mostly of color—languishing in underfunded public schools. I had been promoting the ideals of NCLB in my writings and speeches before the program even existed, but given my new relationship with the administration, it became necessary to disclose the advertising/public relations contract on all of our media outlets, including TV, radio and print. Once the Department of Education started paying me for creating advertising—commercials that were fully disclosed—it didn't occur to me that continuing to espouse my beliefs in my written syndicated column, which the administration was not paying me to write, might be inappropriate and seem like a conflict of interest. They were my beliefs after all. I was getting paid to promote something I believed in, and I promoted it through my other work as well! It seemed like a match made in heaven.

Unfortunately, that's not how dealing with the government works, as I have learned all too well. It doesn't matter what prior beliefs I might have held; it matters how my actions as a public figure are perceived, and whether my negligence could have caused me to do something unethical.

Please understand, I don't mean to excuse my actions in these matters. All of us who hold the public trust as journalists and members of the media should on no account engage contractually with any government agency or entity. (Boy, do I know that now!) The very nature of these arrangements presents an inherent conflict of interest, and controversy will eventually ensue. Under no circumstances will I ever allow myself, or any of my business entities, to engage in compensated government services again.

While I emphasize that our television and radio spots for NCLB were fully disclosed, occasionally mentioning NCLB in my column led Tribune Media Services, which syndicated my column, to sever ties because I never disclosed the professional relationship to them. From there, things snowballed: The mere appearance of impropriety caused the collapse of my entire media platform. Overnight, my life's work crumbled and flaked away. The results were devastating, not only financially, but also to my sense of purpose in life.

As a child I had come across an old proverb that read, "Any man who starts work before dawn each day will become rich." For the vast majority of my life, I carried those words with me not just as an inspiration, but as a source of strength. I awoke every morning before dawn and got started with my workday. It took years, but I accumulated a small media empire. By 2003, my newspaper column was syndicated in over 50 outlets across the country, and so were my television and radio broadcasts. I owned an international public relations firm. I regularly appeared on the news to offer my opinion on the events of the day. I was having the time of my life.

And then, in an instant, it all slipped away.

The rapid descent was disorienting. For as long as I could remember, I had defined myself by my drive for financial security. I had little to no regard for taking the type of rest that would help me collect my thoughts and avoid mistakes that come from chasing heedlessly after economic success.

But now, whether I wanted to or not, I was forced to take a sabbatical—a long, compulsory Sabbath. It wasn't easy. There were moments of despair when I nearly lost myself. In time, however, with hours spent in contemplation, I regained my equilibrium. Along the way, I realized that I had missed something essential in my relentless toiling. There were aspects of my life that had been constructed upon shaky stilts. Every victory, every moment of pre-dawn striving was nothing more than a means to nourish my ego and sense of self-importance. In my published commentaries, I spoke often about morals and religion. While much of my own life had a strong moral base, some of it was being compromised by my desire to acquire wealth and obtain national recognition as a media pundit. Once that material wealth disappeared and I was no longer invited to appear on the cable or national networks, I realized that my life lacked a real foundation from which to judge right or wrong. I had been on this Earth for nearly five decades and the grand sum total of what I had accomplished amounted to little more than a testament to my personal vanity.

I started to attend church more regularly and communicated these feelings to my pastor, Frank Tucker. I told him that I had spent much my life trying to make sure that I never experienced financial or material poverty, but now it seemed that, despite my absolute best effort—every bit of energy that I could muster—I was slipping back down to where I had begun.

"Maybe there is much more to feeling fulfillment in one's life beyond acquiring wealth and materialism," I sighed.

"Probably, it just means that you made a mistake, and that a little rest and spiritual reflection would serve you well," he replied.

He then talked to me about the importance of the Sabbath as an instrument for people to remove themselves from the boorish and egocentric concerns of everyday life. He recounted how the Sabbath law in its original intent was meant to give the Jews a special time to remember God, who brought them out of slavery, and to enhance their well-being through rest (Deuteronomy 5:12).

But it was in Matthew 11:28–30 that he found and paraphrased what perfectly summed up the importance of the Sabbath for me:

"Are you tired? Worn out? Burned out on religion? Come to me. Get away with me and you'll recover your life. I'll show you how to take a real rest. Walk with me and work with me—watch how I do it. Learn the unforced rhythms of grace. I won't lay anything heavy or ill-fitting on you. Keep company with me and you'll learn to live freely and lightly."

What the Pastor Tucker was trying to tell me—in his gentle way—was that no amount of money can truly lessen our human anxiety. Clarity and balance require a calm mindfulness that is honed through the weekly Sabbath. This is more than a ritual; it is a means to briefly remove oneself from society, in order to reconnect with one's deeper truths, and then to figure out how to do good in return.

The time of weekly reflection and relaxation is something that is necessary to the proper functioning of a human being. Taking time out to rest probably would have helped me to do some introspection into what I was doing; I might not have had to experience the turmoil of my ruinous decision.

Fortunately, I was able to learn from my wounds, heal and live long enough to regain what I had lost. And I conduct my life very differently now.

Yet even today, a number of years later, there are people who question my writings and what I say on television or radio, who insist that I'm a media whore, and ask why I should be given space on TV or in print when I violated their trust. Though many have graciously forgiven my actions and have allowed me to put that past behind me, there will always be those who will question my credibility—doubters who will never give me a second chance. Forgiveness is not a free pass from consequences; I accept that it is a price I have to pay.

Benefits of the Sabbath

I'm sure all of us can come up with a situation in which acting rashly has caused more trouble than it was worth, a time when just taking a step back and slowing down a little could have prevented a disaster. This benefit is just one of the perks of observing a weekly Sabbath. As most of us get two days off from work every weekend, we should use one of those days for reflection, preferably on the Creator who encouraged us to observe it in the first place.

In this busy, rushed society of today, we like to cram our schedules so full that there's no time to relax and recharge, and to pursue softer, yet critical matters like family and good friendships. In many cases, we make finances the ultimate goal and neglect all else. However, the world in which we live is driven by relationships, like it or not. Indeed, should some harm befall us, it's usually those we neglected who come to our aid (hopefully).

Taking a Sabbath day gives one the necessary time to protect and, if needed, repair those relationships.

Doesn't it seem odd that we would neglect our safety net? Do you suppose tightrope walkers ever become lax about their safety harnesses, or skydivers about their parachutes? In a world in which we purchase insurance for everything, it seems only logical that we'd want to cultivate the free insurance, or perhaps assurance, that comes from a healthy family relationship and deep friendships. The American Dream is about life, liberty and the pursuit of happiness. Too many of us have tried to replace the third with the pursuit of wealth, but wealth doesn't necessarily bring about happiness, whereas good relationships do. And there is no better way to work on those relationships than during time spent enjoying the Sabbath.

As a nation, we need to bring our focus back to appreciating what's most important in life: our relationships and ourselves. In order to properly cultivate both, we need time. This is why it was suggested so long ago that we take one day out of the week for rest, "Six days shalt thou labour, and do all thy work: But the seventh day is the sabbath . . . in it thou shalt not do any work" (Exodus 20:9–10).

No one truly wants to be an Ebenezer Scrooge, abundantly wealthy, but with no one to call his own.[9] Try to take a Sabbath—if not once a week, then at least once a month—to recharge yourself and reinforce your relationships. See for yourself what a difference a Sabbath can make, and then pass it along to reawaken this virtue in those around you.

❧ "The Morality of Race: The Virtues of Tolerance and Patience"

One of the great moral issues of our time is almost never discussed as such in a reasonable, productive way. Sure, we talk about it often. As a matter of fact, hardly a day goes by without it coming up on one of the major cable news channels or talk radio shows across the nation. It divides Republicans and Democrats and polarizes the parties more than almost anything else. And very few who discuss it do so in a way that makes sense.

I'm talking about racism. And not the mere *existence* of racism, because as long as we're mortal human beings, racism will always exist. The moral issue of racism I'm concerned with here is how poisonous conversations about it have become, to the point where taking a public-policy position, even on something entirely unrelated to race, is seen through the prism of skin color.

That's not to say that *no one* takes the problem of true racism seriously. No doubt many in this country do. Democrats are convinced it's the overriding "issue" or "problem" of our day; although deep down, behind closed doors, it's probably more a function of good retail politics for them, a means to rallying their base and maintaining a constituency, than it is a truly systemic crisis, much less a serious moral concern. Republicans are just as guilty of failing to see it as a moral crisis. They're the ones always on the defensive as alleged racists and respond mostly in talking-point fashion to attacks by Democrats. I guess that's just "politics as usual."

But it shouldn't be. Racism is not just a question of good or bad politics, not just a matter of scoring or losing points in the fight for votes from a constituency. It has profound moral implications, because those who exploit race appeal to the baser, primal aspects of human nature, which pit people against one another in ways we ought to have left behind in the Stone Age.

That is why I believe it is time to counter this unfortunate situation with the twin virtues of tolerance and patience.

Here's the reality: In the United States, if you're a Republican, the left considers you a racist by default, almost no matter what you say or do. If you're a Democrat, your colleagues on the right think you can say or do almost anything—no matter how offensive—and get away with it, virtually guaranteed never to be called a racist.

I bet—and it's crazy to have to think this way—that whether you're a Republican or Democrat, as you read the above paragraph, you likely agreed with it. You Republican readers probably thought to yourselves, "You're right. How sad that my economic and social conservatism makes me a de facto racist;" and you Democratic readers probably thought, "Exactly! Republicans are all racist and I'm not and couldn't possibly be. Your point is?"

Tolerance, or rather the lack thereof, is my point. By automatically labeling one whole segment of the political spectrum as racist, the left has attempted to de-legitimize all conservative thought. It's a red herring. Rather than listen to and consider the true merits or flaws of conservatism, especially in regards to how policies will affect minorities, every idea is labeled as racially insensitive and therefore, inherently bad.

The virtue of tolerance demands that you check your prejudices at the door and consider the person and their beliefs based on their merits. We ask that all people do this when dealing with someone of a different race, yet how quickly we forget to exercise the same ideal when discussing politics.

Let us take the recent health care bill.[10] The prevailing assumption throughout the debate was that Republicans were acting as a monolith—all of them rich, well-to-do whites who themselves, of course, couldn't possibly have known anyone who lacked health coverage—and that their opposition to running a health care system for more than 300 million people out of Washington couldn't have stemmed from a different understanding of economics or public policy. It had to have been motivated by the drive to keep minorities out of their hospitals.

Likewise, during the financial regulation debate, opposition to the Democrats' legislation couldn't have possibly stemmed from fear of overregulation or of stifling the economy, but instead must have had its origin in the massive, white Republican monolith's need to protect its own kind: white bankers on Wall Street. As if Republicans had no skin in the game, and only black and Hispanic Democrats lost their homes and saw their 401(k)s cut in half as a result of the crash!

How can we accomplish anything of major national importance—whether it be helping the uninsured get health coverage or overhauling the financial system—if those who stand on one side of the divide are assumed to be acting and thinking out of a deep hatred for people of color?

The Politics of Race

The fact that a substantial number of black Americans call themselves Republicans should counter the blanket charge that Republicans are racist, but it doesn't. With the growing presence of blacks on the conservative airwaves (Larry Elder, myself and others), in the op-ed sections of major newspapers (e.g., Thomas Sowell, Shelby Steele and Walter Williams), and in the halls of power (Congressmen Tim Scott and Allen West, Supreme Court Justice Clarence Thomas, former Secretary of State Condoleezza Rice and former Republican National Chairman Michael Steele) you would think the idea that Republican policy positions are inherently racist would have dissipated by now.[11] After all, isn't it difficult to believe that such bright, accomplished and well-educated conservative black men and women would be somehow incapable of seeing that their conservatism is in fact a brand of racism? It should be hard to believe, but the sad truth is that black and Hispanic conservatives continue to be stigmatized either as dupes or traitors to their own race.

What you'll often hear from black conservatives like me is that the left's solutions to the problems that ail minority communities are themselves racist, since they operate on the fundamental premise that minorities are incapable. There's almost nothing, according to Democrats, that minorities can accomplish without the help of the government. To hear some Democrats speak, minorities are incapable of doing just about anything without a handout or a leg up.

Believing—as white and black conservatives alike do—that minorities don't need anyone's help to get ahead in life may be naïve, but it is not racist. And it is certainly not as racist as the notion underpinning Democratic policy: that minorities can't make it in this world without free money, special scholarships, quotas, affirmative action, lower admissions standards, and other mechanisms employed to propel them forward. After all, isn't racism defined as a belief in the inherent inferiority of a group of people based on

their skin color? And yet it is somehow, inexplicably, *not* racist if your intentions are good—not to hold them down, but to help them out.

Thus, we black Republicans find ourselves labeled Uncle Toms, race traitors, and Oreos (black on the outside, white on the inside) for daring to say
no, no, no, we don't need anyone's—much less the government's—help to get
ahead in life. We live in a world where saying that we're all equal and no one
person deserves a handout more than the person sitting next to him makes
us a racist.

The litany of accusations can reach absurd proportions. So you want
public schools to focus more on teaching about this nation's founding than on
the history of Swahili in Africa? You're a racist. So you want the government
to stop handing out our tax dollars to companies simply because they're run
by blacks or Hispanics? You must be a racist. And you want to keep health
insurance the way it is, and not turn it all over to politicians and bureau-
crats in Washington? You must be a racist. It sure gets tiresome, doesn't it?

It all goes back to the lack of tolerance for others' beliefs regardless of
race, and the failure to exercise patience in order to understand why Republicans of all colors believe as they do.

Natural Behavior or Racism?

There are many tendencies fundamental to our nature that we must curb,
fight against and work hard to outright overcome. Whether it's shouting at
our bosses, swearing at our spouses, flirting with a married woman or eating a third piece of pumpkin pie on Thanksgiving—whatever the case might
be—we are constantly battling against the unsavory, uncivilized and self-
destructive impulses and appetites that come from within.

Similarly, there are some aspects of seeing people based on color that we
simply are not going to ever eradicate from the human race, even though we
would like to be able to. Some people don't want to hear this—people who
would even consider such a statement racist—so let me start gingerly by discussing other forms of discrimination that don't provoke the same reaction.

No one seems to have a problem with Jews who prefer to date and marry
other Jews, or Catholics who prefer to do the same (or Mormons, atheists,
Democrats, Republicans, and so on). Why? Because it makes sense that people naturally gravitate towards those who share their worldview—or, in the
case of religion, the same Other World view. If, as a devout Catholic, you
believe that those who don't accept Jesus as their savior are going to hell,
you'd naturally prefer to marry someone not destined for fire and brimstone,
and whose presence won't risk hellfire for the children you have together.
Some people might consider such thinking kooky, especially if they're not
religious, but at the very least, they would probably respect the right to see
the world this way and not judge them as bigoted. Most reasonable people

consider it perfectly legitimate for someone to "discriminate" in his or her dating choices by limiting options to those with the same religious beliefs.

Then there are the practical mechanics of making a lifelong marriage work. Marriage is hard enough—there are struggles about finances, parenting philosophy, personality differences and whether to watch the ball game or "Desperate Housewives"—without adding an even bigger struggle over the basic questions of who we are, where we come from, and where we're going when it all comes to an end. So, from a practical standpoint, marriage and dating are simply easier with people with whom you have all this in common.

The same holds true when it comes to politics. No doubt many "intra-political" marriages work just fine, but for the most part, Republicans and conservatives date and marry other Republicans and conservatives. The same typically goes for Democrats and liberals—if only because they usually spend most of their time with like-minded friends and colleagues, making it a sort of self-selecting, self-limited pool of dating prospects.

Most of us understand all of this just fine. Since few seem to have a problem with folks limiting their marital choices based on religion, worldview and maybe even politics, let's turn the discussion up a notch. What about blacks who prefer to marry blacks, Asians who prefer to marry Asians, and whites who prefer to marry whites? Are they racist? Not necessarily. Sure, some might be; that goes without saying, as racists come in all sizes and shapes.

However, I'd argue that the vast majority of them aren't racist. It's more a question of inexpressible taste. When a black person dates only other black people it's more than likely because he happens to be attracted to other black people. There are some black men who might be attracted to white or Hispanic women, and might even casually date them, but would never consider marrying and having children with someone outside their own race. When pushed to explain why, you'd likely get one of two answers: that it could never work socially, including his parents' disapproval; or because, although he may never have thought about this—much less expressed it—he wants his children to look like him.

It may seem unseemly; it may seem unfortunate, and some might even call it wrong for folks to limit their dating and marriage prospects that way. I agree that it's lamentable. What you can't argue, though, is whether it's natural, because the desire to be with others who look and think like you seems to be a fundamental characteristic of human behavior.

If this subconscious desire is truly racist, is it something today's social tinkerers—the progressives who believe that human nature is like a huge chemistry set, and by just changing the equations, they will create a perfect humanity, free of hunger, suffering and violence—can fix through policy?

No. You can't change most things about human nature that way. There are so many nuances to the issue of race relations that it's impossible for policy to get at them all, and I would argue it's not even desirable that we try. Just imagine a bunch of liberal Ivy League grads sitting around a Senate committee conference table to come up with a plan to eradicate subtle racism in American dating. It boggles the mind.

We seem to have lost sight of the real and socially relevant definition of racism: the belief that some people are inferior and, as such, deserve fewer civil-rights protections than others, purely because of the color of their skin. And that is what we should deal with, not some perceived covert racism characterized by interpersonal relationships, but overt racism expressed to the detriment of its intended victims.

Is it true that everyone who marries within their own race or culture or ethnicity specifically does so because they believe others are inferior? Of course not. The real question is—and indeed the only question that matters from a public-policy standpoint—would these same people deny someone employment in their workplace or otherwise repudiate the full humanity of that person because of his or her skin color? That's what matters; that's what we as a society need to be focused on.

The Soft Bigotry of Low Expectations

Liberals are quick to decry legacy admissions to universities (in which the children of alumni—usually big-time donor alumni—are granted admission). They also reject nepotism in the workplace and silver-spoon heirs who take over their fathers' companies—all on the grounds that what should matter most in all of these scenarios is merit, not connections, family trees, and contributions to university coffers. The underlying assumption is: Were it not for these crucial elements, the people who benefit from them would never have been considered. In other words, liberals stereotype all such beneficiaries as unqualified, but for daddy's reputation and checkbook.

Tell me you don't hear this every time a liberal discusses it—in language dripping with contempt, and probably envy, for the obviously *mediocre* family members of important people who capitalize on their family name to get ahead when their own skills wouldn't have allowed it.

And yet somehow in their minds, the race-preferential policies they support don't carry with them the same stigma. Because we're talking about essentially the same problem, aren't we? Chances are, the children of well-educated Harvard graduates are just as well-educated and prepared to be students at Harvard as their parents were—even "legacy" beneficiaries must have stellar scores and resumes to get in—and yet, you don't ever hear liberals conceding that minorities who are pushed through school are widely perceived as less qualified than their white counterparts.

Why the disconnect? The answer is simple: politics.

The reality is that *both* Democrats and Republicans are absolutely right when they decry whichever set of preferential policies they oppose—legacy admissions and nepotism, on the one hand, and race-preferential policies on the other. The key difference is that the former only affects a handful of companies and random individuals who work in and, in some cases, run the "big businesses," while the latter has a vastly negative impact on entire classes of people in our 300-million-plus nation.

So, while the recipient of a legacy admission to Harvard might have to live with a stigma, he also might not. After all, he'll have the Harvard degree, and few of his future employers will be any the wiser that his rich alumnus daddy got him into school; he'll either succeed in the real world or he won't. Likewise, someone who inherits millions, without having done anything to earn it, won't have a tattoo on his forehead spelling out "silver-spoon-fed"— and even if he did, who cares? He'd have millions to play with. Sure, his immediate circle of friends and family will know, but something altogether more pernicious, pervasive and wrong follows around a minority who rises to the top throughout society: *affirmative-action beneficiary.*

With admissions quotas in place at many colleges and universities that require less of minority applicants, that nasty epithet—*affirmative-action beneficiary*—has become commonplace.

Walter Williams of George Mason University in 2002 said of the University of California's race-preferential policy:

> [The policy] is both disgusting and racially condescending. More blacks and Hispanics will be admitted to the University of California by associating them not with academic excellence, but with social and psychological pathology and dysfunction. It teaches black youngsters that victimhood is the ticket to college and academic preparation is a side issue. It's a concession that blacks cannot academically compete and to expect them to do so is racism.

Is it any wonder then that a prospective employer *might* also wonder if a minority applicant treated "academic preparation" as "a side issue" while in school, and whether he or she was unable to "academically compete" with other white applicants? And would white—and even minority—employers be wrong or racially insensitive to ask themselves such questions? I'd argue that they'd be no more wrong than an employer who's skeptical of the abilities of a legacy-admission, silver-spoon-fed white applicant.

Our First Black President

Racism is a funny thing, even though few find the humor in it and it's clearly not a laughing matter when the effects of it are real.

Black comedians from Richard Pryor to Dave Chapelle have made a living pointing out the absurdity of racism that all groups practice.[12] By shining the light on the imbecilic nature of such prejudice, they actually do more to promote a dialogue and understanding than any politician can dream of, including Barack Obama—whose election as president of the United States was no doubt, regardless of your politics, a tremendous moment in the history of our nation.

It was a tough choice for conservatives like me. Obama and I couldn't disagree more on policy, but I admit that I, too, was enamored of his rhetoric of hope, change and healing, and I truly believed he meant it when he said he would bridge the partisan divide in Washington and govern from the center. Like millions of others, I got caught up in his "Yes, we can!" message.

Yes, I voted for Barack Obama.

That's not easy for me to admit. As a long-time observer of and commentator on the political process—and as an inside-the-Beltway resident of Washington—I fell for it. But I comfort myself in knowing that I wasn't alone. As a matter of fact, I'm convinced it's why Obama is president and not Senator John McCain—a lot of people fell for it. Sure, the Democrats voted for him unapologetically, but they would have voted for Hillary Clinton or any other would-be nominee. What won the election for Obama was people like me who were captivated by his persona and, more importantly, wanted to be a part of history—who wanted to vote for the first black president.

So, while I regret my vote, I make no apologies for it. I'm not the first person in history to fall for a politician's empty promises of reasonableness and moderation. But I think the way I voted is instructive on the subject of race in America. It's another example of just how compelling an issue it is, how central to our human nature, that even a conservative like myself could vote for one of the most liberal senators in Congress.

Life certainly hasn't been easy for President Obama since his election. The broad array of constituencies that brought the president to power has proven difficult for him to manage this election season, as he seeks to galvanize a fractured base to defend his party's agenda against a strong Republican onslaught.

Liberals are disappointed because he has not been the transformative progressive they envisioned. Independents are disappointed because he has dramatically increased government spending and raised our national debt to previously unimaginable levels. Internationalists are disappointed because his foreign popularity has not translated into a de-escalation of global conflict.

But of all the complaints about the president from his constituents, some of the most bitter come from black Americans. Obama's 91% approval rating among blacks (according to the Gallup Poll in early 2011) masks a current of ambivalence coursing through the black community. This murmur of frustration speaks loudly about the distorting power of race in presidential politics.

Although they represent only a relatively small part of the overall electorate, blacks came out in record numbers to vote for the president. Consequently, many in the black community feel a sense of ownership of Obama—as if he's "their" president, and not America's. On a recent black journalist's panel, popular radio host Joe Madison went so far as to suggest that Obama recruit a shadow panel of black advisors to guide him through the White House.[13] Still others have pinned the hopes of an entire race on President Obama, a set of expectations that no other American president has ever faced.

In the real world, however, such misplaced hopes actually work against Obama and the black community. If he were to give in to these demands and, say, appoint a special "black cabinet," or implement explicitly race-based policies, he'd quickly lose the rest of America and the White House in short order. Yet despite these stakes, disillusioned blacks have signaled that they would rather not vote at all than heed Obama's recent pleas for renewed enthusiasm to prevent a GOP takeover. "What do we care? Obama's agenda isn't helping us," is the refrain one often hears.

Perhaps more damaging than the average black citizen's disappointment is that powerful factions among black leaders have refused to stir up support for the president. They are sitting on their hands, apparently jealous because Obama skipped to the front of the line ahead of them. This started during the presidential campaign with notable gaffes by Jesse Jackson, and it continues today in more private settings.

The prism of race has obscured a realistic view of the Obama administration. It's not going to solve all of black America's problems—no government, no matter how representatively black, ever will. To put this matter in perspective, the black community is still complaining about the same issues it was griping about 40 years ago—through successive generations of liberal and conservative administrations. What makes anyone think that things will miraculously change because the chief executive happens to have brown skin?

Gripe if you must, but the policies that Obama has managed to pass in the first term arguably benefit blacks disproportionately. He passed health care legislation. Guess which ethnic minority has the largest percentage of uninsured? He passed laws regulating against predatory lending. Who suffers the most from lack of access to affordable credit? He stepped in to ease foreclosures and pressed banks to negotiate with distressed mortgage holders. Which community suffers the most from foreclosures?

Some complain that Obama only appointed four blacks to his cabinet, the same number (although none as high-ranking) as George W. Bush during his first term, and three fewer than Bill Clinton. That equates to 13%, roughly the same percentage as blacks in the U.S. population. Perhaps if Obama had appointed, say, 10 blacks, it would make the community happy. But imagine the outcry from the media and other races and ethnic minorities (not just white, but also Hispanics, who make up over 16% of the population, and Asians, who constitute 3%) over such apparent bias. Would that have truly helped heal the racial divide?

So what else could Obama have done to specifically help blacks without managing to offend the other 87% of the country? Was he supposed to pay their mortgages and bills? Give them raises? Put free food on their tables? Give their children all A grades and then pay for their college educations out of the public treasury?

When it comes to those white Americans who are uncomfortable with a black president, there has been no shortage of racial distortion either. Some have tried to use Obama's skin color and Muslim name to prey upon the fears of a white electorate that has seen its economic prosperity plummet amid an overall decline in America's global influence. Others have even gone so far as to question his citizenship and his birthright. Still others have deliberately misconstrued his political philosophy in a racially tinged manner—asserting that he's an African anti-colonial revolutionary.

While it is fine to disagree with the president's policies, to suggest that his political failures have to do with his race is just plain wrong. The sentiment of disdain voiced by some dissenters about "your black president" ignores the fact that it took a majority of white voters—including disillusioned supporters of the previous administration—to elect him. The broader community should let Obama rise and fall on his own merits, and not make this a litmus test about the fitness of a certain race to lead the country.

On the other hand, Obama's supporters should be careful not to dismiss genuine criticism as an attack on the president's race. The fact is that both major parties have played a role in causing the current economic and social crisis facing America. Say what you want about the Tea Party's racist elements, the movement as a whole provides a forum for people's legitimate concerns about the ongoing bankrupting of America.

As it stands, President Obama is forced to walk the razor's edge. If he is too black, one side gets hysterical. If he is not black enough, the other side wails and laments. But in reality, Obama represents a clear choice that the majority of American voters of all races and ethnic backgrounds made about the type of leadership they wanted at a time of acute crisis in this country. People should hold the president and his administration accountable for their actions. They also have every right to change the country's direction by electing new leaders. However, reducing the Obama presidency to a matter of racial politics trivializes the real reasons he was elected, and obscures the path to our nation's recovery.

The Virtues of Tolerance and Patience

I have touched on many aspects of the race issue. The overarching theme, though, is that some aspects of it are not likely to ever go away entirely, even with the most robust and thoughtful public policy ever imagined. When it comes to race relations, we are overcoming our past failings. The Declaration of Independence proclaimed that all men are created equal, but throughout history, one group has rarely treated others with egalitarianism. Still, we tend to forget that we, as a nation, have made extraordinary progress in living up to ideals articulated by our Founding Fathers.

As Americans, we act like "it only happens here," for better or worse, and often receive foreign criticism as if our sordid, racially divided past were a uniquely American phenomenon. But guess what? Today, most countries have much worse situations—Australia's discrimination of Aborigines, France and Germany's treatment of Muslim immigrants, wholesale slaughter of fellow Africans from other tribes, China's oppression of its non-Han minorities, Japan's underlying prejudice against all gaijin, and so on and so forth. This doesn't excuse America's past or current behaviors; instead, it serves as an illustration that racial discrimination is a long-standing human problem, and one that America addresses quite publicly, for all the world to see. In fact, our determination to deal with our problems with race upfront, even if it makes us uncomfortable, is commendable; we should give ourselves credit for using the ideal that "all men are created equal" as our ultimate goal, expanding the concept well past its original scope to include the whole of humanity.

The virtues we learn from the evils of racism are tolerance and patience—tolerance for others and patience to realize how far we've come. No one can seriously argue that America is not a more tolerant place than it was 50 years ago. The strides we have made are remarkable, not only in regards to race, but also to gender relations and sexual preferences—generally accepting the fact that others are different.

There are signs that even some age-old attitudes are undergoing transformation. All we have to do is look at the dramatic change in how Americans feel about interracial relationships over the past 60 years and the increase in such relationships and marriages. In 1950, 94% of Americans were opposed to interracial relationships. Fast forward to 2007 and 77% of the population approves of such relationships with only 17% opposing. In the past 10 years alone, interracial marriages have risen by 20%. These changes are amazing and ongoing, and they prove that people are becoming more tolerant.

Even on TV, shows like "Scrubs" and "Psych" are built around the best friendships of their black and white stars.[14] The characters riff back and forth, not only on each other, but on racial stereotypes in general. They show interracial friendships as they truly are: just like every other friendship. There is no prejudice to overcome on their part, because it never enters their minds. Unburdened by the fear of racism and drama of overcoming past beliefs, they are free to mock the standard racial conventions. Such shows help stimulate tolerance and understanding just by their example and humor.

But despite these positive developments, we still have people screaming at the top of their lungs that we're in a downward spiral and that Americans are more prejudiced than ever. You know, some of the most intolerant people I've met are those who fiercely promote general tolerance, all the while berating those who do not share their beliefs. "If you are not tolerant of the same things/people/beliefs I am, well, then you are ignorant scum." Does this encourage dialogue and allow us to move forward?

Tolerance is measured by how you deal with those who are different from you and your peers. It is revealed by not acting on some prejudice and discriminating in a negative fashion, and dedicating yourself to treating your fellow men and women with respect, compassion and understanding. This does not mean that one has to like everyone. We all have the right not to like another person. Tolerance also means accepting those feelings respectfully and moving on with your lives. By showing greater tolerance and even forgiveness of those who are different, we hold a mirror up to their own beliefs. In doing so, they come to see that we aren't so different, that everyone is a fallible human being with his or her own dreams and troubles.

The virtue of patience is not only a matter of accepting alternate points of view, skin color, religious values, etc., but also of understanding that prejudice is not overcome in one night. "Rome wasn't built in a day," and neither can we believe that we will wake up tomorrow with all racial issues resolved. Yet this was a trap that many, both black and white, fell into with the election of Obama. We woke up on January 21, 2009 to an America filled with the same racial issues that we always had, and have done so every day since. Just a brief look at history will allow us to measure how far we have come from the days of Dred Scott and Jim Crow laws. We should always use Dr. Martin Luther King's dream as the goal, while judging our progress by comparing the struggles he faced in his life to current societal norms. There is no simple way, but there is progress, hope and, with each successive generation, a greater acceptance that the worth of someone is measured in deeds and character, not skin color.

In order to judge our progress, we're left with a simple tool: common sense. Common sense tells us and history has proven to us that humanity—or at the very least, American society—is marching, even if too slowly for some, toward an age of tolerance and acceptance. The vast majority of people in this nation are not racist. The instances of true racism, in which people are denied fundamental human rights based on the color of their skin, are so few and far between by now that when they spring up, they seem almost contrived or manufactured by race baiters who use them to argue that racism continues to be endemic or systemic in the United States. One example that comes to mind is the "controversy" several years back when Abercrombie & Fitch was accused of racism for not using more black models in its clothing catalogs—this, despite the existence of African-American-owned urban sportswear clothing lines like FuBu (which is commonly thought to be an anagram for "For Us, By Us") and Jennifer Lopez's clothing line targeted almost exclusively (by her own account) to young Latina women.[15]

Looking at today's society, systemic racism within the American populace is largely dead; what little racism remains is likely fomented by government policies that move minorities to the head of the line. This can only prove destructive, as whites understandably wonder why they're passed over in universities admissions and for jobs they'd otherwise get—all because minorities, especially blacks, were poorly treated before their own time. Common sense tells us that affirmative action is ultimately destructive, both for the "soft bigotry of low expectations" that it represents, and for the resentment it creates in members of the white population in this country, the majority of whom were born after the civil-rights era. Common sense tells us that we need to do away with policies that promote set-asides, preferences, quotas and lowered expectations for entire communities in this nation.

This isn't to say that the fight against bigotry is over, and that there isn't major work to be done in order to widen the door to opportunity in this country. Not at all. Far too many minority children are left behind in their sub-standard schools and underfunded communities. But that is a matter of our education system and individual communities needing to be cleaned up. We must be innovative and thoughtful as we attack the problem on a global scale, and not focus specifically on skin color.

If you think about it, race is little more than a human construct. A good friend of mine, a neurosurgeon, likes to say that when he works on someone's brain—the thing that makes a person who he is—it looks the same as everyone else's. The source of all thoughts, desires and actions looks the same whether his patient is black, white, Hispanic, Muslim, Arab, Chinese, Native American, Christian, Hindu or Jewish—you name it. I intentionally mixed religions, ethnicities and nationalities because it simply does not matter what we look like, what we believe or from whence we came; our brains look the same, as do our hearts.

So, rather than spending an inordinate amount of time and energy focusing on race or any other human construct, wouldn't we be better off directing our attention to the issues that really plague the nation?

The vast majority of Americans have moved beyond race in their relations with other people. The question remains: Will their government finally catch up to them?

NOTES

1. Blurb on jacket of Williams, *Reawakening Virtues.*

2. See Williams, interview by Lamb, *Booknotes,* for a transcript of an interview he taped to publicize his first book, *Beyond Blame: How We Can Succeed by Breaking the Dependency Barrier* (New York: Free Press, 1995). In this interview he discusses his upbringing in South Carolina at length but also tells of his frustration with his job at the Department of Agriculture.

3. While Williams's biography as presented in his promotional materials regularly describes the Graham Williams Group as an international public relations, advertising, and media firm, the Center for Media and Democracy's SourceWatch notes that the firm "does not rate a listing in the databases or archives of the major PR trade publications, *O'Dwyers PR Daily,* the *Holmes Report* or *PR Week.*" Center for Media and Democracy. "Graham Williams Group."

4. Toppo, "Education Dept. Paid Commentator."

5. Williams, *Reawakening Virtues,* 15.

6. Astor, "Columnist Group Prez Criticizes."

7. Rosen, "*The Hill* Restores Williams."

8. The No Child Left Behind Act of 2001 was signed by President George W. Bush in 2002. While technically a reauthorization of the Elementary and Secondary Education Act, it is widely known for expanding the role of the federal government in education, particularly by seeking to improve the educational outcomes of disadvantaged students. It mandates annual testing and increases both school and state accountability.

9. *A Christmas Carol* by Charles Dickens was published in 1843. It is the story of Ebenezer Scrooge, a wealthy but miserly businessman who undergoes a spiritual transformation after being visited by several supernatural characters on Christmas Eve.

10. In March 2010 President Barack Obama signed into law the Patient Protection and Affordable Care Act, which was designed primarily to extend health care coverage beginning in 2014 to millions of Americans who were uninsured prior to its passage.

11. Dr. Walter E. Williams is a professor of economics at George Mason University in Fairfax, Virginia. Larry Elder is a conservative (sometimes described as "libertarian") political commentator and radio show host. Thomas Sowell is an African American economist who writes from a libertarian perspective. Shelby Steele is a self-described conservative author and public intellectual. Walter Williams is an academic economist. Congressman Tim Scott was elected from the First Congressional District in South Carolina in 2010; in late 2012 he was appointed to the U.S. Senate to fill out the term of a resigning South Carolina senator. Congressman

380 The Media Generation

Allen West, also elected in 2010, represented the Twenty-Second District of Florida but was defeated for reelection in 2012. Clarence Thomas was appointed to the U.S. Supreme Court in 1991. Condoleezza Rice served as national security adviser from 2001 to 2005 and as secretary of state from 2005 to 2009. Michael Steele chaired the Republican National Committee from January 2009 to January 2011.

12. Richard Pryor (1940–2005) was a stand-up comedian, author, actor, and social commentator. Dave Chappelle (b. 1973) is a comedian, screenwriter, and producer best known for *Chappelle's Show,* a sketch comedy television series that ran from 2003 to 2006. His name is incorrectly spelled in the text of *Reawakening Virtues.*

13. Joe Madison, popularly known as "The Black Eagle," hosts a talk show that is broadcast in Washington, D.C., as well as nationwide on satellite radio.

14. *Scrubs* is a hospital-based comedy series that ran from 2001 to 2010. *Psych* is a comedy-drama series that debuted in 2006.

15. In 2004, Abercrombie & Fitch, a nationwide chain of retail stores, agreed to pay a settlement of $50 million to settle two privately filed class-action lawsuits and a complaint filed by the U.S. Equal Employment Opportunity Commission. The suits alleged that the company's recruiting and hiring practices discriminated against minorities and women.

Afterword: Ty'Sheoma Bethea (b. 1994)

We are just students trying to become lawyers, doctors, congressmen like yourself and one day president, so we can make a change to not just the state of South Carolina but also the world. We are not quitters.

When fourteen-year-old Ty'Sheoma Bethea penned her letter to the "Congressmen of the United States" on February 10, 2009, she joined the ranks of thousands of African American students from South Carolina who over the decades have demanded change, particularly regarding inequities in the state-funded education system. During the Civil War, a group of schoolchildren was among the exuberant throng of black Charlestonians who welcomed Major Martin R. Delany to Charleston shortly after Union troops liberated the city. As the crowd staged a celebratory march that included a hearse for slavery surrounded by black-draped mourners, thousands of schoolchildren proudly carried placards that read, "We know no caste or color."[1]

Nearly a century later, South Carolina's segregated school districts reflected the state's acute awareness of both caste and color through its relegation of African American students to inferior facilities, services, and curricula. In 1950 African American students from Summerton, South Carolina, some of whom were forced to walk as many as eight miles to their ill-equipped schools, became the heart of *Briggs v. Elliott*, a lawsuit that NAACP lawyer

Thurgood Marshall filed to force the state to provide equal transportation and education to all children. *Briggs* eventually became one of five lawsuits in *Brown v. Board of Education,* the successful U.S. Supreme Court class-action desegregation case. The mandate to desegregate with "all deliberate speed" engendered a slow response in South Carolina, however, impelling students such as Jim Clyburn and Jesse Jackson to protest against segregation and discrimination during the 1960s. For example, in 1963 more than 1,350 students who pressured the Orangeburg City Council to require compliance with the *Brown* decision were arrested, filling the jails and nearly emptying the classrooms in an unsuccessful attempt to desegregate Orangeburg's schools. Even after the passage of the 1964 Civil Rights Act, most school districts in South Carolina remained segregated—including those in Ty'Sheoma Bethea's Dillon County District Number 2, where schools were not integrated until the early 1970s.

Bethea was born in Dillon, South Carolina, an impoverished town whose greatest claim to fame may be that it is the hometown of Federal Reserve Board chairman Ben Bernanke. He was the product of the segregated public school system, and the town resources provided to white and to African American children were quite different then as they are now. Bethea attended South Elementary School, a small facility with overflowing classrooms staffed by dedicated teachers who worked diligently to ensure that students received far beyond the "minimally adequate education" mandated by the South Carolina state constitution. The physical plant at the dilapidated 113-year-old J. V. Martin Junior High School she later attended was in worse condition, earning a place in the opening scene of *Corridor of Shame: The Neglect of South Carolina's Rural Schools,* a documentary about South Carolina public schools located along the I-95 highway, which snakes along the eastern portion of the state. At J. V. Martin, students were forced to walk down darkened hallways with paint peeling off the walls, stop classes whenever a train squealed by on the nearby railroad track, and play sports in a gymnasium that lacked heat or air conditioning. Yet J. V. Martin was once the pride of Dillon County. Dillon residents first established a school in a church around 1896. By 1912 they had erected a state-of-the-art classroom and auditorium complex considered to be one of the best in the state. By 1936 a gymnasium, a new auditorium, a home economics department, and two science laboratories were added. In 1958, four years after *Brown v. Board of Education* mandated the integration of America's public schools, the Dillon County schools remained segregated as the town remodeled the old facilities and erected new classrooms and district offices as well as a band room and a cafeteria. In 1970 Dillon built a new high school facility and named the older facility Joseph Vincent Martin Middle School in honor of Joseph

Vincent Martin, who had worked as school superintendent of Dillon County for twenty-nine years. By 1983 the buildings had been renovated, and the school served the needs of seventh and eighth graders. Nearly twenty years later, however, after the decline in South Carolina's textile and agricultural industries had decimated Dillon's economy and the school had fallen into disrepair, J. V. Martin was rated "Unsatisfactory" and "Below Average." By the time Bethea enrolled in the school, the dropout rate hovered around 60 percent, and 85 percent of her classmates lived below the poverty line.

The 2008 presidential campaign put in motion the chain of events that catapulted Bethea and the plight of J. V. Martin students onto the international stage. Presidential candidate Barack Obama visited J. V. Martin twice during the campaign. In his first news conference after being elected president, he referenced the school as the type of institution that could benefit from the $787 billion economic stimulus package he encouraged Congress to approve. Then South Carolina Republican governor Mark Sanford rejected $700 million in federal stimulus aid that was designated for teacher pay and school repairs, reflecting the fractious national debate regarding the federal government's role in funding public education. Amanda Burnette, the principal of J. V. Martin, encouraged her students to become involved in securing stimulus funds to remodel the school. Around the same time, Howard Witt, a *Chicago Tribune* reporter who was conducting research on how schools could benefit from stimulus funding, visited Bethea's social studies class, which met in a rusty mobile trailer, and asked if any of the students knew about the stimulus money. Bethea was one of the few who spoke up. Later that day she went to the Dillon County Library and typed a letter to Congress on a public computer. In it she outlined the students' needs and asked for assistance. The following day, she gave the letter to Burnette, who scanned it and e-mailed copies to South Carolina's representatives in Congress and to the White House. Bethea's letter was selected as one of the few that President Obama reads each day to stay connected with the concerns of average American citizens.

Three days later, President Obama invited Bethea and her mother to visit the White House and sit in the First Lady's box in the House chamber during his first State of the Union address before a joint session of Congress. On February 24, 2009, during a private meeting at the White House, First Lady Michelle Obama assured Bethea that "the power of the pen will take you a long way in life" and that the Obama administration would help publicize the students' plight and lend its support for a new school.[2] Bethea was surprised when President Obama quoted from her letter and asked her to stand during his speech. In recognizing Bethea, Obama quoted a phrase from her letter, "We are not quitters," and then added,

These words and these stories tell us something about the spirit of the people who sent us here. They tell us that even in the most trying times, amid the most difficult circumstances, there is a generosity, a resilience, a decency, and a determination that perseveres; a willingness to take responsibility for our future and for posterity. Their resolve must be our inspiration. Their concerns must be our cause. And we must show them and all our people that we are equal to the task before us.[3]

Bethea did not realize the import of her letter and the international interest her story had generated until she was greeted by a horde of reporters at the airport when she returned to South Carolina. During an appearance on *Good Morning America,* when asked about her career aspirations, Bethea declared that she aspired to become the first woman president of the United States. Major media outlets around the world such as CNN, the *Washington Post,* and the Reuters news agency covered the story. Additionally, educators created lesson plans to teach students how to emulate Bethea's activism.[4] The conservative newspaper the *Washington Times* criticized Bethea for seeking a handout, however, and characterized President Obama as an opportunist who exploited the situation for political gain.[5] South Carolina representative Jim Clyburn came to Bethea's defense, affirming her right to protest appalling conditions in the state's public education system. As J. V. Martin received more publicity, Bethea began to hope that the media attention would provide the momentum needed to secure funding for her school. Conditions at J. V. Martin improved dramatically after Darryl Rosser, president and CEO of the school furniture supplier SAGUS International, Inc., of Chicago, surprised the students by donating $250,000 worth of furniture and labor and remodeling the cafeteria.[6] One year after Bethea attended the State of the Union address, $39.5 million in low-interest loans from the American Recovery and Reinvestment Act of 2009 and grants from the U.S. Department of Agriculture were designated for the building of two new schools, with approximately $25 million allocated for J. V. Martin Junior High School.[7]

Bethea has become a global advocate for rural schools. She also gives speeches to youth groups and churches and makes presentations on abstinence and education for the Unplanned Teenage Pregnancy organization. Bethea has received recognition for her civic activism, including being accorded the title Palmetto Ambassador of Education and Super-Kid by the James Stephens Scholarship Foundation. She donated the jewelry and lavender dress she wore to the State of the Union address to the South Carolina State Museum for its permanent South Carolina Heroes and Leaders exhibit.

In Bethea's letter, presented here, one immediately senses the audacity of hope she exudes in appealing to Congress to help J. V. Martin Middle School students secure better facilities. The frankness of her prose reflects the desperation of their situation and urges immediate action. Bethea asserts that the poor condition of the school limits the effectiveness of the education students are receiving. Throughout her litany of concerns about J. V. Martin, however, runs a sliver of hope reflecting her desire for change, despite the fact that she will be leaving the school within two years. Ultimately, in writing Congress, Bethea exercises her First Amendment right "to petition the government for a redress of grievances."

On April 21, 2011, she joined South Carolina state representative Jackie Hayes (D-Dillon) at a groundbreaking ceremony for the new J. V. Martin Middle School, carrying forth the sentiments of the Charleston schoolchildren who proudly proclaimed, "We know no caste or color." As she reflected on the extraordinary change wrought by her letter, Bethea remarked, "People like me are trying our best to make sure every child's voice is heard. Just don't give up because later things will become better. If we work together as a unit, we can make sure we all get the education and best communities we deserve. *We are not quitters.*"[8]

Dear Congressmen Of The United States,

I am Ty'Sheoma Bethea and I'm a student at J. V. Martin Junior High School[9] in Dillon, South Carolina. As you should know we have a lot of problems with our school. President Obama has visited our school[10] and was able to see why we need a new school.

Some of these problems are we can not afford anything. Our school has gone through budget cuts,[11] and we can no longer afford school trips or have any extracurricular activities. We also have a very poor school. Our lights do not work well and our school is very weak. This school has mobiles[12] that are used for classes, but the mobiles have major problems. The floors inside of the mobiles have holes in them, but we have covered them with rugs.

This is very unsafe for the students, if a student was not to watch his or her step one of them would fall through the floor. This is very dangerous! I also think you should know that the students inside of the school buildings not only have to deal with the bathrooms being out of order, but also they have to deal with the dust falling from the ceiling because the students upstairs are moving around. My school has been standing for many years, and has a lot of great memories. However! I suggest that it is time for the new generation to have a bigger and better school. This would not only benefit the students to look and feel good about their school but the community would also feel good about the education that the students are receiving. It will allow us to provide a better foundation for a better life.

The parents of the students at J. V. Martin have many complaints about the books their children are using because the books need to be upgraded. This is another reason why our school is so left behind in education. People are starting to see my school as a hopeless uneducated school. We are not hopeless or uneducated, and we finally want to prove to the world that we deserve the chance in life just like other students across the nation. We want the chance to feel good about what we are doing because the conditions we are in now does not inspire success in the student body. We are calling on you for help. We are willing to try but our economy is not willing to do much. I'm very concerned about my school's conditions as a student, and its time for me to get involved and do my part.

This is my second and last year at this school and I really want to show how much I care. I also represent my school as a basketball player. Sometimes we have to cancel our home games because the gym ceiling leaks water through the small cracks in the ceiling and our gym court is small. So in the morning during the assembly there is not enough room for students to sit in the gym beside their class. They would have to stand up. I have to remind you that we have a building on our campus that has been standing since the 1800s. We also need teachers because some of our teachers have been teaching for over 40 years. The paintings in my school are becoming so old that they are peeling off of the walls, this is destroying our school.

A major problem that President Obama talked about in one of his speeches about our school is that students that are having class in the mobiles. The teachers have to stop their lesson almost 6 times a day because they can not teach with the train on the tracks. Everyday we (the students) have to repeat our lesson or catch up, which is usually difficult to do because the train breaks our concentration. I'm a loyal student who just loves to take part or help out so I was trying to plan an activity for the school that we can afford like a school dance or prom, but our lights do not work at night. Sometimes they turn off in the daytime during class hours, when this happen we are asked to exit the building whether it's cold outside or hot. We have to go outside until the lights recover and we have permission to return to class.

This is taking away from our learning period of the day. The teachers and the students have all come to a conclusion that we will get in involved, will regain our confidence, and come together to support our school. Now we're just waiting on your consent that you will pitch and with the community, in situations like this we call on congress on their opinions, and I as a 14 years old that attends J. V. Martin Junior High School I have many reasons why I'm so concerned. You as congressmen should also be concerned.

This school means a lot to me and many others and it really upsets the school how the teachers struggle to help us everyday so we can get a good education. Before you (the Congress) come up with an decision I would like you to know that this school has been through a lot and it would make a big difference just to help my school. We are just students trying to become lawyers, doctors, congressmen like yourself and one day presidents, so we can make a change not only in the state of South Carolina but also the world!

We are not quitters because our President has quotes that we use, and that is "Yes we can" and "We can make a change." I hope this list of concerns and why I think you should help our school helps you (the Congress) come up with a good conclusion. Or at least help us to remodel our school so it could look descent. This would not only make us feel good about ourselves but I agree that you will also feel great after you complete this good deed for my school and my community. If you approve this bill it would not only be our school but also yours too.

Thank you very much for having time to read my letter and for any questions you should call.

Sincerely,
Ty'Sheoma Bethea

NOTES

    1. Egerton, *He Shall Go Out Free*, 228.

    2. Ty'Sheoma Bethea, e-mail correspondence, February 1, 2012.

    3. Obama, "Address before Congress," 153.

    4. Hickman, "Using First Amendment Rights"; "Your Government, Your Voice!"

    5. "Yes, Ty'Sheoma."

    6. South Carolina State Department of Education, "Chicago Company Donates New Furniture"; Newsome, "Lesson in Giving."

    7. The American Recovery and Reinvestment Act of 2009 allocated $787 billion to create new jobs and spur economic growth to help the nation recover from recession. Black, "New School Building"; Hadro, "Stimulus Money Reaches School."

    8. Ty'Sheoma Bethea, e-mail correspondence, February 1, 2012.

    9. John Vincent Martin Junior High School, named in honor of former superintendent of the Dillion County Board of Education John Vincent Martin, operated in outdated facilities that included a church built in 1896, an auditorium erected in 1917, and a school gym constructed in 1926 that had originally served as a boxing venue.

10. In 2007 during the presidential election campaign, then U.S. Senator Barak Obama (D-IL) visited J. V. Martin Junior High School, which had been featured in a documentary that examined neglected educational institutions located along interstate 95.

11. Although state law requires the South Carolina Assembly to provide approximately $2,700 per student in the public school system, legislators reduced funding to roughly one-third of that amount during the first decade of the twenty-first century.

12. Mobiles are portable, modular buildings that provide a relatively inexpensive means of expanding classroom space.

Bibliography

An Act Donating Public Lands to the Several States and Territories Which May Provide Colleges for the Benefit of Agriculture and the Mechanic Arts, 37th Cong., Sess. II, Ch. 130 (1862).

An Act to Authorize the People of the Missouri Territory to Form a Constitution and State Government, and for the Admission of Such State into the Union on an Equal Footing with the Original States, and to Prohibit Slavery in Certain Territories, Sess. I, Ch. 22, Stat. 1 (1820).

An Act to Revise and Consolidate the Statutes of the United States, 34th Congress, Sess. 1, Title XIII, Sec. 641 (1870).

American Antiquarian Society. "Lucy Chase's Antebellum Work for Fugitive Slave John Andrew Jackson." *Through a Glass Darkly: Images of Race, Region, and Reform*. Accessed March 28, 2012. http://faculty.assumption.edu/aas/intros/chase jackson.html.

Andrews, William L., ed. *The North Carolina Roots of African American Literature: An Anthology*. Chapel Hill: University of North Carolina Press, 2006.

Astor, Dave. "Columnist Group Prez Criticizes Armstrong Williams Probe." *Editor & Publisher*, April 18, 2005. Accessed November 15, 2012. http://www.editorand-publisher.com/Archive/Columnist-Group-Prez-Criticizes-Armstrong-Williams-Probe.

Barber, J. Max. "The Atlanta Tragedy." *Voice of the Negro* (November 1906): 473–79.

———. "The Monument to Gonzales." *Voice of the Negro* (February 1906): 17–18.

Basler, Barbara. "A Blind and Deaf Infant's Short Life on the Rolls of New York's Homeless." *New York Times*, December 20, 1985.

Basler, Roy P. *The Collected Works of Abraham Lincoln: First Supplement 1832–1865*. Vol. 7. Westport, CT: Greenwood, 1974.

Berman, Jillian. "After They Walk: Eugene Robinson, the Man with the Pen." *Michigan Daily*, March 29, 2010. Accessed November 15, 2012. http://www.michigan daily.com/content/after-they-walk-eugene-robinson.

Bethea, Ty'Sheoma. Letter to the Congressmen of the United States, February 2009.

Bethune, Mary McLeod. "Certain Unalienable Rights." In *What the Negro Wants*, edited by Rayford W. Logan, 248–58. Chapel Hill: University of North Carolina, 1996.

Black, Marlous H. "New School Building in Dillon, South Carolina on the Drawing Board Thanks to a 15 year old Student's Letter to President Obama." *USDA Blog.* Accessed November 8, 2012. http://blogs.usda.gov/tag/ty%E2%80%99sheoma -bethea/.

Blassingame, John W., ed. *Slave Testimony: Two Centuries of Letters, Speeches, Interviews, and Autobiographies.* Baton Rouge: Louisiana Sate University Press, 1977.

Bornstein, Morris. *Manual of Instruction in the Use of Dumb Bells, Indian Clubs, and Other Exercises.* New York: Excelsior, 1889.

Brown, Sue M. Wilson. *History of Central Association of Colored Women.* Des Moines, Iowa: Central Association of Colored Women, 1940.

Bunyan, John. *The Pilgrim's Progress from This World to That Which Is to Come.* London: E. P. Dutton, 1918.

Burns, Rebecca. *Rage in the Gate City: The Story of the 1906 Atlanta Race Riot.* Athens: University of Georgia Press, 2009.

Center for Media and Democracy. "Graham Williams Group." *SourceWatch.* Last modified October 21, 2006. Accessed November 8, 2012. http://www.sourcewatch .org/index.php?title=Graham_Williams_Group

Children's Defense Fund. "About Us." Accessed January 17, 2012. http://www .childrensdefense.org/about-us/.

Clark, Septima. "Literacy and Liberation." *Freedomways* 4, no. 1 (1964): 113–24.

——. "The Role of Women." In *Ready from Within: Septima Clark and the Civil Rights Movement,* edited by Cynthia Stokes Brown, 77–83. Trenton, N.J.: Africa World Press, 1990.

Clyburn, James E. "The Creation of the Student Nonviolent Coordinating Committee (SNCC)." *Civil Rights in America; Connections to a Movement.* Online video. Accessed January 29, 2012. http://topics.gannett.com/civil+rights+video /?template=clarionledger.

——. "Proper Response to Ty'Sheoma's Letter." *Politico,* March 6, 2009. Accessed November 8, 2012. http://www.politico.com/news/stories/0309/19690.html.

——. "Whom Much Has Been Given, Much Is Required." *County Focus* 18, no. 2: 2–4. Accessed November 8, 2012. http://old.sccounties.org/publications/County%20 Focus/2007/CFNum2_07.pdf.

Cochran, John R. *Report of the Joint Investigating Committee on Public Frauds and Election of Hon. J. J. Patterson to the United States Senate Made to the General Assembly of South Carolina at the Regular Session 1877–78.* Columbia, S.C.: Calvo and Patton, 1878.

Coleman, Helen Turnbull Waite. *Banners in the Wilderness: Early Years of Washington and Jefferson College.* Pittsburgh: University of Pittsburgh Press, 1956.

"The Crum Case." *New York Times,* April 28, 1904. Accessed November 15, 2012. http://query.nytimes.com/mem/archive-free/pdf?res=F60815FF395414728DDDA 10A94DC405B848CF1D3.

Curry, Timothy, and Lynn Shibut "The Cost of the Savings and Loan Crisis: Truth and Consequences." *FDIC Banking Review* 13, no. 2 (2000): 26–35.

Daniel, Sadie Iola, and Hallie Quinn Brown. *Women Builders.* New York: G. K. Hall, 1997.

Daniel, Walter C. *Black Journals of the United States.* Westport, CT: Greenwood Press, 1982.

Davis, Russell H. *Black Americans in Cleveland from George Peake to Carl P. Stokes, 1796–1969.* Washington, D.C.: Associated Publishers, 1985.

Delany, Martin Robison. *Martin R. Delany. A Documentary Reader,* ed. Robert Levine. Chapel Hill: University of North Carolina Press, 2003.

Dickerson, Dennis C. "About Us—Our Motto." African Methodist Episcopal Church. Accessed November 8, 2012. http://www.ame-church.com/about-us/motto.php.

Donegan, Lawrence. "The Battle of the N-Word." *Guardian,* January 19, 2002. Accessed November 15, 2012. http://www.guardian.co.uk/education/2002/jan/20/artsandhumanities.highereducation.

Dorrien, Gary J. *The Making of American Liberal Theology: Idealism, Realism, and Modernity, 1900–1950.* Louisville, KY: John Knox Press, 2003.

———. *Social Ethics in the Making: Interpreting an American Tradition.* West Sussex, UK: John Wiley & Sons, 2009.

Drago, Edmund L. *Charleston's Avery Center: From Education and Civil Rights to Preserving the African American Experience.* Charleston: History Press, 2006.

Du Bois, W. E. B. "Returning Soldiers." *Crisis* 18, no. 1 (May 1919): 13–14.

———. *The Souls of Black Folk: Essays and Sketches.* Chicago: A. C. McClurg, 1903.

Du Bois, W. E. B., and Woodrow Wilson. "My Impressions of Woodrow Wilson." *Journal of Negro History* 58, no. 4 (October 1973): 453–59.

Dunlap, David W. "Parting Glance: Brian Lanker, 1947–2011." *New York Times,* March 14, 2011. Accessed November 15, 2012. http://lens.blogs.nytimes.com/2011/03/14/parting-glance-brian-lanker-1947–2011/.

Edelman, Marian Wright. "If the Child Is Safe." In *The Measure of Our Success: A Letter to My Children and Yours,* 79–97. Boston: Beacon Press, 1992

———. *Lanterns. A Memoir of Mentors.* New York: HarperCollins, 2000.

Edgar, Walter. *South Carolina: A History.* Columbia: University of South Carolina Press, 1998.

Egerton, Douglas R. "Forgetting Denmark Vesey; Or, Oliver Stone Meets Richard Wade." *William and Mary Quarterly,* 3rd series, 59, no. 1 (January 2002): 143–52.

———. *He Shall Go Out Free: The Lives of Denmark Vesey.* Lanham, MD: Rowman & Littlefield, 2004.

"Empire Savings and Loan." Open Door, October 1923.

Encyclopedia of Cleveland History. Compiled by David D. Van Tassel and John J. Grabowski. Western Reserve Historical Society and Case Western University. Accessed November 8, 2012. http://ech.case.edu/index.html.

Ferris, William R. *Blues from the Delta.* New York: Da Capo, 1984.

Forbes, Robert Pierce . *The Missouri Compromise and Its Aftermath: Slavery and the Meaning of America.* Chapel Hill: University of North Carolina Press, 2007.

Forty-Eighth Annual Report of the State Superintendent of Education of the State of South Carolina, 1916. Columbia, S.C.: Gonzales and Bryan, 1917.

Fultz, Michael. "'The Morning Cometh': African-American Periodicals, Education, and the Black Middle Class, 1900–1930." *Journal of Negro History* 80, no. 3 (1995): 97–112.

Gatewood, Williard B. "William D. Crum: A Negro in Politics." *Journal of Negro History* 53, no. 4 (October 1968): 301–20.

Gerber, David A. *Black Ohio and the Color Line, 1860–1915.* Urbana: University of Illinois Press, 1976.

Giffin, William W. *African Americans and the Color Line in Ohio, 1915–1930.* Columbus: Ohio State University Press, 2005.

Gordon-Reed, Annette. *Race on Trial: Law and Justice in American History.* Oxford: Oxford University Press, 2002.

Grimké, Archibald. *Right on the Scaffold; or The Martyrs of 1822.* Occasional Papers No. 7. Washington, D.C.: American Negro Academy, 1901.

Grimké, Francis. Introduction to *Recollections of Seventy Years,* by Daniel A. Payne, 5–7. Nashville, Tenn.: Publishing House of the A.M.E. Sunday School Union, 1888.

———. "The Negro and His Citizenship." In *The Negro and the Elective Franchise: A Series of Papers and a Sermon,* 77–90. Occasional Papers No. 11. Washington, D.C.: American Negro Academy, 1905.

Grimké, Francis. Papers. Moorland-Spingarn Research Center, Howard University, Washington, D.C.

Hadro, Matt. "Stimulus Money Reaches School in Need—A Year after Obama's Promise." *Human Events.* Accessed January 28, 2010. http://www.humanevents.com/article.php?id=35371.

Hamilton, James. *Negro Plot. An Account of the Late Intended Insurrection among a Portion of the Blacks of the City of Charleston, South Carolina: Published by the Authority of the Corporation of Charleston.* Boston: Joseph W. Ingraham, 1822.

Hanson, Joyce A. *Mary McLeod Bethune and Black Women's Political Activism.* Columbia: University of Missouri Press, 2003.

Harlan, Louis R. "Booker T. Washington and the *Voice of the Negro,* 1904–1907." *Journal of Southern History* 45, no. 1 (February 1979): 45–62.

Harter, Jim. *World Railways of the Nineteenth Century: A Pictorial History in Victorian Engravings.* Baltimore: Johns Hopkins University Press, 2005.

Helper, Hinton Rowan. *The Impending Crisis of the South: How to Meet It.* New York: Burdick Brothers, 1857.

Hickman, Kyle. "Using First Amendment Rights to Further Equality and Freedom." McCormick Foundation. Accessed March 26, 2012, http://documents.mccormickfoundation.org/Civics/programs/files/pdf/LessonPlanDemonstration_KHickman.pdf.

Holmes, D. O. W. "Phylon Profile IV: Kelly Miller." *Phylon* 6, no. 2 (1945): 121–25.

Hughs, Ina. *A Prayer for Children.* New York: William Morrow, 1997.

Hunter, Jane Edna. *A Nickel and a Prayer,* ed. Rhondda Robinson Thomas. Morgantown: University of West Virginia Press, 2011.

———. "An Opportunity for Club Women to Serve the Underprivileged Girl." Jane Edna Hunter Papers, 1930–1969, Western Reserve Historical Society, Cleveland.

"It's Our Problem: Voters in the Black Belt." Open Door, October 1938.

Jackson, Jesse. 1988 Democratic National Convention Address. Speech delivered at the Omni Coliseum, Atlanta, Ga., July 19, 1988. In *Jesse Jackson's 1988 Presidential Campaign: A Collection of Major Speeches, Issue Papers, Photographs, and Campaign Analysis,* edited by Frank Clemente, 33–39. Boston: Keep Hope Alive PAC and South End Press, 1988.

———. "What Does the Government Owe the Poor?" *Harper's* (April 1986): 35–47.

Jackson, John Andrew. "My Escape." In *The Experience of a Slave in South Carolina,* 23–53. London: Passmore & Alabaster, 1862.

Jackson, Kenneth T. *The Ku Klux Klan in the City, 1915–1930.* New York: Oxford University Press, 1968.

Johnson, Abby Arthur, and Ronald M. Johnson. "Away from Accommodation: Radical Editors and Protest Journalism, 1900–1910." *Journal of Negro History* 62, no. 4 (October 1977): 325–38.

Johnson, Charles S. "The Rise of the Negro Magazine." *Journal of Negro History* 13, no. 1 (January 1928): 7–21.

Johnson, Michael P. "Denmark Vesey and His Co-Conspirators." *William and Mary Quarterly,* 3rd series, 58, no. 4 (October 2001): 915–76.

Jones, Adrienne Lash. *Jane Edna Hunter: A Case Study of Black Leadership.* Brooklyn, N.Y.: Carlson, 1990.

Jones-Wilson, Faustine C., Charles A. Asbury, Margo Okazawa-Rey, D. Kamili Anderson, Sylvia M. Jacobs, and Michael Fultz, eds. *Encyclopedia of African-American Education.* Westport, Conn.: Greenwood Press, 1996.

Kennedy, Lionel H., and Thomas Parker. *An Official Report of the Trials of Sundry Negroes, Charged with an Attempt to Raise an Insurrection in the State of South Carolina.* Charleston: James R. Schenck, 1822.

Kennedy, Randall L. *Interracial Intimacies: Sex, Marriage, Identity, and Adoption.* New York: Pantheon, 2003.

———. *Nigger: The Strange Career of a Troublesome Word.* New York: Vantage House, 2003.

———. "Persuasion and Distrust: A Comment on the Affirmative Action Debate." *Harvard Law Review* 99, no. 6 (April 1986): 1327–46.

King, Martin Luther, Jr. "Statement Regarding the Retirement of Benjamin E. Mays." King Center Archives, Atlanta, Ga., 1967.

Larson, Cedric, and James R. Mock. "The Lost Files of the Creel Committee of 1917–19." *Public Opinion Quarterly* 3, no. 1 (January 1939): 5–29.

Laurens, Edward R. *A Letter to the Hon. Whitemarsh B. Seabrook of St. John Colleton; in Explanation and Defence of An Act to Amend the Law in Relation to Slaves and Free Persons of Color.* Charleston: Observer Press, 1835.

League of Women Voters. "History." Accessed January 13, 2012. http://www.lwv.org/history.

Levine, Robert S. *Martin R. Delany: A Documentary Reader.* Chapel Hill: University of North Carolina Press, 2003.

Logan, Rayford W. *The Negro in American Life and Thought: The Nadir, 1877–1901.* New York: Dial Press, 1954.

Lutz, Tom, and Susanna Ashton. *These "Colored" United States: African American Essays from the 1920s.* New Brunswick, N.J.: Rutgers University Press, 1996.

Maxey, Chester Collins. "The Cleveland Election and the New Charter." *American Political Science Review* 16, no. 1 (February 1922): 83–86.

May, Nicholas. "Holy Rebellion: Religious Assembly Laws in Antebellum South Carolina and Virginia." *American Journal of Legal History* 49, no. 3 (July 2007): 237–56.

Mays, Benjamin E. *Born to Rebel, An Autobiography.* Athens: University of Georgia, 2003.

McCord, David J. "An Act for the Better Ordering and Governing of Negroes and Slaves." In *The Statues at Large of South Carolina; Edited under Authority of the Legislature,* 7:352–65. Columbia, S.C.: A. S. Johnson, 1840.

———. "An Act to Amend the Laws in Relation to Slaves and Free Persons of Color, Act of December 17, 1834." In *The Statues at Large of South Carolina; Edited under Authority of the Legislature,* 7:468–70. Columbia, S.C.: A. S. Johnson, 1840.

McMaster, Susan. *The Telecommunications Industry.* Westport, Conn.: Greenwood Press, 2002.

McPherson, James M., and James K. Hogue. *Ordeal by Fire: The Civil War and Reconstruction.* New York: McGraw-Hill, 2010.

Miller, Kelly. *As to the Leopard's Spots: An Open Letter to Thomas Dixon, Jr.* Washington, D.C.: Hayworth Publishing House, 1905.

———. *The Disgrace of Democracy: Open Letter to President Woodrow Wilson.* Washington, D.C., 1917.

———. "The Practical Value of Higher Education," *Opportunity* 1 (March 1923): 4–5.

———. *Race Adjustment Essays on the Negro.* New York: Neale, 1908.

———. "South Carolina." *Messenger* 7, no. 11 (December 1925): 376–77.

Monaghan, E. Jennifer. *Learning to Read and Write in Colonial America.* Amherst: University of Massachusetts Press, 2007.

National Organization for Women. "The Founding of NOW." Last modified July 2011. Accessed November 8, 2012. http://www.now.org/history/the_founding.html.

"Negroes in Protest March in Fifth Av." *New York Times,* July 29, 1917. Accessed November 15, 2012. http://query.nytimes.com/mem/archive-free/pdf?res=F50F16 FC3B5F157A 93CBAB178CD85F438185F9.

Newsome, Melba. "A Lesson in Giving." *Time,* October 12, 2009. Accessed November 15, 2012. http://www.time.com/time/magazine/article/0,9171,1927265,00.html.

Obama, Barack. "Address before a Joint Session of the Congress." February 24, 2009. National Archives, Public Papers of the Presidents of the United States, 145–53. Accessed February 2, 2013. http://www.gpo.gov/fdsys/pkg/PPP-2009 -book1/pdf/PPP-2009-book1-Doc-pg145-2.pdf.

Ohio Medical Society. "Dudley P. Allen." In *Transactions of the Forty-Eighth Annual Meeting of the Ohio State Medical Society Held at Put-in-Bay, June 28, 29, and 30, 1893.* Cincinnati: Earhart & Richardson, 1893.

Olmstead, Clifton E. "Francis James Grimke (1850–1937): Christian Moralist and Civil Rights." In *Sons of the Prophets: Leaders in Protestantism from Princeton*

Seminary, edited by Hugh Thomson Kerr, 161–75. Princeton: Princeton University Press, 1963.

O'Sullivan, John, and Edward F. Keuchel. *American Economic History: From Abundance to Constraint.* New York: Markus Weiner, 1989.

Pastras, Philip. *Dead Man Blues: Jelly Roll Morton Way Out West.* Berkeley: University of California Press, 2001.

Payne, Daniel A. "The Past, Present and Future of the A.M.E. Church." *A.M.E. Church Review* 1, no. 4 (April, 1885): 318–19.

———. *Recollections of Seventy Years.* Nashville: Publishing House of the A.M.E. Sunday School Union, 1888.

———. "Slavery Brutalizes Man." *Lutheran Herald and Journal of the Fort Plain, N.Y., Franckean Synod* 1, no. 15 (August 1, 1839), 113–14.

Peabody, Francis Greenwood. *Education for Life: The Story of Hampton Institute.* Garden City, N.Y.: Doubleday, Page & Company, 1918.

Perry, Mark. *Lift Up Thy Voice: The Grimké Family's Journey from Slaveholders to Civil Rights Leaders.* New York: Viking, 2001.

Phillips, Kimberley L. "'But It Is a Fine Place to Make Money': Migration and African-American Families in Cleveland, 1915–1929." *Journal of Social History* 30, no. 2 (Winter 1996): 393–413.

"Phillis Wheatley Founder Dies: Jane Hunter Leaves Heritage to Youth." Cleveland Call and Post, Jan. 23, 1971: 1A, 6A. "Hunter, Jane" file. Pendleton Historic Commission, Pendleton, S.C.

Porter, Jane. *The Scottish Chiefs, a Romance in Five Volumes.* London: Longman, et al., 1810.

———. "Community Evolution and Race Relations in Reconstruction Charleston, South Carolina." *South Carolina Historical Magazine* 101, no. 3 (July 2000): 214–33.

Powers, Jr., Bernard E. "Community Evolution and Race Relations in Reconstruction Charleston, South Carolina." South Carolina Historical Magazine 101, no. 3 (July 2000): 214–33.

Reardon, Sean F. *Review of* The Measure of our Success: A Letter to My Children and Yours, *by Marian Wright Edelman. Harvard Educational Review* 63, no. 1 (1993): 111–14.

Robertson, David. *Denmark Vesey: The Buried Story of America's Largest Slave Rebellion and the Man Who Led It.* New York: Vintage, 2000.

Robinson, Charles Frank. *Dangerous Liaisons: Sex and Love in the Segregated South.* Fayetteville: University of Arkansas Press, 2003.

Robinson, Eugene. *Disintegration: The Splintering of Black America.* New York: Doubleday, 2010.

———. "This Consequential Presidency." *Washington Post,* 20 January 2009.

Rodgers, Lawrence R. "Kelly Miller." In *The Concise Oxford Companion to African American Literature,* edited by William L. Andrews, Francis Smith Foster, and Trudier Harris, 290–91. Oxford: Oxford University Press, 2001.

Rogers, David. "On Budget, Jim Clyburn Looks to His Past." *Politico,* May 13, 2011. Accessed January 16, 2012. http://www.politico.com/news/stories/0511/54880 .html#ixzz1PRpxqOdi.

Rosen, Jay. "*The Hill* Restores Armstrong Williams to Legitimacy. Why?" *Huffington Post*, December 23, 2007. Accessed February 1, 2012. http://www.huffingtonpost .com/jay-rosen/the-hill-restores-armstro_b_77979.html.

Rosenberg, Jonathan. "For Democracy, Not Hypocrisy: World War and Race Relations in the United States, 1914–1919." *International History Review* 21, no. 3 (September 1999): 592–625.

Rubin, Hyman III. *South Carolina Scalawags*. Columbia: University of South Carolina Press, 2006.

Rudwick, Elliot M. *Race Riot at East St. Louis: July 2, 1917*. Carbondale: Southern Illinois University Press, 1964.

Safire, William. *Safire's Political Dictionary*. Oxford: Oxford University Press, 2008.

Saxon, Wolfgang. "John C. West, Crusading South Carolina Governor, Dies at 81." *New York Times*, March 23, 2004. Accessed November 15, 2012. http://www .nytimes.com/2004/03/23/business/john-c-west-crusading-south-Carolina -governor-dies-at-81.html.

Scroop, Daniel. *Mr. Democrat: Jim Farley, the New Deal, and the Making of Modern American Politics*. Ann Arbor: University of Michigan Press, 2006.

Shapiro, Herbert. *White Violence and Black Response: From Reconstruction to Montgomery*. Amherst: University of Massachusetts Press, 1988.

Shockley, Megan Taylor. *"We, Too, Are Americans": African American Women in Detroit and Richmond, 1940–54*. Urbana: University of Illinois Press, 2004.

Smalls, Robert. "Election Methods in the South." *North American Review* 151 (December 1890): 593–600.

———. "Hon. Robert Smalls' Speech to the 1895 South Carolina Constitution Convention." In *Journal of the Constitutional Convention of the State of South Carolina*, 473–76. Columbia, S.C.: Charles A. Calvo Jr., 1895.

Smith, Charles Spencer. *A History of the African Methodist Episcopal Church Being a Volume Supplemental to a History of the African Methodist Episcopal Church by Daniel Payne, DD. LL.D., Late One of its Bishops Chronicling the Principal Events in the Advance of the African Methodist Church from 1856–1922*. Philadelphia: Book Concern of the A.M.E. Church, 1922.

Smith, Jessie Carney. *Notable Black American Women, Book 2*. Detroit: Gale Research, 1996.

Snowden, Yates, and Harry Gardner Cutler. *History of South Carolina*, vol. 5. New York: Lewis Publishing Company, 1920.

South Carolina General Assembly. *Report of the Joint Investigating Committee on Public Frauds and Election of Hon. J. J. Patterson to the United States Senate, made to the General Assembly of South Carolina at the Regular Session 1877–78*. Columbia, S.C.: Calvo & Patton, 1878.

South Carolina State Department of Education. "Chicago Company Donates New Furniture to Dillon's J. V. Martin Middle School," News Archive, May 4, 2009. Accessed November 8, 2012. http://ed.sc.gov/agency/news/?nid=1202.

Stephenson, Gilbert Thomas. "The Separation of the Races in Public Conveyances." *American Political Science Review* 3, no. 2 (May 1909): 180–204.

Steward, T. G. Prefatory Note to *A History of the African Methodist Episcopal Church Being a Volume Supplemental to a History of the African Methodist Episcopal Church by Daniel Payne, DD. LL.D., Late one of its Bishops Chronicling the Principal Events in the Advance of the African Methodist Church from 1856–1922*, by Charles Spenser Smith, 504. Philadelphia: Book Concern of the A.M.E. Church 1922.

Tindall, George B. "The Question of Race in the South Carolina Constitutional Convention of 1895." *Journal of Negro History* 37, no. 3 (July 1952): 277–303.

Toppo, Greg. "Education Dept. Paid Commentator to Promote Law." *USA Today,* January 7, 2005. Accessed November 15, 2012. http://usatoday30.usatoday.com/news/ washington/2005–01–06-williams-whitehouse_x.htm.

"Turkish Diplomat to Leave Country." *New York Times,*September 25, 1914. Accessed November 15, 2012. http://query.nytimes.com/mem/archive-free/pdf?res =F10610FB3 F5412738 DDDAC0A94D1405B848DF1D3.

U.S. Department of Commerce, Bureau of the Census. *Negroes in the United States, 1920–32.* Washington, D.C.: Government Printing Office, 1935.

U.S. National Archives and Records Administration. "Teaching with Documents: The Fight for Equal Rights: Black Soldiers in the Civil War." Accessed February 1, 2012. http://www.archives.gov/education/lessons/blacks-civil-war/.

Wallenstein, Peter. "Interracial Marriage on Trial: *Loving v. Virginia,*" in *Race on Trial: Law and Justice in American History,* edited by Annette Gordon-Reed, 177–96. New York: Oxford University Press, 2002.

Washington, Booker T. Letter to Emmet J. Scott, November 4, 1903. In *The Booker T. Washington Papers,* edited by Louis R. Harlan and Raymond W. Smock, 7:328–29. Champaign: University of Illinois Press, 2000.

"Yes, Ty'Sheoma, There Is a Santa Claus." Editorial, *Washington Times,* February 26, 2009. Accessed November 15, 2012. http://www.washingtontimes.com/news/2009/feb/26/yes-tysheoma-there-is-a-santa-claus/.

Weber, Gustavus A. *The Women's Bureau: Its History, Activities, and Organization.* New York: AMS Press, 1974.

White, John H., Jr. *The American Railroad Passenger Car.* Baltimore: Johns Hopkins University Press, 1978.

Wilkerson, Isabel. *The Warmth of Other Suns: The Epic Story of America's Great Migration.* New York: Random House, 2010.

Wilkins, Theresa B. "Section K: Ambrose Caliver: Distinguished Civil Servant." *Journal of Negro Education* 31, no. 2 (Spring 1962): 212–14.

Williams, Armstrong. *Reawakening Virtues: Restoring What Makes America Great.* Sarasota, Fla.: New Chapter Publisher, 2011.

———. Interview by Brian Lamb. *Booknotes.* C-Span. July 16, 1995. Accessed November 8, 2012. http://www.booknotes.org/Watch/65870–1/Armstrong+Williams.aspx.

"Your Government, Your Voice! Grades 5–8: Lessons and Printables." Scholastic Inc. Accessed March 26, 2012. http://www.scholastic.com/browse/article.jsp?id =3750814.

Index